The Management of
Strategic Change

The Management of
Strategic Change

Edited by
ANDREW M. PETTIGREW

Basil Blackwell

First published 1987
First published in USA, 1988.

Basil Blackwell Ltd
108 Cowley Road, Oxford, OX4 1JF, UK

British Library Cataloguing in Publication Data

The Management of strategic change.
  1. Organizational change
  I. Pettigrew, Andrew M.
  658.4'06   HD58.8

ISBN 0-631-15695-X

Library of Congress Cataloging in Publication Data

The Management of strategic change / edited by Andrew M. Pettigrew.
    p.   cm.
      Based on the proceedings of an international research seminar held under the auspices of the Centre for Corporate Strategy and Change at Warwick University, Coventry, England, in May 1986.
    Includes bibliographies and index.
    ISBN 0-631-15695 X . $45.00 (U.S.)
    1. Strategic planning—Congresses. 2. Corporate planning.
—Congresses. 3. Organizational change—Congresses. I. Pettigrew.
Andrew M. II. University of Warwick. Centre for Corporate Strategy and Change.
HD30.28.M311 1988   87–15634
658.4'012—dc19   CIP

Typeset in 10 on 11 pt Ehrhardt
by Photo-graphics, Honiton, Devon
Printed in Great Britain by
T.J. Press Ltd, Padstow, Cornwall

Contents

Preface

This volume has developed from an international research seminar which I organized under the auspices of the Centre for Corporate Strategy and Change at Warwick University, Coventry, England, in May 1986. It was jointly financed by the Industry and Employment Committee of the Economic and Social Research Council, and Coopers and Lybrand Associates.

The first nine chapters in the volume constituted the core of the academic presentations made at the seminar. All of the original papers were revised in the six to nine-month period following the seminar. The nine commentaries published in this book are in many cases substantial developments of the oral responses made at the seminar. They contain pertinent observations not only on the paper to which they respond but also, directly and indirectly, on the theoretical and methodological problems of studying strategic change. The review essays by Andrew Van de Ven and Chris Argyris are developments of the summary and review statements made at the end of the seminar.

For reasons interesting to speculate about but difficult to define, the personal chemistry of the seminar seemed to go remarkably well. The central theme of the seminar, 'The Management of Strategic Change', was sufficiently broad, yet the participants were so chosen as to produce focused discussion and exchanges of high productivity. These high-quality discussions were sustained from beginning to end of the seminar and are a great credit to the international set of participants who gathered at Warwick.

This book was compiled, revised and edited while I was on a period of study leave from Warwick University. I am grateful to Warwick University for granting me the privilege of space to allow me to complete this editing and writing task. Thanks are also due to my colleagues in the Centre for Corporate Strategy and Change, Yvon Dufour, Chris Hendry, Paul Sparrow, Robert Rosenfeld and Richard Whipp, for practical support and assistance in organizing the seminar.

Finally, I would like to acknowledge the important administrative and secretarial assistance provided by Jeanette Whitmore and Gill Drakeley of the Centre for Corporate Strategy and Change, from the period of the seminar's inception through to this final volume.

Andrew M. Pettigrew
Centre for Corporate Strategy and Change
Warwick University

Introduction: Researching Strategic Change

Andrew Pettigrew

The management of strategic change is one of the central practical and theoretical issues of the 1980s. For many organizations in the European and North American economic context, the period since 1979 has been an era of environmentally driven radical change. Large sectors of industry, particularly the mature industries of steel, coal, shipbuilding and engineering, have declined, and the growth prospects of Western economies are poor. Competition for available business is much stronger than before, yet new investment is harder to justify. There have been periodic energy and raw material supply problems, and the costs of those inputs to business rise often unpredictably. Large organizations have been pressured not only by national and international political events and groupings, through mechanisms of regulation and deregulation, but also by environmental and consumer interest groups. These past several years have also witnessed a loss of competitiveness of the advanced industrialized countries relative to the newer industrialized countries and the emergence of so-called 'global markets'.

Among the many managerial responses to the above environmental pressures, the most visible and tangible are selective divestment from product lines not robust enough to survive profitably and the movement of capital and other resources away from home markets to markets and economies offering greater prospects of profitability and growth. Firms have used acquisitions, organic growth and joint ventures to internationalize their businesses, and structural change to reduce numbers of employees and get fixed cost down. Needs for survival have been complemented with needs for regeneration. Through all this, managerial confidence and the capability to sense, articulate, and implement major changes in business strategy, structure, culture and people have become essential requirements of business survival and success.

Recent surveys in the UK context by Thomson, Pettigrew and Rubashow (1985) and in the United States by Severance and Passino (1986) have begun to unravel the anatomy of strategic change in companies. The 1984 Thomson *et al.* survey of 1000 middle and senior executives and directors in 190 companies enquired about changes made since 1979. 33 per cent of the managers reported 'radical changes', with 56 per cent acknowledging 'some change' and 10 per cent indicating little or no change. Factors influencing changes in strategy most notably included the general recession and changing markets. The survey also asked about the methods used to bring about changes in strategy, and the most important group emerged as intensification of marketing and sales effort (69 per cent), reorganization changes (58 per cent), new product development (60 per cent) and tighter financial controls (54 per cent). Those respondents reporting a radically changed strategy had a much higher score for organization changes and rationalization than those reporting the same strategy; non-British company respondents had a higher percentage ranking for new product development than British companies; but the biggest single difference was that the manufacturing companies had a very much higher recording for substantial redundancies as a means of implementing strategic change, mirroring patterns in overall employment change.

The Severance and Passino (1986) survey involved personal interviews with over 50 senior manufacturing executives in 15 firms and then a questionnaire survey distributed to 1500 chief executive officers (CEOs) but completed by only 180. As a prelude to their report, Severance and Passino noted 'recent studies of Fortune 1000 CEOs document strategic planning and implementation to be the area of greatest concern to chief executive officers. It is also the area to which they currently allocate the greatest amount of their time and the one to which they feel that even more of their attention should go' (1986, p. 1). This US survey concludes that the dominant manufacturing strategy of the 1980s has been one of dramatic quality improvements coupled with significant cost reduction achieved through the elimination of inventories and the slashing of direct labour content. The most obvious marketing strategy has been the attempt to increase current market share while offering new products into the market. Strategy implementation has been punctuated by a replacement of the management team and characterized by substantial investments in plant, equipment, R&D, and manufacturing control systems.

Significantly, the Severance–Passino survey also reported on attitudes towards strategic planning and change, with a clear message of CEOs' scepticism towards using formalized strategic planning procedures and an increased sensitivity to more informal processes of leadership, vision building and communicating, and to team and commitment building as sufficient conditions to manage processes of creating strategic change. The importance of such process skills are reported in several of the chapters in this volume.

Thus far, it is evident that the behaviour of many firms is a clear witness to the description of the post-1980 period as an era of substantial change involving people, organizations, markets, industry sectors and national economies. Even with all the doubts and multiplicity of definitions in the management literature of the word 'strategy' (see, for example, Hofer and Schendel, 1978; McGee and Thomas, 1985), there is no question in my mind that the phrase 'strategic change' rests easily and credibly alongside the recent experience of many firms. 'Strategic change' is descriptive of magnitude of alteration in, for example, the culture, structure, product market and geographical positioning of the firm, recognizing the second-order effects, or multiple consequences, of any such changes and, of course, the transparent linkages between firms and their sectoral, market and economic contexts.

But if the management of strategic change is a self-evidently important executive problem, in what sense, and in what way, has it been and is it now a significant area of scholarship and research? In the brief review that follows, the evidence is of comparatively little attention given to the analysis of strategic change, either at the firm or industry sector levels of analysis, and of academics being slow to analyse and understand phenomena that managers and policy-makers have had to grapple with through recent and condensed periods of experience.

RESEARCH ON MANAGEMENT AND STRATEGIC CHANGE: A BRIEF REVIEW

The field of study variously labelled 'business policy and planning', 'business strategy' and 'strategic management' is itself in a period of flux and change, partly at least stimulated by some of the firm and sector-level transformations referred to above. Economists are more explicitly incorporating the language of business strategy, and indeed firm-level behaviour, in their conceptualizations of markets and firms (Moss, 1981; Kay, 1982, 1984). Ideas are being taken from industrial organization research and applied to business policy research to the benefit of both traditions (Porter, 1980, 1981); and organization theorists are contributing by eschewing their traditional concern with the firm and beginning to analyse not only broad sector changes (Lawrence and Dyer, 1983), but also changes in sector-level phenomenon across national boundaries (Walton, 1987). Indeed, it was partly the obvious importance of the topic, plus evidence of an opening up of the field with organization theorists, marketing researchers and business historians more obviously joining economists and business policy researchers to focus on the area of strategy and change, that led to the organization of the seminar on which this volume is based.

But in the narrower fields of strategic management and the study of strategic decision-making and change, what are some of the antecedents of this new and multi-disciplinary enthusiasm for research on strategic aspects of firm behaviour? Broad answers to that question have recently been supplied by the volumes edited by Pennings (1985) and McGee and Thomas (1985). Both of these books illustrate some of the problems of the field, including the bias of existing literature on strategic management towards strategy formulation (the analysis of strategic content); the limited attention given to the implementation of strategy (the analysis of strategic process); the emphasis on prescriptive writing in the field, and the consequent under-concern with description, analysis and understanding; and the definitional problems and conceptualization of what strategy is. In using the term 'strategy', are we talking of intended strategy, implicitly realized strategies, or strategy as a social construction or rationalization used to give meaning to prior activities? Are business strategies to be understood as outcomes, processes or derivatives of peopleless market and economic structures? Where the firm is the focal point of analysis, what model of man and theory of process is understood to drive the strategic development of the firm? Does one lean towards endogenous or exogenous explanations of change? Is, indeed, the firm the correct starting point to explore strategic management, or should one explore strategic groups, industry sectors or product markets? If one decides to analyse more than one level of analysis, what is distinctive and additive about such an approach, and what special methodological challenges does this create alongside the need to find conceptual linkages between and among the levels of analysis so chosen?

In among all these choices and dilemmas, Zajac and Bowman (1985) have recently tried to do an audit of the general perspectives, study domains, sample sizes and research methodologies chosen by empirical strategy researchers. They analysed all the empirical studies published in the *Strategic Management Journal* from its inception in 1980 through 1984, and coded the articles along a variety of dimensions to reveal some of the choices made by research investigators. Although they are careful not to claim that their findings offer conclusive indications of the state of empirical research, they do offer some interesting pointers as to how researchers have conceptualized and studied the topics published in article form in the *Strategic Management Journal*.

Broadly, and perhaps not unexpectedly, Zajac and Bowman found a considerable intercorrelation between their dimensions. Thus, studies that treated the firm as a complex open system were more likely to eschew the more heavily quantitative methodologies and be more hesitant to offer normative suggestions to managers. Equally, strategy implementation researchers (as distinct from those interested in the formulation of strategy) were more likely to use inductive theorizing, small samples and intensive qualitative methodologies. Crucial, however, to our present concern with the analysis and management of strategic change, studies of strategy formulation far exceeded those of strategy implementation. Furthermore, only 6 of the 70 empirical studies were truly longitudinal. 'That is, less than 10% of the studies used either a time series methodology if they were quantitative in nature, or examined trends or patterns in historical archival data if qualitative in nature' (Zajac and Bowman, 1985, p. 20). Unfortunately, Zajac and Bowman did not report how many of the six longitudinal studies actually offered a processual analysis of strategic change of the kind reported elsewhere by Pettigrew (1985a) and Johnson (1987) and provided in this volume by Whipp et al. (chapter 1) and Doz and Prahalad (chapter 2).

Notwithstanding the classic work of Chandler (1962, 1977), the research tradition developed at McGill University by Mintzberg (1978) and others, and recent work by Lawrence and Dyer (1983), Pettigrew (1985a) and Johnson (1987), longitudinal research on the transformation of firms, industries and markets is not yet well established. One way of characterizing the state of knowledge in the field is to map patterns in existing work on to the three broad classes of variables listed in figure 1 below. In this formulation, the management of strategic change involves consideration of not only the content of a chosen strategy, or even of the analytical process which reveals various content alternatives, but also the management of the process of change, and the contexts in which it occurs. Two aspects of context are considered: the inner and outer contexts of the firm. 'Inner context' refers to the structure, corporate culture and political context within the firm through which ideas for change have to proceed. Outer context refers to the economic, business, political and societal formations in which firms must operate. The process of change refers to the actions, reactions and interactions from the various interested parties as they seek to move the firm from its present to its future state. Thus, broadly speaking, the 'what' of change is encapsulated under the label content, much of the 'why' of change is derived from an analysis of inner and outer context, and the 'how' of change can be understood from an analysis of process.

With figure 1 as a reference point, one way of characterizing research on strategic management emanating from industrial organization and business policy and planning is to note the preoccupation with such research with the left-hand side of the triangle. Thus, writers such as Hofer and Schendel (1978), Caves (1980) and Porter (1980) explore in different ways the content–outer context link and substantially ignore the inner context of the firm, while offering an implicit theory of process which is rational in character. Those variants of the literature preoccupied with the content–outer context link perennially treat the formulation and implementation of strategy as discrete and linear activities. This way of conceptualizing the analysis and implementation of strategy not only is increasingly under criticism by process researchers such as Mintzberg (1978), Quinn (1980) and Pettigrew (1985a, 1985b), but also is being discarded at least in the rhetoric of some of the major consultancy firms offering advice on strategic management (Fortune, 1982).

However, the so-called process researchers can have their crimes of omission. There has been a tendency for process scholars from organization

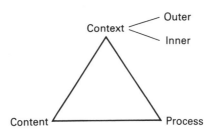

Figure 1

theory and business policy backgrounds to focus on the process–inner context link and thereby to de-emphasize both the explanatory role of outer context variables and the analytical exploration of the alternative content areas for strategic change. In my view, theoretically sound and practically useful research on strategic change should involve the continuous interplay among ideas about the context, the process and the content of change, together with skill in regulating the relations among the three (Pettigrew, 1985a). Research on strategic change which is that analytically broad is still unusual, and one viable approach for taking the field forward is to encourage more research on change that does go beyond the simple content–process dichotomy and brings variability of contexts into the picture.

Drawing the outer and inner context of the firm into the analysis has a number of important benefits. First of all, questions abut the what, why, how and when of firm response to change can be addressed in association with equivalent questions about changes in the structure of sectors, markets and industries. Equally, changes in competitive and co-operative response between competitors need increasingly to be studied in the context of involvements between manufacturers and their suppliers and competitors. As Whitley (1985) and others have pointed out, choosing the level or (more likely) levels of analysis for defined theoretical purposes is a key requirement for effective research on the study of firm behaviour. However, a key and as yet unresolved problem in this area of enquiry is creating the theoretical apparatus to link levels of analysis.

Unstated but central to the mode of analysis implied in figure 1 is the need to explore content, context and process linkages through time. Here there are great practical problems, not only of negotiating access for such intensive analysis, and of finding sponsors for such work, but also of dealing with the challenging methodological issues of collecting time-series data simultaneously in real and historical time over several levels of analysis. The chapters by Whipp, Rosenfeld and Pettigrew (chapter 1), Doz and Prahalad (chapter 2), Tushman and Anderson (chapter 3), Harrigan (chapter 6) and Ghazanfar, McGee and Thomas (chapter 5) reveal alternative forms of longitudinal data collection and analysis majoring at different levels of analysis. Of course, time-series data can be collected without offering an analysis of the processes of decision-making and change, as the Harrigan and Tushman–Anderson chapters illustrate. More work needs to be done testing and developing the relative merits of the various process theories of choice and change now available. Most of these process theories, the so-called boundedly rational, incremental, random, learning and political approaches, have been borrowed, often uncritically, from decision process models. In his view of the seminar proceedings, Van de Ven (chapter 10) rightly points to the work yet to be done in conceptualizing alternative process theories of change. Here there is a recognition that a robust theory of change would simultaneously have to explain forces of stability and change, include exogenous and endogenous sources of change, link phenomena at micro- and macro-levels of analysis and deal with issues about the rate, pace and direction of change.

This brief review has revealed some of the analytical and methodological choices in conducting research on the management of strategic change. It remains for me to illustrate how some of these choices were built into the conceptual structure of the seminar and then exemplified in the chapters, commentaries and review papers in this book.

THE CONCEPTUAL STRUCTURE OF THE SEMINAR AND BOOK

A topic such as the management of strategic change is not containable within the myopia of any particular discipline. Equally, the analysis of strategic change is not reducible to any single level of analysis. Conceptually, the seminar was designed to ensure that discussion did not get trapped at one level of analysis. Thus, the early papers at the seminar and in this volume explore strategic change with the firm as the focal point of analysis; the middle papers (chapters 3–6) concentrate on the industry sector as the unit of analysis; and chapters 7–9 have a bias towards the product market as the unit of analysis. By exposing the analysis of strategic change to these different levels of analysis, not only were different variables and methodologies revealed, but also the theoretical assumptions and limitations of different disciplines. In effect, the move from the beginning to the middle of the seminar (and in this volume) allowed a transition from researchers with business strategy, business history and organization theory backgrounds to scholars using industrial economics perspectives and methodologies. The final chapters open up the proceedings that much more by bringing in researchers with a marketing perspective. Thus, it was challenging to hear economists and industrial organization scholars arguing for the sector as the unit of analysis, in, for example, technological change – 'endogenous and exogenous' provided a useful language to focus this issue; while towards the end of this book Srivastava and Shocker remind us that marketing focuses on customers and competitors, not on managers. This was a reminder that outcomes from strategic decisions and changes are often in the hands of customers and competitors.

The first two chapters that follow report longitudinal case-study work on strategic change processes at the firm level of analysis. Chapter 2 by Doz and Prahalad describes empirical findings from a completed project, while the Warwick chapter (by Whipp, Rosenfeld and Pettigrew) offers the research framework, study questions and some preliminary findings six months into a study of the management of strategic and operational change in mature industries.

The Whipp *et al.* chapter (chapter 1), although focusing on the firm as the unit of analysis, emphasizes the necessity to explore firm-level processes of strategic change in their social, economic and sectoral context. It also argues strongly for longitudinal research combining historical and real time analysis, and for a framework of analysis examining interlinkages between the content, context and process of strategic change. Crucially, in this research strategic change processes are being studied right down to their operational implementation at factory and office level. The sample of firms have been chosen so as to link the process of managerial assessment, choice and change to the relative performance of firms in the automobile, merchant banking, insurance and book publishing industries. Given the early stage of this project, no attempt is made in the chapter to link managerial process to performance; rather, the analytical value of the content–context–process framework is illustrated with reference to case-study work from the automobile and merchant banking sectors.

Chapter 2 by Doz and Prahalad reports a continuation of the authors' work on the transformation of large, complex multinational corporations. Their work seeks both to develop a way of conceptualizing the processes of strategic change in multinationals and to identify the characteristics of the transformation process which lead to success or failure in the adaptation of firms to new environments. Using a data base of 16 case studies, a comparatively large sample for this kind of intensive process research, Doz and Prahalad illustrate how strategic redirections involve complex and difficult processes of managing cognitive, strategic and power shifts within the firm. The association between major change and the challenging of the core beliefs of the top decision-makers by new leaders is a feature of the Doz–Prahalad results, mirrored in earlier work by Pettigrew (1985a), and also signalled in the Whipp *et al.* chapter.

The commentaries by Johnson and Child usefully point to some of the dilemmas of conducting process research of the kind recommended by Whipp *et al.* and Doz and Prahalad. Methodologically, Child would have liked to have seen more evidence of historical investigation and therefore analysis of the antecedents of redirection in the Doz–Prahalad work. Child also points to the important linkage betwen firm-level behaviour and the sectoral networks and influences within which executives may seek to manage the transformation of the firm. In addition, he asks the important question of whether the content of strategic change may influence the character of the process, and he thereby queries the universality of the four-stage process model offered by Doz and Prahalad. Johnson, meanwhile, draws attention to the way the early empirical findings of the Whipp *et al.* chapter bear resemblance to recently published work on strategic change. His commentary usefully asks fundamental questions about the role and purpose of contextualist work of the kind carried out by Whipp and his colleagues. What are some of the relationships between specific, operational decisions and overall patterns of strategy? How do patterns in the process of strategic change vary in different contexts? And what are the detailed mechanisms and processes that release what he calls paradigmatic changes in organizations? These and other more focused areas of enquiry will have to be encouraged if contextualist research on strategic change is to realize its promise.

Chapter 3, by Tushman and Anderson, offers longitudinal data on technological change at the sectoral level of analysis. Here trends are abstracted from the time-series data but no attempt is made to analyse mechanisms and processes of change within the firm. Using data from the US minicomputer, cement and airline industries from their birth through 1980, the authors demonstrate that technology evolves through periods of incremental change punctuated by either competence-enhancing or competence-destroying techno-logical discontinuities. Whereas competence-destroying discontinuities are initiated by new firms and are associated with increased environmental turbulence, competence-enhancing discontinuities are initiated by existing firms and are associated with increased environmental consolidation. These effects decrease over successive discontinuities. Those firms that initiate major technological changes grow more rapidly than other firms.

Pavitt's commentary on the Tushman–Anderson chapter congratulates the authors for the ingenuity of their data sources in a difficult area and for their explicit attempt to test hypotheses. However, Pavitt questions Tushman and Anderson's lack of concern with incremental explanations of technological change, and thereby of the evidence elsewhere for a link between incremental and discontinuous forces of change.

Using mostly secondary time-series data on the strategies of 33 larger firms in the UK cutlery industry, Grant in chapter 4 explores the strategies used by those firms to try to combat low-cost import penetration. Broadly, he found that none of the conventional strategy recommendations for improving international competitiveness in such circumstances was successful. Moreover, heavy investment in strategic adjustment was seen as resource-expensive and risky in a highly competitive, fragmented industry. Profitability was shown to be dependent upon a careful matching of strategy to firm resources and competitive conditions within industry sub-sectors.

Melin's commentary on the Grant chapter not only explores and reveals some of the assumptions of Grant's research but also raises a number of paradigmatic questions about research approaches within the field of strategic management. It can usefully be set alongside the more general questioning about the conduct of research on strategic change offered in this Introduction and in chapters 10 and 11.

Chapter 5, by Ghazanfar, McGee and Thomas, moves us from the fortunes of the UK cutlery industry to a longitudinal study of the impact of technological change on the reprographics industry in the UK. Like Grant's chapter, it reported completed research, but this time there was a more explicit attempt to collect and use primary and secondary data. Ghazanfar *et al.* had sufficient longitudinal data to reveal temporal change in firm and industry structure, and there was some attempt to grasp the content and process of change. Empirically, Ghazanfar *et al.* were able to demonstrate that, with every step change in technology, the main elements of market structure change: cost conditions change, the height of entry barriers changes, and so do the extent and nature of product differentiation. Stoneman's commentary on chapter 5 seeks to link the Ghazanfar *et al.* findings to work by economists in other industries such as shipping, and makes a plea for a greater explanatory role for the endogeneity of technological change than that offered by the authors.

Harrigan's chapter on 'Joint Ventures: A Mechanism for Creating Strategic Change' exposed the definitional approach, methodology and empirical findings from a massive study of how joint ventures have been used to help create structural changes in 23 US industries over the years 1924–85. Harrigan demonstrates how and why decisions to form or not to form co-operative alliances represent key strategic decisions which affect the structure of industries and the fate of individual firms. Her results suggest that co-operative strategies can induce changes in firms' competitive environments by promulgating product standards, developing formal infrastructures in young industries and consolidating excess capacity in mature industries. In his commentary of Harrigan's chapter, Norburn offers a mixture of admiration for Harrigan's exact and cool presentation of her findings plus a request for a more theoretical and practical interpretation of them — probably too much to expect in the space limitations of this volume. He reasonably asks for more exploration of managerial processes of implementing joint venture strategies in future research in this area, also appeals for more research on joint ventures in the context of global industry development and the need to tease out why firms choose joint ventures against other options such as organic growth or outright acquisition.

The final three chapters in this volume, by Mattsson, Srivastava and Shocker, and Easton and Rothschild, move the discussion away from managerial behaviour in the firm and the changing structure of industries to examine market structures, customers and the virtues of product and production flexibility in effecting change. Chapter 7 by Mattsson and chapter 9 by Easton and Rothschild are conceptual in character, offering, in the Mattsson case, a way of conceptualizing markets-as-networks and, in the example of Easton and Rothschild, reflections on the flexibility of the firm drawing on the interests of scholars and practitioners of manufacturing policy and marketing.

Mattsson attempts to link firm and market considerations by conceptualizing the firm in its environment through what he and other Swedish colleagues call the 'markets-as-networks' perspective. In this formulation of co-operative and competitive relationships between firms, strategic change is defined as a major change in a firm's position in its network. In addition to offering a way of thinking about the structure of such networks, through categories such as structuredness, homogeneity, hierarchy and exclusiveness, Mattsson also considers the manner and extent to which network relationships are managed by conscious strategies. Mansfield's commentary on this chapter points to the distinctive contribution of describing a company's strategic position as a network linking suppliers, customers and competitors. However, there are great problems in describing and analysing such networks so as to reveal their dynamic form.

The Srivastava–Shocker chapter (chapter 8) analyses data on parts of the US financial services industry to focus on the role of customer/demand and firm/supply considerations to explain the evolution of product markets. The value of this chapter to the seminar and to this volume lies in its unequivocal introduction of the language of customer and markets into the vocabulary to describe and analyse the formulation of strategy. It demonstrates how data built up from customer perceptions, problems and purposes can help to define both the form of product markets and the choices available to influence the redefinition of product markets. Wensley's commentary on the chapter raises a number of technical, theoretical and philosophical queries about strategic change within a market environment. He questions the extent to which attitude structures are stable, the relationship if any between customer attitudes and behaviour, and the difficulty of linking data about the evolving nature of customer perceptions to the competitive strategy of the firm. There are also difficulties of coming to terms with the very complexity of what is produced by the Srivastava–Shocker approach. As Wensley puts it, knowing this much in this way may not necessarily lead to clear additions in terms of understanding; however, there was no doubt at the seminar, or I believe in Wensley's own mind, that the customer perspective is an important and often neglected one in understanding strategic change in markets and firms.

In Chapter 9, Easton and Rothschild present a conceptual paper at the interface between production and marketing. They examine two aspects of organizational flexibility: flexibility in the production processes a firm may employ, and flexibility in the products it produces. The implications of greater or less flexibility in these two areas of activity are then examined in so far as they relate to marketing strategy. Easton and Rothschild brought out into the open an issue lying just beneath the surface throughout the seminar: do firms have corporate-level strategies, or in discussing strategic changes are we more exactly analysing functional strategies below the corporate level, or some ill-defined mixture of corporate and functional strategies? More narrowly, the chapter also revealed some of the constraints on strategic and operational behaviour at the product market level arising from commitments to manufacturing facilities. However, competitiveness through flexibility is the central prescriptive message for Easton and Rothschild, with the management of change in market positions, products and manufacturing systems representing the means of reaching the competitiveness goal.

In his review of chapter 9, Cunningham doubts that the theme of flexibility is appropriate for all sizes of firms in different markets and technologies. He also raises practical questions about measuring flexibility and thereby demonstrating improvements in flexibility over time, and is sceptical that corporate goals such as flexibility and responsiveness will be able to prevail over the sub-optimal goals driven by marketing and production interests.

In their different ways, the two review essays by Van de Ven and Argyris add considerably to the other chapters in the book. Both authors offer reflections on the content and theoretical perspectives in the earlier chapters, but they also bring to this volume their recent thinking about understanding and managing strategic change processes.

Van de Ven's essay in chapter 10 is an excellent practical statement of some of the key theoretical and methodological issues facing researchers studying processes of strategic change in organizations. In this chapter Van de Ven makes explicit many of the analytical choices that are only implicit in most of the chapters in this book. Critically, he notes that few of the papers at the seminar (and little of the discussion at the time) tried to deal with his fourth requirement for processual analysis: specifying the alternative process theories for making sense of observable process patterns. He points to the need not just for longitudinal research but also for rigorous methods for observing differences overtime; for real time and historical analyses; for sound and coherent ways of organizing and coding time-series data; and, of course, for explicit attempts to develop currently available process theories of change.

Chris Argyris interrogates the bulk of the chapters in this book through some of the questioning from his latest book, *Strategy, Change and Defensive Routines*. He identifies some of the non-trivial executive errors evident in the cases of this book and asks, Why did these executives think and act as they did? Argyris briefly takes us into his thinking about defensive routines in organizations, and pushes us to think about what he calls second-order errors – implicit, undiscussable, and therefore unmanageable errors. It is these second-order errors, combined with organizational defensive routines, that make it difficult for strategic change processes to be managed effectively in organizations. Defensiveness leads to a loss of control by management and thereby to ineffective implementation. If such processes are to be understood and controlled, researchers will have to conduct research on strategic change which is not limited by the tenets of what Argyris calls 'normal sciences'.

REFERENCES

Caves, R. E. (1980) Industrial organization, corporate strategy, and structure: a survey. *Journal of Economics Literature*, 18 (1), 64–92.

Chandler, A. D. (1962) *Strategy and Structure*. Cambridge, Mass.: MIT Press.

—— (1977) *The Visible Hand*. New York: McGraw-Hill.

Hofer, C. W. and Schendel, D. E. (1978) *Strategy Formulation: Analytical Concepts*. St Paul, Minn.: West Publishing.

Fortune (1982) Corporate strategists. *Fortune*, 27 December, 34–9.

Johnson, G. (1987) *Strategic Change and the Management Process*. Oxford: Basil Blackwell.

Kay, N. M. (1982) *The Evolving Firm: Strategy and Structure in Industrial Organisation*. London: Macmillan.

—— (1984) *The Emergent Firm: Knowledge, Ignorance and Surprise in Economic Organisation.* London: Macmillan.

Lawrence, P. R. and Dyer, D. (1983) *Renewing American Industry.* New York: Free Press.

Mintzberg, H. (1978) Patterns in strategy formulation. *Management Science,* 24 (9), 934–48.

McGee, J. and Thomas, H. (1985) *Strategic Management Research: A European Perspective.* Chichester: John Wiley.

Moss, S. J. (1981) *An Economic Theory of Business Strategy.* Oxford: Martin Robertson.

Pennings, J. M. (ed.)(1985) *Organizational Strategy and Change.* San Francisco: Jossey Bass.

Pettigrew, A. M. (1985a) *The Awakening Giant: Continuity and Change in ICI.* Oxford: Basil Blackwell.

—— (1985b) Contextualist research: a natural way to link theory and practice. In E. E. Lawler (ed.), *Doing Research That is Useful in Theory and Practice.* San Francisco: Jossey Bass.

Porter, M. E. (1980) *Competitive Strategy: Techniques for Analyzing Industries and Competitors.* New York: Free Press.

—— (1981) The contributions of industrial organization to strategic management. *Academy of Management Review,* 6 (4), 609–20.

Quinn, J. B. (1980) *Strategies for Change: Logical Incrementalism.* Homewood, Ill.: Richard Irwin.

Severance, D. G. and Passino, J. H. (1986) *Senior Management Attitudes toward Strategic Change in US Manufacturing Companies.* Ann Arbor, Mich.: University of Michigan Press.

Thomson, A., Pettigrew, A. M. and Rubashow, N. (1985) British management and strategic change. *European Management Journal,* 3 (3), 165–73.

Walton, R. E. (1987) *Innovating to Compete: Organisational Change in Seven Countries.* San Francisco: Jossey Bass.

Whitley, R. (1985) The study of firm's behaviour: issues and approaches. Unpublished paper, Manchester Business School.

Zajac, E. J. and Bowman, E. H. (1985) Perspectives and choices in strategy research. Working Paper 85–15, Reginald H. Jones Center for Management Policy Strategy and Organization. The Wharton School, University of Pennsylvania, Philadephia.

1 Understanding Strategic Change Processes: Some Preliminary British Findings

Richard Whipp, Robert Rosenfeld and Andrew Pettigrew

INTRODUCTION

This chapter presents the research framework, study questions and some early findings of a project seeking to link the relative competitive performance of British firms to the capability of those firms to adjust and adapt to major changes in their environment. The research is being carried out at the Centre for Corporate Strategy and Change, University of Warwick, in collaboration with Coopers and Lybrand Associates. It is also part of the Economic and Social Research Council's research initiative on 'The Competitiveness of British Industry'. The paper has four sections. The first gives an outline of our research framework and indicates our analytical point of departure. The middle two sections contain the initial findings of our first studies of strategic change in the automobile and merchant banking sectors, with an exploration of the successive phases of the Rootes/Chrysler UK/Peugeot-Talbot operation in Britain and an examination of the experience of Robert Fleming, a merchant bank. The final section provides a summary and conclusion.

MANAGEMENT, STRATEGIC CHANGE AND COMPETITIVENESS

The unfolding of economic events during the 1970s and early 1980s has drawn further attention to the relative decline of the British economy and the continuing loss of competitiveness of large sectors of British industry. In the search for explanations of Britain's declining competitiveness, a multiplicity

This chapter is derived from research supported by the Economic and Social Research Council.

of factors have surfaced (Pollard, 1982; Caves and Krause, 1980; Wiener, 1981).

But is Britain's declining competitiveness to be explained simply by a mixture that includes national economic policies, macroeconomic variables, the deep-rooted social and cultural biases of UK society, the peculiarities of our financial institutions and our tax system, and the patterns of trade union activity and industrial relations? We think not. Given the substantial changes in the economic, political and business environment of large firms over the past two decades, a critical factor affecting the relative competitive position of British firms must be the capability of firms to adjust and adapt to major changes in their environments and thereby improve their competitive performance. The importance of these adjustment and adaptation processes suggests that the nature of management itself is a crucial aspect of the competitiveness issue. Part of the management task is to identify and assess changing economic, business and political conditions, and to develop and then implement new strategies to improve the firm's competitive performance.

Accordingly, a central proposition of this research is that the way large organizations assess the changing economic, business and political environment around them, and formulate and implement strategic and operational changes, is an important input in the equation leading to the maintenance and improvement of competitive performance. Furthermore, these managerial processes of strategic assessment, choice and change are not just questions of the economic calculation of strategic opportunity carried out by men and women driven by rational imperatives. The process of perceiving and then assessing environmental change and its implications for new strategies, structures, technologies and cultures in the firm is an immensely complex human and organizational process, in which differential perception, quests for efficiency and power, visionary leadership skills, the vicariousness of chance, and subtle processes of additively building up a momentum of support for change and then vigorously implementing change all play their part.

Thus, the objective of this research is to describe and analyse processes of decision-making in selected firms as those firms attempt to manage strategic and operational changes. Strategic decisions and changes will be viewed as streams of activity involving individuals and groups which occur mainly but not solely as a consequence of environmental change, and which can lead to alterations in the core purpose, product market focus, structure, technology and culture of the host organization. 'Strategic' is just a description of magnitude of alteration in, for example, market focus and structure, recognizing the second-order effects, or multiple consequences, of any such changes.

Given the pragmatic requirement for strategic changes to be vigorously and operationally implemented through to the factory or unit level, this research is concerned to identify the processes by which both strategic and more operational changes are made. However, the fact that strategic changes have to be implemented operationally does not have to imply that 'implementation' is a discrete activity which follows the formulation of strategy. Part of the empirical and theoretical focus of this research builds on recent work by Mintzberg (1978), Quinn (1980) and Pettigrew (1985a), which treats the formulation and implementation of strategy as a continuous and iterative process in which additive accumulations of managerial decisions combined with the triggering effects of environmental disturbances can produce major transformations in the firm.

The research focuses on the transformation processes of firms in mature industry and service sectors. Choice and change processes are examined in organizations faced with the twin dilemma of survival and regeneration. This will allow the analysis of the what, why and how of firms surviving with mature products in overcrowded markets while at the same time providing an external and an internal environment, possibly new products, new structures, new systems, new cultures and a new managerial capability to regenerate the firm for the future.

Empirically, the research will examine processes of decision-making and change in a pair of firms in each product market. Using the kind of package of criteria of success adopted by, for example, Lawrence and Lorsch (1967) and Peters and Waterman (1982), one firm will be deemed a higher performer for the product market and the other, relatively speaking, a lesser performer. The chosen firms must also be large for their sector, and each pair must either be both unionized or both non-unionized. A further objective in choosing the sample from mature sectors is to look at two sectors with a history of growth and two with a history of contraction. Thus, for example, automobiles and publishing could represent maturity with contraction, and insurance and merchant banking could represent maturity with a history of growth. The research could thus include a 'higher performing' and a 'lesser performing' firm in each of four sectors of automobiles, publishing, insurance and merchant banking – eight cases in all.

The research will take the perspective and methods of the business historian, business strategist and organization theorist. The intention is to collect longitudinal data gathered in semi-structured tape-recorded interviews, through short periods of observation in each firm, and by the analysis of primary, archival and secondary material. Each of the case studies requires the collection of retrospective and real time data. The project studies change as a continuous process in context, and thus avoid the methodological trap of trying to understand either strategic or operational changes as discrete episodes divorced from the antecedents in the firm, and the ongoing development of the social, political, economic and organizational context influencing and influenced by particular change events (Pettigrew, 1985b).

A basic task is to identify the unit of analysis for the research agenda and, more importantly, the preliminary understanding of the connections between management and competitiveness which it embodies. In short, the unit of analysis is the continuous process of decision-making in selected firms as they seek to manage strategic changes. Yet, as will become clear below, this research will try to describe and analyse these processes as they operate at the level of the firm but within their appropriate contexts both inside and outside the organization. Moreover, far from strategic change being a straightforward rational process, it is best considered as a jointly analytical educational/learning and political process (Pettigrew, 1985a).

At the heart of these analytical and political processes of strategic change are those dominating ideas and frames of thought which provide systems of meaning and interpretation, which in turn filter both intra-organizational and environmental signals. Therefore, the way in which businesses perceive their competitive position, and the decisions they take to adjust their competitive position, must perforce be inextricably linked to those dominating frames of thought which inform an organization's analytical and political processes of strategic change. We are especially concerned with the combined relevance of those rational/objective and political/subjective aspects of strategic change processes to competitive performance.

In order to extend this understanding of the link between competitiveness and strategic change, the subject of competitiveness itself deserves further attention. There are useful distinctions to be made between the levels at which competitiveness may be understood and their dynamic nature across time. Three major levels are involved: the firm, the sector and the national/international levels (Pettigrew, Whipp and Rosenfeld, 1987). It is insufficient, however, to approach competitiveness according to a fixed hierarchy. Rather, the bases of competition at each level, and hence the rules for competing, are not stable or constant: on the contrary, they change over time and seemingly (in the 1980s) with increasing speed, as will become evident in both the automobile and banking examples that follow.

It would be reasonable to maintain that, following this hierarchical and dynamic understanding of competitiveness, the ability of an enterprise to compete at any given moment and within whatever prevailing market configuration relies on (1) the capacity of that organization to identify and understand the nature of competition and how it changes, and (2) the potential of a business to mobilize and manage the resources necessary for whatever response is chosen. Irrespective of the decision that is made, the capacity to carry out the changes it implies depends on the critical ability to manage that process of change. Furthermore, adopting a contextual and processual approach to the management of strategic and operational change enables our research to embrace both the vertical and the horizontal axes of competition. The contextualist mode of enquiry addresses the competitive forces that operate at the firm, sector or national/international levels; the processual mode captures the changing bases of competition at each level and across time.

In order to elaborate on the relevance of a contextual and processual approach to the relationship between the management of strategic change and competitive performance, it is necessary to outline what a possible research framework might look like. If management's general task is to assess changing economic, business and political conditions, and to identify and implement new strategies which improve the firm's competitive performance, this implies that its especial responsibility becomes the management of three related areas: the content of a chosen strategy, the process of change, and the contexts in which it occurs (Pettigrew, 1985a). The three related areas may be expressed in simple diagrammatic form as in figure 1.1. Each of these three areas contains a collection of research themes and issues.

There are four groups of issues which arise in relation to the content of a specific strategy: the dominating frames of thought within the organization; the strategy's central objectives; the source of the strategy; and the extent to which the strategy anticipates the means of implementation. The extent to which these components provide a cohesive knowledge base and tactial repertoire for the business as a whole are also of concern; and the role of specialist advisors in forming competitive attitudes should be accounted for.

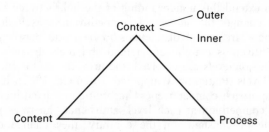

FIGURE 1.1   Outline analytical framework

The second main area of the research framework relates to the contexts in which any strategic change occurs. There are two contextual levels: the inner and the outer contexts of the firm. The inner context consists largely of the structure, culture and politics of an organization. Structure here refers not only to the formal framework of relationships within a company but also to the multiple structures produced by the composite actions of individuals within an organization. The culture of an organization includes the beliefs, meanings and rationales used to legitimate action, together with the languages, codes and rules that inform those actions. The politics of an enterprise relates both to the internal distribution of power and to the plurality of contenders involved. Each has a direct or indirect bearing on competitive performance by the way they shape company strategies in either their mode of creation or their execution. The outer context of strategic change processes comes closer to the macro- and national-scale approaches to competitive performance. It may be conveniently divided into four areas: the economic, business, political and societal formations in which firms must operate.

The third, and perhaps most critical, yet elusive, area of the research framework concerns the processual dimension of strategic change. It is through this dimension that research can capture the dynamic aspects of strategic assessment, choice and change as well as competitive performance. In essence, we are interested in the long-term pattern of events by which strategies are conceived and their competitive purposes put into operation. We need to ascertain, therefore, who champions and manages new strategies; what decision arenas and processes they emerge from; what models of change govern the conception and implementation; and how appropriate they are to the contexts in which the firm operates (Pettigrew, 1985a; Whipp and Clark, 1986).

As much of the foregoing implies, contextual research into competitiveness at the level of the firm hinges on the relationship between managerial perception, action and the contexts in which management operates. The analytical challenge is to connect up the content, contexts and process of strategic change with competitive performance. We have suggested a range of possible linkages. Perhaps the most critical connection for our research is the way managers mobilize the contexts around them and in so doing provide legitimacy for change. The contexts in which management operate are not inert or objective entities. Just as managers perceive and construct their own versions of those contexts, so they subjectively select their own versions of the competitive environment together with their personal visions of how to re-order their business to meet those perceived challenges.

In essence, this research hopes to extend our comprehension of that relationship by maximizing the use of an integrated conception of the problem combined with a flexible approach and methodology. Put briefly, the research employs a synthesis of a contextualist and processual orientation to strategic change in order to discover how managing that change relates to the different levels of competition. Such a synthesis raises the possibility of moving beyond those accounts of competitiveness which focus solely on the firm, or the sector or societal unit of analysis (Hart, 1983). More especially, a research agenda that takes such a conceptual starting point would hope to highlight both the subjective bases and the more objective definitions of competitiveness: it would also expect to reveal the way these conceptions change interactively with the essentially human process of managerial assessment, choice and change.

STRATEGIC CHANGE AND THE ROOTES/CHRYSLER/ PEUGEOT–TALBOT UK OPERATION

The need to study the management of strategic change in the British auto industry in general and across the successive phases of the Rootes/Chrysler/ Peugeot–Talbot operation is compelling. A lengthy list of academic and press articles, government inquiries and specialist reports notwithstanding, detailed explorations of strategic and operational change in individual motor manufacturers are rare (Whipp and Clark, 1986). The upheaval in the UK motor industry of the last fifteen years has been as severe as anywhere in the world (Berg, 1985).

The Rootes/Chrysler/Peugeot story provides a notable opportunity to examine how British, US and French management attempted to make the necessary assessments, choices and changes within the 'new competition' of the 1970s (Abernathy *et al.*, 1981). Although attracting widespread attention during the many crises within the Chrysler UK era, most accounts have dealt with the outcomes of these episodes (Young and Hood, 1977).

The example of Rootes/Chrysler/Peugot–Talbot raises a set of issues of special relevance to students of strategic change. These include the difficulties of strategic redirection when management of different nationalities are involved; the way in which the social and technical characteristics of large organizations can both facilitate and retard different aspects of given strategies; and how the means of creating and operationalizing such strategies have been found wanting when confronted by recent market and technological changes. In short, this section will try to explain the relatively poor competitive performance of Rootes/Chrysler/Peugeot–Talbot not only by reference to the stated content of the strategies employed, but also by relating their formation and fate to the contexts in which they arose together with their processes of operation. Even at this interim point in the research, the complexity of these processes of strategic change is daunting. What follows, therefore, is a very compressed treatment of the processes, which by no means considers every dimension of our research framework. Caution is necessary for one further reason; reconstructing the events and relationships involved, after the climactic events of 1964–78 especially, might be likened to piecing together the fragments of a bomb.

Strategic Events: A Profile of Rootes/Chrysler/Peugeot–Talbot

A central proposition within our research is that the formulation and implementation of strategy is a continuous and iterative process. However, in order to come to terms with such a process, it is necessary to establish an outline description of the main strategic events and acts. There are, strictly speaking, three eras involved: Rootes between 1898 and 1964, the Chrysler era from 1964 to 1978, and the Peugeot–Talbot phase from 1979 to the present.

The origins of the Rootes group can be traced to the establishment in 1898 of William Rootes's business selling cars in Hawkhurst, Kent. In 1926 the company began what we now know was to become a lengthy series of acquisitions as it moved from servicing the industry to manufacturing cars and commercial vehicles in its own right. Up to 1939, Rootes was able to buy into manufacturing relatively cheaply, as the purchase of Humber–Hillman, Karrier Motors and Sunbeam–Talbot was of companies that were virtually bankrupt or in receivership. Rootes realized that capital restructuring and reorganization of the new additions would not ensure a profit. Their strategy was therefore 'one of growth and expansion'. By the Second World War

Rootes had grown in sales terms by almost 600 per cent and the company accounted for 10 per cent of the UK car market (Talbot, 1983).

During the postwar years of high replacement demand and a marked expansion of the world market, Rootes embarked on a second phase of acquisition in the 1950s. Yet, as the replacement boom gave way to more uneven cyclical demand and increased competition in the 1960s, Rootes's strategy of expansion raised a major coincidence of problems. Rootes had to rationalize a diverse mixture of companies, plants and sales networks. Yet at the same time, the Rootes Group in total did not have the sales levels that would allow them to benefit from such reorganization (Whipp and Clark, 1986). This was to be a key difficulty for all three eras of Rootes, Chrysler and Peugeot–Talbot. In 1963 Rootes took a major step in opening a new 1.6 million square foot plant at Linwood in Scotland in order to extend their model range to include the growing small car market. Political considerations apart, Linwood was symptomatic of the difficulties Rootes faced. While the logic for such an attempt to increase their range and market share was reasonable, the company was unable to realize the sales objectives on which their strategy depended. Profitability suffered accordingly (Young and Hood, 1977).

Between 1964 and 1967, Chrysler Corporation progressively bought control of Rootes. Up to 1974, successive managements wrestled with the problem-set inherited from the Rootes Group. In tackling those problems, two sets of additional difficulties arose. One related to the worsening position of the UK economy and motor car industry which led to mounting losses between 1969 and 1973; the second occurred in 1974 as the world auto industry slumped disastrously following the oil price escalation, allied to a marked decline in the fortunes of the Chrysler Corporation in the USA. In 1975 Chrysler Corporation, the parent company, decided to offer Chrysler UK to the British government; if the government was uninterested, Chrysler would close the UK operation. The ensuing negotiations and debate were matched in intensity only by those surrounding the government's parallel rescue of British Leyland (HMSO, 1976). At the end of 1975 an agreement was signed between the Corporation and the government in which both underwrote Chrysler's UK's losses for four years, and provided loans and capital injections of the order of £121 million. Against continuing losses in the UK and elsewhere, Chrysler Corporation retrenched. In August 1978 the Corporation negotiated an agreement to sell its European companies in France, Britain and Spain to Peugeot SA.

The operation of Peugeot–Talbot UK really falls into two sub-phases, each with a distinct character. In the initial phase from 1978 to 1981, Peugeot–Talbot's managers addressed a nest of major problems which had accumulated during the traumatic years of the mid-1970s. These ranged from low productivity to a declining dealer organization. Not two years into addressing these problems, the company was engulfed by the combined effect of the Iranian revolution and war, a world recession and the strength of

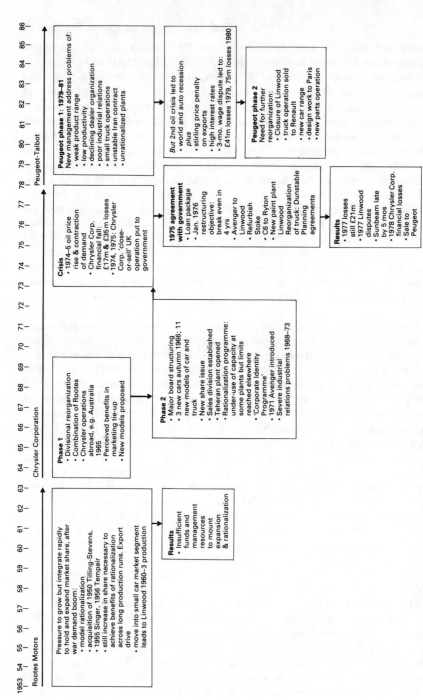

FIGURE 1.2 Rootes Chrysler Peugeot–Talbot strategic event chart

of the Rootes Group and those of the Chrysler Group, in terms
lines, manufacturing facilities and marketing organization, are
ith each other rather than in conflict, and the pattern of the two
uch that association as provided by the agreement assures the
rength essential to a strong competitive position in the world market.

t overlooking of the major differences in market structure,
igns, product life-cycles and managerial practices between Britain
industries is revealing. It is critical in accounting for the way
rporation's initial strategy of merely financing and giving help
to by Rootes between 1964 and 1967 failed, and why its reformed
after was always trying to recapture lost ground. Chrysler's early
towards Rootes is especially remarkable given the reaction of a
epresentative at the unveiling of the prototype of the Hillman
1964. The Rootes family acclaimed the model. The euphoria was
by the Chrysler man who remarked: 'Gentlemen, we are now
an obsolescent automobile' (*Motor*, 1978). When Rootes losses
o more than £10 million in 1966–7, Chrysler realized that more
rvention was necessary.

me had been lost. After taking effective control of the company in
967, Chrysler management found that Linwood was operating at
city while the Imp and Hunter models had failed against the
t products of Ford, BMC and Vauxhall. As they publicly admitted
ootes 1967 Annual Report, they faced the difficult task of: 'two
eous programmes. On the one hand we are retrenching, making
es, reducing costs and reshaping our structure. On the other hand,
e-equipping our plants to meet new programmes and to arrange our
cturing capabilities to match the best techniques.'
lost time and long-term weaknesses of Rootes meant that Chrysler
the company was renamed in 1970) strategy was always a defensive
best aimed at catching up with the other domestic producers. Although
Avenger model introduced in 1970 was a sales success, the cost of
g the car into production meant that Chrysler UK lost over £10 million
0. Tiny profits between 1971 and 1973 were insufficient to fund new
s. Furthermore, the fact that the company was highly geared and relying
sively on short-term bank loans made for an insecure financial base. As
as February 1971, the managing director's reports to the board begin
l with conclusions that 'these negative points are largely beyond direct
ational control.' Liquidity became an increasing problem as credit lines
withdrawn and the parent corporation ran into financial difficulties.
he years 1976–8 saw, after the government rescue package, a major
ucturing as the basis of a strategy for breaking even in four years. The
main components hinged on the transfer of the Avenger from Coventry
Linwood and the introduction of the Chrysler-France-developed Alpine
). Continued industrial relations problems and a failure to produce to

sterling and high interest rates in the UK. As a result, the company made
major strategic changes between 1981 and 1983. These included the closure
of Linwood, the disposal of its truck plants to Renault, the integration of
Peugeot and Talbot sales in the UK, the transference of engineering and
stylling functions to Paris, and the progressive replacement of Chrysler's
model range with six Peugeot vehicles. The UK operation is now described
as 'somewhat peripheral' to Peugeot SA's main activities, and its future is
unclear (Casson, 1985).

Figure 1.2 depicts the sequence of strategic events outlined above and can
be used as a simple map to guide the exploration of the content, contexts
and process of strategic change in Rootes/Chrysler/Peugeot–Talbot which
follows. Table 1.1 and figure 1.3 indicate the course of the companies' market
share and profitability across the period.

TABLE 1.1 Market shares of main producers in the UK auto industry, 1965–85(%)

	Rootes/ Chrysler/ Peugeot– Talbot	Brit. Motor Corp./ Brit. Leyland	Ford	Gen. Motors	Fiat	Volkswagen– Audi group
1985	4.0	18.1	25.9	16.6	2.9	5.7
1984	4.0	18.3	27.8	16.2	2.9	5.5
1983	4.4	18.6	28.9	14.6	2.8	5.6
1982	4.8	17.8	30.5	11.7	3.1	5.9
1981	5.7	19.2	30.9	8.6	4.2	5.4
1980	6.0	18.2	30.7	8.8	3.4	4.5
1979	6.9	19.6	28.3	8.2	4.6	4.4
1978	7.0	23.5	24.6	9.7	5.3	4.0
1977	6.0	24.3	25.7	10.4	5.7	3.5
1976	6.4	27.4	25.3	10.1	4.3	3.4
1975	8.0	30.9	21.7	8.3	3.8	4.0
1974	10.8	32.7	22.7	8.0	3.8	3.1
1973	11.4	31.9	22.6	9.0	3.2	3.8
1972	11.6	33.1	24.6	10.0	3.1	4.1
1971	10.5	40.1	18.7	10.7	2.8	3.8
1970	10.4	38.1	26.5	9.9	2.1	3.4
1969	9.2	40.2	27.3	11.6	2.1	2.1
1968	11.3	40.5	27.2	13.1	NG	NG
1967	11.9	40.7	25.3	13.1		
1966	11.7	45.2	25.0	11.2		
1965	11.9	44.5	26.3	11.8		

Sources: Society of Motor Manufacturers and Traders, Annual Reports on the UK Industry, New Registrations; Statistics Yearbook, Peugeot–Talbot, 1984.

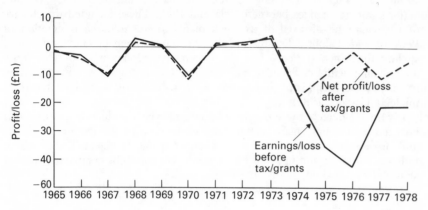

FIGURE 1.3   Chrysler UK profit/loss profile, 1965–78 (unadjusted)
Source: Annual Reports.

Content: Expansion, Integration and Retrenchment

In order to explore and explain the nature of strategic change in the Rootes/
Chrysler/Peugeot–Talbot example in the space available, the rest of this
section examines the content, contexts and process involved, separately and
sequentially. First, the key objectives and sources of the main company
strategies will be displayed and their internal logic exposed. Second, the main
components of these policies and changes will then be related to two main
contexts: the inner or organizational setting from which they emerged, and
the outer context, which those policies were supposed to address. The third
part of this exploration of strategic change turns to the dynamic aspect. This
attempts to show how corporate intentions and contextual forces interacted
across time.

The outline of the postwar Rootes policies and problems was given earlier.
The need to rationalize newly acquired facilities while at the same time
increasing market share to make scale economies within those plants possible
remained constant. However, by the very nature of the companies that Rootes
Motors had acquired (Humber, Sunbeam and Clement Talbot and Singer),
their model range was directed towards the quality end of the car market.
So, although the company appeared aware of the growing market of the
postwar era, and of their own internal need to increase sales, it was firmly
located in the quality market areas. Here, by definition, sales could never
match the popular volume end, and scale economies would always prove
difficult to reach.

Moreover, given the considerable problem of facilities and company
rationalization within the Rootes Group, the family-dominated board was

schedule led to continuing losses in a severely contracting market and to the sale to Peugeot SA in 1978.

The financially strong Peugeot company mounted a strategy in 1979 which was really yet another attempt to tackle the problems in the UK operation within the existing structure set by Chrysler. Peugeot therefore addressed the weak product range, low productivity, a declining dealer organization, the poor industrial relations record, the instability of the Iran contract and the persistent problem of scattered manufacturing plants with underused capacity. After the second oil crisis and the world recession it triggered in 1978–9, Peugeot took radical action. As set out above in the outline of strategic events, the old Chrysler UK structure was drastically reduced. By 1983 the Ryton plant in Coventry assembled three French-developed models, of which 22 per cent of the components came from Peugeot. There is a question mark in 1986 over Peugeot's UK business. Will it invest further in Britain when faced with major problems across its European operations? Most critically, Peugeot 'faces too many serious problems', namely: there are too many products competing in the same range (see table 1.2); the company benefits from few advantages of scale; and the group is falling short on spending to maintain its three product lines. The Group must rationalize quickly 'if it is not to become totally uncompetitive' (Bhaskar, 1979).

Contexts: From Amateurism to Professionalism in a Cold Climate

As the foregoing account of the content of Rootes/Chrysler/Peugeot–Talbot's strategies has suggested, it is impossible to explain the changing policies of the companies without reference to the contexts in which they occurred. An examination of the internal structure, leadership style and dominating frames of thought show why Rootes was slow to react to market changes, how the Chrysler management found its knowledge unsuited to UK conditions, and how a timely change in chief executive under Peugeot ensured the implementation of a drastic new strategy. At the same time, two broad features

TABLE 1.2   Peugeot SA Model Range 1983, Cars

Segment	Talbot UK	Peugeot	Citroen
Mini			2CV/Dyane
Small	Samba	104	LNA/VISA
Light/medium	Horizon	205/305	GSA
Large	Solara/Alpine	504	BX
Executive		604	CX
Luxury			
Specialist	Rancho		

Sources: Peugeot SA, Annual Reports; Press Release File, Peugeot–Talbot UK

of the outer context deserve attention: first, the fundamental changes in markets and second, government intervention.

Inner Context   Throughout the process of acquisition and expansion, the Rootes Group management remained heavily dependent on the Rootes family. In the early stages, Billy and Reginald (sons of William Rootes, who began the Rootes motor retail business) provided twin direction until 1939. Billy won a wide reputation as an entrepreneur, while Reginald's skill lay in 'administration and finance'. After the Second World War, their sons joined them in senior management. Geoffrey and Brian, the sons of Billy, eventually became managing directors of manufacturing and overseas operations, respectively; Timothy, son of Reginald, was director of sales and service. These family members personally controlled the boards of each member of the Group. As the success of many German family firms (including BMW) shows, there is no necessary reason why such enterprises should not succeed (Bruce, 1984).

However, in the case of the Rootes company, the personal backgrounds and motivations proved decisive and reveal why their strategic orientation became outdated and left Chrysler with such a nest of problems. The attempt to retain personal control, allied to certain family dispositions, meant that the development of managerial expertise in key areas remained undeveloped. Allowing for the state of contemporary product management in the UK, Rootes product planning in the 1950s and 1960s was still resting on procedures better suited to the earlier era of quality/specialist car demand. The second generation of the Rootes family saw themselves as fitted for management by war service and vacation work in the company's plants. None had specialist management education, something they had in common with the managers they recruited in the immediate postwar era. Nor was this pattern greatly disturbed, as the lengthy career profiles at Rootes show: over 10 per cent of Rootes staff had over 25 years' service in 1966.

Others have pointed to the undeveloped nature of industrial relations and production management at Rootes in the conditions of labour shortages (especially skilled workers) (Tolliday, 1986). Indeed, in a sellers' market, and with help from suppliers such as Pressed Steel, for example, Rootes could survive, albeit modestly, on such a basis. However, when the market changed and models in new market segments were required, these accumulated weaknesses were sorely exposed between 1960 and 1964.

The mixture of new British and US managers that Chrysler brought in from 1967 onwards faced a formidable task which grew progressively more difficult. At the outset, Chrysler Corporation was not renowned for its managerial excellence. Unlike the strategies of Ford and GM in the USA, Chrysler attempted to make periodic, radical product innovations, a course that involved greater risks and led to several crises. Moreover, as Chrysler began its association with Rootes in 1965, the parent company experienced a sales slump and corruption scandal among its top management. Coalmineowner George Love saved the Corporation with a capital injection; 70,000 of the US white-collar staff were fired, and Chrysler was forced to adopt the less risky evolutionary, incremental styling policy of its major competitors. In addition, Chrysler Corporation was doubly ill-equipped to meet the problems it would face in the UK. Not only was its management recovering from a crisis in 1965, but the Corporation had little experience or skills associated with vertical or, to an extent, horizontal integration. Compared with Ford's well proven integrated growth from a central stem, Chrysler US was still using over 30,000 independent suppliers in 1978 (Whipp and Clark, 1986; Casson, 1985).

Yet, as we saw in the sub-section on the content of Chrysler UK's strategy, the US management lost three years as they gave Rootes's existing leadership the benefit of the doubt. When they assumed control in 1967, the full scope of the problem shocked the Detroit Corporation. According to those responsible, it was not so much a question of what strategy to choose but rather, how they could develop a company structure and management remotely capable of carrying out a chosen course of action. In simple terms, Chrysler UK did two things: first, it decided on a US-inspired divisional structure with a set of 'modern' accounting and organizational methods; second, it brought in senior management from its US operations with junior management recruited from Ford UK. The three divisions were Overseas, Passenger Cars, and Commercial Vehicles. It took three major attempts to create an organizational structure around the idea of a board, administrative committee, policy committees and functional divisions and departments. Financial planning and accounting procedures, and management training and product planning models, were introduced virtually from scratch.

While trying to create a corporate structure which resembled contemporary US or European standards and appointing senior executives with international experience, the problems facing Chrysler UK intensified at a frightening pace. At the same time as grappling with what the new managing director Hunt saw as retrenching and re-equipping, the company did well to launch the Avenger in 1970. However, a combination of internal developments was decisive in leading to the crisis of 1975. The problems of low profits arising from the development costs of the Avenger and the resulting liquidity pressures have already been mentioned. Three further factors stand out. Critical obstacles emerged in the areas of (1) industrial relations, (2) suppliers, and (3) Chrysler UK's connections with the other Chrysler companies in Europe.

On the first two counts, US management found the British fragmented bargaining structure and the chaotic collection of small independent suppliers bordering on the incomprehensible. But elements of the firm's outer context served only to worsen the position in the 1970s. As inflation hit record levels in the early 1970s and workers attempted to match wages to prices, disputes reached similar peaks in both vehicle and component suppliers (Whipp, 1986). Contrary to the general orthodoxy, it was the undeveloped nature of Rootes and other car companies' industrial relations structures (not union strength) which led to widespread disruption and the continual inability to meet production targets. Symptomatic of these problems were the 150 major components which had to be dual-sourced in October 1971 and the 185 of Chrysler's 390 suppliers who did not have any 'labour agreement'. Between 1970 and 1973, the dispute record of Chrysler UK spoke for itself (see table 1.3). On the third count, what should have been a major help to the supply situation and Chrysler UK's scale economies, the integration of Chrysler Europe, was slow to develop.

TABLE 1.3   Chrysler UK's industrial disputes, 1970–3

	1970	1971	1972	1973
Man-hours lost	566,458	497,029	1,599,271	1,751,103
Vehicles lost	23,152	37,914	43,358	90,541

The 'crash' of 1975, with its consequent effects on morale among Chrysler UK's management and its market position, only made their task more difficult in 1976–8 as the price inflation and wage parity pressures continued. At this stage of the research, identification of the key internal changes of Peugeot–Talbot is still only partially developed. Thus far, it would appear that the introduction of a chief executive with both UK and international car industry experience was critical. What is seen within the organization as his 'courage' to make the decisions to rationalize the UK operation and take speedy action to reorder the entire dealer network, raise productivity, transform product quality and reliability and introduce new pay and bargaining arrangements coincided with a return to profit in five years of a savagely reduced company.

Outer Context   A comprehensive account of the elements that made up the outer context which the strategies of Rootes/Chrysler/Peugeot–Talbot addressed lies outside the scope of this chapter. In order to understand the character and fate of those strategies, however, two main aspects of the firm's outer context deserve mention: the major changes in the auto industry in the UK and abroad, and the course of government attempts to manage the UK economy.

First, the transition from the postwar years of replacement demand to the problem-filled decades of the 1960s and 1970s changed the character of competition fundamentally in the UK auto industry (McNalty, 1954). Productive capacity among the Western producers outstripped demand; fierce competition ensued with the abolition of European tariff barriers and the twin oil price shocks of 1973–4 and 1979. In Britain the problem was magnified by the car industry's accumulated disadvantages. The effect was devastating.

Import penetration rose from 6 per cent in the late 1960s to a colossal 40 per cent by 1975 in the UK market (Bloomfield, 1978; PEIDA, 1984).

It has already been shown how Rootes embodied so many of the deficiencies of the UK producers. Chrysler inherited those deficiencies but, while trying to tackle them, was also required to respond to arguably the most serious dislocation of the world industry in the postwar era. It is unsurprising, therefore, given what we have revealed of the source and internal setting of Chrysler UK's strategies, that they resulted in even greater deficits (Jones, 1981). The second broad feature of the outer context of Rootes/Chrysler/Peugeot–Talbot relates to the macroeconomic level and the role of government policy. What has been termed the 'stop–go' nature of these policies has made planning in the UK especially difficult compared with other countries (Dunnett, 1980). Summarizing the situation, the managing director of Chrysler UK told his board on 15 January 1975 of 'The very changing pattern of our industry to-day, which makes any form of forecasting difficult to the point of being practically impossible. ... The business world is changing rapidly in ways which most of us have not experienced before.'

Since 1979, the effects of government monetarist policy have added to the difficulties of the UK motor industry and to Peugeot especially. In spite of some easing of sterling from 1981/2 onwards, British inflation and exchange rates have been high compared with European norms. From 1978 Britain's competitiveness deteriorated by 35–55 per cent compared with Germany, France, Belgium and the Netherlands. In order to compete with Japan on real exchange rates in October 1983, Britain's sterling rate of exchange would have had to have fallen by nearly 60 per cent (Bhaskar, 1979).

Process: Some Dynamics of Strategic Change

Further into our research programme, it will be possible to construct a map which will chart the full richness of strategic change across three different enterprises. Such a chart would reveal the multiple linkages between the conception and execution of successive policies and their relevant contexts. It would also include the way the rhythm of internal development and crisis in the firms in question intersected with the wholly exceptional course of change within the auto sector and the international economy.

At present, our analysis of such courses and conjunctions are but partially formed. None the less, on the evidence presented here, some interesting insights into the nature of strategic change emerge. An appreciation of how the interaction of the contents and contexts of the strategies of Rootes, Chrysler and Peugeot–Talbot propelled this process of strategic change can be derived from key examples of managerial assessment, choice and change.

In common with other domestic auto manufacturers, Rootes appear to have made a number of assessments in the 1950s which were based on outdated methods. This led to choices which were notable for their limited relevance to market trends. In contrast to the period of expansion prior to the Second

World War, the implementation of even those changes that Rootes had seen as necessary was decreasingly successful. Put simply, Rootes's strategic capacity no longer matched up to the environment in which it had to operate.

However, in Chrysler UK's case the picture is not so straightforward. As a result, some of the orthodox conclusions are shown to be unfounded. As we saw, Chrysler Corporation's assessment of first Rootes and then the British car market was misplaced; hence the damaging pause of 1964–7 and the scale of the task that faced Hunt and his management from 1967 onwards. Yet, in some ways the speed of introducing critical 'competitive skills' to the organization which Chrysler inherited was impressive. The creation of long-range planning, project management and competitor monitoring procedures, for example, were almost entirely new to the British industry. On the basis of assessments made using these new tools, choices that led to successful cars such as the Avenger in 1970 and the award-winning Alpine in 1976 seem logical and defensible. At first, the ability to implement the necessary changes worked adequately, at least in the case of the Avenger.

But the mounting losses of the early 1970s should not lead to an easy dismissal of Chrysler UK's ability to assess and implement change. Bardou *et al.* (1982) argue that all the Western car producers' growth projections were wrong in the early 1970s, in spite of alternative forecasts which suggested a market downturn *before* the oil crisis. Moreover, if we bring together the range of obstacles that brought the market leaders almost to their financial knees, then Chrysler's fate takes on a slightly different appearance. Briefly put, while implementing necessary changes to meet the conditions of the British market, Chrysler UK was swamped by a tidal wave of external problems. A financial crisis in the parent corporation and a climactic transformation of the world auto market, combined with mounting difficulties in basic areas of supplies, industrial relations and government policy, overwhelmed Chrysler UK's original strategy. Furthermore, it is completely inappropriate to assume that Chrysler faced a single crisis or problem set. Reconstruction of internal reporting, and in particular the managing director's quarterly board reports across time (that is, in 1967–78), reveals a cumulative, almost 'rolling', sequence of radically new obstacles, as the managing director's comment from January 1975 showed.

The temporal dimension assumes an important significance within the analysis which goes beyond either Chrysler or the auto sector. It is vital therefore not only to set strategic change within a long-term historical perspective, but also to go beyond that in order to discover the critical alterations of the *pace* of change. Understanding the Chrysler example and the interaction of content and contexts hinges on this point. There are perhaps three phases involved. In the early 1970s, Chrysler management's attempt to redress the uncompetitiveness of Rootes found the increase in European competition, arising from overcapacity, outstripping them. Second, the speed at which events thwarted Chrysler's adjusted strategies during 1973–5 was exceptional, as parent company losses were followed by two large-scale strikes in 1973, the oil crisis, liquidity failure and the prolonged trauma of a government rescue throughout 1975. Third, the intensification of competition across the world auto industry through and beyond this second phase led to totally new bases of competition. Radically new production technology, international component sourcing and manufacturing and a wholesale reworking of the design process, with the related reduction of product cycles and lead times, appeared. Neither Chrysler UK in 1976–8 nor Peugeot Talbot in Britain in 1978–81 was able to develop managerial capacities which could make the appropriate assessments, choices and changes. In truth, the speed at which those assessments, choices and changes have to be made, and the vast capital sums they entail, has increased markedly. Indeed, few car manufacturers outside Japan can be at all confident of their capacity to mobilize their competitive skills at such speed in the future.

THE STRATEGIC DEVELOPMENT OF A MERCHANT BANK

Introduction

Research into the merchant banking sector began in January 1986. Discussion in this section centres on the context, content and processes of strategic changes that have occurred at one merchant bank, Robert Fleming Holdings Limited. Given the cumulative nature of strategic change over time, the analysis will follow a longitudinal approach, identifying specific aspects of the content, context and process relevant during a particular time period.

Strategic change at Robert Fleming has come about persistently through an evolutionary process. Much consideration is given to determining whether a 'fit' exists between the personalities of the individuals and organizations involved. An additional factor in understanding the way in which Robert Fleming has evolved is the overall stability of leadership within the organization. Of the six chairmen at Robert Fleming since its incorporation in 1909, three have been members of the Fleming family. The issue of compatibility is paramount at Fleming's. According to the firm's top management, this compatibility is crucial to successful ventures. Compatibility is seen as the degree of congruence between people, personalities, experience and environment.

Foundations of Fleming's Strategy

Robert Fleming was a bookkeeper for a Scottish textile firm in Dundee which specialized in the import of jute fibre. In 1870, at the age of 25, he travelled to America to survey economic conditions there. He found that the dollar had depreciated considerably as a result of the efforts being made to recover from the Civil War. Upon his return to Scotland, he initiated, in 1873, an investment trust, called the Scottish American Investment Trust, which was the first trust in Scotland to invest in US railroad bonds. The offering for this venture was highly oversubscribed and was followed by the start-up of two more trusts to invest in US railroad bonds.

The economic environment at the time was clearly ready for the kind of service Fleming was offering. Scottish businessmen were faced with a declining business in the jute trade and were anxiously looking around for alternative investments. Given his experience in jute, Fleming was already known to many of the potential investors. From Fleming's standpoint, the level of risk involved was relatively low since he was already aware that he would have clients lined up for this product, once it was established. This approach of introducing new products when a need was perceived among its clients was to hold throughout the development of the company and is still maintained today.

Owing to the popularity of investing in the USA at the time, Robert Fleming focused his attention primarily upon US investment opportunities. The emphasis placed during this period upon investing in North American securities has also been maintained throughout the years. By 1888 Fleming had opened an office in London, and by 1909 he was headquartered in London. Also in 1909, Robert Fleming & Co was registered as a partnership between Robert Fleming and Walter Whigham. They described themselves as 'one of the strongest agencies which offered to investment trusts the advantage of cooperative management, purchasing and underwriting participations' (Fitzherbert, 1983, p. 14). In 1911 Robert Fleming's son Phillip joined the partnership, at the age of 22. By 1928 it was reported that Robert Fleming was able to influence 56 trusts, with a total valuation of £114.8 million.

The First Reorganization

The first major reorganization of the company came in 1932 when the partnership was split into two limited companies: London & Lochside Investment Trust Limited, which managed the investment trust side of the business, and Robert Fleming & Co. Limited, which focused on the merchant banking side. It was perceived that there was the potential for a conflict of interest between the trust side of the business and the banking side. It would be unethical if the trust side were to buy or sell investments on the basis of confidential information which the banking side had received in the course of its work with clients. Though these firms were to remain separate until 1974, the top management of both organizations was largely the same. It was at the account management level that the separation had to be most clearly seen. In modern parlance in the City of London, this can be viewed as an early attempt to construct a 'Chinese Wall' of confidentiality.

In 1933 Robert Fleming, the founder, died at the age of 88. He was succeeded by his long-time partner Walter Whigham until he passed away at the age of 70, in 1948. Upon Whigham's demise, Robert Fleming's son Phillip assumed chairmanship. Phillip Fleming retired in 1966.

Fleming's strategy during this period was defensive in that the emphasis remained on the fund management business. After the Second World War, corporate finance activity increased dramatically in the UK, and Fleming's operated in this area as well. However, the firm was only moderately succssful owing to its hesitancy to commit the necessary financial and managerial resources. Earnings during this period were featured by slow, steady growth in terms of share capital and pre-tax profits. As the firm was family-owned, its dividend policy was to extract only enough money from the company to maintain the Fleming family.

During this stage of slow growth, the strategies remained unstated, with the exception of a strong belief that Fleming's should continue to service its clients' financial needs as they requested them. The expansion of the business was seen as being 'customer-led'. This approach was supported by the directors at the time (a majority of whom were members of the Fleming family), who desired to see the firm remain profitable enough to support the family at large, and therefore were unwilling to stake too much of their accumulated capital on any risky or capital-intensive venture.

The outer context within which Fleming's had to operate changed slowly during this period. There was a gentlemanly approach to competition within the City at that time. Members of the Fleming family were close friends with the families running other merchant banks, such as Baring Brothers, Kleinwort & Co., and Robert Benson/Lonsdale. Links were also maintained through cross-directorships with other firms and financial institutions.

The competitive atmosphere started to change in the later part of the 1950s as the merchant banks recognized that, in order to survive, greater financial strength would be required. Up to this point, profits had generally derived from helping domestic clients with their financial transactions. This was reinforced by the passing of the Foreign Exchange Control Act in 1947, which severely limited the fredom of investors to transfer their funds overseas. By the late 1950s, merchant banks were beginning to merge with one another in an attempt to provide a fuller range of services to clients. Table 1.4 illustrates some merchant banking mergers during the 1950s and 1960s.

During this period of realignment among the merchant banks, Fleming's had also been tempted by a merger proposal with de Stein, a bank that had done business with Fleming's earlier. Its chairman, Sir Edward de Stein, approached Fleming's but was turned down by Phillip Fleming and his second-in-command, Sir Archibald Jamieson. Eventually, de Stein merged with Lazard's in 1960.

The inner context of Fleming's changed very little during this period. The directors (called 'partners' within the firm) tended to work very closely with one another. They worked together in a large room, and therefore most decisions were made informally. Work was carried out on a reciprocal basis with everyone 'pitching in' when required. As leaders, Walter Whigham, and Phillip Fleming after him, saw themselves as less autocratic than Robert Fleming, and they were hesitant to make any change to the business itself.

TABLE 1.4   Merchant banking mergers during the 1950s and 1960s

Participant	Year	Major services	Accepting Houses committee member
S. G. Warburg	1956	CF (**)	No
Seligman Brothers		B (**) CF (*)	Yes
J. Henry Schroder & Co.	1960	B (***) I (*) CF (*)	Yes
Herbert Wagg & Co.		CF (***)	No
Kleinwort & Co.	1961	B (***) I (*) CF (*)	Yes
Lonsdale Investment Trust (Robert Benson & Co.)		I (*) CF (***)	No
Lazard Brothers	1960	B (***) CF (*)	Yes
Edward de Stein		CF (***)	No
Phillip Hill, Higginson & Co.	1959	B (*) CF (***)	No
Erlangers		B (**) CF (*)	Yes
Phillip Hill, Higginson, Erlangers & Co.	1965	B (**) CF (***)	Yes
M. Samuel & Co.		B (**) I (*) CF (*)	Yes

Key
B   Banking (mainly acceptances)
CF   Corporate finance services in new issues, and advisory services in mergers and acquisitions
I   Investment management
*   Denotes relative strength
Source: Robinson (1976, p. 42).

This unwillingness to change was the underlying factor behind the haphazard approach to expansion and diversification. An example of the hesitancy with which Fleming's approached new strategic opportunities concerns the growth of corporate finance business.

In 1956, Fleming's was asked by one of its clients, Aberdare Cables, to help them by underwriting a new rights issue. The Fleming's manager who handled this affair recounts this story: 'I went and saw Richard [Fleming], and told him that it was done and all underwritten and he said, "what do you think we ought to charge them?" I said I have no idea; it's the first one we have done. He said, "Well, why don't we charge them £500 and that will teach them we don't like this sort of business"' (Fitzherbert, 1983, p. 91). Having charged Aberdare Cables £500 for what amounted to a relatively large operation, the firm came back again and again.

Owing to its success in handling a small number of such corporate finance issues, other companies who used Fleming's for investment management purposes began to approach the firm to take on similar work. The difficulty was that Fleming's did not have the specialist personnel to handle such work, and whenever such a task was accepted, staff had to be taken off their normal work to deal with it. Eventually, a team evolved out of the staff at Fleming's which would handle corporate finance activity as it came up. This consisted of Richard Fleming (who later became chairman) and a few others. Early corporate finance clients included Britain Petroleum, Burmah Oil and ICI. An effect of the haphazard approach to corporate finance work at the time is the work done for ICI in 1961 on the unsuccessful bid for Courtaulds. The bid was not managed well, and when the offer failed it was viewed within the City as a poor reflection upon Fleming's reputation. This experience was repeated again in 1963 during the ill-fated takeover attempt of Pergamon Press by Leasco. The result was that it highlighted the need to acquire more individuals with expertise to handle the increasingly complex business of corporate finance.

Inner Contextual Change: A New Type of Leader

In 1966 Richard Fleming became chairman. In reality, he had already assumed much of the day-to-day running of Fleming's owing to his charismatic style of leadership. Largely through his initiative, the organization began to grow and diversify into new business areas. Before assuming the chairmanship, Richard Fleming had become interested in corporate finance and had seen the potential in allocating more resources and expertise to this area. At the same time the passing of the Trustee Investments Act in 1963 permitted firms such as Fleming's to widen the type of issues in which they could place their funds. Under the new ruling they would be permitted to invest in a wider range of equities and commercial bonds domestically, as well as internationally.

The 1960s was a time when new potential was being recognized within the merchant banking sector. The Eurodollar market was being created, corporate finance was becoming more active in conjunction with the rise in mergers and acquisitions within British industry in general, and merchant banks were perceiving greater opportunities in the fee-generating business of fund management.

During this period, many of the merchant banks adopted diversification strategies, moving out of their area of origin (i.e. trade financing) into a wide variety of other financially based activities. Aside from expansion overseas, normally to areas with which the merchant bank has some historical link, the diversification included life insurance, insurance broking, employee benefits consultancy, property investment and management, shipbrokers, oil and gas exploration, unit trust operations and advertising.

Beginning in the late 1970s and early 1980s, London started to attract an increasing number of foreign banks and financial services companies to start up operations. One reason for coming to the UK was to participate in the growth of the Eurocurrency markets. Within a relatively short space of time, the international banks, especially US-based banks, came to dominate the international currency markets, as well as servicing the overseas financial needs of US multinationals. Not surprisingly, these foreign financial entities soon started to compete directly with UK financial institutions for domestic sterling-denominated business.

From the mid-1960s, Fleming's adopted a more competitive stance, diversifying away from its core investment management business by undertaking more banking and corporate-finance-related activity. Unfortunately, the firm was a late arrival in a competitive market, and it proved difficult to woo clients away from other merchant banks. Throughout Richard Fleming's tenure as chairman, he brought into the organization individuals with expertise in the various areas of banking and corporate finance to provide the knowledge base necessary to function adequately in this area.

An example of an endeavour that encountered difficulty owing to lack of resources was the expansion into the USA through the firm's wholly owned subsidiary, Robert Fleming, Inc. (RF, Inc.). Initially, this operation was to participate in the underwriting of equity and bond issues in the USA in much the same way as domestic US investment houses do. When RF, Inc. commenced operations in 1969, the stock markets in the USA were peaking and a good return was made very quickly. However, within two years the markets had turned sour. Coupled with this was the advent of 'negotiated commissions', which served to reduce the profit margin on underwriting participations (Walmsley, 1985). Survival in this market now required more capital to undertake a greater number of participations. A higher level of risk also had to be accepted, as it would be necessary to participate in many more issues to resume the previous levels of profitability. Given the restricted financial and managerial resources available at the time, RF, Inc. evolved into a representative office for Fleming's rather than as a domestic US securities house.

Another endeavour undertaken by Fleming's during this period was the creation in 1969 of Jardine Fleming, a joint venture with the Jardine Matheson Group of Hong Kong. Within the Fleming organization today, this venture is viewed as an example of unforeseen success, not only for the profit it has contributed, but also for the boost it gave to expanding the investment horizons beyond the UK and the USA.

Fleming's interest in the Far East was awakened by requests the firm had received from its investment clients regarding potential opportunities in Far Eastern markets. In fact, 'it was put to Fleming's by some of these clients that unless they were able to provide advice on Far Eastern markets as well as that traditionally provided for American, Australian, and other overseas markets, they might be obliged to either develop the research themselves or look elsewhere for guidance' (Fitzherbert, 1983, p. 91).

Through already existing family and financial connections, Richard Fleming was approached by the chairman of Jardine Matheson (JM), Henry Keswick, to participate in a joint venture to provide merchant banking facilities to companies operating out of the Far East. Initially, the operation would be in Hong Kong and would expand throughout the Far East as market opportunities suggested.

An agreement was reached between Richard Fleming and Henry Keswick following which a Fleming's person was appointed managing director and arrived to set up the operation as Jardine Fleming (JF) in Hong Kong in September 1969.

As a joint venture, Jardine Fleming benefited from its association with JM primarily in the new issue area, as many of the new companies coming to the market were connected with the JM Group. JF's role was to underwrite and bring to market companies who wished to expand their business, raise capital, raise money through rights issues and carry out amalgamations. It quickly developed into a fully fledged corporate finance business. At its peak, in late 1972 and early 1973, JF would be bringing new issues to the market at the rate of one per week, with subscriptions for these issues amounting to ten times the amount offered.

Jardine Fleming was highly profitable and served to raise the reputation of Fleming's from a conservative City-based investment house to something more like that of an international merchant banker. The success of JF had three effects upon the course of strategic developments at Fleming's. First, it made the directors realize that JF should not be considered as an ephemeral development in which to maintain an equity stake, but as one that has become a major element of the Fleming group of activities, by internationalizing their activities. Second, it pointed out the profitability that could accrue to developing a successful merchant banking business rather than maintaining primarily an investment management function. The expertise that was being accumulated through JF could be brought back to London and used to expand the banking side of the business there. This became especially important in 1979–80, when Fleming's was faced with the new banking legislation, requiring it to become a 'recognized' bank. Third, JF's successful record in the Far East brought a number of valuable new investment clients to Fleming's investment operations in London, customers who would not otherwise have been able to distinguish Fleming's from any of its competitors.

Change in the Inner Context: The Second Reorganization

The need for more capital upon which to base any expansion of activities of Robert Fleming in the UK and elsewhere was addressed by a restructuring of the company in 1974 into the present organizational form. The structure

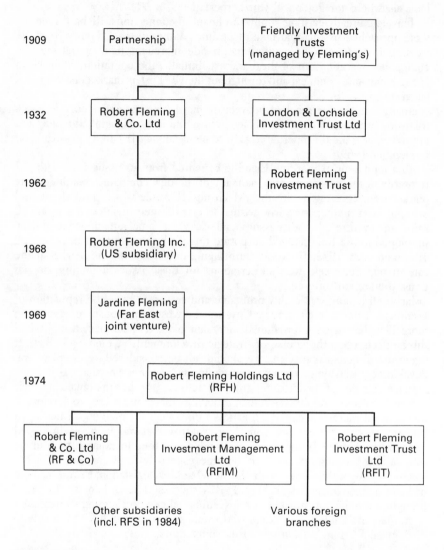

1909	Partnership — Friendly Investment Trusts (managed by Fleming's)
1932	Robert Fleming & Co. Ltd — London & Lochside Investment Trust Ltd
1962	Robert Fleming Investment Trust
1968	Robert Fleming Inc. (US subsidiary)
1969	Jardine Fleming (Far East joint venture)
1974	Robert Fleming Holdings Ltd (RFH)
	Robert Fleming & Co. Ltd (RF & Co) — Robert Fleming Investment Management Ltd (RFIM) — Robert Fleming Investment Trust Ltd (RFIT)
	Other subsidiaries (incl. RFS in 1984) Various foreign branches

FIGURE 1.4 Re-structuring of the Robert Fleming group of companies (simplified)

of the organization since 1932 had addressed the potential difficulties that could arise owing to a conflict of interest between the investment trust side of the business (first renamed London & Lochside Investment Trust, but then renamed Robert Fleming Investment Trust Limited in 1962), and the banking side of the company, Robert Fleming & Co. By the beginning of the 1970s, it was becoming clear to the board that a choice had to be made: either to reduce the need for capital by cutting back in the capital-intensive banking business, to obtain additional capital by diluting ownership of the company through a rights issue, or to re-combine the banking and investment trust side of the company into a large holding company with various divisions. Given the demand for Fleming's to offer a complete investment/banking service, it was felt that no cutback should be made to the banking initiatives already under way. The alternative of obtaining external financing through a rights issue was not considered, since the Fleming family did not wish to dilute control any further. In addition, owing to poor stock market performance in the UK during this period, the amount of internally generated funds in Robert Fleming & Co. was down substantially. Therefore, it was decided to set up a holding company, Robert Fleming Holding Ltd (RFH), with a variety of wholly owned subsidiaries: Robert Fleming & Co. (RF & Co), which would carry on the banking/corporate finance activities; Robert Fleming Investment Trust Ltd (RFIT), which would assume control of all Fleming's own investments; and Robert Fleming Investment Management Ltd (RFIM), to provide investment management and research advice to clients. The reorganization served to create a larger company (RFH) which had a more substantial capital foundation upon which to base expansion of the group's international activities as well as enter into new areas of business. Figure 1.4 illustrates the changing structure of Fleming's.

In December 1974, Richard Fleming retired as chairman of RFH and was succeeded by his deputy chairman, Bill Merton. This change of leader, as well as leadership style, marked an important strategic change at Fleming's. Where Richard Fleming assumed the style of benevolent autocrat and primary decision-maker, Bill Merton preferred to be less interventionist, letting the subsidiary companies run their own operations with relatively little interference. Merton's management philosophy was to whittle down the main board of RFH to a smaller 'executive committee'-type board.

Change in Strategic Content: An Incremental Approach

The period from the mid-1970s to 1979 can be viewed as a continual process of building up the personnel, expertise and capital necessary to expand into a full-service merchant bank operating on an international scale. Officially, RF & Co. could not be viewed as an 'official' merchant bank since it had not applied for 'authorized bank' status under Bank of England regulations. The rationale was that banking was never viewed as a particularly profitable business, given the competition with the clearing banks as well as with foreign banks, and therefore was not worth the trouble of meeting the strict requirements that had been set down. Within Fleming's, it was felt that to make money in banking would require the firm to incur large overhead costs. A third reason behind the hesitancy to enter banking was that it would require employing many more people and thereby would reduce the close-knit relationships that had developed among members of the RF group.

By the mid-1970s, RF and Co. had started to feel some pressure from the Bank of England to become an 'authorized' bank. Up until this point, Fleming's had 'authorized depositary' status. Following the 1974 'secondary banking' crisis, the Board of Governors of the Bank of England decided that they would have to play a larger part in the supervision of banking activity in the City and to cut down on the scope of activities that could be undertaken by financial institutions that were not authorized banks (Channon, 1977).

Within Fleming's, the success of Jardine Fleming had shown that profits could be made in banking and that potential business was being lost because of a lack of banking services. The inconvenience of remaining an 'authorized depositary' was also becoming clear. Fleming's could not buy foreign unquoted securities for clients without Bank of England permission, and because the firm was very much involved with the foreign investment business, it was having to go to the Bank of England more and more often. So Fleming's decided to apply for 'authorized' bank status, which at that time meant that it could deal in foreign exchange without requiring Bank of England approval for every transaction. RF & Co became an 'authorized' bank on 2 October 1979. However, three weeks later, on 23 October, exchange controls were lifted and the benefits of achieving 'authorized' status became redundant. Coinciding with the abolition of exchange controls in the UK was the introduction of the 1979 Bank Act, which modified the status of banks. All those banks that had 'authorized' status prior to the introduction of the Act were automatically given 'recognized' bank status.

The lifting of exchange controls had a great effect on Fleming's. The government's rationale behind this move was that the riches being derived from the North Sea Oil would temporarily distort the UK economy by building up a substantial surplus on the current account for at least ten years. In order to protect the non-oil-related sectors of the economy from the uncompetitive effects of a rising pound, it was decided to permit UK institutions (in particular, insurance companies and pension funds) to build up their foreign investments so that, when the effect of the oil revenues start to decline, the dividends and interest payments flowing back to the UK from these foreign investments would help prop up the value of the pound. An indication of the effectiveness of this tactic was that between 1979 and 1984 Britain's stock of overseas assets rose from £12.5 billion to £70 billion, equivalent to a rise from 6.5 to 22 per cent of gross domestic product (Plender and Wallace, 1985).

Having spent most of the 1960s and 1970s handling the financial capital of other countries within the UK, in particular the oil-related currencies from the Middle East, City institutions could now also turn their attention to increasing their role as exporters of Britain's capital. This marked the first salvo in what is now called the 'City Revolution'. It provided merchant bankers with enormous flexibiity in the types and range of business they could participate in: all the various permutations of currency and commercial paper, for both domestic and foreign clients. It also opened up the scope for arbitrage (taking advantage of differing rates of return on similar financial instruments in a variety of global financial centres).

The profits being made in the City were due largely to the overall growth of the financial services sector in general rather than to any increase in the competitive approach adopted by the merchant banks themselves. For instance, the failure of UK merchant banks to win and maintain any real share of the Eurobond market is indicative, especially when one considers that the merchant bank S. G. Warburg (now part of Mercury Securities) played a pioneering role in establishing the market during the late 1960s and 1970s, along with, to a lesser extent, Rothschild. By the early 1980s, Warburg was the only British merchant bank with any substantial portion of this market, and it amounted to only 3 per cent. *Euromoney* magazine, which publishes a league table of the major Euromarket dealers, reported that in 1984, Credit Suisse–First Boston (CSFB) was at the top with 12 per cent (more than all the British banks combined) and all the other major participants in this market were foreign. Of the top ten, five were American: Morgan Guaranty, Merrill Lynch, Morgan Stanley, Salomon Brothers and Goldman Sachs.

The various business areas in which the merchant banks have focused their efforts have become increasingly domestic and relatively low-risk. Perhaps the most profitable, as well as most glamorous, business has been in the corporate finance/mergers and acquisitions arena, advising clients on how to take over and fend off other companies. The difficulty with this market sector is that it requires a large capital base to support the acquisition of stock on behalf of clients or the underwriting of debt issues. An advantage to participating in this sector of the market is that, by becoming associated wih the 'winners' in a corporate takeover battle, a merchant bank can more than likely obtain further business from a grateful management by managing corporate finance bond issues or stock deals. Additional 'spoils' that merchant banks were keen to acquire included the generally substantial fee-earning income which could be generated from managing an organization's pension fund.

Through the management of company pension plans, merchant banks controlled the largest share of the investment advisory business. This had grown dramatically since the early 1970s after the former Conservative government of Ted Heath introduced a pay policy which provided employers and unions with an inducement to agree to improve pension benefits in lieu of direct pay increases – an area in which Fleming's, through its RFIM subsidiary, benefited greatly.

Despite a relatively profitable period, the UK merchant banks were beginning to perceive themselves as increasingly hemmed in by the encroachment of their traditional markets in corporate finance and investment management. Long-standing relationships with company clients ceased to guarantee preferential treatment as competition became more cut-throat and corporate treasurers 'shopped around' for the best deal. In fund management, pension fund trustees also became more demanding, splitting up pension funds between a number of merchant banks or investment houses, as well as changing fund managers if their performance should falter.

Following the upgrading of RF & Co. to 'recognized' bank status by the Bank of England. Fleming's was now eligible to become a member of the prestigious Accepting Houses Committee (AHC) of the Bank of England. The AHC serves as a select 'club' within which the top merchant bankers can influence Bank of England policy on issues that affect them. Current members of the AHC are listed in table 1.5 in descending order of total assets.

A complication that RF & Co. faced when asked to join the AHC was that, up until this time, RF & Co. had always disclosed its true profits in its financial statements, as all companies are required by law to do. Merchant banks that are members of the AHC, however, are granted special dispensation from this regulation and are permitted to report their earnings on a cumulative basis after transfers to (or from) inner reserves, and taxation. The rationale has been that merchant banks exist primarily on the strength of their reputation within the financial community. Any fall in their reported profits in any particular year could undermine investor confidence in the firm as well as

TABLE 1.5 Members of the Accepting Houses Committee for year ending 31 March 1985
(In descending order of total assets)

	Total assets ($£m$)	% change 1980–4	Disclosed profits ($£m$)	% change 1980–4
Kleinwort Benson	4701	+ 52.3	30.3	+ 32.3
Morgan Grenfell	3941	+117.0	20.4	+183.1
Schroders	3920	+ 86.1	15.1	+ 84.0
Samuel Montagu (Midland)	3461	+100.6	5.0	0.0
Hambros	3305	+ 61.5	17.1	− 2.3*
Hill Samuel	3195	+ 82.4	31.9	+182.5
Mercury Securities	2458	+ 79.2	28.2	+129.2
N. M. Rothschild	2590	+171.7	3.0	+100.0
Lazard Frères	1367	+ 62.7	4.4	− 21.0
Baring Brothers	1208	+107.9	1.6	+ 82.4
Charterhouse Japhet	1124	+107.8	9.0	+124.4
Robert Fleming	1024	+256.8	18.5	+153.1

* In 1983–4, Hambros made a loss of $£9.2$ million.

the sector in general. Owing to the nature of the business they are in, there may be years when profits are extremely high and so overstate what the true financial picture is. To overcome this problem, the AHC convinced the Bank of England and the Department of Taxation that members of the AHC should be allowed to transfer to a secret account (entitled 'inner reserves') whatever amount of money they feel is necessary to 'even out' the reported profits. In bad financial years, they would be permitted to 'top up' their reported profits by drawing upon their inner reserves. Though there has been much speculation about the inner reserves maintained by the merchant banks, little information has emerged.

In order to comply with the AHC regulations regarding inner reserves, RF & Co applied to the then Department of Taxation for special status in line with the other accepting houses. This permission was granted in early 1982, and RF & Co's financial reports from financial year 1981 onwards show profits on an after-tax and transfer-to-inner reserves basis only.

At the end of 1981 the chairman of RFH, Bill Merton, retired and was succeeded by his deputy chairman Joe Burnett-Stuart. Burnett-Stuart is similar to Bill Merton in that both men tend to prefer a consensus-seeking approach to management. Following his appointment, Burnett-Stuart added five additional people to the board of directors. This move was seen as a recognition that the business was becoming increasingly large and complex. These internal board appointments were made to provide the various specialized areas with a more knowledgeable voice at the top.

An Outer Contextual Change: the Big Bang

In July 1983, secret negotiations were undertaken between the Stock Exchange (represented by Sir Nicholas Goodison) and the Department of Trade (represented by the then Secretary of State for Trade, Cecil Parkinson). The outcome of these negotiations was that the government agreed to call a halt to the court case examining the restrictive practices of the Stock Exchange and to exempt the Stock Exchange from the Restrictive Trade Practices Act of 1976 in return for reforms to its Rule Book. In particular, the Stock Exchange was to permit outsiders to join the Stock Exchange Council and to dismantle the minimum commissions structure by 31 December 1986.

An important part of the Stock Exchange regulations prior to the July 1983 negotiations was the requirement for 'single capacity'; i.e., no single organization could assume the functions of a stockbroker and jobber at the same time. The argument for this system was that it afforded investors some protection in that brokers had to select the best price offered by the variety of jobbers. The underlying agreement, dating back to the Stock Exchanges deed of settlement in 1802, was that brokers had to bring all their business to the Stock Exchange and to deal with recognized jobbers only. In other words, by delivering the jobbers an assured flow of orders, jobbers would not approach the investing public directly, thereby undercutting the broker's commission.

In effect, the whole system regulated itself, the protection deriving from the fact that jobbers competed only among themselves for brokers' business while brokers had no incentive to overcharge the client.

The ending of the system of fixed commissions signalled the demise of the single-capacity system as well. Once brokers' profits came under risk owing to the entry of other sorts of firms on to the Stock Exchange (merchant banks, foreign stock brokers, foreign banks, etc.), the brokers would be increasingly tempted to cut the jobber out by matching purchases to sales on an in-house basis to reduce jobbers' commission costs. To the extent that they would fail to match up exactly, brokers would then have to take positions in particular shares in the same way as a jobber would. Alternatively, the jobbers were now under no restriction to deal solely with brokers and could approach brokers' clients directly and compete for their business.

The procedure for permitting negotiated commissions and dual capacity was to involve the phasing-in of these changes over a period of time in different parts of the market (gilts, equities, foreign stocks, etc.). However, this was quickly seen as unworkable and a date was set for the implementation of these reforms: 27 October 1986, a day which was very quickly nicknamed 'Big Bang'.

Reactions to Change in the Outer Context

Though Fleming's has always laboured under the feeling that it has drifted along without any explicitly stated strategy, the announcement of the imminent 'Big Bang' focused the firm's attention very strongly upon the potential effects this could have upon its business. The options available to Fleming's at this time were essentially the same as those faced by all the other merchant banks: (1) do nothing, i.e., watch the world change and then decide; (2) bet your company on the 'Big Bang', i.e., buy a stockbroker, jobber or gilt trader; or (3) take a middle-of-the-road stance, expanding your banking activities more or less on an in-house basis, while maintaining a diversified base.

The first of these options – do nothing – was adopted by merchant banks such as Hambros, Lazards and N. M. Rothschild. Though each of these has admitted some change in its strategy (for instance, Hambros has decided to buy the provincial estate agency chain Barstow Eves, and Rothschild has bought stockjobbers, Smith Brothers), these investments have been relatively small compared with the large sums of money other merchant banks are spending on realigning their businesses.

At the other extreme are the merchant banks that see the dangers that the large international securities houses such as Merrill Lynch, Goldman Sachs, Citibank, Deutsche Bank, Credit Suisse/First Boston and Normura Securities can inflict upon the traditional sources of business of the UK merchant banks. These merchant banks have decided to undertake a major expansion of their securities' trading functions while at the same time running down their non-banking businesses such as insurance broking, shipping and oil exploration.

The managements of these firms could be said to have 'bet their company' on 'Big Bang' and the industry shake-out that they expect to occur. This rationalization, they feel, will be based upon the extensiveness of their range of banking and securities services, as this range of services is what is being offered by the large international securities houses.

The risk with this strategy is that, to upgrade itself into an organization ready to take on the large capital-backed international houses, these merchant banks must make very large capital investments in new information technology, personnel and adequate working capital. For instance, S. G. Warburg, now part of the reorganized Mercury Securities, has been rumoured to have paid over £100 million for its purchase of a stockbroker and gilt jobber. Another associated risk with the strategy of 'buying-in' firms of jobbers and/or brokers is that these acquisitions are only as strong as the people who have built up their reputation, and there already is much evidence that a certain amount of 'raiding' is occurring between the organizations for their top personnel. There are stories of whole departments being wooed away from one merchant bank or security house to another for sizeable 'golden handshakes'. Merchant banks that have moved in this direction, despite the risks involved, include Mercury Securities, Kleinwort Benson, Morgan Grenfell, Barclays deZoete Wedd (part of Barclays Bank Group) and County Bank (part of the NatWest Group).

The third strategy that has become evident is to move forward cautiously towards becoming a full-scale international securities house through in-house expansion in selective areas of the banking business. Merchant banks adopting this strategy believe they do not have a sufficient capital base to risk a large proportion of it on acquiring businesses with which they are unfamiliar. However, they all realize that the era of deregulation does have important implications for them in that, without offering a more complete securities trading service to their clients, they will be losing business to those that can offer such a service. In response to this dilemma, these merchant banks have chosen to develop some sort of stockbroking and jobbing facility in-house, preferring to use their limited capital as working capital rather than pay out large sums to partners of stockbrokers and jobbers. There are a number of risks associated with this approach. First, because of their limited capital base, these merchant banks may not be able to undertake the large international financial risks that firms like Citibank, Deutsche Bank and Mercury Securities may undertake. Second, these in-house services may not attain a sufficiently high reputation quickly enough to draw clients to them, leaving the firms with an expensive, yet underused, trading facility. Third, the increased competition in the deregulated trading markets may provoke a price-cutting period in which the most cost-effective (or largest) trading firms may survive because of their established capital base and ability to sustain a temporary loss. In order to provide a measure of security against such risks, these merchant banks have been keen to expand their non-banking areas of business as well, so as to provide a measure of profits not dependent upon the newly developing, highly competitive market. Merchant banks that have chosen this route include Schroders, Samuel Montagu and Robert Fleming.

At Fleming's, two decisions were made in response to the Big Bang. The first was to create a presence on the retail banking side by starting a High Interest Chequing Account in association with Save & Prosper. As Fleming's already owned 53 per cent of Save & Prosper, this was seen as a way to acquire synergy from two (up until now) separate parts of the organization. Of greater strategic significance in a capital-using sense, it was decided to form an in-house market-making operation in response to the deregulation of the Stock Exchange. The decision was to create a new subsidiary, Robert Fleming Securities Limited (RFS). As a market-maker, RFS serves as a combined stockbroker/jobber in that it buys large lines of particular stock and then sells directly to clients.

Though the creation of RFS was viewed as a strategic decision within RFH, the development of a market-making operation can also be viewed as an evolutionary development, and therefore as being more in line with previous 'strategic' changes. Given Fleming's strength in the investment management business, over the years the firm had also developed a very strong expertise in the investment research area, culminating in the creation of the subsidiary RFIM, which provides the research to clients. The in-house research group had originally been developed because Fleming's wished to reduce its reliance upon outside research as developed by various stockbroking firms. RFIM has analysts in all the major market sectors as well as overseas, with large research departments in the USA (RF Inc.) and Tokyo (through Jardine Fleming).

A second factor providing the evolutionary backdrop to Fleming's move into market-making was the experience gained through the strong association with Jardine Fleming. Some years earlier, Jardine Fleming had moved into stockbroking and in fact had become the largest foreign-owned stockbroker on the Tokyo Exchange, accounting for about half of all the business transacted by foreign dealers.

A third important factor relating to the entry into market-making was Fleming's dissatisfaction with the system already in place (i.e., brokers and jobbers). The problem Fleming's confronted with the present system was that it was very difficult to obtain large lines of particular stocks which the firm required for its large investment fund management role. Fleming's fund managers would contact a broker who would then contact a jobber, who would then come back and quote a price for a relatively small amount of shares. This was generally seen as insufficient, given that the portfolios that Fleming's manages total between £12 and £14 billion. The problem lay in the origins of the jobbing system; by and large, the jobbers had remained privately owned and therefore their capital base had not expanded sufficiently to cope with the astronomical growth of the funds under investment. Therefore these firms were unwilling to take the huge positions in stocks now demanded by firms such as Fleming's without getting more capital or expensive bank financing.

Fleming's saw an opportunity to create a new business in an area that was linked to the firm's knowledge of the investment business as well as its experience in the Far East. The choice was to determine whether it should purchase a stockbroker/jobber, as many of the other merchant banks were doing, or develop an in-house capability. Fleming's chose to develop an in-house market-making business for five reasons. First, the stock market had been relatively bullish for a number of years and the prices being paid for stockbrokers and jobbers were reflecting their recent highly profitable records which, in Fleming management's opinion, were highly inflated. Second, despite Fleming's reorganization in 1974 to create a company with a larger capital base, the firm was still relatively small in terms of total assets when compared with some of its competitors, which restricted the amount of capital that was available to be spent on market-making. This resulted in an inclination to start small and to let RFS grow primarily on its own profits. Third, within Fleming's, there were already a number of individuals who had come from a stockbroking background. These individuals championed the move to create a market-making function internally and provided the needed experience to organize the operation. A fourth reason to proceed on this small scale was that the reason for the market-making operation was seen as initially to provide for Fleming's own needs for large lines of stock, therefore reducing the need to attain a very high profile quickly. A fifth, and more intangible, reason was the general hesitancy which Fleming's has always shown when considering entries into new business areas. Historically, the firm has preferred to limit its risk through joint ventures. In this case, owing to the number of links already being made by other merchant banks and the high cost of acquiring potential partners, it was decided to view the market-making operation as an 'experiment'. As the chairman, Joe Burnett-Stuart, stated,

> We wanted to learn this business of being a broker, and a dealer, and a market maker, all at the same time, becaues it is what all stock exchange members are going to have to learn after all the changes take place. It's an experiment on our part, rather than something that is going to be anything in the way of a substantial business on its own account before the stock exchange changes.

During 1986, Fleming's moved out of their long-time offices into a futuristic new building expressly designed for the firm, which offers the very latest in information technology, linking up its offices world-wide. The move is seen as part of a new beginning within Fleming's. The firm is entering a new phase of increased uncertainty regarding its overall competitiveness. To cope with this uncertainty, Fleming's management has become hesitant to commit themselves to any long-term strategic plan. The consensus appears to be that, by expressing any strategic preference now, they would be unnecessarily restricting their options as new opportunities emerged.

The strategic history of Robert Fleming Holdings Limited has been only very briefly summarized here. The full richness and extent of the data must be presented elsewhere. Three elements can be offered at this stage as a stepping-stone to understand the nature of strategic change at RFH. First, strategic change appeals to the organization most when the change is 'demand-led', that is, when top management accept that there is a large enough demand for a particular service. This decision process is a key facet of the firm's approach to strategic decision-making. Second, successful instances of change occur when there is an interaction between people, personalities, experience and environment. Third, top management at Fleming's have consistently emphasized stability of the organization, and are unwilling to expand too quickly or change the face of the organization too radically. The maintenance of Fleming's as a 'family' is seen as a prime objective in considering any strategic alternative.

SUMMARY AND CONCLUSION

The authors of this paper wish to be quite explicit about the limitations of what has been presented here. We are seven months into a three-year empirical study exploring the links between the relative competitive performance of British firms and the capability of those firms to manage long-term processes of strategic and operational change. The data we have collected so far from four firms in two quite different sectors provide us with confidence that we are pursuing a critical and relatively unexplored theme as well as helping to understand the relative competitiveness of British firms; but the limitations of our comparative perspective on our data at this time mean we cannot here at length link up competitiveness and strategic change. Instead, we have chosen in this chapter to do three things: first, to reveal aspects of the research agenda and study questions we are pursuing; second, to expose the context, content and process meta-framework which is guiding our research; and third, to explore the utility of that framework by connecting it to the strategic development of the Rootes/Chrysler UK/Peugeot–Talbot operation and the experience of Robert Fleming Holdings Limited.

A critical starting-point for this research is the notion that theoretically sound and practically useful research on strategic change should involve the continuous interplay between ideas about the *context* of change, the *process* of change and the *content* of change, together with the skill in regulating the relations between the three. The analytical importance of the context, content and process framework, plus its managerial corollary that formulating the content of a strategic change crucially entails managing its context and process, suggests that managerial processes of assessment, choice and change are at the heart of the strategic development of firms (Pettigrew, 1985a, 1985c). Such processes of assessment, choice and change can be revealed only through the brand of contextual and processual research advocated in this paper. If, indeed, it is the case that major shifts in the economic, social and business environment of firms require conceptual shifts in the minds of managers and ultimately in their beliefs and behaviour, then such processes obviously require time-series data which explore the inner and outer context of the firm. Our framework allows such a dynamic and contextually sensitive analysis of the processes of strategic and operational change to occur.

Furthermore, our approach allows us to question one of the restrictive orthodoxies in the strategy literature, that strategies are first formulated and then implemented through rational linear processes. Thus, in microeconomics strategic planning in organizations is conceived of as being dominated by powerful entrepreneurs. Meanwhile, in some of the earlier views of business policy and planning, and even in later reformulations of that view, strategy formulation is still portrayed as a rational linear process (Andrews, 1971; King and Cleland, 1978). As applied to the formulation of strategy, the rational approach describes and prescribes techniques for identifying current strategy; analysing environments, resources and gaps; revealing and assessing strategic alternatives; and choosing and implementing carefully analysed and well-thought-through outcomes. Depending on the author, explicitly or implicitly, the firm speaks with a unitary voice, can be composed of omnipotent, even heroic, general managers or chief executives, looking at known and consistent preferences and assessing them with voluminous and presumably apposite information, which can be organized into clear input–output relationships. Bourgeois and Brodwin (1984) have recently and appropriately labelled this the 'commander model' of formulating and implementing strategy.

But does this 'commander' view of rational choice and change processes equate with what we know of top management behaviour? Does organizational action derive so singularly from decisions taken at the top, or do many senior executives find either that the levers they are pulling are being pushed and pulled in different directions by their peers or subordinates, or that, in the tasks of strategy implementation, the levers they are pulling are not connected up to anything or anybody? Indeed, is it the case that, as far as senior executive behaviour is concerned, thinking big is not the same as acting big?

Certainly the empirical process research published in the 1970s by, for example, Bower (1970) and Mintzberg (1978), and more recently by Quinn (1980) and Kanter (1983), has made a number of descriptive contributions to the understanding of strategic change processes. Strategic processes of change are now more widely accepted as multi-level activities and not just as the province of a few, or even a single, general manager. Outcomes of decisions are no longer assumed to be a product of rational or boundedly rational debates, but are also shaped by the interest and commitments of individuals and groups, forces of bureaucratic momentum, and the manipulation of the structural context around decisions and changes. With the view that strategy development is a continuous process, strategies are now thought of as reconstructions after the fact, rather than just as rationally intended plans. The linear view of process explicit in strategy formulation to strategy implementation has been questioned, and with that questioning has come both an additional awareness of the substantial but limited power of chief executives in implementing strategic change and new attempts to develop models and processes of implementation other than the simple commander model.

Our approach seeks to build on and develop the above process research: first by means of our context, content, process framework, a feature absent in the Bower (1970), Mintzberg (1978), Quinn (1980) and Kanter (1983) work; second, by conducting more explicitly longitudinal research which reveals the dynamics of changing as well as the exploration of change outcomes; and finally, by seeking to connect the capability of firms to effect strategic and operational changes and the maintenance, loss or improvement in their competitive performance. In so doing, the management of strategic change will be understood as a jointly analytical, political and learning process which weaves together the content and context of change.

Focusing for a moment on our work in the automobile sector, we can make the following summary points. Existing treatments of the profound changes of the past two decades in the auto industry are deficient when they deal with strategic change. Few, if any, of the oft-quoted studies attempt to discover how or why given strategies have been generated, formed and adapted through to their ultimate fate. Otherwise painstaking accounts of market and industry-wide changes ignore or assume the internal processes involved, and, more importantly, the relationship between such processes and environmental change.

Bhaskar (1984) and Jones (1981) have drawn attention to the litany of defects in UK auto firms. The list is by now familiar: low productivity, poor quality, outdated models, weak distribution arrangements and disastrous industrial relations. Studies of individual projects apart, the role of management or the complex process of strategic change across the enterprises concerned is left untreated. The much-quoted Central Policy Review Staff Report (HMSO, 1975a), and other studies, (HMSO, 1975b) dwells on the same accepted schedule of 'the problems of the auto industry'. The report pointed to the responsibilities of managers, yet showed no appeciation of how management could better understand or manage strategic or operational change. Our analytical framework suggests the possibility of offering insights that are outside the current literature on the UK auto industry; also, because of the framework's treatment of the dynamic interrelationship between variables at the firm and the sector, our framework is well able to cope with the strategic challenges and responses of firms in the 'new competition' of a global industry.

In the merchant banking sector, where our fieldwork is barely two months off the ground, we have a rare opportunity not only to analyse retrospectively any patterns in the processes of strategic change in our chosen firms, but also to conduct real time analyses of the differential strategic response of those firms to the deregulation of the City of London in autumn 1986. Research in the merchant banking sector is much less advanced or visible than equivalent work in the auto industry. As yet, we have not uncovered any study that deals with the interplay between the context, content and processes of strategic change in merchant banks, although the strategic responses of US investment banks has been and continues to be studied by Hayes *et al.* (1983) and Crane and Eccles (1986). Our research in merchant banking has drawn support from an increasingly internationally competitive financial services sector. The high degree of strategic change presently being viewed in the City of London has focused attention on the need to improve the internal processes of assessment, choice and change in merchant banks.

While it is premature to look for patterns of strategic change across the two cases from autos and merchant banking revealed in this chapter, it is clear that changes in outer and inner context triggered strategic changes in both firms. It is also clear that leadership behaviour was critical, even fateful, for predisposing or inhibiting change in both cases. Furthermore, both firms had to 'unlearn' past patterns of belief and behaviour at a time when they had also to appreciate and then learn new skills and behaviour for the future. And they had to understand the cultural constraints that can limit the success of particular strategic changes and to find ways of managing strategic change which were sensitive to the differential contexts in which they continue to operate. Further observations about constancy and variability in processes of managing strategic and operational change within and across our cases will have to await the fruits of what we regard as some extremely interesting and exciting comparative case-study work.

REFERENCES

Abernathy, W., Clark, K. and Kantrow, A. (1981) The new industrial competition. *Harvard Business Review*, September–October, 69–81.

Andrews, K. (1971) *The Concept of Corporate Strategy*. Homewood, Ill.: Richard D. Irwin.

Bardou, J. P., Chanaron, J. J., Fridenson, P. and Laux, J. M. (1982) *The Automobile Revolution: The Impact of an Industry*. Chapel Hill, NC: University of North Carolina Press.

Berg, M. (1985) Government policy and its impact on the motor industry. *Long Range Planning*, 18 (6), 40–7.

Bhaskar, K. (1979) *The Future of the Motor Industry*. London: Kogan Page.

—— (1984) *A Research Report on the UK and European Motor Industry*. Norwich: University of East Anglia, Motor Industry Research Unit (Bath, Sewells).

Bloomfield, G. (1978) *The World Automotive Industry*. London: Bergman.

Bourgeois, L. and Brodwin, D. (1984) Strategic implementation: five approaches to an elusive phenomenon. *Strategic Management Journal*, 5, 241–64.

Bower, J. (1970) *Managing The Resource Allocation Process*. Cambridge, Mass.: Harvard University Press.

Bruce, P. (1984) Growing pains of the business. *Financial Times*, 17 April.

Casson, M. (1985) Foreign divestment and international rationalisation in the motor industry: the sale of Chrysler UK and Peugeot. *University of Reading Discussion Papers in International Investment and Business Studies*, no. 86, May.

Caves, R. E. and Krause, L. B. (eds), 1980 *Britain's Economic Performance*. Washington DC: The Brookings Institution.

Channon, D. F. (1977) *British Banking Strategy and the International Challenge*. London: Macmillan.

Crane, D. B. and Eccles, R. G. (1986) Organizational design in investment banking. Working Paper 87-028, Harvard Business School.

Dunnett, P. (1980) · *The Decline of the British Motor Industry*. London: MacMillan.

Fitzherbert, N. (1983) Robert Fleming Holding: a work of research. Unpublished paper.

Hart, P. E. (1983) Competition and efficiency in British industry. Paper presented to ESRC Workshop on Competitiveness, 18–19 November.

Hayes, S., Spence, A. and Van Praag Marks, D. (1983) *Competition in the Investment Banking Industry*. Cambridge, Mass.: Harvard University Press.

HMSO (1975a) *The Future of the British Car Industry*. London: Central Policy Review Staff.

—— (1975b) *British Leyland: the next decade*. Abridged version of a report presented to the Secretary of State for Industry by a Team of Inquiry led by Sir Don Ryder. London.

—— (1976) *Public Expenditure on Chrysler UK Ltd, Minutes of Evidence* Expenditure Committee, Session 1975–76 London, 15 January 1976.

Jones, D. (1981) *Maturity and Crisis in the European Car Industry: Structural Change and Public Policy*. Brighton: Sussex University Press.

Kanter, R. (1983) *The Change Masters: Innovation for Productivity in the American Corporation*. New York: Simon & Schuster.

King, W. and Cleland, D. (1978) *Strategic Planning and Policy*. New York: Van Nostrand.

Lawrence, P. R. and Lorsch, J. W. (1967) *Organisation and Environment*. Cambridge, Mass.: Harvard University Press.

McNalty, J. (1954) A quarter-century of progress in Ford production methods. *Institution of Production Engineers, Proceedings*, 1954–55 Session, p. 243.

Mintzberg, H. (1978) Patterns in strategy formulation. *Management Science*, 24 (a), 934–48.

Motor (1978) Chrysler supplement – Banking on the future. *Motor*, 29 October.

PEIDA (1984) The UK vehicle manufacturing industry. *London Planning and Economic Consultants*, 36–42.

Peters, T. J. K. and Waterman, R. H. (1982) *In Search of Excellence: Lessons from Americas Best Run Companies*. New York: Harper.

Pettigrew, A. M. (1985a) *The Awakening Giant: Continuity and Change in ICI*. Oxford: Basil Blackwell.

—— (1985b) Contextualist research: a natural way to link theory and practice. In E. Lawler *et al.* (eds), *Doing Research that is Useful in Theory and Practice*. San Francisco: Jossey Bass.

—— (1985c) Examining change in the long-term context of culture and politics. In J. M. Pennings (ed.), *Organizational Strategy and Change*. San Francisco: Jossey Bass.

—— Whipp, R. and Rosenfeld, R. (1987) Competitiveness and the management of strategic change process: a research agenda. In A. Francis and M. Tharaken (eds), *European Competitiveness: Country Policies and Company Strategies*.

Plender, J. and Wallace, P. (1985) *The Square Mile: A Guide to the New City of London*, London: Century Publishing.

Pollard, S. (1982) *The Wasting of the British Economy: British Economic Policy 1945 to the Present*. London: Croom Helm.

Quinn, J. B. (1980) *Strategies for Change: Logical Incrementalism*. Homewood, Ill.: Richard D. Irwin.

Robinson, D. (1976) Strategy and structure of some major merchant banks. Unpublished MA thesis, Manchester Business School.

Talbot Company (1983) History of the company. Peugeot Talbot UK. mimeo.

Tolliday, S. (1986) High-tide and after: Coventry Engineering workers and shopfloor bargaining, 1975–80. In W. Lancaster and A. Mason (eds), *Coventry Life and Labour*. Coventry: Cryfield Press.

Walmsley, J. (1985) New York's big bang – 10 years after. *The Bankers*, March, 35–9.

Whipp, R. (1987) Democracy and the design cycle, in McGoldrick, J. (ed.), *A Business Case File in Behavioural Science*, Wokingham, Van Nostrand Reinhold, pp. 1–16.

—— and Clark, P. (1986) *Innovation and the Auto Industry*. London: Frances Pinter.

Wiener, M. (1981) *English Culture and the Decline of the Industrial Spirit, 1850–1980*. Cambridge: Cambridge University Press.

Young, S. and Hood, N. (1977) *Chrysler UK: A Corporation in Transition*. London: Praeger.

Commentary on Chapter 1
Gerry Johnson

The paper by Whipp, Rosenfeld and Pettigrew employs a processual and contextualist methodology to examine issues of competition and strategic change. As such, it is a valuable and welcome contribution to the developing literature on processes of strategic change in organizations. As one strongly committed to the aims of contextualist research (Johnson, 1987), I begin from a position of interest and sympathy with the purpose, methodology and content of the approach. However, the role of a commentary is to extend and develop issues, and with that in mind the aim here will be to advance some ideas about the ways in which research into processes of strategic change might be further advanced.

Far from agreeing with the authors that it is 'premature to look for patterns of strategic change' (p. 53) from within the paper, one of the interesting features of the study seems to be the extent to which it confirms the patterns of strategic change emerging from the literature on processes of strategic management. However this, in itself, raises some questions of the additive value of such studies.

PATTERNS OF STRATEGIC CHANGE

Borrowing Mintzberg's (1978) terminology, it is possible to discern some common features in different phases of strategic change. There are likely to be periods of relative *continuity* or *incremental* change, which may well be long in duration, in which a momentum (Miller and Friesen, 1980) will tend to persist, strategies being formulated on the basis of the interpretation of stimuli in terms of organizational history and paradigms (Pfeffer, 1981; Sheldon, 1980; Johnson, 1987) or interpretive schemes (Bartunek, 1984), industry recipes (Grinyer and Spender, 1979a, 1979b; Spender, 1980), and through the predominance of organizational routines (Nelson and Winter, 1982), within an essentially social and political arena (Pettigrew, 1973, 1985) in which bargaining and solicitation processes predominate (Mintzberg *et al.*, 1976;

Lyles, 1981). Moreover, the cultural artefacts of each organization – the language and stories, rituals, ceremonies and symbols – will tend to legitimize the current modes of thinking and behaviour (Dandridge *et al.*, 1980; Wilkins, 1983), will act to insulate them from contradictory evidence or pressures for change (Abravanel, 1983) and will bind individuals together in the organization (Trice and Beyer, 1984). Organizational structures may well become 'segmentalist' (Kanter, 1983) in nature, preserving their own ways of doing things and relatively impervious to outside influence. Managers in organizations which demonstrate such characteristics might well see themselves as being continually adaptive in changing strategy when, in fact, they are adjusting strategy only within the dominant paradigm or recipe (Grinyer and Spender, 1979a; Ouchi, 1980), a process likely to give rise, over time, to 'strategic drift' (Johnson, 1987).

Over years or decades, then, organizations may drift apart from environmental 'realities' as they enact their own reality (Weick, 1979). In time this may result in growing signs within the organization and from outside it – from shareholders, government, customers and so on – of disquiet with the prevailing strategy. The organization is likely eventually to enter a period of *flux*, characterized by a lack of clarity of strategy as pressures for change come into conflict with political groupings resistant to such change (Fahey, 1981; Pettigrew, 1985). In such circumstances there may be a break-up of traditional political alliances and apparent destructive activity which 'abolishes, discredits, suppresses or otherwise renders useless an organisational structure' (Biggart, 1977). The result will be a good deal of 'pain' (Schein, 1985) as management is faced with discontinuity and a lack of problem definitions or solutions. This phase may also be characterized by largely iterative problem definition and search for solutions (Mintzberg *et al.*, 1976; Lyles, 1981), a tightening of control systems, and an attempt to cut costs (Grinyer and Spender, 1979a, 1979b) as the utility of the current paradigm fades.

In time, a point is likely to be reached where the extent of drift is undeniable: a point of perceived crisis. More *global* change may be triggered in such circumstances. Global change is characterized not by a change of strategy within the dominant paradigm but by a change in the paradigm itself. In these circumstances there is likely to be outside intervention (Grinyer and Spender, 1979b), perhaps in the form of a takeover or the appointment of a new chief executive, the re-configuration of political structures and alliances and not only the assertion of new strategies, but the introduction of changed organizational routines and symbols which signal a break with the past (Johnson, 1987).

The extent to which the studies of Rootes/Chrysler/Peugeot and Flemings bear resemblance to such patterns is marked and usefully adds further confirmatory weight to the patterns themselves. However, in so doing, the question of the role of further similar studies has to be raised. What is the continuing role for contextualist research, and how might it most usefully add to our understanding of processes of strategic change?

SOME ISSUES FOR RESEARCH IN MANAGING STRATEGIC CHANGE

There is no doubt that, in trying to understand how organizations manage strategic change more or less effectively, we need to encourage research that examines processes of change in an historical and organizational context. A contextualist approach is most valuable in developing an understanding of patterns of organizational behaviour and, within these, appreciating the relevance and impact of specific phenomena. To take one example, studies that have examined strategic change processes in context have demonstrated the importance of management cognition and ideational culture as a likely source of inertia and barrier to change (Bower, 1970; Grinyer and Spender, 1979a; Pettigrew, 1985; Johnson, 1987). However, here we face something of a problem: a contextualist approach, concerned quite properly with surfacing and explaining how years of history combine with organizational dramas to form strategy, is unlikely to provide for a detailed structural study of any one specific phenomenon. Yet studies of specific phenomena out of context are likely to provide only partial and crude explanations of process. How is this problem to be resolved?

First, we need to be clearer as to what the central issues are for more specific processual research. When Fredrickson (1983) listed 28 'high priority questions for strategic process research', well over half of them were questions which derived from a concern that rational models did not describe the processes he and others observed in organizations. We do not need to continue to concentrate on such questions: we no longer need to demonstrate that the rational models are inadequate descriptions of process. As has been said, there are other questions which arise out of processual studies which are more significant. Indeed, one useful task is to identify more clearly what these issues are and to design research which studies them more specifically and in greater depth. Some of the issues emerge out of the more generalizable patterns of process described above. For example:

1   What relationship exists between specific, often operational, decisions, organizational routines and overall patterns of strategy? In this sense historical mapping of strategy would benefit from being even richer, perhaps within shorter time periods, so as to examine the anatomy of adaptive evolutionary patterns of strategy.

2   For specific strategic decisions, are the patterns of iteration which researchers such as Mintzberg *et al.* (1978) and Lyles (1981) have begun to note confirmed? Moreover, building on the work by Hickson *et al.* (1986), how do these vary in different contexts?

3   Just how do managers manipulate the systems and routines of the organization to resist or promote change? In particular, while there is a growing amount of research on management behaviour as it contributes to adaptive or incremental patterns of change, there remains little work on

the management processes associated with more fundamental strategy reformulation.

4 Cognitive models clearly play a central role in strategy formulation. What perceptions and rationalities do managers have of their internal or external organizational worlds, of organizational issues and problems or of competition, for example? To what extent are these perceptions and rationalities similar between individuals or sub-groups or, indeed, between organizations in apparently similar environments? In other words, what is the level of aggregation of cognitive models and in what contexts does this vary? How do such models change over time? And to what extent can differences be accounted for by managerial backgrounds, job experience, personality types and so on? Given this much deeper understanding, how then do we understand managerial cognition within processes of strategic change?

5 The questions that arise around the notion of the paradigm are considerable. Is the phenomenon detectable in different organizational contexts? What sorts of constructs make up the paradigm in different contexts? What is the nature of paradigm constructs, and how do they differ by context? Do levels of paradigm homogeneity differ by organization? How does paradigmatic change come about?

6 What are the links between cognitive models and organizational action, for example in terms of the ways in which symbolic artefacts preserve and legitimize the paradigm, and also its links to political structures and behaviour?

7 Further work is also needed on the role of symbolic activity in the context of strategic management. For example, the extent to which the achievement of paradigm shifts and strategy reformulation may be facilitated by symbolic intervention or the current paradigm 'preserved' by symbolic artefacts.

8 What are the processes and effects of intervention in strategic management processes by 'outsiders' such as new executives or consultants? Which intervention processes seem to be more effective than others, and why?

9 The studies of so-called 'excellent' companies have been somewhat anecdotal in nature. The management behaviour and systems of organizations that have demonstrated a consistent record of profits and strategic change would benefit from a rather more structured research approach.

Such issues have been addressed in the past but usually without clear contextual reference points. On the other hand, when contextual studies have addressed such issues they have, perhaps understandably, avoided highly structured enquiry on specific phenomena. There are few studies which combine longitudinal and contextual work with structured, integrated investigations of particular process issues. However, if we are to progress further in understanding complex issues of process, there is a strong case that just such methodological triangulation is required. Researchers might usefully consider constructing contextualist research around more focused issues, for example. Or, within a research programme, those interested in longitudinal, contextualist research might usefully canvass the support and help of psychologists interested in cognitive processes, anthropologists interested in cultural systems, accountants or operational researchers interested in control systems and microeconomists interested in decision-making routines.

However, such collaboration could be taken further. The more the importance of such studies becomes recognized, the stronger the argument is for much greater co-operation between researchers at different institutions. This is already underway through the growing number of conferences and workshops that take place, but such events usually review only output. The need is for a greater degree of planning between institutions and research teams about how the focus and tasks of investigation can usefully be split up between them. Moreover, in such areas the traditional reluctance of one institution to protect its access to data from other institutions is more questionable in research in which data collection is such a time-consuming process. There is also a strong argument for the prior planning of contexts of research between institutions such that useful comparisons and contrasts can be made.

Funding agencies also have a role to play. The sort of work on processual issues, central as it is to the understanding of managerial process, may none the less be unattractive to many funding agencies. Time scales may be long, resource requirements given small sample sizes may appear extremely high, and output (hitherto) rather generalized. Yet if such work is to continue, there needs to be investment in the time to do it. The funding agencies could play a major role in the setting of criteria for such work that demand that institutions demonstrate the extent to which they are co-operating in data collection and interpretation, involving others in the more specific areas of research that are possible within larger studies and building in triangulated methodologies.

CONCLUSION

Until the 1980s, virtually all the research into processual aspects of strategy was concerned with what Pettigrew (1985) would denote as an examination of issues of 'change' rather than the processes of 'changing'. Only latterly has there been a growing recognition of the value of longitudinal, contextual research approaches. For those who seek to develop research into processes of strategic change, this historical division might appear to constitute a conflict of focus. The one offers the facility to invesigate specific aspects of strategic change in depth but, uneasily, in an ahistorical and a aprocessual manner; the other emphasizes relevant context but runs the risk of largely reconfirming patterns of change and failing to address more specific issues in any depth.

The argument in this commentary is that this is an essentially historical divide, traditionally fuelled by epistimelogical debate and conflict. If we are to develop profitably a study of processes of strategic change, there is an increasing need to design research programmes that consciously seek for methodological and theoretical triangulation.

REFERENCES

Abravanel, H. (1983) Mediating myth in the service of organisational ideology. In L. R. Pondy, P. J. Frost, G. Morgan and T. C. Danbridge (eds), *Organisational Symbolism*. Greenwich, Conn.: JAI Press.

Bartunek, J. M. (1984) Changing interpretive schemes and organisational restructuring: the examples of a religious order. *Administrative Science Quarterly*, 29, 355–72.

Biggart, N. W. (1977) The creative–destructive process of organisational change: the case of the Post Office. *Administrative Science Quarterly*, 22, 410–26.

Bower, J. L. (1970) *Managing the Resource Allocation Process*. Cambridge, Massachusetts: Harvard University Press.

Dandridge, T. C., Mitroff, I. and Joyce, W. F. (1980) Organisational symbolism: a topic to expand organisational analysis. *Academy of Management Review*, 5, 77–82.

Fahey, L. (1981) On strategic management decision processes. *Strategic Management Journal*, 2, 43–60.

Frederickson, J. W. (1983) Strategic process: questions and recommendations. *Academy of Management Review*, 8, 565–75.

Grinyer, P. H. and Spender, J. C. (1979a) *Turnaround: Managerial Recipes for Strategic Success. The Fall and Rise of the Newton Chambers Group*. London: Associated Business Press.

—— (1979b), Recipes, crises and adaptation in mature businesses. *International Studies of Management and Organisation*, 9, 113–123.

Hickson, D. J., Butler, R. J., Cray, D., Mallory, G. R. and Wilson, D. C. (1986) *Top Decisions: Strategic Decision Making in Organisations*. Oxford: Basil Blackwell.

Johnson, G. (1987) *Strategic Change and the Management Process*. Oxford: Basil Blackwell.

Kanter, M. (1983) *The Change Masters: Innovation for Productivity in the American Corporation*. New York: Simon & Schuster.

Lyles, M. A. (1981) Formulating strategic problems – empirical analysis and model development. *Strategic Management Journal*, 2, 61–75.

Miller, D. and Friesen, P. (1980) Momentum and revolution in organisational adaptation. *Academy of Management Journal*, 23 (4), 591–614.

Mintzberg, H. (1978) Patterns in strategy formation. *Management Science*, May, 934–48.

——, Raisinghani, O. and Theoret, A. (1976) The structure of unstructured decision processes. *Administrative Science Quarterly*, 21, 246–75.

Nelson, R. R. and Winter, S. G. (1982) *An Evolutionary Theory of Economic Change*. Cambridge, Mass.: Harvard University Press.

Ouchi, W. G. (1980) Markets, Bureaucracies and Clans. *Administrative Science Quarterly*, 25, 129–141.

Pettigrew, A. M. (1973) *The Politics of Organisational Decision Making*. London: Tavistock.

—— (1985) *The Awakening Giant*. Oxford: Basil Blackwell.

Pfeffer, J. (1981) Management as symbolic action: the creation and maintenance of organisational paradigms. In L. L. Cummings and B. M. Staw (eds), *Research in Organisational Behaviour*, Vol. 3, pp. 1–15. Greenwich, Conn. JAI Press.

Schein, E. H. (1985)   *Organisational Culture and Leadership*. San Francisco: Jossey Bass.

Sheldon, A. (1980)   Organisational paradigms: a theory of organisational change. *Organisational Dynamics*, 8 (3), 61–71.

Spender, J. C. (1980)   Strategy making in business. PhD thesis, University of Manchester.

Trice, H. M. and Beyer, J. M. (1984)   Studying organisational cultures through rites and ceremonials. *Academy of Management Review*, 9 (4), 653–69.

Welck, K. E. (1979)   *The Social Psychology of Organizing*. Reading, Mass.: Addison-Wesley.

Wilkins, A. L. (1983)   Organisational stories as symbols which control the organisation. In L. R. Pondy, P. J. Frost, G. Morgan and T. C. Dandridge (eds), *Organisational Symbolism*. Greenwich, Conn.: JAI Press.

2 A Process Model of Strategic Redirection in Large Complex Firms: The Case of Multinational Corporations

Yves L. Doz and C. K. Prahalad

This paper examines the process of strategic redirection in large complex multinational corporations (MNCs). There has been an abundant literature on the organizational forms taken by MNCs (Stopford and Wells, 1972; Davis, 1979; Franko, 1976) relating the overall corporate structure to product diversity and geographical scope. There has also been a rich literature on the internationalization strategies of MNCs (Hymer, 1976; Vernon, 1966; Dunning 1974; Brooke and Remmers, 1970). Implicitly or explicitly, much of this literature approaches the internationalization of firms and their subsequent strategic choices at the level of individual businesses. Yet, the nature of strategic choices by MNCs in individual businesses and the management structures used in these businesses have seldom been studied together (Doz, 1979). Even scarcer are studies of strategic change processes in MNCs. Stopford and Wells (1972), for instance, in their classic book on MNCs, show stages in the structural evolution of MNCs, but do not describe the process of transition from one stage to another. Similarly, other researchers have described the evolution of major corporations as long periods of relative strategic and structural stability punctuated by shorter periods of transformation (Mintzberg, 1978, Miller and Friesen, 1980).

We also believed, at the outset of our long research, that attention to shift in formal structures, as descriptors of the consequences of strategic changes, was an oversimplification, and that the process of change, as well as that of controlling a global business in a steady state, or even more critically of providing for flexibility in dealing with multiple tradeoffs, implied in at least some categories of businesses, called for a richer view of organization than could be encapsulated by structural categories (Doz, 1976; Bower and Doz, 1979). A matrix structure, for example, is, by design, neutral *vis-à-vis* strategic direction, and the formal organization of a matrix tells little about how it is managed and what strategies individual businesses follow within the matrix organization.

The purpose of this paper is to explore the processes of strategic and organizational transformation in MNCs and to develop a process framework of these transformations. Beyond proposing a framework, we also set out to research which characteristics of the transformation process lead to sucessful adaptation to new environments and which prevent or block successful adaptation. Our research is also managerial in focus. In our view, the overly deterministic views of both planned adaptation (as typically represented in the usual business policy and strategic management literature) and population ecology (as most fully represented by Hannah and Freeman, 1977) are misguidedly simplistic: whether a large complex firm adapts or not to new environmental conditions depends on its ability to manage a strategic transformation.

Beyond the specific problems of MNCs, therefore, this paper also attempts to make a contribution to the broader literature of strategic change. In particular, it hopes to address some of the drawbacks of much of the organizational change and business policy literatures as failing to relate content, context and process of change (Pettigrew, 1985, ch. 2).

The research reported here specifically analyzes the process through which MNCs adapt from a geographically fragmented environment – in which trade barriers prevent substantial product cross-shipments from country to country – to an internationally competitive environment where strong competitive benefits accrue to the firms that can specialize their manufacturing operations in various countries and manage them as a tightly co-ordinated network. We selected this process of specialization and co-ordination because it constitutes a change of major magnitude in the strategy of the MNC. It encompasses changes of strategic direction, of management structures and systems and of organizational culture. Yet, from company to company, the content of the change and its underlying techno-economic rationale are quite similar, at least throughout Europe (the territory where our research was mainly conducted). All the changes we analyzed were made under competitive pressure and many under duress, as a strategic response to a weakening strategic position in the wake of new lower-cost competitors taking a more international view of their business. As we will discuss later, however, the true extent of new competitive pressures and the threat they constitute were not widely understood, or shared, within the companies we studied. The strategic position was weakening, but this had not yet resulted in a serious financial performance crisis in most of the businesses we studied; or, conversely, these businesses had been low performers for sufficiently long for their poor performance to be seen not as a crisis, but as 'business as usual'.

RESEARCH METHODOLOGY AND DESIGN

Our approach was chosen to generate conceptual frameworks, not to test *a priori* empirical hypotheses. Since the views of strategic change, particularly as it affects multinational corporations, were so underdeveloped, we traded off empirical validation for a deeper longitudinal and processual understanding of the dynamics of change over time. A first pilot study was carried out in 1975 in a large chemical company (Prahalad, 1975). It yielded a first-cut conceptual framework within which to analyze changes in relative power within a matrix organization (Prahalad, 1976). In parallel with this work, a study of the same issues in the medical electronics business of Hewlett Packard was carried out (Salter *et al.*, 1975). It provided a relatively detailed analysis of the management tools used to regulate the distribution of power in matrix organizations. Following these two initial studies, a more detailed comparative analysis was carried out of selected businesses in four companies (Brown Boveri, GTE, LM Ericsson and Philips). While not all the businesses studied were undergoing strategic change, several were – in particular, at Brown Boveri (small motors), at GTE (main exchange switchgear) and at Philips (Hi-fi sets and integrated circuits). These studies enabled the development of a more systematic methodology.

In each business studied, data were gathered on the change process over time through interviews and documentary archival evidence. Wherever possible, interviews took place at different times as the change process was evolving within a single business, with some managers thus interviewed repeatedly over several years. When this was not possible, and our study was thus retrospective, we used documents to evoke or challenge recollections from key participants in the change process and to try to overcome *ex post* rationalization and selective recollection. We also cross-checked recollections and interpretations of various participants. As much as we could, we attempted to reconstitute cause-and-effect relationships by avoiding bunched 'snapshot' interviews and by not relying only on the interviewees' memory. In each of the businesses studied interviews numbered between 15 and 60 depending on the complexity of the process and of the business. Interviews took place both at headquarters and in foreign subsidiaries, and in some cases key actors who had left the company or retired were also interviewed. Where appropriate, joint venture partners and host government officials were also interviewed. Interviews lasted on average over two hours.

Archival evidence included strategic plans, minutes from meetings, proposals for resource allocation, memoranda between key actors, market and strategic studies, and reports concerning the strategic change and the attending organizational changes themselves. We also collected material used in meetings (e.g., transparencies used for presentations) or in communication (e.g., internal announcements of changes to employees, documents given to unions). While companies varied greatly in how comprehensive the written evidence they provided was, we had access to key documents in all the companies studied, at various levels in the organization (e.g., from the famous 'blue letters' used for investment requests to the board at Ford, to minutes of product standardization meetings between assistant product managers at Philips).

To a large extent, the desire for quality of access drove us to be opportunistic in our sample. The amount of work also implied that doctoral students using our frameworks contributed their own research and findings to the generalization presented here (e.g., Bartlett's study of Corning, or the work of Peter Mathias). The constraints of access, and the limits on the researchers' own time, meant that the sample evolved and grew over time as we accumulated more individual studies of strategic redirection. While a more rigorous sampling procedure might have yielded more structured results, it might not have been feasible in practice, given the high quality of required access. Our sample now counts 16 businesses in several industries. Table 2.1 presents the sample.

In all 16 cases, we kept the content of the change process similar (from a fragmented nationally responsive collection of individual subsidiaries to a globally co-ordinated network of manufacturing centers and sales operations), but otherwise we made no effort to achieve uniformity in the sample. On the contrary: after our initial studies, we looked for deviant cases from which we could challenge our emerging framework, modify and enrich it, or establish its boundaries. Our only domain constraint was to stay with manufacturing multinationals rather than study service businesses, financial institutions or other non-manufacturing multinationals (e.g., trading companies).

The data gathered on each change process observed were structured into a detailed chronology of actions – obviously including symbolic actions which gave meaning but resulted in no immediate operational or strategic change. These chronologies were then collapsed into protocols where we focused our 'key events' (to the best that we could identify these) and their consequences. These in turn were categorized in terms of our framework, and analyzed. For each of the change processes observed, we extracted from the data a single summary protocol, such as the one presented in table 2.2.

These summary protocols are the most aggregate form of data we used to compare the change processes. We also, obviously, carried out more detailed comparisons of individual steps in the change process. When authorized by the company, detailed case histories were written on individual redirection processes. Sometimes only pedagogical material more narrowly focused, or less detailed, was allowed. In some cases, the companies insisted on full anonymity and did not let us circulate detailed descriptions.[1] The longitudinal emphasis of our study aims at uncovering the sequence of changes that took place, the cause and effect relationships between them, and the pace at which the overall change process evolved.

Ex post, we have characterized the change processes as 'successful' and 'unsuccessful'. To a large extent this is a judgemental characterization made by the researchers based on the outcome of the observed processes. The business circumstances were too different from one situation to another to

TABLE 2.1 The sample of businesses studied

Company code	Industry	Timing of redirection	Company origin	Result of attempted redirection	Observations
A	Petrochemicals	1972–6	America	Success	
B	Electrical motors	1972–7	Europe	Failure	Some early improvements but no completed redirection; several phases to change process, no complete success
C	Telecom. equipment	1974–7	America	Success	
D	Automobiles	1974–83	America	Success	
E	Trucks	1974–81	Europe	Failure	
F	TV tubes	1973–80	America	Failure	
G	Farm equipment	1972–80	America	Failure	
H	Office equipment	1971–9	America	Success	
I	Automobiles	1968–78	America	Success	
J	Electronics	1970–6	America	Success	
K	Pigments	1981- ongoing	Europe	Failure (?)	Unlikely to be successful
L	Pharmaceuticals	1975–82	Europe	Failure	
M	Coatings	1981- ongoing	Europe	–	
N	Car components	1984- ongoing	North America	–	
O	Consumer electronics	1969–78	Europe	Success	
P	Electronic components	1972–80	Europe	Success	

use more usual methods of relating the change process to measures of performance. As can be seen from table 2.1, some of the more recently studied change processes are still incomplete, and thus cannot be characterized. The normative yardstick we used to assess success was the completion of a change process yielding a co-ordinated and specialized network of subsidiaries. This in itself, though, is not sufficient to guarantee long-term competitive success.

TABLE 2.2 Chronological Sequence of Changes: Company E

No.	Months	Mechanism used	Dimension	Strength	Narrative comments
1	1	Key manager	Power	Strong	Respected manager with personal leadership characteristics, past experience of managing mergers and rationalizations, commitments to foster competitiveness through rationalization
2	6–12	Strategic planning	Strategic	Strong	Formulation of manufacturing and engineering rationalization plan
3	6–12	Information system	Cognitive	Strong	Efficient scale analysis
4	6–12	Integrator	Cognitive	Strong	Functional co-ordinators
5	6–12	Capital appropriation	Power	Strong	Major commitment of resources to rationalization plan
6	6–12	Business teams	Cognitive	Strong	Management advisory committee composed of functional co-ordinators and heads of major national companies
7	18	Planning process	Strategic	Weak	Lack of precise accounting information makes planning process difficult after initial rationalization plan was carried out
8	30+	Patterns of socialization	Cognitive	Strong	One-week convention, meeting of all managers; top management stresses need to continue rationalization
9	36	Management development	Cognitive	Strong	Internal management training program stresses needs for integration
10	36+	Budgeting systems	Power	Weak	Lack of agreement on accounting/budgeting procedures
	48				Consultants called in

Further, corporate priorities may shift for reasons independent from the performance of the given business studied. Indeed, some of the companies we studied early in our research process subsequently divested the business(es) that had been successfully redirected. Some of the change processes we studied comprised multiple phases, where a particular change process was salvaged following a crisis. We might have broken down these complex multi-phased change processes into several separate observations (one per phase). We chose not to do so, because (1) we wanted to bring the historical context into clear perspective and to look at long-term change, and (2) we could not always define clear phase categories and establish beginning and ending points. Indeed, while the periods indicated on table 2.1 give a clear sense of beginning and end, reality is a lot more muddled, and we selected only the end of a period of strategic stability as the beginning point and the establishment of a co-ordinated network of specialized subsidiaries as the end point. To a large extent, in our data collection we went beyond the beginning point to understand the underlying stability of the strategy, organization and management processes that preceded the strategic redirection we studied. Based on the judgemental success criteria described above, our sample comprises eight successes, six failures and two situations in which events are still unfolding.

A PROCESS MODEL OF STRATEGIC REDIRECTION

As our research evolved, we developed a four-stage process model of strategic redirection. We can label these four stages 'incubation', 'variety generation', 'power shifts' and 'refocusing'. Each stage consisted of a series of steps in each company. While the sequence of individual steps varied from company to company, and from business to business, the four-stage sequence was observed in all businesses that successfully went through the kind of strategic redirection we studied. Conversely, we can point out where, in the sequence of these phases, specific redirection processes lost momentum and went astray, and why. In this section we present the process model that we developed from the data.

Four stages

1 *Incubation* Over time, whether its origins were planned or unintended (Mintzberg, 1978), a stable strategy becomes an intellectual construct, an explicit logic of how to compete, of how to commit resources and mobilize the energies of the corporation toward competitive advantage. In effectively managed companies, strategies are reflected in current management structures and processes. In the businesses we observed, the explicit strategy that preceded redirection had typically been one that can best be characterized as national responsiveness: each national subsidiary operated by and large on its own, in a discrete national competitive environment, with headquarters mainly

providing the technology and raising the funds. In many cases, the subsidiaries self-funded their growth and developed a set of strong technical competencies, thus decreasing their dependence on headquarters over time. A decentralized structure, devolving key strategic decisions to the subsidiaries, was the natural outcome of the strategy of national responsiveness.

The lowering of trade barriers in the 1970s allowed a different type of strategy to emerge. This strategy was predicated on cost reduction opportunities provided by economies of location (e.g., the early successes of the Japanese industry; the move 'offshore' of part of the electronics industry) and on economies of scale obtained by serving multiple geographical markets from single large-scale plants using the most cost-effective high-volume processes (e.g., from batch to continuous automated production of ball bearings). With a few notable exceptions (e.g., Otis in the elevators business), these new strategies were initially adopted by newcomers to an industry. Typically, these were producers who had not invested internationally and tried to succeed via exports. Of course, Japanese companies often played the key role, but not always: in small electrical motors, for example, the new competitors were Eastern European. Generally, even among new competitors, these strategies were emergent rather than intended strategies (Doz and Lehmann, 1986; Abegglen, 1985).

The companies we analyzed in this research were comparatively slow not only to respond – we will discuss later why strategic transitions are relatively slow processes – but even to perceive the needed change. Indeed, the very fragmentation of their organization into autonomous subsidiaries, which served them so well in a fragmented world market, impaired their vision of new competitors. The total pattern of actions by a given competitor was not easily perceptible to subsidiaries focused mainly on their own national markets. Further, new competitors seldom launched a frontal attack; rather, they eroded the well established multinationals' positions in peripheral markets, capturing new markets the development of which went almost unnoticed by established companies (Hamel and Prahalad, forthcoming). New competitors also made early blunders which, wrongly, diminished the credibility of their later development (e.g., Toyota's ill-fated first attempts at penetrating the US market).

Competitive shifts were also relatively slow, change being incremental rather than radical. In most of the cases we studied there was no perception of immediate crisis. Performance was deteriorating slowly, for reasons that were not sufficiently clear to arouse questioning or discrediting of the past strategy. Indeed, if anything, performance deterioration led to a reinforcement of the past strategy, for instance by establishing tightly measured and strongly motivated strategic business units within the subsidiaries. This only reinforced the local 'patch' orientation of operating managers in subsidiaries. Further, in many of the companies studied, managerial tenures in any one position were relatively short – home country managers moved not only between countries but also between businesses – and thus made an in-depth perception of long-term competitive and strategic deterioration less perceptible. In some others, conversely, local national 'barons' had managed subsidiaries for a long time and were rather insensitive to global perspectives.

Further, any departure from the status quo was likely to undermine the existing autonomy of the subsidiaries, on which the success of the company had been built and the careers of the most senior executives made. In some companies, managing larger and larger national affiliates was the privileged route to corporate managing directorship; in others, local 'barons' stifled any change that could endanger their power.

Finally, the management systems in use focused operating managers' attention and interest toward success at the local level rather than toward global performance, which was ignored. The management systems were – predictably – consistent with sustaining the strategy of national responsiveness. A typical set of management systems used in the companies pursuing a strategy of national responsiveness is presented in table 2.3. It is directly borrowed from company B.

Successful strategic redirection thus faced enormous odds! Contrary to a strategic redirection in the opposite direction, impetus was unlikely to come successfully from the ranks. Although individual product managers, and managers within subsidiaries, could occasionally become aware of the need for strategic redirection, they lacked access, influence and data to put their

TABLE 2.3 Multi Dimensional Organization map of Company B's motors business

	Orientation		
Organizational change mechanism	*Cognitive*	*Strategic*	*Power*
– Reorganization of B into 5 groups			National
– Identifying country organizations as profit centers	National		
– Creation of corp. staff groups		Global	
– export marketing co-ordination by			
– Corp. marketing	Global		
– Corp. finance			National
– Corp. planning		Global	
– Legal			National
– Management committee			
– business committee	Global		
– product committee	Global		
– Career progression			National
– Executive compensation			National

position forward, and usually did not find receptive ears in their own hierarchy. Status quo endured. In *all* the successful cases of strategic redirection that we observed, the status quo was broken only by the appointment at a senior position (typically, head of European or international operations in the business group studied among US companies, and division head in the European companies) of an executive pregnant with a different vision. Most often, though, the appointment was not made because of that vision, but just because the executive was next in line!

These senior executives brought a different vision with them. In the course of our research we could not trace precisely the origins of that vision. It seemed to be the result of early exposure to global perspectives, either outside the company (e.g., diplomatic or consulting experiences) or in one of its outposts exposed among the earliest to global competition (e.g., in foreign markets where Japanese competition was first felt). Visions were not blueprints: early on, they remained relatively general and vague, more along the lines of 'we ought to take better advantage of our global scope to reduce costs and improve market positions', rather than assuming the form of detailed action programs. They provided a sense of direction, not an action agenda or a blueprint, of the desired outcome of the strategic transformation. The vision was further developed and refined in the redirection process itself.

Based on our limited sample, the appointment of a new key executive bringing a different vision appears a necessary – but not sufficient – condition for successful strategic redirection. In our sample we have observed two cases of strategic redirection processes being started without a new key executive being appointed – and bringing with him a new vision – and both went quickly astray. These findings are consistent with observations of major strategic changes in other settings.

The first difficulties the newly appointed key executives faced was to succeed in communicating, refining and eliciting commitment to a vision that went against the accepted – still apparently successful – strategic logic of the business and challenged its management structure and processes, and thus the power base of other key executives.

2   *Variety generation*   Newly appointed key managers started working toward providing legitimacy to their vision and undermining the legitimacy of the prevalent conventional wisdom. Yet, early on, their new vision was not always openly discussable as it was still too tentative and too fragile. They had to trade off obtaining the data needed for sustaining the vision – normally not provided by the management systems (since these were set to sustain a different straegic direction) – and starting to communicate that vision to operating managers in the organization. In the situation we observed, strategic redirection started with cognitive shifts, i.e. with the discovery, development, communication and acceptance of a new perspective – a new 'world view' on the business situation. This was needed for actual change to take place.

Rather than try to 'sell' their vision right away, key managers involved in successful change processes first generated both variety and pressure. Pressure was generated by creating a sense of impending crisis, by emphasizing and reinterpreting performance decline or the risk of performance decline. In several of the change processes, reports were generated which emphasized the competitive weakness of the firm in that business and its high-cost position, and analyzed the success of competitors following different approaches. This was obviously easier where precedents of strategic shifts by competitors could be identified (e.g., GM could use the rationalization and integration of Ford of Europe as a justification for similar changes). True competitive innovators faced greater difficulty, since they had to create a new vision from scratch rather than be inspired by some competitor's actions.

Variety was created by broadening the choice of discussable options, and occasionally by outlining extreme options, if only to prompt rejection. Although the transformation processes varied widely in their detailed chronologies, the approach used in the various cases shared common characteristics. First, discussion arenas were used, e.g., product planning groups, worldwide 'conferences' for manufacturing or technology, product standardization committees. These arenas were usually newly created, and were clearly signalled as important by the new key manager, who participated in them. Second, the discussion arenas were specialized enough so that debate could be analytical rather than discursive, and so that progress could be accomplished on narrow fronts. The need for strategic redirection was not tackled in its entirety, but various facets were explored and, when possible, preconditions for change were established (e.g., product specification compatibility, common costing methods). Each precondition was promoted as 'making sense' in its own right, independently from the total strategic redirection.

The debate during the variety generation phase also allowed the key executive to develop his vision more fully by acquiring relevant information from the subsidiaries and integrating such information into the overall vision. Learning took place by rubbing multiple cognitive orientations and strategic priorities. Debate also provided the opportunity for operating managers to contribute actively to the development of the overall vision, and in this way to make it acceptable, or even in some cases to take ownership for it. Also, functional specialists from the various subsidiaries could usually better perceive the need for strategic redirection than could subsidiary top management, and could see a personal opportunity in it rather than a threat to their own status and power.

Once the legitimacy of the possible strategic redirection is recognized in part, it becomes easier to make the overall strategic shift discussable and systematically to provide information to explore and analyze other facets of the shift. The completion of stage 2 is often marked by formal alteration to information and accounting systems.

3 *Power shifts* In the successful redirections we observed, this stage consisted of a series of relatively minor reallocations of decision and

implementation authority. For instance, in several of the cases we studied the new key executive quickly acted on export markets, bringing subsidiaries to share in supplying them when previously they had been supplied only from the home country. This usually provided direct benefit to the subsidiary managers – within the context of their existing measurement and evaluation systems – by increasing their capacity utilization rates. Often it also assuaged host government concerns. Yet, at the same time, becoming part of a centrally determined export flow made the subsidiaries hostage to the new executive who now controlled at least some of the variability in their economic performance, particularly in situations of oversupply which many of the companies in our sample were facing. In turn, co-ordination of exports required similar product specifications, common pricing policies and, increasingly, similar costing and transfer pricing approaches.

Typically, this stage involved no formal organizational change; rather, the shift in power took place as the result of a sequence of seemingly minor and beneficial decisions that could not easily be opposed by any of the executives involved. Yet, through that sequence subsidiary executives became increasingly dependent on decisions and policies made centrally. The quid pro quo was better support from headquarters to foreign operations, and a structured input from the subsidiaries into headquarter decisions. For instance, several of the businesses studied had their management create 'key country teams' to help and guide the development and introduction of new products for multiple geographic markets.

Whether formally or informally, the businesses studied all put in place matrix-like organizational overlays that allowed worldwide business priorities and local responsiveness priorities to be identified jointly and traded off. The relative importance of various overlays changed over time, with some linkages becoming more important and others less so.

4 *Refocusing* This stage mostly involved registering the legitimacy of the change process, i.e., modifying the formal management systems and communicating the true meaning of the change. Some activities that had been initially carried out off-line through special task forces (e.g., for international product planning) were now folded into a permanent formal process. In other words, information and planning systems, budgeting and resource allocation processes were formally modified to allow the change to be anchored permanently into the administrative infrastructure of the business.

More critically, key managers were often moved in this stage. First, some managers just left the businesses and the companies involved, as they realized that their status and influence would be eroded. Conversely, other managers in the subsidiaries started to look forward to positions at business group headquarters, now seen as more desirable and more influential than subsidiary positions. Consistent with this shift, the business group top management made efforts, at this stage, to move managers from one subsidiary to another, to widen the perspective of individual managers.

A SEQUENCE OF CHANGES

In the cases we observed, strategic redirection was managed as a sequence of changes over time – changes being broken down in a series of relatively minor steps. Our observation runs contrary to the textbook view of redirection being achieved through rapid comprehensive restructuring. Restructuring – when it takes place (and it does not always do so) – is the consequence rather than the cause of redirection; it is imprinting an already achieved redirection into the permanent administrative infrastructure of the company.

The evidence we gathered sheds some light on the process of change. First, we did not observe change as being continuous and incremental. The periods of transformation we studied followed long periods of stability. Our findings thus support more the view of Mintzberg and others (e.g., Miller and Friesen) rather than the 'logical incrementalism' view (Quinn, 1980).

The transformation process itself, though, is largely incremental. To a large extent it is a learning process, both for the manager who brings the new strategic vision (he has to refine that vision through the process and to learn about the organization), and for the managers he is trying to influence. In that transformation process, perceptions change first. In other words, a precondition for strategic redirection seems to be a change of perspective on the environment, a shift in the cognitive maps in use within the organization. Our observations tend to confirm views of strategic change as a learning process (Normann, 1976; Argyris, 1985). Based on the experiences of the companies we studied, it seems that attempting to provide a new strategy, or to implement a reorganization, without having first achieved a cognitive shift that provides a new strategic context consistent with the new strategy and/or organization is unlikely to succeed. Legitimacy is needed for a new strategy to take root.

To succeed in this initial stage of cognitive redirection usually requires stepping out of the existing management processes – since these processes are set to sustain the 'old' cognitive perspective. It also requires creating a non-threatening context, where managers can learn.

Strategic redirection follows cognitive redirection. Once a new strategic context is constructed, and accepted within the organization, the strategy of integration, rationalization and global rather than local competitive advantage become an obvious choice. In some of the businesses we studied it even became the too-obvious choice, probably leading to less depth and care in articulating and communicating the new strategy than might have been achieved. This was particularly true of 'follower' firms who could follow the trend set by their competitors. This sometimes led businesses in our sample to prepare for the current situation – ignoring the time needed for the new strategy to be implemented – rather than exercise strategic foresight (Hamel and Prahalad, 1985).

To take hold, strategic redirection requires power reallocation, as was observed in our very first longitudinal study (Prahalad, 1975). Yet, power reallocation can be accomplished only when the need for it has been widely recognized, and when one's resistance is seen by other managers as personal opportunism rather than a genuine legitimate difference in priorities.

We can thus overlay on the four-phase process described above a view of the *content* of change as made of three dimensions, each managed through a sub-process of change. The dimensions are: cognitive perspective, strategic priorities, and power allocation. In the successful redirection we observed, they changed in sequence.[2]

The sequence of change was managed not only by developing a new cognitive perspective and a new strategy 'off-line' but also by the carefully orchestrated use of a whole range of management tools over time.

MANAGEMENT TOOLS

These tools can be grouped into three categries: data management tools, managers' management tools, and conflict management tools. Data management tools provide and structure the data pertinent to the critical strategic decision and to the global and local performance of the company. By structuring such data and focusing the attention of executives on specific aspects, these tools transform raw data into useful information for decision-making and strategic control. Managers' management tools shape executive perceptions of self-interest and of their expectations by defining 'rules of the game' within the firm. Promotion and appointment processes, individual evaluations, rewards and punishment and management development processes, for instance, all help to communicate rules of the game to the various senior and middle-level executives within the firm. Finally, conflict management tools provide channels and structures for contentious decisions to be made, in particular decisions for which the priorities of global integration and of national responsiveness have to be traded off carefully. Table 2.4 provides a list of the typical management tools clustered into these three categories.

Not all management tools influenced redirection along the three dimensions equally. Data management tools were used to sustain and refine the new strategic priorities relatively early in the change process and to provide the infrastructure needed for the multiple minor power reallocation instances managed in stage 3 (power shift). Managers' management tools varied greatly in use. The 'softer' managers' management tools, such as socialization and management development, were used early in the change process – as a way to help unlock and challenge the dominant perspectives and to manage variety generation (stage 2). The 'harder' management tools – such as changes in measurement and rewards and shifts in appointments and patterns in career paths – were not used until late in the process, as a way of making power shifts visible and stable. Conflict resolution tools were used mostly in stages

TABLE 2.4 A typical repertoire of management tools

Data management tools	*Managers' management tools*	*Conflict resolution tools*
1 Information systems	1 Choice of key managers	1 Decision responsibility assignments
2 Measurement systems	2 Career paths	2 Integrators
3 Resource allocation procedures	3 Reward and punishment systems	3 Business teams
4 Strategic planning	4 Management development	4 Co-ordination committees
5 Budgeting planning	5 Patterns of socializations	5 Task forces
		6 Issue resolution processes

2 and 3 (variety generation and power shifts) to enable the sharing of new perspectives and the reallocation of power to take place.

Table 2.5 presents a schematic of the overall redirection process. While no one of the change processes observed followed exactly the same sequence of steps as any other, the composite pattern that is yielded by comparative analysis of change protocols was used as the basis for the table. The usual limitations to generalizing from field observations are therefore in order: our research is inductive and interpretative in the tradition of 'grounded theory' field research. The change process model developed above is thus an inductively derived model in which the researchers have attempted to give a conceptual structure to the observed patterns of change.

TIMING

As can be seen already in table 2.1, the redirection processes we observed were slow, lasting from three to ten years! And this period does not include the incubation phase. The reasons for this relatively slow unfolding of successful redirections are clear from the analysis of the change processes made above. First, and importantly, the new key executives we observed had a vision but no 'game plan' – they did not plan the sequence of actions we observed. None of the managers who masterminded strategic redirections started with a detailed planned sequence of how he would manipulate the organization and its members. Each step that was initiated had its own local rationale at the time in the total sequence, but managers seldom planned more than a very few steps at any one time. While the vision was relatively clear, the route toward it was not mapped clearly, and managers whom we

TABLE 2.5   A process model of strategic redirection

Change process stages	Change content		
	Cognitive perspective	*Strategic priority*	*Power allocation*
1 Incubation	New vision brought by new executive, often appointed for unrelated reasons		
2 Variety generation 3 Power shift	Data management and 'soft' management tools used to consider change	Different strategic priorities emerge, new vision is refined, need for redirection becomes seen as legitimate; conflict resolution tools are used to make change legitimate	Short-term self-interest of operating managers aligned with new strategy through series of relatively minor changes
4 Refocusing			'Hard' management tools used to make power reallocation clear; changes in information and administrative infrastructure

observed managing successful transformations showed a constancy of purpose but great flexibility in carrying out their moves. They thus waited to gauge the impact of each step, or short sequence, before deciding on the next ones.

In the second place, management tools are slow to take effect. Different tools can have an impact more or less quickly, and can be changed or redirected more or less rapidly. A change of single key executive usually has an impact in less than a year, while the slower reshaping of patterns of career paths for middle-level executives takes several years to reach critical mass. Individuals also adjust slowly, and require a long time to shift world views, develop new strategic perspectives and accommodate redistributions of power. A new appointment is not, on its own, sufficient.

Data management tools also have a relatively long lead time. A new planning and control system takes a few years, from initial design, introduction and evolution, to become a widely accepted and trusted tool for senior and middle executives alike. Typically, it takes at least three or four years to reach this stage.

In most companies we analyzed, individual managers' adjustment to newly reset managers' management tools and the lead times involved in building reliable data management tools, or in restructuring them, were the key pacing factors of strategic redirection.

During this relatively slow transformation, a number of risks exist for the process to run astray and/or lose momentum. The six cases of failed strategic redirection which we studied allow us to point out a few tentative hypotheses to explain failure.

SUCCESSFUL AND UNSUCCESSFUL REDIRECTIONS

In this section we focus on the 'failures' in our sample and draw from their study some tentative propositions that may have more widespread implications. The causes of failure are described below.

Lack of key executive The analysis of two of our cases suggest that failure is attributable to the lack of a key executive as initiator and focal point of the change process. Changes initiated by corporate staff groups and run as a collective exercise in an existing constellation of executives did not succeed. They made progress so long as they could strike a happy compromise between the interests of the various executives involved, but wherever power reallocations would have been required to make further progress, these changes bogged down. In one case, the very lack of a senior executive driving the change process reflected the lack of top management commitment. In the other, top management commitment was present, but the nature of the transformation was seen as technocratic rather than political, and it progresses on the narrow front of data management systems without being defined broadly enough. In neither case was strategic redirection accomplished: the process had stalled after two to three years.

Confused strategic logic A contributing factor in five of our cases of failure was the inability to formulate a clear logic for the redirection process. In two cases problems arose because of intense interdependencies between businesses and conflicting priorities for these businesses. One (small) unit was seen as supporting another (more important) one; it was difficult to establish a clear logic for the smaller business being-independent from the larger one, and such logic could not take hold in the organization, particularly since in that company the capabilities to manage interdependencies between businesses were lacking. In another company various segments of the same business had very different priorities but also shared many operations, and the strategic logic for the whole business was unclear. In other cases the issues were more that both national responsiveness and integration were important, but that these two sets of needs were seen as mutually exclusive. In other words, the strategic solution was constructed as *either* responsiveness *or* integration, but each of these 'solutions' had such drawbacks that it could not be seen as successful. Rather than reformulate the strategic problem as one of gaining advantages from both responsiveness *and* integration, the either/or view led to a zero-sum game approach to very real strategic tradeoffs. This made it impossible to recognize the need for both responsiveness and integration.

Infrastructure lag   The most prevalent cause of failure was a widening gap in the process between the broad cognitive shift and the administrative infrastructure needed to support it. In other words, the key executive attempted to make progress despite and against management systems that had not changed at all – or were in a state of confusion – and did not support the change process. Data management systems were not sufficiently well developed to allow the need for a possible shift in strategic direction to be analyzed and justified, and thus the credibility of the new vision declined rapidly. Vision cannot outpace action by too great a margin, and action is difficult, in a large complex multinational company, when it cannot rely on management system infrastructure and yet needs to involve many subsidiaries, functions and product lines. In one case of failure the underlying administrative infrastructure did not change at all. In other cases it did evolve, but too slowly and with too much confusion.

Departure of key executive   In two of the cases of failure, this was a critical factor. In one, the key executive who had initiated the change process reached mandatory retirement age in the middle of the process and retired, and his successor did not elicit sufficient respect, or probably did not have enough organizational savvy, to carry the change through. In the other case the key executive in charge was abruptly brought back to domestic operations – a stop-gap firefighting move – to solve a critical crisis. No one was ready to step in to continue to manage the redirection, and it lost momentum by default of leadership.

Inability to shift power   In one of our cases, direct clear conflict erupted toward the end of the process between the key executive who had masterminded the process and some increasingly reluctant, but strong, subsidiary managers. The senior executive involved had not succeeded in bringing about a real cognitive shift, or in tilting the balance of power away from the old geographical base of the company. The chief executive officer (CEO), who had succeeded by turning around an increasingly important national affiliate, did not uphold the key executive, and the change process not only stalled, but reverted to a position of national responsiveness. More generally, in specific phases of multiphase processes, attempts to shift power without having first legitimized a new cognitive perspective, and developed an alternative strategy, were abortive.

SUMMARY AND CONCLUSION

We started by arguing that both the strategic management and the population ecology approaches probably had too deterministic a view of strategic adaptation as a planned teleological process or as fortuitous with the exception of unlikely 'mutations', respectively. The part of our research work on multinational companies reported here sheds some light on this debate. Based on our observation of strategic redirection processes in 16 multinational businesses, we can argue that strategic adaptation is possible, but fraught with difficulties. Major strategic redirections involve such interwoven changes in cognitive, strategic and power-sharing processes among executives, such careful and well trained use of management tools, as to be extremely difficult to implement. Changes are also dependent on one focal individual obtaining a position of leadership and bringing with him a new vision. Further, in six of our 16 cases the strategic transformation process did not succeed, and in two of the remaining 10 cases, while the process has not stopped, it is making only slow progress.

At least three possible avenues of exploration are suggested by the difficulty of strategic redirection, but they pull in somewhat different directions. Can the frequency or/and unit cost of strategic redirection be reduced? One inference is that strategy life-cycles have to be long since strategic direction cannot be changed easily. A critical aspect in the robustness of strategies thus must be their durability. Another possibility is to reduce the cost and difficulty of strategic redirection by providing for greater flexibility in managing multinational operations and by substituting for formal structures and management systems more cultural regulation modes in headquarter–subsidiary relationships. A third possibility is to preserve some benefits of multinationality, but administer them through less tightly coupled organizational arrangements than multinational companies.

From 'heterarchic' MNCs (Hedlund, 1986) to networks of firms, various such arrangements have been proposed. How they can operate practically deserves more research.

NOTES

1 This is why the companies in the sample are letter-coded, in particular to protect the anonymity of the most recently studied companies where events are still unfolding or are still too fresh to be publicized.

2 It is important to note that we observed changes under pressure, but not changes in situations of immediate crisis. While some of the businesses we studied had very poor financial performance, they were part of a larger corporation which did not explicitly consider their divestiture at that time. Although they were under pressure, the new key executives had time to develop and manage an incremental

transformation process over several years and did not have to achieve an immediate financial turnaround. Change processes under condition of immediate crisis and threats of demise may be quite different.

REFERENCES

Abegglen, James (1985)   *Kaisha: The Japanese Corporation.* New York: Basic Books.
Argyris, Christopher (1985)   *Strategy, Change and Defensive Routines.* Marshfield, Mass.: Pitman.
Bartlett, Christopher and Yoshino, Michael (1981)   *Corning Glass Works International,* Harvard Business School Case Series, nos. 381-160, –161, –162, –163, –164, –112.
Bower, Joseph L. and Doz, Yves L. (1979)   Strategy formulation: a social and political process. In Dan Schendel and Charles Hofer (eds), *Strategic Management: A View of Business Policy and Planning.* Boston: Little, Brown.
Brooke, Michael Z, and Remmers, H. Lee (1970)   *The Strategy of Multinational Enterprise.* London: Longman.
Davis, Stanley M. (1979)   *Managing and Organizing Multinational Corporations.* New York: Pergamon Press.
Doz, Yves L. (1976)   *National policies and multinational management.* Doctoral dissertation, Harvard Business School.
—— (1979)   *Government Control and Multinational Strategic Management.* New York: Praeger.
—— and Lehmann, J.-P. (1986) The Strategic Management process: the Japanese example. In Erich Pauer (ed.), *Silkworms, Oil and Chips,* Bonn: Bonner Zeitschrift Für Japanologie, Vol. 8.
Dunning, John H. (ed.) (1974)   *Economic Analysis and the Multinational Enterprise.* London: George Allen & Unwin.
Franko, Lawrence G. (1976)   *The European Multinationals.* Stanford, Conn.: Greylock.
Hamel, Gary and Prahalad, C. K. (1985)   Do you really have a global strategy? *Harvard Business Review,* July–August, 139–148.
—— (forthcoming), Unexplored routes to competitive revitalization.
Hannah, M. T. and Freeman, J. H. (1977)   The Population Ecology of Organizations. *American Journal of Sociology,* 82, 5, 929–65.
Hedlund, Gunnar (1986)   The hypermodern MNC – a heterarchy. *Human Resource Management,* 25 (1), 9–36.
Hymer, Stephen H. (1976)   The international operations of the national firm. Cambridge, Mass.: MIT Press.
Mathias, Peter (1978)   The role of the logistics system in strategic change: the case of the multinational corporation. Doctoral dissertation, Harvard Business School.
Miller, Danny and Friesen, Peter (1980)   Archetypes of organizational transitions. *Administrative Science Quarterly,* 25, 268–99.
—— (1984)   *Organizations: A Quantum View.* Englewood Cliffs, NJ: Prentice-Hall.
Mintzberg, H. (1978)   Patterns in strategy formation. *Management Science,* 24, 9, 934–48.
Normann, Richard (1976)   *Management and Statesmanship.* Stockholm: SIAR.

Pettigrew, Andrew (1985) *The Awakening Giant: Continuity and Change in Imperial Chemical Industries*. New York: Basil Blackwell.

Prahalad, C. K. (1975) The strategic process in a multinational corporation. Doctoral dissertation, Harvard Business School.

—— (1976) Strategic choices in diversified MNCs. *Harvard Business Review*, July–August, 67–78.

Quinn, James Brian (1980) *Strategies for Change*. Homewood, Ill.: Richard D. Irwin.

Salter, Malcolm, Hamermesh, Richard and Doz, Yves L. (1975) *Medical Product Group (A), (B) and (C)*. Harvard Business School Case Study no. 2–375–312, –313, –314.

Stopford, John M. and Wells, Louis T. (1972) *Managing the Multinational Enterprise*. New York: Basic Books.

Vernon, Raymond (1966) International investment and international trade in the product cycle. *Quarterly Journal of Economics*, 80, 190–207.

Commentary on Chapter 2

John Child

The pressing need which many firms have faced in recent years to effect a strategic and organizational transformation has served to highlight the paucity of research into how this process is achieved. It is Doz and Prahalad's intention to explore the process of strategic redirection in large complex multinational corporations (MNCs) and to develop a framework for analysing this. In particular, they aspire to redress the failure of much previous literature to relate the content, context and process of change.

They studied 16 MNCs which were attempting to change from operating through a fragmented, nationally-oriented collection of subsidiaries to a globally co-ordinated network of specialized manufacturing centres. While this was a rational change in terms of permitting advantage to be taken of production scale economies and the international division of labour, it amounted to a major upheaval within the corporations, both cognitively in terms of what had constituted normality, and politically in terms of what had been established positions of power. It is one of the merits of Doz and Prahalad's analysis that it gives saliency to the cognitive reorientations and power shifts required to achieve successful strategic redirection. Another strength of their work is that they were able to include in their collection of cases some corporations that failed to achieve the change. This comparison of success and failure allows for a more precise identification of likely causes of failure which are discussed in the last part of their paper.

The heart of Doz and Prahalad's analysis is a four-stage 'process model of strategic redirection'. The four stages are labelled 'incubation', 'variety generation', 'power shifts' and 'refocusing'. They see the key to incubation as the implantation of a new strategic 'vision' – as they put it, 'strategic redirection follows cognitive redirection.' In all the successful cases of strategic redirection, the introduction of the new vision against the status quo required that an executive 'pregnant' with this vision be appointed to a senior position. The generation of discussable options (variety), accompanied by the creation of a sense of urgency, then follows as a means of undermining adherence to older embedded views and refining the new vision. Power shifts in terms of reallocations of authority, typically incremental and often at the time seemingly minor, form the third stage. The last stage involves registering the legitimacy of the change through formal modifications to systems and structures, and key managerial appointments.

In presenting this as a new process model, Doz and Prahalad stress its contrast to the conventional treatment in 'textbooks' on business policy and strategic redirection. Their analysis is not, however, so novel as they seem to think. They draw a contrast between their model and Quinn's (1980) notion of 'logical incrementalism', on the basis that the transformations they studied followed long periods of stability rather than exhibiting continuing incrementalism. That may be so, but Quinn's somewhat more prescriptive approach identifies comparable process stages in regard to the articulation of a new vision, the generation of variety and commitment, the occupancy of key posts and the formalization of a new orthodoxy. It is not apparent, either, how the authors have advanced beyond Pettigrew's more comprehensive analysis of strategic change processes (1985, ch. 11). Theirs is an admittedly concise and neat model, but these qualities have been achieved at the cost of some simplification. For example, little is said about the role in the implementation of strategic redirection played by key agents at somewhat lower levels of the organization – key in terms of the technical knowledge, ideological concept-generating ability or process-facilitating skills that they possess.

There are clearly limits to what can be contained within a single paper, and Doz and Prahalad refer to forthcoming publications which may offer a richer fare. This is to be hoped for, since their research design *per se* is well conceived, incorporating a variety of corporate experiences in tackling a common strategic move, and, unusually, offering the benefits of comparison between a relatively large number of cases. The authors' present paper is nevertheless over-economical in its offering of the illustrative contrasts between successful and unsuccessful processes of strategic redirection that would both give life to their model and indicate some of its practical applications. The model suggests, for instance, that to embark upon strategic change from a weak power base, and to articulate that change overtly in a comprehensive formal plan, is to invite failure. Empirically, this implies that firms should not rely upon total rationalization plans drawn up by corporate planning staff specialists, or entrust the implementation of major strategic projects to a lower-level co-ordinator. It would have been helpful to have been offered some specific empirical grounding of this kind.

One of the more important contributions of the Doz–Prahalad paper lies in its discussion of the 'visions' with which the process commences. This is a fruitful concept for several reasons. First, it draws attention to the key agent of strategic change, and in all the authors' successful cases this was a newly appointed senior executive. At the initiating stage it appears that an individual incomer to the established cultural and political mould has a far greater chance of distancing himself from it than, say, a committee of people drawn from the existing set-up. This accords with the observed high degree of association between chief executive turnover and the onset of strategic change (cf. Pennings *et al.*, 1985).

Second, as Doz and Prahalad point out, visions are not blueprints or game plans. They have the capacity to inspire cognitive reformulation in the minds of other managers but retain flexibility with regard to the form and timing of their application. This flexibility allows others to work on the specification of the vision and in so doing to attach their commitment to it. Thus, in the case of a major rationalization within a large food corporation which I recently studied, the specification of the strategic vision behind it proceeded through two stages. The vision itself was publicly articulated by top management in terms of simple watchwords such as 'concentrate on core businesses' and 'reduce headcount'. Headcount reduction, a theme vigorously espoused by a newly appointed managing director, was translated into an annual target which in his own words 'wasn't a very scientific figure but people got it into their heads that it was about 1000 a year ... and that was pretty well how it turned out'. A second stage in specification then arose with regard to organization since certain practices had to be adopted to run plants with a severely reduced headcount, such as the enlargement of jobs and a flexible team mode of working. The two stages of specification were undertaken by less senior managers and engineers, often working in project teams.

A further utility of vision as a concept is that it draws attention to the question of its origins. Doz and Prahalad were not able to throw any precise light upon these. In so far as vision in this context constitutes a challenge to existing strategic frames, it must derive from exposure to other perspectives either through experience outside the corporation or at least in one of its subsidiary outposts or boundary roles. The import of outside personnel into senior positions, and the circulation of managers between outpost and core units, would seem to be the practical recommendations which follow as an insurance against strategic rigor mortis. The paradox is that corporations perhaps most require the challenge of a new strategic vision at that point when their perceived wellbeing is at its height, when existing policies have attained a high level of consensus and have become firmly anchored in formalized practice. How else, given the long time span that Doz and Prahalad (and others) found to attend acceptance and implementation of a new vision, can corporations adjust in time to suit the present pace of change in their contexts? The problem is that such exposure to discomforting ideas at a time when threat appears distant goes against all the natural political and psychological tendencies of corporate life. It presents a major challenge to the ingenuity of advisors on the management of strategic change.

Understanding the origin and specification of strategic vision requires more attention to the contribution of social networks than is accorded by Doz and Prahalad or most other strategic management writers. The network between the corporation and the sector(s) in which it operates can be important here. Sectors are not just populations of competitors; they are also networks of actual and potential collaborators (Child, 1988). Since the sector can be a fruitful source of exemplars for the revision of a corporation's strategy, its social network may provide the channels for the transfer of strategic visions through the inter-corporate mobility of executives, through industry trade associations, economic development committees and so forth. Spender (1980) was for this reason able to map distinct sector strategic 'recipes' which appeared to be widely shared at least in relatively homogeneous industries. Collaborative transactions can also furnish the experience required to implement strategic change. For example, in the field of information technology, the use of which in its modern forms is certainly of strategic significance, the suppliers of equipment and systems may play a significant role in assisting the specification of their client's strategic intentions (cf. Vollering and Waarts, 1986). The role of the sector social system in which the corporation is located deserves more attention from those interested in the management of strategic change.

The MNCs studied by Doz and Prahalad were attempting 'to specialize their manufacturing operations in various countries and manage them as a tightly co-ordinated network'. One of the capabilities necessary for the successful implementation of this strategic redirection is that of being able to devise a suitable mode of organization to cope with these requirements, and this involves internal social networking. The simultaneous specialization and co-ordination sought by the MNCs echoes Peters and Waterman's (1982) fundamental recommendation of 'simultaneous loose–tight properties'. Doz and Prahalad do not report on how the corporations successful in achieving strategic redirection organized for this, though they do cite lags in adjusting 'infrastructural' organizational support as a cause of failure. It would be interesting to know, for example, whether they adopted a 'participative' form of organization along the lines described by Grinyer and Spender (1979). Within the large diversified multi-level corporation, this form attempts to combine co-ordination with a capacity for strategic learning by intensifying internal relations beyond arm's-length modes to a level of discourse and social contact somewhat reminiscent of the Japanese stereotype.

Doz and Prahalad have focused on only one type of strategic change, large in magnitude but introduced fairly incrementally and not in an atmosphere of crisis. The question therefore arises of whether a different model is required to describe the steps taken to achieve more radical changes within a context of perceived threat to corporate survival, or to account for the situation where inherited cultures and structures have become so entrenched that they have to be destroyed before a new strategy can be introduced (cf. Biggart, 1977). I suspect that a portfolio of models will be required, and that in the future the art of managing strategic change will become informed by much more sophisticated analyses which take into account the historical legacy of the organization, the external conditions which present themselves, and the character of the change which as a consequence is being sought.

REFERENCES

Biggart, N. H. (1977) The creative–destructive process of organizational change: the case of the Post Office. *Administrative Science Quarterly*, 22, 410–26.

Child, J. (1988) On organizations and their sectors. *Organization Studies*, 9/1 (forthcoming).

Grinyer, P. H. and Spender, J-C. (1979) *Turnaround*. London: Associated Business Publications.

Pennings, J. M. and Associates (1985) *Organizational Strategy and Change*. San Francisco: Jossey-Bass.

Peters, T. J. and Waterman, R. H. Jr (1982) *In Search of Excellence*. New York: Harper & Row.

Pettigrew, A. M. (1985) *The Awakening Giant*. Oxford: Basil Blackwell.

Quinn, J. B. (1980) *Strategies for Change*. Homewood, Ill.: Richard D. Irwin.

Spender, J-C. (1980) *Strategy-making in Business*. Unpublished PhD thesis, University of Manchester.

Vollering, J. B. and Waarts, E. (1986) The relationship between time and success in administrative automation projects – a study in decision-making. *Organization Studies*, 7, 381–9.

3 Technological Discontinuities and Organization Environments

Michael L. Tushman and Philip Anderson

Since Barnard's (1938) and Selznick's (1949) seminal work, one of the richest streams of research in organization theory has centered on organization–environment relations. (See Starbuck, 1983, for a thorough review of this literature.) Recent work on organization life-cycles (Miller and Friesen 1984; Tushman and Romanelli, 1985), organization adaptation (Aldrich and Auster, 1986), population dynamics (Freeman, 1982), executive succession (Carroll, 1984) and strategy (e.g. Harrigan, 1983) hinges on environment–organization linkages. Environments pose constraints and opportunities for organization action (Hrebiniak and Joyce, 1985).

If organization outcomes are critically influenced by the context within which they occur, then a better understanding of organization dynamics requires that we understand more fully the determinants of environmental change. While there has been substantial research on environmental conditions and organization relations (see Downey and Ireland's 1979 review), relatively little research has examined how competitive environments change over time. While it is agreed that environmental conditions are shaped by competitive, legal, political and technological factors (e.g., Porter, 1980; Starbuck, 1983), there are few data on how these factors change over time or how they affect environmental conditions.

This paper focuses on technology as a central force in shaping environmental conditions. As technological factors shape appropriate organization forms (McKelvey, 1982), fundamental technological change affects the rise and fall of populations within organizational communities (Astley, 1985). Basic technological innovation affects not only a given population, but also those populations within technologically interdependent communities. For example, major changes in semiconductor technology affected semiconductor firms as well as computer and automotive firms. Technology is, then, an important source of environmental variation, and hence a critical factor affecting population dynamics.

This paper investigates patterns of technological change and their impact on environmental conditions. Building on a considerable body of research on

A version of this chapter appeared in *Administrative Science Quarterly*, 31 (1986), 439–465.

technological change, we argue and empirically demonstrate that patterned changes in technology dramatically affect environmental conditions. There exist measurable patterns of technological change which generate consistent patterns of environmental change over time, across three diverse industries. Whilst technology is but one force driving the course of environmental evolution, it is a key building block in our attempt to understand better how environments, and ultimately organizations, evolve over time. (See Noble, 1984, and Horwitch, 1982, for thorough analyses of the interplay between technology, politics and legal factors in shaping competitive environments.)

TECHNOLOGY AND TECHNOLOGICAL DISCONTINUITIES

Technology can be defined as those tools, devices and knowledge which mediate between inputs and outputs (process technology) and/or which create new products or services (product technology) [Rosenberg, 1972]. Technological change has an unequivocal impact on economic growth (Solow, 1957; Klein, 1984) and on the development of industries (Lawrence and Dyer, 1983). The impact of technology and technological change on environmental conditions is, however, less clear.

For over thirty years, technology and work flows have been central concepts in organization theory (e.g., Gerwin, 1981). Most studies of technology in organization theory, however, have been cross-sectional in design (e.g. Woodward, 1965), have taken place in technologically stable settings (e.g. public and not-for-profit settings), or simply have treated technology as a constant (Astley, 1985). Since technology has been taken as a given, there has been a conspicuous lack of clarity concerning how and why technologies change, and how technological change affects environmental and/or organization evolution. (See Brittain and Freeman, 1980, for a major exception.)

There is a substantial literature on technological evolution and change (e.g. Sahal, 1982; Dutton and Thomas, 1985; Mensch, 1979). Some suggest that technological change is inherently a chance or spontaneous event driven by technological genius. (See Taton's 1958 discussion of penicillin and radioactivity, or Schumpeter, 1961.) Others suggest that technological change is a function of historical necessity (e.g., the multiple independent discoveries of sail for ships: Gilfillan, 1931), while still others view technological progress as a function of economic demand and growth (Schmookler, 1966; Merton, 1968). An analysis of many different technologies over years of evolution strongly indicates that none of these perspectives alone captures the complexity of technological change. Technology seems to evolve in response to the interplay of history, individuals and market demand. Technological change is a function of both variety and chance as well as structure and patterns (Morison, 1966; Sahal, 1982).

Case studies across a range of industries indicate that technological progress constitutes an evolutionary system punctuated by revolutionary change.

Discontinuous product (e.g. jets or xerography) and/or process (e.g. float glass) technological break-throughs are relatively rare, and tend to be driven by individual genius (e.g. C. Carlson and xerography; A. Pilkington and float glass). These relatively rare discontinuities trigger a period of technological ferment. As a new product class opens (or following product or process substitution), the rate of product variation is substantial as alternative product forms compete for dominance (e.g., competition between electric, wood and internal combustion engines in automobiles, or the competition between incompatible video-cassette and/or microcomputer technologies). This techno-logical experimentation and competition persists within a product class until a dominant design emerges as a synthesis of a number of proven concepts (Abernathy, 1978; Utterback and Abernathy, 1975).

A dominant design reflects the emergence of product class standards and ends the period of technological ferment. Alternative designs are largely crowded out of the product class, and technological development focuses on elaborating a widely accepted product or process; the dominant design becomes a guidepost for further product/process change (Sahal, 1982; Abernathy and Clark, 1985). Dominant designs and associated shifts in product/process change have been found across industries. The Model T, the DC-3, the Fordson tractor, the Smith Model 5 typewriter and the PDP-11 minicomputer were dominant designs which dramatically shaped the evolution of their respective product classes.

Once a dominant design emerges, technological progress is driven by numerous incremental, improvement innovations (Dutton and Thomas, 1985; Myers and Marquis, 1969). For example, while the basic technology underlying xerography has not changed since Carlson's model 914, the cumulative effect of numerous incremental changes on this dominant design has dramatically improved the speed, quality and cost/unit of reprographic products (Dessauer, 1975). Similarly, Yin and Dutton (1986) document the enormous performance benefits of incremental process improvement in oil refining.

Incremental technological progress, unlike the initial break-through, occurs through the interaction of many organizations stimulated by the prospect of economic returns (see Hollander's 1965 discussion of rayon, or Tilton's 1971 study of semiconductors, or Rosenbloom and Abernathy's 1982 study of VCR technology). These incremental technological improvements enhance and extend the underlying technology, reinforcing an established technical order (see figure 3.1).

Technological change is a bit-by-bit, cumulative process until punctuated by discontinuous advance. Such discontinuities offer sharp price/performance improvements over existing technologies. Discontinuous innovations represent technical advance so significant that no increase in scale, efficiency or design can make older technologies competitive with the new technology (Sahal, 1982; Mensch, 1979). Product discontinuities are reflected in the emergence of new product classes (e.g. airlines, automobiles, plain-paper copiers), in product substitution (e.g. transistors vs vacuum tubes; diesel vs steam locomotives), or in fundamental product improvements (e.g. jets vs turbojets; LSI vs VSLI semiconductor technology). Process discontinuities are reflected in either process substitution (e.g. mechanical vs natural ice; thermal vs catalytic cracking in crude oil production; artificial vs natural gems) or in process innovations which result in radical improvements in industry-specific dimensions of merit (e.g. Dundee kiln in cement; Lubbers machinery in glass) (see figure 3.1).

These major technological shifts can be classified as *competence-destroying* or *competence-enhancing* (see also Abernathy and Clark, 1985). The former require new skills, abilities and knowledge in both the development and the production of the product. The hallmark of competence-destroying discontinuities is that mastery of the new technology fundamentally alters the set of relevant competences within a product class. For example, the knowledge and skills required to make glass using the float glass method are quite different from those required to master other glass-making technologies. Diesel locomotives required new skills and knowledge that steam manufacturers did not typically possess. Similarly, automatic controlled machine tools required wholesale changes in engineering, mechanical and data processing skills. These new technical/engineering requirements were well beyond and qualitatively different from those skills necessary to manufacture conventional paper-punched machine tools (Noble, 1984).

Competence-destroying changes	Competence-enhancing changes
Product	

New product class:
   Airlines (1924)
   Cement (1872)
   Plain-paper copying (1959)
	Major product improvements:
	   Jet → turbofan
	   LSI → VSLI semiconductors
	   Mechanical → electric typewriters
	   Continuous aim cannons
	   Nonreturnable → returnable bottles
	   Thin-walled iron cylinder block engine

Product substitution:
   Vacuum tubes → transistors
   Steam → diesel locomotives
   Piston → jet engines
   Records → compact disks
   Punched paper → automatic control machine tooling
   Discrete → integrated circuits
   Open → closed steel auto bodies
	Incremental product changes
	
	 Dominant designs:*
	   PDP-11, VHS technology
	   IBM 360, DC-3
	   Numerical control machine tools

Process	

Process substitution:
   Natural → mechanical ice
   Natural → industrial gems
   Open hearth → basic oxygen furnace
   Individual wafer → planar process
   Continuous grinding → float glass
   Thermal cracking → catalytic cracking
   Vertical → rotary kiln
   Blown → drawn window glass
	Major process improvements:
	   Edison kiln
	   Resistive metal deposition (semiconductors)
	   Gob feeder (glass containers)
	   Catalytic cracking → catalytic reforming
	
	 Incremental process improvements:
	   Learning by doing; numerous process
	   improvements

*Some dominant designs are incremental improvements (e.g. PDP-11), while others a e major improvements (e.g. DC-3, IBM 360).

FIGURE 3.1 A typology of product and process technological changes

A competence-destroying *product* discontinuity either creates a new product class (e.g. xerography or automobiles), or substitutes for an existing product (e.g. diesel vs steam locomotive; transistors vs vacuum tubes). Competence-destroying *process* discontinuities represent a new way of making a given product. For example, the float glass process in glass manufacture substituted for continuous grinding and polishing; mechanical ice-making substituted for natural ice harvesting; planar processes substituted for single-wafer process in semiconductors. In each case, the product remained essentially unchanged while the process by which it was made was fundamentally altered. Competence-destroying process break-throughs may involve combining previously discrete steps into a more continuous flow (e.g. float glass) or may involve a completely different process (e.g. man-made gems) (see figure 3.1).

Competence-destroying discontinuities are so fundamentally different from previously dominant technologies that the skills and knowledge base required to operate the core technology shift. Such major changes in skills, distinctive competence and production processes are associated with major changes in the distribution of power and control within firms and industries (Barley, 1986; Chandler, 1977). For example, the ascendence of automatically controlled machine tooling increased the power of industrial engineers within the machine tool industry (Noble, 1984), while the diffusion of high-volume production processes led to the rise of professional managers within more formally structured organizations (Chandler, 1977).

Competence-enhancing discontinuities are order-of-magnitude improvements in price/performance which build upon existing know-how within a product class. Such innovations substitute for older technologies, yet do not obsolesce skills required to master the old technologies. Competence-enhancing *product* discontinuities represent an order-of-magnitude improvement over prior products, yet building on existing know-how. For example, IBM's 360 series was a major improvement in price/performance and features over prior models, yet it was developed via the synthesis of familiar technologies (Pugh, 1984). Similarly, where the introduction of fan jets or the screw-propeller dramatically improved the speed of jets and ocean-going steamships, aircraft producers and boatyards were able to take advantage of existing knowledge and skills and rapidly absorb these complementary technologies (Headrick, 1981; Davies, 1972).

Competence-enhancing *process* discontinuities are process innovations which result in an order-of-magnitude increase in the efficiency of producing a given product. For example, the Edison kiln was a major process innovation in cement manufacture which permitted enormous increases in production capacity, yet it built on existing skills in the cement industry (Lesley, 1924). Similarly, major process advances in semiconductor integration, strip steel and glass production eliminated barriers to future growth in their product classes. These advances built on existing knowledge and skills and provided the core for subsequent incremental improvements (Dutton and Thomas, 1985) (see figure 3.1).

Both technological discontinuities and dominant designs are known only in retrospect – technological superiority is no guarantee of success. The dominance of a substitute product (e.g. Wankel engines, supersonic jets or bubble memory) or substitute processes (e.g. continuous casting), or a dominant design (e.g. beta vs VHS videocassette systems) is a function of technological, market and legal/social factors which cannot be fully known *ex ante.* For example, the choice by vacuum tube makers such as RCA, GE and Philco to concentrate on a dominant design for electron tubes in the early transistor days turned out, in retrospect, to have been an error (Tilton, 1971). Similarly, choices between standard record speeds, widths of railroad track, automatic control machine tool technologies or automated office equipment standards are often less a function of technical merit than of market or political power (Noble, 1984).

Multiple-product class case studies indicate that technology progresses in stages through relatively long periods of incremental, competence-enhancing change elaborating a particular dominant design. These periods of increasing consolidation and learning-by-doing may be punctuated by competence-destroying technological discontinuities (i.e., product or process substitution) or by further competence-enhancing technological advance (e.g. revitalizing a given product or process with complementary technologies). Technological discontinuities trigger a period of technological ferment culminating in a dominant design and, in turn, to the next period of incremental, competence-enhancing, technological change.

Hypothesis 1 Technological change within a product class will be characterized by long periods of incremental change punctuated by discontinuities.

Hypothesis 1(a) Technological discontinuities are of two types: (1) competence-enhancing (building on existing skills and know-how) and (2) competence-destroying (requiring fundamentally new skills and competences).

Competence-destroying and competence-enhancing discontinuities dramatically alter previously attainable price–performance relationships within a product class. Both create technological uncertainty as firms struggle to master an untested and incompletely understood product or process. Existing firms within an industry are in the best position to initiate and exploit new possibilities opened up by a discontinuity if it builds upon competence they already possess. Competence-enhancing discontinuities tend to consolidate industry leadership; the rich are likely to get richer.

Competence-destroying discontinuities, in contrast, disrupt industry structure (Mensch, 1979). Skills that brought product class leaders to pre-eminence are largely obsolesced; new firms founded to exploit the new technology will gain market share at the expense of organizations which, bound by traditions, sunk costs and internal political constraints, remain committed to outmoded technology (Tilton, 1971; Hannan and Freeman, 1977).

Hypothesis 2 The locus of innovation will differ for competence-destroying vs competence-enhancing technological change. Competence-destroying discontinuities will be initiated by new entrants, while competence-enhancing discontinuities will be initiated by existing firms.

TECHNOLOGICAL DISCONTINUITIES AND ORGANIZATIONAL ENVIRONMENTS

To what extent will technological discontinuities affect environmental conditions? Building on Dess and Beard's (1984) review of environmental dimensions, we examine two critical characteristics of organizational environments: uncertainty and munificence. Uncertainty refers to the extent to which future states of the environment can be anticipated or accurately predicted (Pfeffer and Salancik, 1978); munificence refers to the extent to which an environment can support growth. Environments with greater munificence impose fewer constraints on organizations than those environments with resource constraints.

Both competence-enhancing and competence-destroying technological discontinuities generate uncertainty as firms struggle to master an incompletely understood product and/or process. Technological break-throughs trigger a period of technological ferment as new technologies are tried, established price/performance ratios are upset and new markets open. During these periods of technological upheaval, it becomes substantially more difficult to forecast demand and prices. Technological discontinuities will, then, be associated with increases in environmental uncertainty.

Hypothesis 3 Competitive uncertainty will be higher after a technological discontinuity than before the discontinuity.

Technological discontinuities drive sharp decreases in price/performance or input/output ratios. These factors, in turn, fuel demand in a product class. The role of technological progress in stimulating demand is well documented (e.g. Solow, 1957; Mensch, 1979). As both competence-enhancing and competence-destroying discontinuities reflect major price/performance improvements, both will be associated with increased demand and environmental munificence.

Hypothesis 4 Environmental munificence will be higher after a technological discontinuity than before the discontinuity.

Environments can also be described in terms of different competitive conditions (Scherer, 1980). Important dimensions of competitive conditions include entry–exit patterns and the degree of order within a product class. Orderliness within a product class can be assessed by inter-firm sales variability. Those environments with substantial net entry and substantial inter-firm sales variability will be very different competitive arenas from those environments where exits dominate and there is minimal inter-firm sales variability.

Competence-destroying technological discontinuities have quite different effects on competitive conditions from competence-enhancing discontinuities. Competence-enhancing advance permits existing firms to exploit their competence and expertise and thereby gain competitive advantage over smaller and/or newer firms. Competence-enhancing discontinuities consolidate leadership in a product class; the rich get richer as liabilities of newness plague new entrants. These order-creating break-throughs increase barriers to entry and minimum scale requirements, resulting in relatively fewer entries relative to exits and a decrease in inter-firm sales variability: those remaining firms will share more equally in product class sales growth.

Competence-destroying discontinuities break the existing order. Barriers to entry are lowered; new firms enter previously impenetrable markets by exploiting the new technology (Astley, 1985; Abernathy and Clark, 1985). These discontinuities favor new entrants at the expense of entrenched defenders (Miles and Snow, 1978). New entrants take advantage of fundamentally different skills and expertise, and gain sales at the expense of formally dominant firms burdened with the legacy (i.e., skills, abilities and expertise) of prior technologies and ways of operating (Astley, 1985; Tushman and Romanelli, 1985). Competence-destroying discontinuities will be associated with increased entry/exit ratios and an increase in inter-firm sales variability.

Hypothesis 5 Competence-enhancing discontinuities will be associated with decreased entry/exit ratios and decreased inter-firm sales variability. These patterns will be reversed for competence-destroying discontinuities.

If competence-destroying discontinuities do not emerge to alter a product class, successive competence-enhancing discontinuities will result in increased environmental orderliness and consolidation. Each competence-enhancing break-through builds on prior advances and further raises barriers to entry and minimum scale requirements. As product classes mature, the underlying resource base becomes ever more limited by physical and resource constraints. Successive competence-enhancing discontinuities will have smaller impacts on uncertainty and munificence as successive advances further exploit a limited technology and market resource base.

Hypothesis 6 Successive competence-enhancing discontinuities will be associated with smaller increases in uncertainty and munificence.

Environmental changes induced by a technological discontinuity present a unique opportunity/threat for individual organizations (Tushman and Romanelli, 1985). Technological discontinuities alter the competitive environment and reward those innovative firms that are the first to recognize and exploit technological oportunities. The superiority of a new technology confronts organizations with a stark choice: adapt or face decline. Those firms that are among the first to adopt the new product or process proceed down the learning curve ahead of those that follow. The benefits of volume and experience provide early movers with a competitive edge not easily erased (Porter, 1985; MacMillan and McCaffrey, 1984).

Hypothesis 7 Those organizations that initiate discontinuous innovations will have higher growth rates than other firms in the product class.

RESEARCH DESIGN AND MEASURES

Three product classes were selected for study: scheduled passenger airline transport in the US, Portland cement manufacture, and minicomputer manufacture (excluding firms which merely add peripherals and/or software to another firm's minicomputer and resell the system), representing assembled products, non-assembled products and services.[1] This product class diversity increases the generalizability of our results. The industries were also selected because most participants had historically been undiversified, so environmental conditions outside the industry had little effect on these firms. Data on each product class were gathered from the niche's inception (1872 for cement, 1924 for airlines and 1956 for minicomputers) through 1980.[2]

Technological Change

A thorough review of books and trade publications permitted the identification of price–performance changes and key technological events within the three product classes. Technological change was measured by examining key performance parameters for all new kilns, airplanes or minicomputers introduced in each year of the industry's existence. For cement and airlines, percentage improvement in the state-of-the-art was calculated by dividing the seat-mile/year or barrel/day capacity of the most capable plane or largest kiln in existence in a given year by the same capacity figure for the most capable plane or largest kiln in existence the previous year. This review of new equipment also permitted the identification of initiators and early adopters of significant innovations.

The key performance parameter in cement production is kiln capacity in barrels of cement per day. For every new kiln, this capacity is reported by the manufacturer and is widely published in trade journals and industry directories. For airlines, the key economic factor is the number of passenger seat-miles per year a plane can fly, calculated by multiplying the number of seats normally in an aircraft model by the number of miles per year it can fly at normal operating speeds for the average number of flight hours per year it proved able to log. These figures are reported in Davies (1972) for all aircraft models flown by US airliners. In minicomputers, a key performance parameter is the amount of time required for the central processing unit to complete one cycle; this is the primary determinant of computer speed and throughput capability. Both *Computers and Automation*, a leading trade journal and industry directory, and the International Data Corporation (IDC), a leading computer industry research firm, report cycle time for all minicomputers.

Uncertainty

Uncertainty is typically measured as a function of variance measures (Dess and Beard, 1984). As environmental uncertainty refers to the extent to which future states of the environment cannot be predicted accurately, we measured uncertainty in terms of forecasting error – the ability of industry analysts to predict industry outcomes. Published forecasts for every SIC code are collected and indexed in *Predicasts Forecasts*. For each of the three niches, published one-year demand growth forecasts were collected and compared with actual historical results. Forecast error is defined as:

$$\frac{|\text{ Forecast demand growth } - \text{ actual demand growth }| \times 100}{\text{Actual demand growth}}$$

Munificence

Munificence was measured in terms of demand, the basic resource available to niche participants. Annual sales growth in units was obtained from the Civil Aeronautics Board (CAB) and Bureau of Mines for the airline and cement niches, respectively. Minicomputer sales data were obtained from the International Data Corporation and from *Computers and Automation*. Since sales figures grow as a result of both inflation and growth in the economy as a whole, these factors were eliminated by dividing demand figures by an index of real GNP growth.

Entry/Exit

Entry and exit data were gathered from industry directories and books chronicling the histories of each product class. An entry was recorded in the year when a firm first began cement production, an airline flew its first passenger-mile or a firm produced its first minicomputer. An exit was recorded when a firm ceased producing cement, flying passengers or producing at least one minicomputer. Bankruptcy was recorded as an exit only if production ceased. An exit was recorded whenever a firm was acquired; an entry was recorded only if the acquiring firm did not already produce cement, fly passengers or produce minicomputers. An entrant was classified as 'new' if the company sold no products prior to its entry into the industry, or as an existing firm if it had sold at least one product before entering the industry. Entry/exit statistics are not calculated for the airline industry from 1938 through 1979, as entries were forbidden by the CAB and exits depended more on regulatory action than on market forces. Table 3.1 provides measures, data sources and summary data for each variable.

RESULTS

Hypothesis 1 suggested that technological evolution would be characterized by periods of incremental change punctuated by either competence-destroying or competence-enhancing discontinuities. Hypothesis 2 argued that competence-destroying advances would be initiated by new entrants, while competence-enhancing advances would be initiated by existing firms. Table 3.2 summarizes the key technological discontinuities for each niche, while figures 3.2 (a)–(c) provide more detailed data on key performance dimensions over time.

The cement, airline and minicomputer niches opened in 1872, 1924 and 1956, respectively. After the three niche openings, we observe six competence-enhancing technological discontinuities and two competence-destroying discontinuities (see table 3.2). Each discontinuity had a marked effect on a key measure of cost or performance, far greater than the impact of other, more incremental, technological events.[3]

Figure 3.2 (a) documents the three significant technological changes that have punctuated the history of the Portland cement industry. Portland cement, invented in Europe, was first made in the USA about 1872, but early attempts to compete with established European brands were largely failures. Two events effectively established the US industry. The development of the rotary kiln made the manufacture of large volumes of cement with little labor practicable, and the invention in 1896 of a method for creating a continuous flame fed by powdered coal meant that a high-quality, uniform cement could be made without expensive hand-stoking.

During the following decade, rotary kilns 60 ft in length were standard. In 1909 Thomas Edison patented a technique for making kilns over 150 ft in length, enormously increasing the production capacity of a kiln, and the industry rapidly adopted the new 'long kiln'. Subsequent progress though was gradual; kiln capacity increased greatly over a period of decades, but in a series of incremental advances. In 1960 the industry began experimenting with computerized control of kilns. The introduction of computers permitted the construction of huge kilns, much larger than any that had preceded them. The experimental models of the early 1960s culminated in the enormous Dundee kiln in 1967; previously kilns of such capacity could not have been used because their huge size and weight made them impossible to regulate.

The revolution that brought powdered coal and rotary kilns to the industry was competence-destroying, almost completely obsolescing the know-how required to operate wood-fired vertical kilns. A totally new set of competences was required to make cement, and most vertical kiln operators went out of business. The Edison and Dundee kilns were competence-enhancing innovations; each markedly extended the capability of coal-fired rotary kiln technology. A good deal of investment in new kilns and process control equipment was required, but existing cement-making techniques were not

TABLE 3.1 Summary of variables, measures and data sources

Variable	Industry	Measure	Data source	N	Range	Mean	SD
Technological change	Cement	% improvement in bbl/day production capacity of largest kiln	Published specifications of new kilns in *Rock Products*	90	0–320%		
	Airlines	% improvement in seat-miles/yr capacity of most capable plane flown	Davies (1972)	54	0–248%		
	Minicomputers	Central processor unit speed	Published specification in *Computers and Automation*	24	2–9000		
Locus of innovation	Cement	Proportion of new firms among earliest to adopt an innovation	Reports on new kilns in *Rock Products* and trade directories	4	0.1–1.0		
	Airlines		Davies (1972), CAB annual studies of airplane purchases	4	0–0.9		
	Minicomputers		Published specifications in *Computers and Automation*	3	0–0.5		
Uncertainty	Cement	Mean percentage error of 1 yr demand growth forecasts	*Predicasts Forecasts*	28	5.2–266.9	52.0	61.6
	Airlines			88	0.1–381.4	59.2	58.4
	Minicomputers			36	3.5–811	138.1	167.1

		Measure / description	Source	N	Range	Mean	SD
Munificence	Cement	Annual cement consumption (tons)	US Bureau of Mines	101	8–85513	30296	27103
	Airlines	Annual passenger-seat-miles (m)	Civil Aeronautics Board	52	0.1–156.6	34.6	46.1
	Minicomputers	Annual minicomputer sales (000)	International Data Corporation	16	0.1–168	47.3	49.6
Entries	Cement	No. of firms producing for first time (mean, range and SD are entries per year, N is number of entries)	Cement Industry Trade Directory; Rock Products	281	0–24	2.8	4.2
	Airlines		Davies (1972); CAB annual reports	147	1–33	11.3	9.8
	Minicomputers		Computers and Automation; International Data Corporation	173	3–30	10.8	7.3
Exits	Cement	No. of firms acquired or no longer producing (mean, SD and range are exits per year, N is number of exits)	Cement Industry Trade Directory; Rock Products	218	0–23	2.2	3.9
	Airlines		Davies (1972); CAB annual reports	126	1–28	9.7	8.2
	Minicomputers		Computers and Automation; International Data Corporation	82	0–14	5.1	4.2
Inter-firm sales variance	Airlines	Unweighted variance in 5 yr sales growth % among all firms in the industry	Same as munificence measure	4	2.0–13.4	5.5	4.6
	Minicomputers		Same as munificence measure	4	2.6–21.3	11.2	8.6
Firm growth rate	Airlines	Firm sales at end of 5 yr era divided by sales at beginning of 5 yr era	CAB annual reports	46	−269–346	61.4	79.9
	Minicomputers		International Data Corporation	67	−96–11900	635.6	1561.6

TABLE 3.2 Significant technological discontinuities

Industry	Year	Event	Importance	Type of discontinuity	Locus of Innovation		Probability
					New firms	Existing firms	
Cement	1872	First production of Portland cement in the United States	Discovery of proper raw materials and importation of knowledge opens new industry	Niche opening	10 of 10	1 of 10	
	1896	Patent for process burning powdered coal as fuel	Permits economical use of efficient rotary kilns	Competence-destroying	4 of 5	1 of 5	0.333
	1909	Edison patents long kiln (150 ft)	Higher output with less cost	Competence-enhancing	1 of 6	5 of 6	0.001*
	1966	Dundee Cement installs huge kiln far larger than any previous	Use of process control permits operation of very efficient kilns.	Competence-enhancing	1 of 8	7of 8	0.000*
Airlines	1924	First airline	Mail contracts make transport feasible	Niche opening	9 of 10	1 of 10	

1936	DC3 airplane	First large and fast enough to carry passengers economically	Competence-enhancing	0 of 4	4 of 4	0.005*
1959	First jet airplane in commercial use	Speed changes economics of flying	Competence-enhancing	0 of 4	4 of 4	0.005*
1969	Wide-body jets debut	Much greater capacity and efficiency	Competence-enhancing	0 of 4	4 of 4	0.005*
Minicomputer manufacture						
1956	Burroughs E-101	First computer under $50,000	Niche opening	1 of 8	7 of 8	
1965	Digital Equipment Corp. PDP-8	First integrated-circuit minicomputer	Competence-destroying	3 of 6	3 of 6	0.019*
1971	Data General Supernova SC	Semiconductor memory much faster than core	Competence-enhancing	0 of 7	7 of 7	0.533

* $p < 0.01$.

Note: Fisher's exact test compares the pool of firms that are among the first to enter the niche with the pool of firms that introduce or are among the first to adopt a major technological innovation. The null hypothesis is that the proportion of new firms is the same in each sample; probability is the probability of obtaining the observed proportions if the null hypothesis is correct.

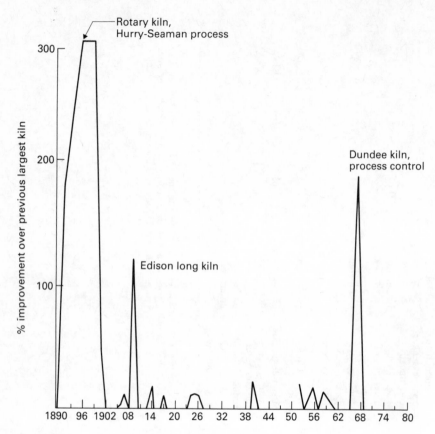

FIGURE 3.2(a)   Barrels-per-day production capacity of the largest US cement kiln, 1890–1980

obsolesced, and the leading firms in the industry proved most able to make the necessary capital expenditures.

New developments in aircraft construction have been the major technological break-throughs that have affected the economics of the airline industry, as illustrated in figure 3.2 (b). Numerous flimsy, slow aircraft were flown until the early 1930s, when a flurry of development produced the Boeing 247, Douglas DC-2 and Douglas DC-3 in a span of three years, each a significant improvement on its immediate predecessor. The DC-3, which incorporated some 25 major improvements in aircraft design (Davies, 1972), superseded all other models to become so dominant that by the outbreak of the Second World War 80 per cent of US airliners in service were DC-3s. Further

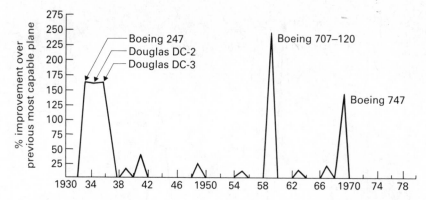

FIGURE 3.2(b) Seat-miles-per-year capacity of the most capable plane flown by US airlines, 1930–78.

aircraft improvements were incremental until 1959, when the debut of jet aircraft, with their considerably greater speed and size, again changed the economics of the airline industry. The final discontinuous event was the introduction in 1969 of the Boeing 747, beginning an era dominated by wide-bodied jets.

All three of these discontinuous advances were competence-enhancing from the perspective of the air carriers (though not from the perspective of aircraft manufacturers). Each advance generated significant economies of scale; airlines could carry many more passengers with each plane than was possible before. Though new skills were required to fly and maintain the new machines, airlines were able to build on their existing competences and take advantage of increased scale economies permitted with new aircraft.

In contrast to cement and airlines, established firms built the first inexpensive computers (usually as an extension of their accounting machine lines). These early minicomputers were based on vacuum tubes and/or transistor technology. The first transistor minicomputer was far faster than its vacuum-tube predecessors, but transistor architecture was replaced by integrated circuitry within two years, and thus never diffused widely. Sales were meager until integrated circuit minicomputers were introduced by a combination of new and older firms. Figure 3.2 (c) depicts the enormous impact of transistors, immediately followed by integrated circuitry, on computer performance. Integrated circuitry increased minicomputer speed more than 100 times between 1963 and 1965, while size and assembly complexity also decreased substantially. Integrated circuits permitted the construction of compact machines at a greatly reduced cost by eliminating most of the wiring associated with transistors. Integrated circuit technology was competence-destroying, since expertise in designing, programming and assembling transistor-based

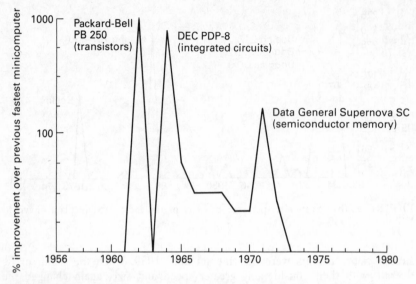

FIGURE 3.2(c)　Central-processor-unit cycle time of the fastest minicomputer in production, 1956–80.

Note: The vertical scale is logarithmic, because the impact of transistors and integrated circuitry on processor speed was so great.

computers was not especially transferable to the design and manufacture of integrated circuit machines (Fishman, 1981).

The introduction of semiconductor memory in 1971 caused another abrupt performance improvement (see figure 3.2 (c)), but did not challenge the fundamental competence of existing minicomputer firms; most companies were able to offer customers versions of their existing models equipped with either magnetic core or semiconductor memory. The effect of semiconductor memory was to increase order in the product class as existing firms were able easily to incorporate this innovation into their existing expertise. (Note that semiconductor memory was a competence-destroying discontinuity for memory manufacturers.)

These patterns of incremental technological progress punctuated by discontinuities strongly support hypothesis 1. As suggested in hypothesis 2, the locus of technological innovation for competence-enhancing break-throughs significantly differs from that for competence-destroying discontinuities. The first cement and airline firms were overwhelmingly new start-ups, not existing companies entering a new industry (table 3.2). No product classes existed in 1872 or 1924 whose competences were transferable to cement manufacture or flying airplanes. In contrast, early minicomputers were made by accounting machine and electronics manufacturers, who found that their existing know-how was readily transferable to the first small, crude computers. New industries can be started by either new organizations or established ones from other industries; a key variable seems to be whether analogous product classes with transferable competences exist when a new product class emerges.

Patterns in the locus of innovation for discontinuities subsequent to product class openings are remarkably consistent. The two competence-destroying discontinuities were largely pioneered by new firms (i.e., 7 of 11), while the six competence-enhancing discontinuities were almost exclusively introduced by established industry members (i.e., 35 of 37) (Fisher's exact test; $p = 0.0002$). Across these three industries, competence-destroying break-throughs are significantly more likely to be initiated by new firms, while competence-enhancing break-throughs are significantly more likely to be initiated by existing firms. Similarly, within each industry, Fisher's exact tests indicate that the proportion of new firms that initiate competence-destroying discontinuities is significantly greater than the proportion of new firms initiating competence-enhancing discontinuities (see last column in table 3.2).

Hypothesis 3 suggested that environmental uncertainty would be significantly higher after a technological discontinuity than before. To test this hypothesis, the mean forecast error for the five-year period before each technological discontinuity was compared with the mean forecast error for the five-year period following the discontinuity[4] Since systematic forecasts are not available before 1950, only four of the eight technological discontinuities could be tested. In three of the four cases examined, mean forecast error after the discontinuity was significantly higher ($p < 0.05$) than before the discontinuity (see table 3.3). Except for the period following the introduction of semiconductor memory in minicomputers, the ability of experienced industry observers to predict demand one year in advance was significantly poorer following technological disruption than before. In the semiconductor case, forecast errors were very high both before and after the discontinuity.[5]

Hypothesis 4 suggested that environmental munificence would be higher after a technological discontinuity than before. Mean demand growth was calculated for five-year periods before and after each technological discontinuity. The results in table 3.4 strongly support the hypothesis. In every case, demand growth following the discontinuity was significantly higher than it was immediately prior to the discontinuity. Further, these demand data indicate the enormous impact of initial discontinuities on product class demand. Initial discontinuities were associated with, on average, a 529 per cent increase in product class demand. Subsequent discontinuities spark smaller (though still relatively large) increases in demand (226 per cent, on average). Technological discontinuities were, then, associated with significantly higher demand after each discontinuity; this effect, though significant in each case, was smaller over successive discontinuities (except for minicomputers, where demand increased substantially after both technological discontinuities).[6]

Hypothesis 5 argued that competence-enhancing discontinuities would be associated with decreased entry/exit ratios and decreased inter-firm sales

TABLE 3.3   Forecast error over time

Industry	Era	Mean forecast error (%)	$t(1)^a$	d.f.	$t(2)^a$	d.f.
Airlines	1955–9	16.15	1.78*	18		
	1960–4	77.81				
Airlines	1965–9	18.52	4.35**	66	1.91*	54
	1970–4	49.13				
Cement	1963–7	38.31	1.85*	26		
	1968–72	80.26				
Minicomputers	1967–71	146.31	−0.14	34		
	1972–6	136.12				

* $p < 0.05$; ** $p < 0.01$.
[a] t (1) compares mean forecast error of the first period with the mean forecast error of the second period; t (2) compares 1960–4 with 1970–4.

TABLE 3.4   Demand before and after technological discontinuity

Industry	Era	Mean annual demand	t^a
Cement	1892–6	168	−3.16**
	1897–1901	1,249	
	1905–9	9,271	−6.35**
	1910–14	15,612	
	1963–7	63,348	−2.16*
	1968–72	77,122	
Airlines	1932–6	2,326	−3.01**
	1937–41	8,019	
	1955–9	244,625	−3.68**
	1960–4	355,678	
	1965–9	742,838	−4.42**
	1970–4	1,165,943	
Minicomputers	1960–4	435	−1.96**
	1965–9	2,181	
	1967–71	7,274	−4.60**
	1972–6	47,149	

* $p < 0.05$; ** $p < 0.01$.
[a] t-statistic compares mean demand of first period with mean demand of second period. In each case, there are 8 degrees of freedom.

variability. Opposite effects were hypothesized for competence-destroying discontinuities. Entry-exit ratios were calculated for five years before and after each discontinuity (except for the 1938–79 period in airlines). Results in table 3.5 are partially supportive of hypothesis 5. The ratio of entries to exits was higher in each of the five years before a competence-enhancing discontinuity than during the five subsequent years. None of the differences is statistically significant, though pre-discontinuity entry/exit ratios range from 1.15 to over 7 times greater than post-discontinuity entry/exit ratios. Entry/exit ratios prevailing before a discontinuity are markedly shifted in favor of exits following competence-enhancing discontinuities.

It was expected that entry/exit ratios would rise following the two competence-destroying discontinuities: the opposite was observed. Entry/exit ratios were quite high folowing these competence-replacing innovations, but were smaller than the extremely large entry/exit ratios prevailing just before the discontinuity. Many firms entered and few departed the cement and minicomputer niches in the 1892–6 and 1960–4 periods, respectively. Both of these eras were themselves periods of technological ferment in emerging product classes – rotary kilns began to replace vertical kilns in the early 1890s, and transistors began to replace vacuum tubes in the early 1960s. It may be that the rush of new firms to enter emerging product classes confounds the effects of competence-destroying discontinuities.

Entry/exit patterns are consistent across these three divergent industries. Entries dominate exits early on, reflecting the rush of new entrants. After competence-enhancing discontinuities in cement and airlines, exits dominate entries, reflecting industry consolidation. In minicomputers, while entry/exit ratios decrease over time, entries dominate exits throughout this 20-year period.

Hypothesis 5 also suggested that competence-enhancing discontinuities would decrease inter-firm sales variability as those remaining firms adopt industry standards in both products and processes. Small firms drop out of the industry, entry barriers are raised, and firms exploiting similar existing competences experience relatively similar outcomes. Following competence-destroying discontinuities, though, we expect marked variability in sales growth as firms compete with each other on fundamentally different bases; some firms' sales grow explosively, while others experience dramatic sales decline.

The results in table 3.6 for airlines and minicomputers support this prediction. In minicomputers, integrated circuits triggered explosive growth in the product class and increased inter-firm sales variability. Following the other three competence-enhancing discontinuities, though, inter-firm sales variability decreased significantly; niche occupants experienced similar results as they built upon their existing competences to exploit demand growth.

Hypothesis 6 suggested that successive competence-enhancing discontinuities would be associated with relatively smaller effects on uncertainty and munificence. Because forecast data are not available before 1950, this hypothesis could be only partially tested in the case of uncertainty. As

TABLE 3.5   Entry/exit ratios before and after discontinuity

Industry	Era	Entry/exit ratio[a]	Discontinuity type
Cement	1872–96	3.25	Niche opening
	1892–6	46.00	Competence-destroying
	1897–1901	12.00	
	1905–9	1.489	Competence-enhancing
	1910–14	0.814	
	1963–7	1.250	Competence-enhancing
	1968–72	0.160	
Airlines	1913–30	1.730	Niche opening
	1930–4	0.820	Competence-enhancing[b]
	1935–9	0.714	
Minicomputers	1956–60	Not finite[c]	Niche opening
	1960–4	5.500	Competence-destroying
	1965–9	2.917	
	1967–71	4.933	Competence-enhancing
	1972–6	2.708	

[a] The difference between the pre-discontinuity entry/exit ratios and the corresponding post-discontinuity entry/exit ratios, while consistent, do not reach statistical significance, owing to the large variance between individual years.
[b] Airline data for subsequent periods were not reported, because entry and exit were regulated.
[c] Six entries, no exits.

TABLE 3.6   Inter-firm sales variability before and after discontinuity

Industry	Era	Discontinuity type	Inter-firm variance	F[a]	d.f.
Airlines	1955–9	Competence-	79.24	2.726*	12,12
	1960–4	enhancing	29.07		
	1965–9	Competence-	103.63	4.096**	11,11
	1970–4	enhancing	25.30		
Minicomputers	1960–4	Competence-	5,599.32	−17.480**	8,11
	1965–9	destroying	97,873.25		
	1967–71	Competence-	86.26	9,960**	9,35
	1972–6	enhancing	8.65		

* $p < 0.05$; ** $p < 0.01$.
[a] The F-statistic compares the ratio of inter-firm sales variance before the discontinuity with inter-firm sales variance after the discontinuity.

predicted, the mean forecast error in airlines for the 1960–4 period is higher than that for the 1970–4 period ($t = 1.91$; $p < 0.05$; see table 3.3). Hypothesis 6 receives stronger support with respect to munificence. In cement and airlines, mean growth rates in demand are smaller for each successive competence-enhancing discontinuity. These differences are significant for two of the three comparisons (see table 3.7). These data suggest that as technology matures, successive competence-enhancing discontinuities increase both uncertainty and munificence, but not as much as those discontinuities that preceded them in establishing the product class. These data, as well as those entry/exit data in table 3.5, suggest that successive competence-enhancing advances result in increased product class maturity, which is reflected in decreased uncertainty, decreased demand growth rates and increased product class consolidation.

Hypothesis 7 argued that those firms initiating technological discontinuities would have higher growth rates than other firms in the product class. The growth rates of the first four adopters were available for airlines after 1955 and for minicomputers.[7] Table 3.8 compares five-year growth rates for the four early adopters with all other firms before and after technological discontinuities. As hypothesized in each of the four comparisons, early adopters experienced more growth than other firms. Early adopters had significantly higher five-year growth rates than other firms in the airline industry. For jets, early adopters had similar growth rates to others before the discontinuity, while for wide-bodied jets, the early adopters had higher sales growth before and after the discontinuity (see table 3.8). In minicomputers, early adopters had annual percentage growth rates that were 105 percentage points higher, on average, than other firms. Technological discontinuities are, then, sources

TABLE 3.7 Demand patterns following successive competence-enhancing discontinuities

Industry	Era	Mean growth[a] (%)	t (1)	d.f.
Cement	1910–14	48.3	12.03**	8
	1968–72	8.4		
Airlines	1937–41	161.5		
	1960–4	33.4	30.79**	8
	1970–4	32.3	.75	8

** $p < 0.01$.
[a] Mean growth is the average annual *percentage* gain in sales for the industry (in contrast to table 3.4, which measures demand in units). The *t*-statistic compares consecutive post-discontinuity periods; e.g., a comparison of mean percentage growth for 1910–14 with mean percentage growth for 1968–72 yields a *t*-statistic of 12.03, failing to support the null hypothesis that there is no difference in percentage growth rates between successive post-discontinuity eras.

TABLE 3.8 Relative sales growth of first four adopters of a major innovation

Industry	Innovation[a]	Era	Mean sales growth first 4 adopters (%)	Growth all others (%)	t [b]	d.f.
Airlines	Jet aircraft	1955–9	38.1	22.2	1.268	10
		1960–4	44.3	12.3	2.121**	10
	Wide-body jets	1965–9	101.1	19.2	2.487*	9
		1970–4	16.1	1.0	2.642*	9
Minicomputer	Integrated circuits	1960–4	n.a. (new firms)			
		1965–9	339.2	179.6	.44	10
	Semiconductor memory	1967–71	n.a. (new firms)			
		1972–6	238.0	188.4	.14	34

* $p < 0.05$; ** $p < 0.06$.

[a] The first four adopters in each case are: *jet aircraft*: American, TWA, United, Eastern; *wide-body jet*: American, TWA, Continental, United; *integrated circuits*: Digital Equipment, Computer Control Co, Scientific Data Systems, Systems Engineering Laboratories; *semiconductors*: Data General, Digital Computer Controls, Interdata, Microdata.

[b] The t-test compares the mean annual percentage growth rates of the four firms who first introduced or adopted each innovation with the mean annual percentage growth rates of all other firms in the industry. Two periods do not yield interpretable statistics because annual growth for new firms cannot be calculated when the base year contains zero sales.

of opportunities (or threats) for firms. While dominant technologies cannot be known in advance, those firms that recognize and quickly adopt a discontinuous break-through grow more rapidly than others.

DISCUSSION

The purpose of this chapter has been to explore the nature of technological evolution and to investigate the impact of technological evolution on environmental conditions. A better understanding of technological evolution may increase our understanding of a range of phenomena at the population (e.g., structural evolution, population dynamics, strategic groups) as well as the organization level of analysis (e.g., organization adaptation, executive succession patterns, executive demographics and political dynamics) [Astley, 1985; Tushman and Romanelli, 1985].

Longitudinal data across three diverse industries indicate that technology evolves through relatively long periods of incremental change punctuated by relatively rare innovations which radically improve the state-of-the-art. Such discontinuities occurred only eight times in the 190 total years observed across three industries. Yet in each product class these technological shifts stand out clearly, and significantly alter competitive environments.

The effect of discontinuous technological change on the two fundamental dimensions of uncertainty and munificence is unambiguous. Environmental conditions following a discontinuity are sharply different from those that prevailed before the technical break-through: the advance makes available new resources to fuel growth within the niche, and renders observers far less able to predict the extent of future resource availability. Major technical change opens new worlds for a product class, but requires niche occupants to deal with a considerable amount of ambiguity and uncertainty, as they struggle to comprehend and master both the new technology and the new competitive environment.

It is also clear that technological discontinuities are not all alike. Competence-enhancing discontinuities significantly advance the state of the art, yet build on, or permit the transfer of, existing know-how and knowledge. Competence-destroying discontinuities, on the other hand, significantly advance the technological frontier, but with a knowledge, skill and competence base that is inconsistent with prior know-how. Where competence-enhancing discontinuities build on existing experience, competence-destroying discontinuities require fundamentally new skills and technological competence.

The locus of innovation and the environmental consequences of competence-destroying vs competence-enhancing discontinuities are quite different. Competence-enhancing break-throughs are overwhelmingly the children of existing, successful firms. Competence-enhancing discontinuities result in greater product class consolidation, which is reflected in relatively smaller entry/exit ratios and decreased inter-firm sales variabiilty. As competence-enhancing discontinuities build on existing know-how, it appears that the rich get richer, while new firms face liabilities of newness (Stinchcombe, 1965). Product class conditions become ever more consolidated over successive order-creating discontinuities.

Competence-destroying discontinuities are more rare than competence-enhancing technological advances. Competence-destroying break-throughs are watershed events in the life of a product class; they open up new branches in the course of industrial evolution (Astley, 1985). These discontinuities are initiated by new firms and they open the product class up to waves of new entrants unconstrained by prior technologies and organization inertia. Where liabilities of newness plague new firms confronting competence-enhancing break-throughs, liabilities of age and tradition constrain existing, successful firms in the face of competence-destroying discontinuities. While the data were limited, competence-destroying discontinuities seem to break the grip of established firms in a product class. Inter-firm sales variability jumped after integrated circuits were introduced in minicomputers, as new firms and established firms pursued different strategies with markedly different results. Similarly in cement, new firms initiated rotary kilns and went on to dominate the industry.

These patterns are seen most vividly in minicomputer manufacture. The first inexpensive computers were built by established office equipment firms (e.g. Monroe), electronics firms (e.g. Packard-Bell) and computer firms (e.g. Burroughs). This new product class limped along until the advent of integrated circuits. Without exception, established firms floundered in the face of a technology based on active components. Integrated circuits rendered obsolete much of the engineering knowledge embodied in the first minicomputers. Office equipment and the existing computer firms were unable to produce a successful model embodying semiconductor technology. Only the few firms founded explicitly to make minicomputers (e.g. DEC) were able to make the transition. By 1965, almost every firm that had produced early minicomputers had exited the product class.

Technological discontinuities, whether competence-destroying or competence-enhancing, appear to afford a rare opportunity for competitive advantage for firms willing to risk early adoption. In all four cases, early adopters of discontinuous innovations had greater five-year growth rates than the rest of the product class. While these data are not unequivocal, firms that recognize and seize opportunities presented by discontinuous advance gain first-mover advantages. Those firms that do not adopt the innovation early, or, worse, increase investment in obsolete technology, risk failing as product class conditions change so dramatically after the discontinuity.

Technological advance seems to be an important determinant of market as well as intra-organizational power. Competence-enhancing discontinuities are order-creating in that they build on existing product class know-how. These break-throughs increase the market power of existing firms as barriers to entry are raised and dependence on buyers and suppliers decreases in the face of larger and more dominant producers. Competence-destroying technological advance, on the other hand, destroys order in a product class. These discontinuities create fundamental technological uncertainty as incompatible technologies compete for dominance. New firms, unconstrained by prior competence and/or history, take advantage of technological opportunities and the lethargy of organizations stuck with the consequences of prior success. Given the enormous impact of technological advance on product class order, future research could explore the politics of technological change as interest groups attempt to shape technological progress to suit their own competences (e.g. Noble, 1984).

Within the firm, technological discontinuities affect the distribution of power and, in turn, decision-making processes. Those who control discontinuous technological advance (whether competence-destroying or -enhancing) will gain power at others' expense (e.g. Morison, 1966; Pettigrew, 1973). As technological dominance is rarely known *a priori*, the control of technological assumptions and the locus of technological decisions will be an important arena for intra-organizational political processes. Shaping technological advance may be a critical organization issue as technology affects both intra- and inter-organization bases of power.

Technology may also be an important lever affecting organization adaptation. Investment in R&D and technological innovation may be an instrument that organizations can use to shape environmental conditions and, in turn, organization fate. Initiating or quickly adopting either competence-destroying or competence-enhancing discontinuities are direct actions which shape environmental conditions in early movers' favor. While technological dominance can not be predicted *ex ante* (e.g., Wankel engines, bubble memory), organizations that create technological variation (or are able quickly to adopt technological change) maximize their probability of being able to move with a changing technological frontier; organizations that do not contribute to and/or keep up with multiple technological bases may lose their ability to be aware of and deal with technological evolution (Dutton and Thomas, 1985).

Organization design, executive leadership succession and strategic reorientations are levers which may enhance organization adaptation in the face of technological change. Venture teams, independent business units and venture units are organization design variations which permit technological experimentation uncoupled from ongoing business (Burgelman and Sayles, 1986). Given the politics of inertia, executive succession coupled with organization-wide change also enhances organization learning. Longitudinal research on firms in the minicomputer industry suggests that strategic reorientations are a necessary conditon for organization effectiveness in technologically turbulent industries (Tushman *et al.*, 1985). These organization-wide transformations are driven either by a visionary CEO coupled with executive team change (e.g. K. Olsen at DEC) or by a new CEO (usually from outside the firm) along with a substantial executive team change (Virany and Tushman, 1986). These patterns are also found in other industries (e.g. Pettigrew, 1985). The difficulty of managing complex organization designs and organization-wide transformations puts premium not only on executive leadership's vision, but also on its ability to manage strategic change (Tushman *et al.*, 1986; Tushman and Nadler, 1986).

The patterns of technological change are similar across these three diverse industries. It appears that new product classes are associated with a wave of new entrants, relatively few exits and substantial technological experimentation. Competence-destroying discontinuities occurred early in both cement and minicomputer manufacture. After competence-destroying break-throughs, successive competence-enhancing discontinuities result in an ever more consolidated and mature product class. While we have no data, subsequent competence-destroying discontinuities may, in turn, break up a mature product class and restart the product class's evolutionary clock (e.g., microcomputers vs minicomputers, or compact disks vs records).

Competence-destroying discontinuities initiate a period of technological ferment as alternative technologies compete for dominance. This period of technological competition lasts until a dominant design emerges as a synthesis of prior technological experimentation (e.g., Dundee kiln, DC-3, PDP-11). Dominant designs reflect a consolidation of industry standards. These designs crowd out alternative designs and become guideposts for incremental product as well as major process change (Utterback and Abernathy, 1975). Thus, quite apart from major technological advance, the establishment of a dominant design may also be an important lever in shaping environmental conditions and, in turn, organization fate.

While these data indicate that technological discontinuities exist and that these discontinuities have important effects on environmental conditions, they are not conclusive. Though the data are consistent across three diverse industries, the number of cases is relatively small and some of the tests were limited by data availability. Future research needs to focus more closely on patterns of technological change. If technology is an important determinant of competitive conditions, we need to know more about differences between competence-destroying and competence-enhancing technological advance, what distinguishes major improvements from discontinuous improvements, what are dominant designs and how they occur, and what are the impacts of competence-destroying advances in mature product classes.

Equally important, the effects of non-technological discontinuities must be examined to understand more fully how competitive environments change. Technological change does not occur in a vacuum. It frequently sparks a response from the legal, political and/or social environments. For example, bioengineering, automatic control machinery, nuclear power and supersonic transportation each have been directly affected by a complex set of interactions between technological and political/social/legal considerations (e.g. Noble, 1984; Astley and Fombrun, 1983; Horwitch, 1982). Further, periods of incremental technological change and standardization may become turbulent for non-technological reasons (e.g. airline deregulation, or the outlawing of basing-point pricing in cement). More complete analyses of the technology–environment linkages must also take into account the linkages between technological change and these other important social, political and legal forces.

While this research raises many questions, it seems clear that technological evolution affects organization environments and, in turn, organizations. Beyond exploring more deeply the nature of technological change, future research could also explore the linkage between technological evolution and population phenomena (e.g. structural evolution, mortality rates, strategic groups) as well as organization issues (e.g. adaptation, succession, political processes). Technology may be a strategic lever in proactively shaping environmental conditions and, in turn, organization adaptation.

CONCLUSION

Technology and technological change are important determinants of environmental conditions. This research indicates that technological change proceeds through periods of stability punctuated by discontinuous advance. These discontinuities are either competence-destroying or competence-enhancing; they either build on or destroy existing technological know-how. These discontinuities have significant impacts on environmental conditions over long periods of time in diverse industries. While technology is not the only major determinant of environmental conditions, it clearly wields an important influence. These results underscore the importance of technology and technological change in our quest to better understand environments and, in turn, organizations.

NOTES

1 This research was generously supported by funds from the Strategy Research Center at Columbia University, the Center for Entrepreneurial Studies at New York University and the Center for Innovation Management Studies at Lehigh University. We would like to thank Graham Astley, Ellen Auster, Robert Drazin, Kathryn Harrigan and anonymous *Administrative Science Quarterly* reviewers for their helpful comments.
2 The three populations studied included all US firms which produced cement, flew airplane passengers or produced minicomputers. These industries were chosen partly because archival sources exist permitting a complete census of population members over time. Two outstanding books (Lesley, 1924; Davies, 1972) chronicle the history of the cement and airline industries and include meticulously researched profiles of early entrants into those product classes. In the airline industry, CAB lists of entries and exits after 1938 are definitive, owing to licensing requirements. In cement, the very high degree of agreement among two trade journals and two industry directories from 1900 on suggests substantially that all firms that ever

produced cement are included. Similarly, in minicomputers, the very high degree of agreement among trade journals, an exhaustive annual industry directory in *Computers and Automation* and International Data Corporation (IDC) product listings indicate that virtually all firms that ever produced a minicomputer are included. All sources included very small firms which survived only briefly; any firms that might have been overlooked in this study have never received published mention in three industries thoroughly covered by numerous archival sources.

3 Technological discontinuities were relatively easy to identify because a few innovations so markedly advance the state-of-the-art that they clearly stand out from less dramatic improvements (see figures 3.2 (a)·(c)). Other industries may not exhibit such marked differences, and eventually a coefficient of technological progress could be developed to help distinguish incremental from discontinuous change; one approach might be to pool annual percentage improvements and select those more than two standard deviations above the mean.

4 The choice of five-year-periods is arbitrary. Major technological changes do not have an overnight impact; it takes several years for their effect on uncertainty and munificence to appear. Yet in the longer run, extraneous events create demand fluctuations whose noise can drown out the patterns generated by discontinuous technological advances. Since the industries selected included discontinuities seven and ten years apart, five years was selected as the maximum practicable period of observation that would not create serious overlap problems between the era following one discontinuity and the era preceding another.

5 Since the entire population of published forecasts, annual growth in demand and entry/exit data are available, sampling error is not an issue; one could simply report the differences between populations. However, the critical question here is whether consistent differences between pre- and post-discontinuity environments can be discerned. The significance tests show that the probability is small that chance processes could have produced the reported differences between pre- and post-discontinuity eras (Blalock, 1979, p. 241).

6 Two possible objections may be raised to comparing the means of five-year periods preceding and following a discontinuity. First, if there is a strong upward trend in the time series, then for practically any year chosen, demand in the five succeeding years will be significantly higher than demand in the five preceding years. If this is so, there is nothing special about the eras surrounding a technological discontinuity. On the other hand, it may be that the findings are very sensitive to the exact year chosen to mark the discontinuity. If results are significant comparing, for example, 1960–4 with 1965–9, but not significant if the comparison is between 1959–63 and 1964–8, or between 1961–5 and 1966–70, then the finding is not robust.

Accordingly, the difference-of-means test was performed for every possible combination of two adjacent five-year periods for each industry. In each industry, it was found that eras of significant before/after demand shift are rare. Sixteen of 96 possible comparisons were significant at the 0.05 level in the cement industry (17%), 17 of 45 possible comparisons of airline demand (38%), and 2 of 7 possible comparisons of minicomputer demand (28%). This suggests that technological discontinuities are not the only events that seem to be associated with sharp increases in demand. However, neither do such shifts occur frequently or at random. And in each case, a difference of one year either way in identifying the discontinuity would have made no difference; the demand shift is not particularly sensitive to the specific year chosen as the discontinuity.

In summary, at a few comparatively rare periods in the history of an industry, one can locate a demand breakpoint, an era of two or three years during which average demand for the five years following any of these critical years significantly exceeds the average demand in the five years preceding the chosen year. Some of these critical eras are not associated with technological discontinuities. Without exception, every technological discontinuity is associated with such a demand shift.

7 The number of early adopters chosen was arbitrary. Four were selected to provide a group large enough for a mean to be meaningful, yet small enough to argue reasonably that the firms considered were quicker to adopt the innovation than the rest of the industry.

REFERENCES

Abernathy, William (1978) *The Productivity Dilemma*. Baltimore: Johns Hopkins University Press.
—— and Clark, Kim B. (1985) Innovation: mapping the winds of creative destruction. *Research Policy*, 14, 3–22.
Aldrich, Howard and Auster, Ellen R. (1986) Even dwarfs started small: liabilities of age and size and their strategic implications. In Thomas L. Cummings and Barry Staw (eds), *Research in Organizational Behavior*, vol. 8, pp. 165–198. Greenwich, Conn.: JAI Press.
Astley, W. Graham (1985) The two ecologies: population and community perspectives on organizational evolution. *Administrative Science Quarterly*, 30, 224–41.
—— and Fombrun, Charles (1983) Technological innovation and industrial structure: the case of telecommunications. In Robert Lamb (ed.), *Advances in Strategic Management*, vol. 1, pp. 205–29. Greenwich, Conn.: JAI Press.
Barley, Stephen R. (1986) Technology as an occasion for structuring: evidence from observations of CT scanners and the social order of radiology departments. *Administrative Science Quarterly*, 31, 78–108.
Barnard, Chester (1938) *The Functions of the Executive*. Cambridge, Mass.: Harvard University Press.
Blalock, Hubert (1979) *Social Statistics*. New York: McGraw-Hill.
Brittain, Jack and Freeman, John (1980) Organizational proliferation and density-dependent selection. In John R. Kimberly and Robert Miles (eds), *The Organizational Life Cycle*, pp. 291–338. San Francisco: Jossey-Bass.
Burgelman, Robert and Sayles, Leonard (1986) *Inside Corporate Innovation*. New York: Free Press.
Carroll, Glenn R. (1984) Dynamics of publisher succession in newspaper organizations. *Administrative Science Quarterly*, 29, 93–113.
Chandler, Alfred D., Jr (1977) *The Visible Hand: The Managerial Revolution in American Business*. Cambridge, Mass.: Belknap Press.
Davies, R. E. G. (1971) *Airlines of the United States Since 1914*. London: Putnam.
Dess, Gregory, G. and Beard, Donald W. (1984) Dimensions of organizational task environments. *Administrative Science Quarterly*, 29, 52–73.
Dessauer, John H. (1975) *My Years with Xerox*. New York: Manor Books.
Downey, H. Kirk and Ireland, R. Duane (1979) Quantitative versus qualitative: environmental assessment in organizational studies. *Administrative Science Quarterly*, 24, 630–7.

Dutton, John and Thomas, Annie (1985)   Relating technological change and learning by doing. In Richard D. Rosenbloom (ed.), *Research on Technological Innovation, Management, and Policy*, vol. 2, pp. 187–224. Greenwich, Conn.: JAI Press.

Fishman, Katherine (1981)   *The Computer Establishment*. New York: Harper & Row.

Freeman, John (1982)   Organizational life cycles and natural selection processes. In Barry Staw and Larry Cummings (eds), *Research in Organizational Behavior*, vol. 4, pp. 1–32. Greenwich, Conn.: JAI Press.

Gerwin, Donald (1981)   Relationships between structure and technology. In Paul Nystrom and William Starbuck (eds), *Handbook of Organizational Design*, vol. 2, pp. 3–31. Oxford: University Press.

Gilfillan, S. Colum (1931)   *Inventing the Ship*. Chicago: Follett.

Hannan, Michael and Freeman, John (1977)   The population ecology of organizations. *American Journal of Sociology*, 82, 929–64.

Harrigan, Kathy (1983)   *Strategies for Vertical Integration*. Lexington, Mass.: D. C. Heath, Lexington Books.

Headrick, Daniel (1981)   *The Tools of Empire*. Oxford: University Press.

Hollander, Samuel (1965)   *The Sources of Increased Efficiency*. Cambridge, Mass.: MIT Press.

Horwitch, Mel (1982)   *Clipped Wings: A Study of the Supersonic Transport*. Cambridge, Mass.: MIT Press.

Hrebiniak, Lawrence G. and Joyce, William F. (1985)   Organizational Adaptation: Strategic Choice and Environmental Determinism. *Administrative Science Quarterly*, 30, 336–49.

Klein, Burton (1984)   *Wages and Business Cycles: A Dynamic Theory*. New York: Pergamon Press.

Lawrence, Paul and Dyer, Davis (1983)   *Renewing American Industry*. New York: Free Press.

Lesley, Robert (1924)   *A History of the United States Portland Cement Industry*. Chicago: Portland Cement Association.

MacMillan, Ian and McCaffrey, M. L. (1984)   Strategy for financial services: cashing in on competitive inertia. *Journal of Business Strategy*, 4, 58–73.

McKelvey, Bill (1982)   *Organizational Systematics – Taxonomy, Evolution, Classification*. Berkeley: University of California Press.

Mensch, Gerhard (1979)   *Stalemate in Technology: Innovations Overcome the Depression*. Cambridge, Mass.: Ballinger.

Merton, Robert (1968)   *Social Theory and Social Structure*. New York: Free Press.

Miles, Raymond and Snow, Charles (1978)   *Organizational Strategy, Structure and Process*. New York: McGraw-Hill.

Miller, Danny and Friesen, Peter (1984)   *Organizations: A Quantum View*. Englewood Cliffs, NJ: Prentice-Hall.

Morison, Elting E. (1966)   *Men, Machines, and Modern Times*. Cambridge, Mass.: MIT Press.

Myers, Sumner and Marquis, Donald G. (1969)   *Successful Industrial Innovations*. Washingon, DC: National Science Foundation.

Noble, David (1984)   *Forces of Production: A Social History of Industrial Automation*. New York: Alfred A. Knopf.

Noyce, Robert (1977)   Microelectronics. *Scientific American*, 234, no. 9, 63–9.

Pettigrew, Andrew (1973)   *Politics of Organizational Decision-Making*. London: Tavistock Press.

—— (1985) *The Awakening Giant.* Oxford: Basil Blackwell.
Pfeffer, Jeffrey and Salancik, Gerald (1978) *The External Control of Organizations.* New York: Harper & Row.
Porter, Michael (1980) *Competitive Strategy: Techniques for Analyzing Industries and Competitors.* New York: Free Press.
—— (1985) *Competitive Advantage: Creating and Sustaining Superior Performance.* New York: Free Press.
Pugh, Emerson W. (1984) *Memories that Shaped an Industry: Decisions Leading to the IBM System 360.* Cambridge, Mass.: MIT Press.
Rosenberg, Nathan (1972) *Technology and American Economic Growth.* Armonk, NY: M. E. Sharpe.
Rosenbloom, Robert, and Abernathy, William (1982) The climate for innovation in industry: the role of management attitudes and practices in consumer electronics. *Research Policy*, 11, 209–25.
Sahal, Devendra (1982) *Patterns of Technological Innovation.* Reading, Mass.: Addison-Wesley.
Scherer, Frederick (1980) *Industrial Market Structure and Economic Performance.* Boston: Houghton-Mifflin.
Schmookler, Jacob (1966) *Invention and Economic Growth.* Cambridge, Mass.: Harvard University Press.
Schumpeter, Josef (1961) *History of Economic Analysis.* New York: Oxford University Press.
Selznick, Philip (1949) *TVA and the Grass Roots: A Study of Politics and Organization.* Berkeley: University of California Press.
Solow, Robert M. (1957) Technical change and the aggregate production function. *Review of Economics and Statistics*, 39, 312–20.
Starbuck, William (1983) Organizations and their environments. In M. Dunnette (ed.), *Handbook of Organizational and Industrial Psychology*, pp. 1069–1123. New York: John Wiley.
Stinchcombe, Arthur (1965) Social structure and organization. In James G. March (ed.), *Handbook of Organizations*, pp. 142–93. Chicago: Rand McNally.
Taton, Rene (1958) *Reason and Chance in Scientific Discovery.* New York: Philosophical Library.
Tilton, John W. (1971) *International Diffusion of Technology: The Case of Semiconductors.* Washington DC: Brookings Institution.
Tushman, Michael and Nadler, David (1986) Managing strategic organizational change. Columbia University working paper.
Tushman, Michael, Newman, William and Romanelli, Elaine (1986) Convergence and upheaval: managing the unsteady pace of organization evolution. *California Management Review*, 24, 29–44.
Tushman, Michael and Romanelli, Elaine (1985) Organizational evolution: a metamorphosis model of convergence and reorientation. In Thomas L. Cummings and Barry Staw (eds), *Research in Organizational Behavior*, vol. 7, pp. 171–222. Greenwich, Conn.: JAI Press.
Tushman, Michael, Virany, Beverly and Romanelli, Elaine (1985) Executive succession, strategic reorientations and organization evolution. *Technology in Society*, 7, 297–314.
Utterback, James and Abernathy, William (1975) A dynamic model of process and product innovation. *Omega*, 33, 639–56.

Virany, Beverly and Tushman, Michael (1986) Top management teams and corporate success in an emerging industry. *Journal of Business Venturing*, 4, 261–74.

Woodward, Joan (1965) *Industrial Organization: Theory and Practice*. Oxford: University Press.

Yin, Zun-Sheng and Dutton, John M. (1986) System learning and technological change: the evolution of 20th century US domestic petroleum-refining processes. Working Paper, New York University Graduate School of Business Administration.

Commentary on Chapter 3

Keith Pavitt

The chapter by Tushman and Anderson has two major merits. First, it addresses interconnected subjects that are central to our understanding of the nature, dynamics and strategic implications of technical change. Second, its authors have taken the time and the trouble to collect data from a wide variety of disparate sources, in order to test their hypotheses. I could spend some time questioning the quality, validity or the interpretation of the statistical data, but this would not be very productive; working in a policy-oriented research organization, I am only too aware of the difficulties of collecting and interpreting empirical evidence on little explored subjects. On this score, I think that the paper does a fine job.

Instead, I shall concentrate on the conceptual model of technical and organizational change underlying the paper, which has clearly been influenced by recent work on organization and strategic change. I carry a rather different intellectual baggage, growing out of empirical studies of the nature, determinants and impact of technological innovation, and of evolutionary theories of change (cf. Pavitt, 1984; Nelson and Winter, 1982). These stress the firm-specific nature of technological change, which means that I applaud the central importance given by Tushman and Anderson to firm-specific competence.

However, these traditions of analysis also stress the importance of the differentiated nature of this technological knowledge: depending on their starting points, firms evolve technologically in different directions. Empirically observed patterns of technical change over time do not confirm that all sectors and product groups pass through the same, or similar, technological and market cycles. This conclusion is at variance with the hypotheses put forward by Tushman and Anderson, and with the elegant and influential 'product cycle' model on which it draws (Utterback and Abernathy, 1975).

The essential hypotheses put forward by Tushman and Anderson are: (1) that technical change consists of both continuous incremental change and occasional major discontinuities; (2) that these discontinuities can be either competence-enhancing or competence-destroying; (3) that competence-enhancing innovations are accompanied by increasing stability, with the reinforcement of existing firms, and competence-destroying innovations by increasing volatility and the appearance of new entrants into the competitive game; (4) that whether competence-enhancing or -destroying, major discontinuities increase uncertainty and munificence, and first-comers do best in the competitive game.

I shall question these hypotheses, first by discussing the relationship between incremental and major technological change, and second by questioning the validity of the distinction between competence-enhancing and competence-destroying technical changes. I shall also suggest an alternative explanation for the patterns empirically observed by Tushman and Anderson.

To begin with, the distinction between incremental and major innovations is a useful one, both conceptually and operationally. However, it is misleading to describe all (or even most) major innovations as discontinuities, since they depend heavily on the incremental technical changes that precede and follow them, for four sets of reasons.

1   Accumulated incremental change over a long period can be difficult to distinguish from radical change, since it can lead to a different product, for a different market, designed and made with a different mix of skills. This assertion can best be illustrated by an example cited by Tushman and Anderson: the development of video cassette-recorders (VCRs) as analysed by Rosenbloom and Abernathy (1982). Over a period of 15 years, Japanese firms transformed the cumbersome and expensive Ampex machine, used by television companies, into the convenient and cheap consumer durable, complementary to television viewing. This transformation required continuous incremental innovation in product design, components and materials, and production methods: there was no observable technological discontinuity. Numerous similar examples can be found in the development of synthetic chemicals, and in electrical and electronics products.

2   Major technological changes often grow directly out of experience in the use of earlier vintages of technology, and build cumulatively upon them. Rosenberg (1982) has shown how the design of the Boeing 747 depended strongly on airlines' operating experience with the 707, in such parameters as engine reliability and servicing, and metal fatigue. In addition to such 'learning by using', the spectacular history of the development of electronic chips shows the importance of 'learning by doing'. Since the days of the earliest transistors, each successive jump in the capacity to manipulate and store information, as well as each reduction in cost, has depended strongly on experience in design, manufacture and quality control in the preceding vintage of technology.

3   The exploitation of major innovations very often depends critically on subsequent incremental improvements if it is to be competitive with existing vintages. The commonly held assumption (shared by Tushman and Anderson) that new vintages of technology immediately reach economically superior performance is rarely borne out in practice: witness the earliest experiences

with the transistor, jet transport, oxygen steel making, and even the steam engine. A period of trial, error, learning and associated incremental change is necessary before a major new technology begins to reach its potential.

4   Even when major innovations do comprise some radically new technology, they rarely displace all the skills and knowledge related to earlier vintages of technology. Thus, IBM's considerable electro-mechanical and marketing skills were still critical after the advent of computing, just as incremental innovations in established design, production engineering and mechanical engineering remain essential in the automobile industry, after the advent of electronics in computer-aided design, robots and flexible manufacturing (Pavitt, 1986a).

From these characteristics of incremental and major technical innovations I shall draw five conclusions.

First we should not expect first adopters of major innovations always to grow fastest, since economic exploitation often depends on subsequent improvement in the technology, where followers rather than the leader may perform better. Teece (1986) has recently given examples where first-comers failed with major innovations (Comet, EMI Scanner), and where later comers succeeded (VHS videos, IBM PC). He ascribes this to differential rates of incremental learning after initial commercial launch, and also to differential access to complementary assets (e.g. finance, distribution, after-sales service). This conclusion is not inconsistent with the empirical results presented by Tushman and Anderson, who show that the first *four* adopters – not the *first* adopter – of major innovations grow relatively quickly (see Tushman and Anderson's table 3.8 above).

Second, we should expect relatively few competence-destroying innovations, given the mutually dependent links between major and incremental innovations and the complementary links between old and new technologies. Tushman and Anderson nowhere develop a direct measure of competence-destroying or competence-enhancing innovations. I find most of the examples of competence-destroying innovations in figure 3.1 unconvincing, and could find numerous examples of old-established firms that have performed very well with such innovations (including IBM, Rolls Royce, Hoesch and Pilkington). And in the three industries examined in detail, only three out of the eleven 'significant technological discontinuities' appear as 'competence-destroying' in the sense that the main locus of innovation was new firms. All three happened in 1924 or earlier (see table 3.2).

This last observation leads to the third conclusion: namely, that, as Tushman and Anderson themselves point out, organizations with strong and varied in-house technological capabilities are less likely than others to be surprised or defeated by unforeseen or unmastered major innovations developed elsewhere. In-house R&D can, in this context, be seen as both an insurance policy and a capacity to adjust. Mowery (1983) has found a greater stability among larger firms in the USA in precisely the period since 1930, when in-house R&D activity has grown rapidly. Tushman and Anderson's identification of major innovations associated with new entrants in 1924 and earlier periods is consistent with both Mowery's observation and our prescriptive conclusion.

Fourth, the Tushman/Anderson model can, in my view, be made more robust by dropping the distinction between competence-destroying and - enhancing innovation, and concentrating on the positive links between major innovations, munificence and uncertainty. Given uncertainty, even established firms with high technological competence can miss major innovations, and given munificence, new entrants can thereafter establish strong positions. Thus, IBM missed xerography and Kodak missed instant photography, and these two firms had difficulty re-establishing themselves, not because of their lack of technological competence, but of the strong patent position established by Xerox and Polaroid. This suggests that degrees of appropriability by innovators should be included in any models of competitive dynamics.

Finally, I conclude that we do not yet have a satisfactory theory to describe the essential characteristics of the entrepreneurial function – or the capacity to deal with both incremental and continuous change – within firms. In dealing with discontinuities, Tushman and his colleagues identify the importance of the qualities of the CEO – in particular, the vision and the capacity to implement.

(N.B.: the same point has been made before: '... there is nothing more difficult to carry out, nor more doubtful of success, nor more dangerous to handle, than to initiate a new order of things. For the reformer has enemies in all those who profit by the old order, and only lukewarm defenders in all those who would profit by the new order ... arising partly from fear of adversaries ... and partly from the incredulity of mankind, who do not truly believe in anything new until they have had actual experience of it.' (N. Machiavelli, 1950 edn, p. 21). My thanks to C. Freeman for drawing my attention to this passage.)

However, while such explanations may be relevant to small firms, or to business units, they do not explain the ability of large and established firms – particularly in the chemicals and the electrical/electronics industries – to undertake both major and incremental innovations, and even to establish new divisions and products based on them, over very long periods. Given their size and their continuity, the salient features of these organizations must inevitably go beyond the characteristics of the CEO. Elsewhere, I have suggested that they should include the volume and distribution of technological and related skills (defining possible directions of opportunity), organizational forms (both for implementation and for exploiting inter-divisional synergies), and evaluation systems (especially for entry into new areas) (Pavitt, 1986b). There are probably many other factors and hypotheses that could be generated. Given the importance of the subject, they deserve attention and debate.

REFERENCES

Machiavelli, N. (1950 edn) *The Prince*, Modern Library College Editions. London: Random House.

Mowery, D. (1983) Industrial research and firm size, survival, and growth in American manufacturing, 1921–46: an assessment. *Journal of Economic History*, **43**, 953–80.

Nelson, R. and Winter, S. (1982) *An Evolutionary Theory of Economic Change.* Cambridge, Mass.: Belknap press.

Pavitt, K. (1984) Sectoral patterns of technical change: towards a taxonomy and a theory. *Research Policy*, (6), 343–74.

—— (1986a) Chips and trajectories: how does the semiconductor influence the sources and directions of technical change? In R. Macleod (ed.), *Technology and the Human Prospect*, pp. 31–53. London: Frances Pinter.

—— (1986b) Technology, innovation and strategic management. In J. McGee and H. Thomas (eds), *Strategic Management Research: A European Perspective*, pp. 171–90. Chichester: John Wiley.

Rosenberg, N. (1982) Learning by using. *Inside the Black Box: Technology and Economics*, pp. 120–40. Cambridge: University Press.

Rosenbloom, R. and Abernathy, W. (1982) The climate for innovation in industry: the role of management attitudes and practices in consumer electronics. *Research Policy*, (4), 209–26.

Teece, D. J. (1986) Profiting from technological innovation: implications for integration, collaboration, licensing and public policy. *Research Policy*, 15 (6), 285–306.

Utterback, J. and Abernathy, W. (1975) A dynamic model of process and product innovation. *Omega*, 3, 639–56.

4 Business Strategy and Strategy Change in a Hostile Environment: Failure and Success among British Cutlery Producers

Robert M. Grant

INTRODUCTION

Mature industries are characterized by a low growth in demand and a comparatively long-established and well-known technology. This does not imply that such industries have static environments. In common with other industries, they are in a constantly evolving state through two processes. The first is *natural competition*, involving the displacement of firms whose characteristics are less well suited to the prevailing circumstances by firms that are better suited. The second is *strategic competition*, involving conscious and planned adjustment by firms to improve their competitive position *vis-à-vis* rivals. The strategic management literature has tended to see the principal problems of strategic change as being the internal constraints on change arising from organizational, cultural and political factors. However, when the processes of natural and strategic competition are operating simultaneously, a further issue is whether, by strategic change, established firms can achieve competitiveness with emerging rivals.

In the case of mature manufacturing industries, this question is especially pertinent. A major factor in the decline of the manufacturing base of Western Europe and North America over the past two decades has been the declining

This paper has benefited from the research assistance of Stephen Downing and comments from Charles Baden Fuller. The research was undertaken at the Centre for Business Strategy at London Business School. Financial support for the research was provided by the Centre and by the ESRC (grant no. F20250003).

competitiveness relative to the newer industrialized countries.[1] The shift of production from more to less advanced countries is seen by economists as a natural consequence of the product life-cycle. Comparative advantage in international trade has been shown to depend most importantly upon factor proportions. The advanced industrialized countries (AICs), with a relative abundance of capital, technological resources and labour skills, have a comparative advantage in technology and skill-intensive goods – typically, products in the early stages of their life-cycles. Less advanced countries, with a relative abundance of unskilled labour, have a comparative advantage in labour-intensive products requiring limited technological know-how or sophisticated labour skills – typically, mature products. For empirical evidence, see Thorakan *et al.*, 1978; Aquino 1981.)

This tendency for production to shift from the AICs in the course of the product life-cycle does not imply, however, that mature industries in these countries are sentenced by the iron laws of economics to inevitable demise in the face of competition from the newly-industrializing countries (NICs). Business academics, most prominently those of Harvard Business School, have argued that, challenged by new and more efficient overseas competitors, firms have the capacity for 'dematurity' (Abernathy *et al.*, 1983), 'renewal' (Lawrence and Dyer, 1983) and 'restoring competitive edge' (Hayes and Wheelright, 1984). The underlying theme is that comparative advantage is not determined exogenously by resource endowments, but is created by firms themselves through investing in strategic change.

The capacity of firms successfully to re-establish competitiveness against apparently unfavourable international trends depends crucially upon the resources that firms have at their disposal. A feature of existing empirical studies is their focus upon large firms in relatively concentrated industries.[2] This is true both of the industry studies, notably of automobiles (Abernathy *et al.*, 1983, Altschuler *et al.*, 1985), steel (Aylen, 1983, Messerlin and Saunders, 1983), shipbuilding (Mottershead, 1983) and consumer electronics (Turner, 1982), and of the empirical investigations into strategy–performance relationships; these have focused upon large firms either explicitly (e.g. Hall, 1980) or implicitly by use of the PIMS data base, where most of business units are members of relatively large corporations (e.g. Hambrick and Schecter, 1983; Anderson and Zeithaml, 1984).[3] However, many of the mature industries facing the greatest pressure from low-cost international competition are fragmented industries, where small firm size and absence of market power limit firms' strategic capability and constrain their room for manoeuvre in adjusting to new competitive forces.

To gain a clearer insight into how firms in mature, fragmented industries can respond to the growth of low-cost international competition, a study was made of business strategies and firm performance in the UK cutlery industry during the period 1974–83.[4] The industry was selected for study because it represented an extreme case of a 'problem industry' in terms of its high degree of fragmentation and its near-devastation by import competition. The

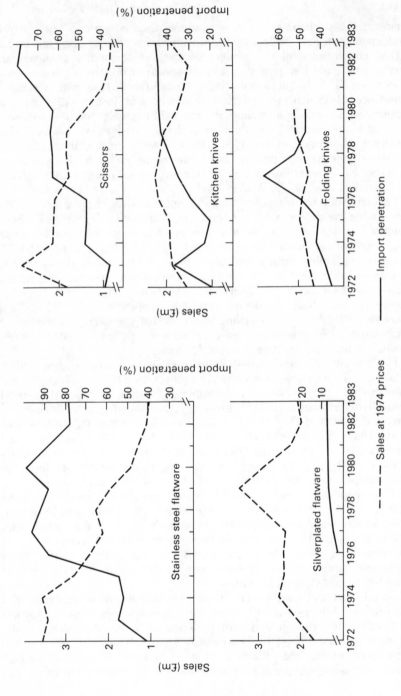

FIGURE 4.1 Sales growth and import penetration by industry sector

– – – Sales at 1974 prices   —— Import penetration

object of the study was to identify which strategies, by which firms and in what circumstances were conducive to survival and profitability.

The paper is organized as follows. The next section describes some key features of the cutlery industry. The following section examines the sources of profit, identifies the key role of competitive advantage and proposes a number of hypotheses predicting the impact of business strategy upon firm peformance. There is then a description of the empirical testing of the hypotheses, followed by a presentation of the results. The final section draws conclusions.

THE CUTLERY INDUSTRY

The cutlery industry was defined to include the producers of cutlery (knives), flatware (spoons and forks) and metal holloware (teapots, jugs, serving dishes, etc.). The industry, both in North America and in Western Europe, has been subject to severe competitive pressures from more recently industrializing countries. As the former chairman of a large British cutlery company observed, 'For a wide variety of newly industrializing countries, from Taiwan and South Korea to Israel and Brazil, cutlery has been one of the first manufacturing industries which they have established – it is ideally suited to countries which have a plentiful supply of unskilled labour and easy access to supplies of steel.'

Between 1974 and 1983, output and employment in the UK cutlery industry approximately halved, largely as a result of increased import penetration. The most dramatic increases in import penetration were in stainless steel products, where UK production was largely displaced by imports from the Far East (Japan, Hong Kong, Taiwan and South Korea). Import penetration has also increased from Western Europe. Here imports have included table cutlery, kitchen knives, scissors asnd pocket knives and have been directed primarily at the higher-quality end of the market. Figure 4.1 shows the trends in sales volumes and import penetration for some product segments.

The sample consisted of 33 cutlery firms with sales in excess of £100,000 in 1974. They ranged in size from Viners Ltd, with 460 employees in 1974, to very small family businesses, such as William Whiteley and Sons Ltd and Walter Trickett Ltd, which employed fewer than ten persons. The sample and the principal characteristics of the companies are shown in table 4.1.

Intense competition in the industry was reflected in a dismal overall profit performance. Between 1974 and 1982 the mean pre-tax return on capital employed was 12.2 per cent, well below the average for the manufacturing industry as a whole and below the average long-term rate of interest during the period. Moreover, return on capital declined during the period, from 14.4 per cent in 1974–7 to 10.0 per cent in 1980–4.

At the same time, there was considerable inter-firm variability of performance. While some firms were consistent loss-makers and six companies either failed

TABLE 4.1 UK cutlery industry: principal characteristics of study sample

Firm	Parent company	Major product segments[a]	Principal acquisitions, 1974–83	Average Annual Sales		Net return on capital		Gross return on sales		Notes
				1974–7 (£000)	1978–82 (£000)	1974–7 (%)	1978–82 (%)	1974–7 (%)	1978–82 (%)	
Viners	–	TC	(OrFevrere St Merlord, Glatman & Lander	9,245	11,305	16.0	1.4	11.5	6.8	Liquidated 1982.
Hawker Marris	–	H		2,867	3,583	12.1	-1.8	12.3	8.6	
Oneida Silversmiths	Oneida (USA)	TC	Old Hall	2,757	3,413	-6.1	-10.0	4.7	3.2	Financial data estimated 1978–82
Richards of Sheffield	Imperial Knife (USA)	PK, KK	Rogers Westenholme	2,488	3,666	24.0	-19.5	21.6	-2.9	Receivership 1983
Hiram Wild	Walter Lawrence	TC		2,275	3,401	6.9	1.6	4.7	2.9	Financial data estimated for 1980–2
Old Hall	Prestige/Oneida	H, TC		1,891	2,391	-8.4	-4.5	6.1	6.2	Sold to Oneida; ceased production 1984
Pinder Brothers	–	TC	Arundel Stainlessware	1,463	1,763	11.4	10.7	5.2	6.1	
Arthur Price & Co.	–	TC	Pepper & Hope, J. Stephenson	1,357	2,488	13.3	-4.0	10.3	9.1	
George Butler	Ingersoll/T. Mason	TC		1,241	2,030	8.5	11.6	14.4	12.4	Acquired by Heron group, subsequently by T. Mason
Harrison Fisher	–	KK	T. Frost & Co. J. Sanderson	1,187	2,050	8.3	9.1	9.8	11.1	

Company										
Roberts & Belk	C. J. Vander		SPTC, SPH	1,126	2,127	26.8	7.8	18.9	11.3	
Cooper Brothers	Richardson (USA)		TC	1,101	1,364	14.9	−13.5	7.1	3.9	Acquired by Frank Cobb 1983
Westall Richardson	Acme (USA)		KK	1,023	2,649	15.2	22.4	8.7	11.7	
Surmanco	–		S	819	1,288	27.1	21.7	15.1	14.3	ROC estimated. Cutlery production terminated 1984
J. Billam			TC	774	899	20.6	3.0	18.5	5.0	
Parkin Silversmiths	–	Elkington	SPH, SPTC	714	959	17.0	1.3	11.8	7.8	
Turners (Eyre St.)	–		B	643	1,056	6.1	2.8	12.6	10.1	
Slack & Barlow	–		SPTC	602	1,574	42.4	23.1	10.6	7.4	
R&J Hopkinson	–		TC	574	833	20.0	7.3	11.9	11.0	
Gee & Holmes	–		SPTC	380	512	66.2	11.4	24.6	25.0	
Sheffield Metal Co.	–		B	375	398	8.5	−5.8	16.6	6.8	Liquidated
A. Deeley	–		TC	354	762	0.5	8.4	8.4	9.9	
Nickel Blanks	–		B	346	672	45.5	39.7	24.9	22.8	
Ernest Wright & Sons	–	MAB	S	339	467	14.2	9.7	13.6	14.7	
J. Clarke & Son	–		PK	318	431	37.9	11.0	24.8	14.3	
Jessop & Smith	–		B	294	498	15.8	2.1	14.6	9.5	
Beatson Drake	–	Erysea	Handles	275	584	56.4	21.2	41.0	9.5	Formed from merger of F. Beatson and Erysea
K. Bright	–	H. Hutton	SPTC	269	432	13.9	4.9	9.4	11.4	
William Whitely	–		S	267	374	24.4	5.2	17.0	9.5	
Frank Cobb	–	Cooper Bros.	SPH	142	341	−4.1	13.8	8.6	16.7	
Walter Trickett	–	T. Gilpin	SPTC	139	245	16.1	10.1	13.4	12.9	
J. Elliot & Sons	–	Dewsnap Bowler	KK	*	*	1.8	−14.8	*	*	Limited partnership till 1979
Harris Miller	–		SSTC	*	1,523	*	16.5	*	13.7	

a TC, table cutlery; H, holloware; B, blanks; KK, kitchen knives; PK, pocket knives; S, scissors; SS, stainless steel; SP, silver plated.

or ceased production before the end of 1984, some firms achieved quite satisfactory profitability and sales growth. The standard deviation of average pre-tax return on capital over the period 1974–82 was 13.2 percentage points.

BUSINESS STRATEGY, COMPETITIVE ADVANTAGE AND THE DETERMINANTS OF PROFIT

The Sources of Profit

The focus of the research was to see how far differences in performance between firms could be explained in terms of the strategies which the firms had adopted. A first stage of the analysis was to examine the determinants of firm profitability. Figure 4.2 provides a simple framework: it shows that profit (above the competitive rate) may arise either as a result of a favourable industry environment, or by possessing competitive advantage over rivals.

The industry-level factors determining profitability have been cogently analysed by Porter (1980). Rate of return on capital may exceed the risk-free rate of interest as a result of three principal factors:

1   market power arising from high seller concentration and barriers to the entry of new competitors;
2   risk;
3   a high level of output relative to capacity. (Conversely, when demand is weak and excess capacity is present, losses are likely.)

In the cutlery industry none of these factors is likely to be conducive to profitability; nor are they likely to give rise to substantial differences in profitability between different industry segments. Fragmentation, low entry barriers and excess capacity are general to all parts of the international cutlery industry. Hence, competitive advantage is the key to profitability and the basis for survival in the industry.

Competitive Advantage

Competitive advantage – the ability of a firm to earn a superior profitability to that of its rivals – is, in Porter's (1985) framework, a consequence either of *cost advantage*, arising from superior efficiency, or *price advantage*, arising from greater or more effective product differentiation.

Competitive advantage is the product of a number of factors, some of which are exogenous to the firm and others of which are endogenous. In the context of an internationally competitive industry, national factors such as factor supplies, exchange rates, infrastructure and government policies are key determinants of competitive advantage between firms located in different countries. The principal endogenous factor is firms' deployment of available resources through business strategy.

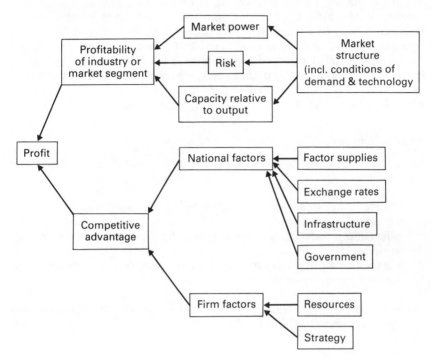

FIGURE 4.2   The determinants of firm performance

Thus, in the cutlery industry, competitive advantage between firms may be examined, first, in terms of the *national*-level factors, which are of primary importance in determining competitive advantage between countries, and second in terms of the *firm*-level factors, which determine competitive advantage between individual producers.

The national-level factors influencing the relative competitiveness of domestic and overseas cutlery producers are primarily those that determine international factor cost differentials. A comprehensive analysis would seek to measure the impact of each cost factor on firms' competitive performance. Since, however, the focus of this study is on the role of firms' strategies, for the purposes of the empirical analysis I have assumed that comparative advantage between domestic and overseas suppliers is indicated by the level of import penetration in individual product segments.

A number of empirical studies have shown industry profit rates to be negatively related to the level of industry import penetration, with import penetration having a much weaker effect in fragmented than in concentrated industries.[5] However, these studies have not distinguished between import competition from different sources. Where there is a substantial cost differential between imported and domestically produced products, import competition can have a substantial impact on both margins and output, even in a fragmented industry. Hence, profitability between different product segments in the cutlery industry depends upon both the level of import penetration and the extent to which imports are from low-cost producing countries or from other AICs.

Business Strategies to Create Competitive Advantage

In analysing the impact of business strategy on firm performance, three issues are central:

1   whether some strategies are generally more successful than others;
2   whether the effectiveness of different strategies varies according to the competitive conditions in individual industry segments (strategy–environment fit);
3   whether certain strategies may be more effective for some firms than for others (strategy–resource fit).

For any strategy to be generally successful in creating advantage *vis-à-vis* international competitors, it is likely to be based on exploiting country-specific advantages.

Such an approach suggests four strategies which might be conducive to success, all of which are familiar themes in recent calls for improved national competitiveness by business and political leaders.

1   *Cost reduction through capital investment*   Where firms face the disadvantage of high labour costs, cost competitiveness is attainable through increased capital intensity, which has the effect of substituting (relatively cheap) capital for (relatively dear) labour and exploiting the productivity benefits from process innovations embodied in up-to-date equipment. The need to increase investment has been a near-universal theme in nearly all commentaries upon declining manufacturing industries in Britain and the USA.[6] In the case of the British cutlery industry, a report noted with dismay that the average age of machinery in the industry was over 20 years (Oldfield and Robinson, 1978, p. 58).

2   *Product differentiation*   If the comparative advantage of the NICs in mature industries is low production cost, the principal competitive advantage possessed by firms in the AICs is market proximity, established brand names and a knowledge of the market. Hence, the principal route by which domestic firms can achieve competitive advantage over low-cost imports is by using

differentiation (marketing, brand promotion, product innovation and design) to earn a price premium. It has further been argued that firms in AICs with relatively large domestic markets are able to differentiate their products without losing the benefits of scale economies (Dreze, 1960).

3 *Up-market movement into higher-quality product segments* In mature industries, the cost advantage of the NICs is most readily exploited in standardized products at the lower end of the quality spectrum. High-quality products have been identified as providing attractive niches for domestic firms on the basis of lack of price sensitivity and the need for good market intelligence, effective marketing and skilled labour. A failure to move into higher-quality, higher value-added products has been identified as a general source of competitive weakness of the British manufacturing industry (Connell, 1980).

4 *Broadening market scope through product and geographical diversification* Where declining sales volumes make the exploitation of scale economies difficult, product and geographical diversification may be effective in utilizing spare physical and managerial capacity as well as exploring economies of scope. In the cutlery industry, market diversification is likely to be a profitable adjunct to differentiation and niche strategies. Investments in brand promotion offer economies of scope by diversifying into other cutlery and tableware products, while the costs of investments in design and specialized production facilities can be spread by expanding export sales.

The Fit between Strategy and Competitive Environment

Within most industries, competitive conditions vary between different industry segments (Porter, 1980, ch. 7). In the cutlery industry there are some clear differences in competition between product segments determined primarily by the source and the extent of import penetration. While scissors and stainless steel table cutlery and holloware are subject to very heavy low-cost import penetration, in quality table cutlery, holloware and kitchen knives import penetration is lower and is primarily from other AICs.

Such product segment differences have important implications for the likely effectiveness of different strategy variables.

1 Cost reduction through capital investment is likely to be less effective in creating cost advantage in product segments subject to strong low-cost import competition than in less heavily penetrated segments, since in the former the extent of the cost differential between domestic and overseas producers is likely to render ineffective a strategy based exclusively on cost efficiency.

2 Product differentiation is likely to be more effective in establishing a price advantage in segments subject to high levels of low-cost, low-quality

import penetration than in segments where import competition is primarily from other AICs (e.g. kitchen knives, folding knives), where the effectiveness of product differentiation may be limited by overseas firms' occupancy of the positions of high quality and brand leadership.

3   Quality is likely to provide a profitable basis for focus by cutlery firms, both because of the tendency for these segments to be sheltered from low-cost competition and because of the lower price elasticity of consumer demand in quality products. It should be noted, however, that the success of up-market specialization is dependent upon not too many firms pursuing the same direction of adjustment. As with product differentiation, a quality focus is likely to be more successful in market segments where overseas competition is from low-cost producers.

The Fit between Strategy and the Firm's Resources

Among firms pursuing similar strategies in the same industry segment, different performance is to be expected, depending upon each firm's resource base. Resources are of two types: tangible assets, purchased or hired on input markets, and intangible assets – resources such as technical know-how, brand goodwill, marketing expertise and organizational skills that are specific to the firm. These intangible assets have been referred to as 'specific assets' (Caves, 1971), and 'distinctive competences' (Lenz, 1980; Hitt and Ireland, 1985).

A firm's command over resources available from the market is dependent upon its financial resources which are related, *inter alia*, to its size. Since larger firms have a greater access to resources than smaller firms, they face a wider opportunity set and at the same time are capable of exploiting economies of scale. Hence it might be expected that large firms would possess a competitive advantage over small firms.[7]

A firm's intangible assets are dependent upon its past strategic investments reinforced by experience effects. Thus, a firm that has engaged in past brand advertising and promotion of its products to customers is better placed to pursue market-oriented product differentiation than one that has not previously marketed its brand. The development of specific assets in the form of brand and customer goodwill, market and customer knowledge and production know-how are key elements of 'first-mover advantages' accruing to established firms. The implication, therefore, is that in competing in a product–market segment, or through any particular strategic approach, firms that already occupy such a market position will be at an advantage over firms that are shifting their competitive position.[8]

The sustainability of a competitive advantage based upon such firm-specific competences depends upon the speed and cost at which other firms can reproduce the intangible assets required. One of the major barriers to the imitation by competitors of the strategy of a successful firm may be lack of information. Nelson and Winter (1982, pp. 96–136) have examined the difficulty facing the firm in obtaining sufficient knowledge of the 'organizational routines' of the successful firm, while Lippman and Rumelt (1982) point to the uncertainty inherent in such strategy imitation.

The hypothesis to be tested can be summarized as follows.

The influence of import competition

H1 Firm performance is negatively related to the level and growth of import penetration into firms' market segments.

H1 (a) Import penetration from low-cost manufacturing countries has a bigger impact on performance than import penetration from countries with a similar cost structure to that of the UK.

The influence of strategy variables

H2 Firm performance is positively related to:
   (a) capital investment;
   (b) product differentiation;
   (c) product quality;
   (d) product and geographical market scope.

The fit between strategy and environment

H3 (a) Capital investment is more effective in industry segments with low levels of low-cost import penetration than in segments subject to intense low-cost import competition.

H3 (b) Product differentiation and up-market movement into higher-quality segments are more effective in segments with high levels of low-cost import penetration.

The fit between strategy and firm resources

H4 Large firms earn superior profits to small firms.

H5 Among firms pursuing similar strategies,

   (a) firms established in a strategic position are at an advantage, and hence can earn superior profits, to firms that are adjusting towards that position;
   (b) the extent of the advantage is dependent upon barriers to imitation.

EMPIRICAL TESTING

The Data

The financial performance and business strategies of 33 larger firms in the cutlery industry in 1974 were tracked over the following nine years. The principal data sources were company accounts, trade directories and interviews with the companies and their customers.

The data were subject to a number of imperfections which arose mainly because the empirical measures of the variables did not correspond precisely to the variables specified in the hypotheses. The limitations of financial performance measures based upon published company accounts are well known. To avoid these problems a measure of gross profit was defined to correspond to an overall surplus over operating costs. To limit multicollinearity and to increase degrees of freedom, the marketing-related product differentiation variables (advertising expenditure, introduction of new designs, product innovation, operation of retail outlets) were combined arithmetically into a composite product differentiation variable. To remove the effects of short-term fluctuations in the values of variables, averages were taken over two parts of the study period: 1974–7 and 1978–82. Each of these periods corresponded, roughly, to similar phases of consecutive economic cycles. The performance and strategy variables measured are shown in table 4.2.

Empirical Analysis

Empirical testing of the influence of adjustment strategies on firm performance was primarily through multiple regression. The analysis comprised a testing of both static and dynamic relationships.

First, firms' average performances were regressed on the average values of strategy variables and import penetration (table 4.4). Although my interest was in adjustment by firms, i.e. the effect of strategy change upon performance, it was apparent that firms' adjustment to import competition was gradual and long-term, and for most firms had begun before the beginning of the study period. Hence the average values of performance and strategy variables could be seen as outcomes of the adjustment process.

The second stage of the regression analysis attempted to measure the effect of the adjustment behaviour on performance by regressing performance in the second part of the period on first-period performance and changes in the values of the independent variables (table 4.5).

Finally, because it was hypothesized that the relationship between strategy and performance was contingent upon the competitive conditions in different product markets, the sample was split into above-median and below-median import penetration firms and the regressions of second-period profitability on strategy change were run separately for each group (table 4.6).

However, the regression analysis was subject to several deficiencies. First, firm performance is an outcome of a large number of factors, many of which operate interactively rather than independently. The small size of the firm sample meant that there were insufficient degrees of freedom to test a full model of firm performance, even if the full set of variables could be specified and measured. Second, some of the independent variables were highly correlated (e.g. firm size and product differentiation), which made separating

TABLE 4.2 Variables included in the regression analysis, their definitions and their sources

Variable	Definition	Source
Performance		
Gross *ROC*	Profit (before deduction of interest, tax, depreciation and directors' remuneration)/(capital employed + overdrafts)	Company accounts
Gross *ROS*	Gross profit (as above)/sales revenue	Company accounts
SALES	Sales revenue 1978–82/sales revenue 1974–7	Company accounts
Strategy		
I/S	Expenditure on plant and equipment/sales revenue	Company accounts
ADV	Media advertising expenditure	MEAL
RET	Number of retail outlets operated	Interviews
PI	Introduction of product innovation (dummy variable)	Interviews
ND	Introduction of new product designs (dummy variable)	Interviews
PDIFF	Index of product differentiation (composite variable)	$(\sqrt{ADV} + \sqrt{RET} + PI + ND)$
PQUAL	Index of quality (scale: 1 (low)–5 (high))	Interviews, sales literature
DIV	Number of product segments	Buyers' guides,
EX/S	Exports/sales revenue	Company accounts
Resources		
SIZE	Average sales revenue 1974–7	Company accounts

their individual influences very difficult. (Table 4.3 shows correlations between variables.) Third, performance is not a deterministic outcome of a set of environmental, strategy and resource variables: performance is crucially dependent upon the effectiveness of strategy implementation, which is primarily a function of managerial capabilities in terms of leadership, motivation and co-ordination.

For these reasons, the study did not rely exclusively on statistical testing. Use was made of generalizations and exceptions based upon the experiences of the individual firms within the sample, although there is space to quote only a few examples in this chapter.

TABLE 4.3 Correlations between variables

Between average values of variables, 1974–82

	Gross ROC	Gross ROS	△ SALES	IMPEN	LCIMP	I/S	SKTO	log PDIFF	QUAL	DIV	EX/S
Gross ROS	0.671										
△ SALES	0.255	0.198									
IMPEN	−0.235	−0.253	−0.450								
LCIMP	−0.404	−0.526	−0.531	0.701							
I/S	−0.019	0.161	0.139	−0.071	−0.120						
SKTO	0.692	0.288	0.203	−0.080	−0.275	−0.068					
log PDIFF	−0.475	−0.328	−0.074	0.076	0.311	0.099	−0.403				
QUAL	0.184	0.122	0.145	−0.717	−0.518	−0.215	0.124	0.021			
DIV	−0.241	−0.284	−0.172	0.168	0.149	−0.253	−0.105	0.319	0.123		
EX/S	−0.158	−0.054	0.376	0.300	0.105	0.179	−0.158	0.291	−0.197	−0.006	
log SIZE	−0.510	−0.530	−0.341	0.420	0.674	0.133	−0.325	0.613	−0.320	0.435	0.152

Between changes in values of variables, 1978–82/1974–7

	△ Gross ROC	△ Gross ROS	△ SALES	△ LCIMP	△ I/S	△ SKTO	△ PDIFF	△ QUAL	△ DIV	△ EX/S
△ Gross ROS	0.354									
△ SALES	0.292	0.069								
△ LCIMP	0.164	0.111	−0.300							
△ I/S	−0.010	−0.288	−0.005	0.038						
△ SKTO	0.096	−0.588	0.431	−0.058	0.050					
△ PDIFF	0.227	0.139	0.009	0.270	0.144	−0.102				
△ QUAL	−0.278	−0.162	−0.221	0.139	0.197	−0.107	0.386			
△ DIV	0.023	−0.067	−0.101	0.038	0.220	−0.084	0.524	0.444		
△ EX/S	0.038	0.107	0.030	−0.145	−0.252	0.159	−0.121	−0.066	−0.189	
log SIZE	0.050	−0.075	−0.341	0.583	0.262	−0.203	0.462	0.258	0.274	0.024

TABLE 4.4 Average performance over the period, regressed on levels of independent variables

Dependent variable	Constant	LCIMP	I/S	log PDIFF	QUAL	DIV	EX/S	Adjusted R^2
Gross ROC	41.7***	−66.1**	−0.278	−5.97**	5.22*	−1.54	0.087	0.224
Gross ROC	19.8***		0.887	−7.09***	0.98	0.251		0.174
Gross ROC	117.3***		0.602					0.149
Gross ROS	15.6***	−20.7**	0.374	−0.310		−0.486		0.210
Gross ROS	32.1***				−0.25		−0.126	0.235
△SALES	2.43***	−2.56***	−0.0112	0.0539	−0.0854	−0.0353		0.208
△SALES	2.00**	−2.39***	−0.00388		−0.0626	−0.0251	0.048	0.175

*   Significant at 90 per cent level
** Significant at 95 per cent level
*** Significant at 99 per cent level

TABLE 4.5 Second-period performance, regressed on first-period performance and changes in the values of independent variables

Dependent variable, 1978–82	Constant	Dependent variable, 1974–7	△LCIMP	△I/S	△PDIFF	△QUAL	△DIV	EX/S	Adjusted R^2
Gross ROC	5.07	0.510***	−43.09	−0.546	1.52	−25.3**	−3.37		0.627
Gross ROC	8.94*	0.550***		−0.499	1.10	−24.6**	−2.63	0.141	0.622
Gross ROC	6.39	0.507***	−35.8		1.58	−24.5**	−3.70		0.648
Gross ROS	9.63**	0.401***		−0.974***	0.202	4.71	−1.93**	−1.43*	0.348
Gross ROS	12.1***	0.106	−16.1*		0.930	−1.41			0.199

*   Significant at 90 per cent level
** Significant at 95 per cent level
*** Significant at 99 per cent level

TABLE 4.6 Regression of performance on changes in strategies for high- and low-import penetration sub-sample

Dependent variable, 1978–82	Constant	Dependent variable, 1974–7	$\Delta I/S$	$\Delta QUAL$	$\Delta PDIFF$	ΔDIV	SIZE	Adjusted R^2
Firms facing low-cost import penetration above the median level								
Gross ROC	−0.124	0.647***	−2.18**	−5.84				0.805
Gross ROC	−3.09	0.690***	−2.02**	−9.61	0.889*			0.813
Gross ROC	8.68	0.626***	−2.23**			−0.154	−1.28	0.780
Gross ROS	31.0**	−0.0360			0.925**	−2.17**	−3.35***	0.455
Gross ROS	12.7***	−0.729***	−0.877**	−7.88**	0.767***			0.583
Firms facing low-cost import penetration below the median level								
Gross ROC	0.96	0.579***	0.112	−65.2*	1.48	−4.50		0.429
Gross ROC	82.6*	0.570***	0.189	−59.3*	3.34		−11.9	0.405
Gross ROS	8.83***	0.121	−1.08**	14.2**	0.386	−0.488		0.362
Gross ROS	10.4***	0.785	−1.13***	24.2***	0.497			0.659

* Significant at the 90 per cent level
** Significant at the 95 per cent level
*** Significant at the 99 per cent level

THE RESULTS

Import Competition

Firm performance was regressed upon both overall import penetration (*IMPEN*) and low-cost import penetration (*LCIMP*).[9]

The finding that overall import penetration had a weak negative influence on profitability was consistent with previous studies' findings that import competition is more influential in concentrated rather than unconcentrated industries. The consistent, significant impact of low-cost import penetration upon both return on sales and return on capital supports the view expressed by managers in the industry that competition from the Far East has been the principal source of the industry's poor performance and explains the support they have given to import restrictions. It was interesting that there was no significant relationship between changes in import penetration and changes in profitability between the first and the second periods. This would appear to be because declining sales during the second part of the period were due more to the severe 1979–82 recession than to increased import penetration, and the fall in sales was greatest in those product segments where growth of import penetration was comparatively low.

Investment in Plant and Machinery

Static regression analysis showed an insignificant relationship between the investment/sales ratio and both profitabiilty and, more surprisingly, sales growth. Clearer results emerged in the analysis of second period performance; here, changes in investment/sales ratios were negatively related to second-period profitability.

It was apparent from table 4.6, however, that the negative impact of increasing capital investment on profitability was most apparent in industry segments facing above-median levels of low-cost import penetration (consistent with prediction).

My interviews were able to shed further light on the relationship. In the first place, it was apparent that heavy investment in plant and equipment was not synonymous with cost reduction. Several firms had pursued vigorous cost reduction strategies through the modification, upgrading and efficient utilization of existing capital equipment and showed only modest investment/sales ratios.

Conversely, a number of firms (including two large firms which went into liquidation – Viners and Hawker Marris) had invested heavily in units of modern equipment (presses, automated polishing machines, computers and automated plating baths) but had been unable to produce long enough runs to utilize the new machinery efficiently. In several of the firms visited it was notable that mechanized production processes had been abandoned in favour of traditional, labour-intensive methods in the face of declining run lengths.

The finding that capital investment failed to generate improved profit returns is not unique to this study. A wealth of case studies and industry studies points to the absence of a strong relationship between capital investment and competitiveness.[10] Using PIMS data, Anderson and Zeithaml (1984) found investment to have a negative impact on profitability among firms in declining industries, although Hambrick and Schecter (1983) found that newness of plant and equipment was a characteristic of turn-around businesses in mature industries.

Product Differentiation

Product differentiation emerged as having a clearly negative association with return on capital (table 4.4), although the high correlation between firm size and product differentiation led to difficulties in identifying their independent influences. Changes in product differentiation over the period had an insignificant effect on second-period return on capital, but a weak positive relationship with second-period return on sales was evident (table 4.5).

The apparent ineffectiveness of a differentiation strategy in the cutlery industry is explicable in terms of the high threshold costs of advertising and marketing in relation to small firm size. While only the largest firms engaged in media advertising and investment in retail outlets, such activities necessitated costs that were heavy relative to sales volumes and become more onerous as sales volumes declined over time. Conversely, some of the most profitable firms in the table cutlery sector incurred virtually no costs of marketing and brand promotion, choosing instead to supply a limited number of customers for resale under their own names (e.g. Garrards, Mappin and Webb, Foulerton).

The effectiveness of a market-orientated differentiation strategy clearly depends on the nature of the competitive environment. In industry segments exposed to low-cost import competition, product differentiation had a significantly positive effect on return on sales – indicating the potential for differentiation to create a price advantage. In industry segments with low levels of low-cost import penetration, where the major competitive threat was from other Western European manufacturers, differentiation had an insignificant relationship with profitability (table 4.6).

This demonstration that the effectiveness of differentiation is contingent upon the characteristics of the competitive environment may help explain the inconsistencies between different findings on the relationship between differentiation and firm performance. While most US evidence points to the importance of product differentiation as a route to profitability and market share in mature and declining industries (Hall, 1980; Buzzell and Wiersema, 1981; Hammermesh and Silk, 1979), Anderson and Zeithaml (1984) have shown that, as markets move from maturity to decline, so marketing variables become either insignificant or negative in their impact.

Quality

In the static regressions, the relationship between product quality and performance was difficult to identify because of the high inverse correlation between quality and low-cost import competition. Quality showed a weak positive association with return on capital (table 4.4).

A clearer link was evident between changes in quality and second-period performance (table 4.5). Up-market shifts by firms into higher-quality segments were associated with significant *reductions* in return on capital.

From interviews and closer observation of the experiences of specific firms, two factors explain this surprising result. First, the high-quality segments were principally silver-plated cutlery and tableware; the movement of a large number of firms into this narrow market segment put pressure on margins and volume. Second, mobility barriers into this segment, arising from the difficulties of newcomers establishing a reputation as suppliers of high-quality products, meant that established suppliers possessed a competitive advantage over entrants.

Further light was shed on the impact of quality change on profitability by the separate regressions for high- and low-import penetration sectors (table 4.6). In segments subject to a high level of low-cost import penetration, quality change had no significant relationship with profitability. In segments where low-cost imports were not a major problem, quality increases enabled improvements in sales margins but simultaneously resulted in lower returns on capital. The likely explanation is that, while in these segments higher quality permitted a price premium to be earned, the tendency for many firms to move up-market resulted in higher capital/output ratios with a consequent deterioration in return on capital.

Thus, in contrast to Woo and Cooper (1981), who identified high quality as a general feature of effective low-share businesses, the study found that the effectiveness of a strategy of quality focus is crucially dependent upon the characteristics of the individual firm and its competitive environment.

Market Scope

There was a general tendency for firms in the industry to broaden their product ranges over the period, although very few of them attempted diversification outside the confines of the cutlery and tableware industry. Differences in the level of product diversity were unrelated to differences in profit and sales performance over the period (table 4.4). However, diversification of product range was negatively related to second-period profitability (table 4.5). The direction of causation appeared to be two-way. Diversification required investment while offering little synergy in production (although some economies were available from spreading fixed costs of administration, marketing and distribution). At the same time, poor sales and profit performance were an incentive for product diversification. While the regression results showed no performance benefits from product diversification, interviews revealed that for several firms the primary objective of broadening product range was to reduce market risk.

Export/sales ratio showed no consistent or significant relationship (table 4.4). It is noteworthy, however, that its coefficient was positive in regressions of return on capital and negative in regressions of return on sales, indicating that exports tend to earn a lower margin than domestic sales but can improve return on capital by augmenting sales.

Firm Resources

Despite *ex ante* arguments for the benefits of firm size and market share, large firms were consistently outperformed by smaller firms. Initial firm size was negatively related to average profitability over the period and changes in profitability between the first and second periods. The poor performance of large firms was also indicated by the high failure rate among the largest firms: of the four largest in the industry in 1974, three had entered receivership by 1984.

However, it is difficult to separate the influence of firm size from that of the strategy variables. It is likely that the poor performance of larger firms was due not to any inherent disadvantages of size, but to the fact that it was the large firms in the industry that attempted the most ambitious strategy adjustments with regard to capital investment, product differentiation and diversification. In addition, some of the largest firms (notably, Viners and Richards of Sheffield) experienced particular difficulties of management succession during the 1970s.

The role of 'intangible assets' was also difficult to identify – mainly because they were not measurable. At the same time, there was a good deal of fragmentary and indirect evidence to show that these assets were key factors in determining firm performance. The positive association between quality and profit and negative association between changes in quality and changes in profit were supported by the hypothesis that barriers to the acquisition of specific assets give established firms an advantage over newcomers in any particular strategic position within an industry. The individual company experiences underlined the importance of a close fit between the specific skills and experiences of managers and the strategies pursued by the firm. Such a fit was apparent in the two most successful firms in the industry, Westall Richardson and Terence Mason Investments (the parent company of George Butler Silverware). Westall Richardson's outstandingly successful strategy of product innovation and capital-intensive, cost-efficient production of kitchen knives (where it claims to be Europe's largest supplier) was firmly based upon the engineering and technical skills of the firm's managing director, Bryan Upton. Terence Mason Investments' emergence as market leader in the table cutlery and silverware sector has rested upon a marketing-based, brand-orientated strategy which has utilized the marketing skills of the company's founder and chairman. It is noteworthy that both these CEOs brought to their companies experience gained outside the industry, and both have tended to shun the traditions and conventional wisdoms of the industry.

CONCLUSIONS

The study fails to identify any strong, significant relationships between business strategy and firm performance in the UK cutlery industry. No 'generic strategy', 'strategy recipe' or 'critical success factor' conducive to profitability was apparent. Moreover, of the business strategies conventionally advocated for enhancing international competitiveness, capital investment, product differentiation and quality improvement tended to be negatively or insignificantly related to performance.

It does not follow, however, that business strategy was an unimportant influence on firm performance. The findings underline the crucial importance of 'strategic fit' – that strategy must be carefully tailored both to the firm's resource base and to its competitive environment.

With regard to the fit of strategy and competitive environment, it is apparent that the success of a particular strategy is determined primarily by the underlying competitive positions of domestic relative to overseas suppliers; a cost reduction strategy is doomed if overseas firms hold an unassailable cost advantage.

Equally important is the fit between the firm's resources and its strategy. The failure of many of the firms pursuing the most ambitious adjustment strategies was a consequence of their lack of financial resources, small sales base and limited management skills. Conversely, the successful firms tended to be those that matched the resource requirements of their strategies to the resource base of the firms.

One of the problems of strategic adjustment which the results point to is that firms that already occupy a particular competitive position are at an advantage over firms shifting towards that position; thus, while a quality orientation was associated with higher profitability, firms moving towards higher-quality segments experienced declining profitability.

The high risks associated with investment in strategic adjustment and the key role of fit between strategy, resources and environment arise from the basic character of the cutlery industry. In a fragmented industry facing strong international competition, investment in change involves risks; the combination of limited firm resources and narrow profit margins means that the costs of strategic investment tend to increase the firm's vulnerability to any unanticipated downturn in profits. The turbulence of the period studied, in terms of the fluctuations in demand, interest rates, metal prices and exchange rates, further increased the difficulties of pursuing investment in long-term competitive advantage.

While the results of the study are specific to the industry and the period under investigation, I believe that the problems of competitiveness and the strategy issues which arise are likely to be common to other industries, countries and time periods. The factors that have determined the character of competition in the UK cutlery industry – fragmentation and intense competition from low-cost imports – are common to a number of mature industries in Western Europe and North America.

NOTES

1 By contrast, most strategic management research into declining industries has focused on industries where overall demand is declining; see in particular Harrigan (1980).
2 Most studies of trade adjustment in mature industries have been concerned with public policy rather than business policy issues; see, for example, Toyne et al. (1984), Turner and McMullen (1982), Shepherd *et al.* (1983), Cable (1983), Ballance and Sinclair (1983), De la Torre (1980).
3 Most of these strategy–performance studies have failed to reveal strong and consistent relationships for mature and declining industries.
4 For a full account of the study, see Grant and Downing (1985).
5 See, for the UK, Turner (1980); for the USA, Eposito and Eposito (1971) and Pugel (1980); for Belgium, Jacquemin *et al.* (1980); for Ireland, Hutchinson (1981).
6 British approaches to national industrial strategy have long placed central emphasis on the need to step up capital investment (see, for example, Department of Industry, 1974). In recent years exhortation of the imperative for increased investment has shifted to the USA (see for example Scott and Lodge, 1985, and the President's Commission on Industrial Competitiveness, 1985).
7 It might further be expected that subsidiary firms would have a better access to resources than independent firms, particularly where the parent company was an overseas manufacturer of cutlery. However, since this would depend upon the nature of the relationship between parent and subsidiary, ownership was not included as an explanatory variable in the empirical analysis.
8 It could be argued that the superior return derived from a competitive advantage conferred by specific assets is not really a profit, but derives from the fact that firms' specific assets are not capitalized in their accounts.
9 Overall import penetration is not included in the tables of regression results for simplicity of presentation. Simple regressions of firm performance on both total import penetration ($IMPEN$) and low-cost import penetration ($LDCIM$) gave the following results:

$$\text{gross } ROC^{74-82} = \quad 44.4 \quad - \quad 37.13 \quad IMPEN^{74-82} \qquad \bar{R}^2 = 0.024$$
$$(4.88) \quad (-1.34)$$

$$\text{gross } ROS^{74-82} = \quad 14.3 \quad - \quad 8.42 \quad IMPEN^{74-82} \qquad \bar{R}^2 = 0.032$$
$$(7.41) \quad (-1.41)$$

gross ROC^{74-82} = $\quad$ 49.77 $-\quad$ 93.16 $\quad$ $LCIMP^{74-82}$ $\quad$ $\bar{R}^2 = 0.136$
$\qquad\qquad\qquad$ (6.40) $\quad$ (-2.42)

gross ROS^{74-82} = $\quad$ 16.34 $-\quad$ 25.50 $\quad$ $LCIMP^{74-82}$ $\quad$ $\bar{R}^2 = 0.252$
$\qquad\qquad\qquad$ (10.50) $\quad$ (-3.33)

Δgross ROC $\quad$ = -0.875 $-\quad$ 0.83 $\quad$ $\Delta LCIMP$ $\quad$ $\bar{R}^2 = 0.000$
$\qquad\qquad\qquad$ (-6.59) $\quad$ (-0.63)

$\Delta gross\ ROS$ $\quad$ = -0.852 $-\quad$ 0.601 $\quad$ $\Delta LCIMP$ $\quad$ $\bar{R}^2 = 0.000$
$\qquad\qquad\qquad$ (-8.46) $\quad$ (-0.60)

$\Delta SALES$ $\quad$ = $\quad$ 1.97 $-\quad$ 1.95 $\quad$ $LCIMP^{74-82}$ $\quad$ $\bar{R}^2 = 0.257$
$\qquad\qquad\qquad$ (16.8) $\quad$ (3.37)

10 Caves (1980) found capital intensity to be insignificant in explaining US/UK productivity differentials; while attempts during the 1970s at boosting productivity by heavy capital investment in the British steel, shipbuilding and auto industries were all dismal failures (see Grant, 1984).

REFERENCES

Abernathy, W. J., Clark, K. B. and Kantrow, A. M. (1983) *Industrial Renaissance: Producing a Competitive Future for America.* New York: Basic Books.

Anderson, C. R. and Zeithaml, C. P. (1984) Stage of the product life cycle, business strategy and business performance. *Academy of Management Journal*, 27, 5–24.

Altschuler, A. et al. (1985) *The Future of the Automobile*, Cambridge, Mass.: MIT Press.

Aquino, Antonio (1981) Changes over time in the pattern of comparative advantage in manufactured goods. *European Economic Review*, 15, 41–62.

Aylen, Jonathan (1983) International competitiveness and industrial regeneration: the lessons of British Steel. SSRC workshop on competitiveness and the regeneration of British industry, London, 18–19 November.

Ballance, R. and Sinclair, S. (1983) *Collapse and Survival: Industry Strategies in a Changing World*, London: George Allen & Unwin.

Bothwell, J. L., Cooley, T. F. and Hall, T. E. (1984) A new view of the market structure-performance debate. *Journal of Industrial Economics*, 32 (4), 397–417.

Buzzell, R. D., Gale, B. T. and Sultan, R. G. M. (1975) Market share – a key to profitability. *Harvard Business Review*, January–February, 97–100.

Buzzell, R. D. and Wiersema, F. D. (1981) Successful share building strategies. *Harvard Business Review*, January–February, 135–44.

Cable, Vincent (1983) *Protectionism and Industrial Decline.* London: Hodder and Stoughton.

Caves, R. E. (1971) International corporations: the industrial economics of foreign direct investment. *Economica*, 38, 1–27.

—— (1980) Productivity differences between industries. In R. E. Caves and L. B. Krause, *Britain's Economic Performance*, Washington DC: Brookings Institution.

Connell, D. (1980) The UK's performance in export markets: some evidence from international trade data. Discussion Paper no. 6. London: NEDO.

De la Torre, Jose (1980)   Decline and adjustment: public intervention strategies in the European clothing industries. INSEAD Working Paper no. 80/07.

Department of Industry (1974)   *The Regeneration of British Industry.* Cmnd 5710. London: HMSO.

—— (1980)   *Report of the Working party on the Cutlery and Flatware Industry.* London: HMSO.

Dess, G. G. and Davis, P. S. (1984)   Porter's (1980) generic strategies as determinants of strategic group membership and organisational performance. *Academy of Management Journal,* 27, 467–88.

Dreze, J. (1960)   Quelques reflexions sereines sur l'adaptation de l'industrie belge au Marché Commun. *Comptes rendues des Travaux de la Société d'Economie Politique de Belgique,* 3–26.

Eposito, L. and Eposito, F. (1971)   Foreign competition and domestic industry profitability. *Review of Economics and Statistics,* 53, 343–53.

Gale, B. T. (1972)   Market share and rate of return. *Review of Economics and Statistics,* 54, 412–23.

Grant, R. M. (1984)   Business strategies for adjusting to low-cost international competition in mature industries. Centre for Business Strategy, Discussion Paper, London Business School, September.

— and Downing, S. (1985)   Industry adjustment, business strategy and firm performance: the UK cutlery industry 1973–83. Centre for Business Strategy Working Paper, London Business School.

Hall, W. K. (1980)   Survival strategies in a hostile environment. *Harvard Business Review,* September–October, 75–85.

Hambrick, D. C. and Schecter, S. M. (1983)   Turnaround strategies for mature industrial-product business units. *Academy of Management Journal,* 26, 231–48.

Hammermesh, R. and Silk, S. (1979)   How to compete in stagnant businesses. *Harvard Business Review,* September–October, 161–68.

Harrigan, K. R. (1980)   *Strategies for Declining Businesses.* Lexington, Mass.: D. C. Heath.

Hayes, R H. and Wheelwright, S. C. (1984)   *Restoring our Competitive Edge: Competing through Manufacturing.* New York: John Wiley.

Hitt, M. A. and Ireland, R. D. (1985)   Corporate distinctive competence, strategy, industry and performance. *Strategic Management Journal,* 6, 274–94.

Hutchinson, R. W. (1981)   Price-cost margins and manufacturing industry structure. *European Economic Review,* 16, 247–67.

Jacquemin, A. *et al.* (1980)   Concentration and profitability in a small open economy. *Journal of Industrial Economics,* 29, 131–144.

Lawrence, P. L. and Dyer, D. (1983)   *Renewing American Industry,* New York: Free Press.

Lenz, R. T. (1980)   Strategic capability: a concept and framework for analysis. *Academy of Management Review,* 5, 225–34.

Lippman, S. A. and Rumelt, R. (1982)   Uncertain imitability: an analysis of interfirm differences under competition. *Bell Journal of Economics,* 13, 418–38.

Messerlin, P. and Saunders, C. (1983)   Steel: too much investment too late. In Shepherd *et al. (1983).*

Mottershead, P. (1983)   Shipbuilding: adjustment-led intervention or intervention-led adjustment. In G. Shepherd, F. Duchene and C. Saunders (eds), *Europe's Industries: Public and Private Strategies for Change.* London: Frances Pinter.

Nelson, R. and Winter, S. (1982) *An Evolutionary Theory of Economic Change.* Cambridge, Mass.: Harvard University Press.

Oldfield, E. A. and Robinson, J. (1978) *Study of the Cutlery Industry.* Sheffield: Cutlery and Allied Trades Research Association.

Porter, M. (1980) *Competitive Strategy.* New York: Free Press.

Porter, M. (1985) *Competitive Advantage.* New York: Free Press.

President's Commission on Industrial Competitiveness (1985) *Global Competition: The New Reality.* Washington DC: US Government Printing Office.

Pugel, T. (1980) Foreign trade and US market performance. *Journal of Industrial Economics,* 29, 119–29.

Scott, B. and Lodge, G. (1985) *US Competitiveness in the World Economy.* Cambridge, Mass.: Harvard University Press.

Shepherd, G., Duchene, F. and Saunders, C. (1983) *Europe's Industries: Public and Private Strategies for Change.* London: Frances Pinter.

Thorakan, P. K. M. *et al.* (1978) Heckscher–Ohlin and Chamberlain determinants of comparative advantage: an empirical analysis of the penetration of manufactures from the developing countries in the European markets. *European Economic Review,* 11, 221–39.

Toyne, Brian *et al.* (1984) *The Global Textile Industry.* London: George Allen & Unwin.

Turner, P. P. (1980) Import competition and the profitability of UK manufacturing industry. *Journal of Industrial Economics,* 29, 155–65.

Turner, L. (1982) Consumer electronics: the colour television case. In Turner and McMullen (1982).

—— and McMullen, N. (1982) *The Newly Industrialising Countries: Trade and Adjustment.* London: George Allen & Unwin.

Woo, C. Y. and Cooper, A. C. (1981) Strategies of Effective Low Share Businesses. *Strategic Management Journal,* 2, 301–18.

Commentary on Chapter 4

Leif Melin

What understanding about strategic change is provided us by scientific explanation derived from traditionally patterned research and directed by the rules of positivism? Within the entire field of management research, it is time to discuss the distinction between *explaining* reality and *understanding* reality. What do we actually comprehend about the processes of strategic change when we prove significant causal relationships between, for example, performance and a specific strategy type? The purpose of scientific research is to build knowledge, and an understanding of reality ought to be implicit in such knowledge. The research method predominantly applied to the field of management has been to employ and follow the rules and methods set forth by the paradigm of positivism, most often without reflecting on the choice of the research method as such. The usual procedure is to formulate hypotheses derived through deduction and to measure empirically the existence of causal relationships between the variables included in the hypotheses. When a statistically sound relationship has been established, the researcher assumes it to be an explanation. The dilemma is that we seem to be able to produce explanations without increasing our enlightenment. But can we then understand phenomena in real-world organizations and produce cumulative knowledge without traditional scientific explanations? The emerging paradigm of interpretation and understanding is based on a belief that this is indeed possible.

A good illustration of the difference between explaining reality and understanding it is provided in the above paper by Robert Grant. Grant's intent is to show how differences in performance can be explained by differences in the strategy chosen. But to obtain an understanding of his results, he must filter them through supplementary data about events in the studied industry, data that are more qualitative than the data used in his test.

The chapter by Grant is perhaps less interesting for its conclusions than for the several important paradigmatic questions it raises concerning research approaches within the field of strategic management. In the comments that follow, I will use Grant's paper mainly as a springboard for a rather general discussion of certain problems and shortcomings connected with this approach to research, an approach which for the most part is based on the competitive view of the industrial world held by Porter (1980, 1981) and other industrial economists who have redirected their attention to the field of business policy. I share the opinion that we need influences from the field of industrial organization when we study structure–strategy–performance relationships. But we must strive to be more conscious of the underlying assumptions of the industrial organizational paradigm when we try to develop strategic management theory. We would also benefit by having influences from many other approaches and viewpoints.

RESEARCH ON STRATEGY CONTENT

Fahey and Christensen (1986) have presented an evaluation of research carried out on strategy content which is worth considering in this context. In the present section I will relate some aspects of Grant's work to that of Fahey and Christensen. The research field devoted to strategic management is currently dominated by research emphasizing strategy *content* (i.e., what decisions are made concerning corporate and competitive strategy), at the expense of research on strategic *process* (i.e., how strategic change takes place and how decisions of strategy are arrived at in an organizational setting). Fahey and Christensen pose the typical research question concerning strategy content: 'What performance results arise from the following specific strategies under different conditions?' The research approach to strategy content is to a large extent expressed in the 'model' shown in figure 4c.1, developed from Fahey and Christensen (1986, p. 170).

FIGURE 4C.1   The dominating model for strategy research

Almost every study of strategy content examines external conditions, while very little attention is paid to the firm's internal circumstances. This fact is not surprising if we bear in mind that the model shown in figure 4C.1 is almost identical to the old industrial organization model of Bain (1968): industry *structure* determines the *conduct* of firms, which in turn determines the *performance*. In this model the individual organization is treated as a black box, with the exception of conduct, which is expressed in terms of some identified strategic actions.

Grant's study fits in very well in the mainstream of research on strategy content. This means that it also suffers from some of the deficiencies that Fahey and Christensen have identified. In other studies of the maturity stage, parameters delineating maturity have often been reduced to one or two variables. In Grant's study, the maturity situation is described only by low growth of demand and familiarity with technology. However, the main external force in his study is competition from low-cost import, which has no direct relation to an industry's maturity.

Fahey and Christensen found that performance has been almost exclusively operationalized in financial terms; they also noted that the absence of other legitimate organizational goals has been a weakness. Grant's study is no exception. Furthermore, profitability is not always a good measurement of the value of a changed strategy. In some cases a changed strategy may be absolutely necessary for survival, even if it causes a decline in profitability.

Fahey and Christensen also discovered that the temporal context of performance has been neglected in research dealing with strategy content. I found the time perspective in Grant's study very unclear. The success or failure of a changed strategy is said to be determined by increased or decreased profitability, but nothing is said about the time perspective. When did the strategy changes occur, and when did the profit curve change? The time elapsing between changed strategy and measured effects on performance must be an important factor to consider, a point demonstrated by Chandler (1962). For example, Grant found investments to have a negative impact on profitability. In the short range, the influence of investments on capital costs may exceed increased revenue. It also takes time to win new market shares. One measured strategy was to move up to a higher-quality segment, which will certainly not give results in the short term. The customer's image of the product seems to be very stable; it takes time to communicate a shift in quality, especially to the consumers on the end-user market.

There is, of course, a time-lag between the implementation of a new strategy and the reaping of its full effect. A longitudinal approach is necessary. The advantage of the longitudinal approach used by Grant, however, is almost eliminated when he combines his time series to obtain the average of two periods. Furthermore, I don't think a pure longitudinal approach will suffice to manage this empirical problem. The study must also be process-oriented; in other words, we must try to capture the processes of change in a qualitative way.

THE USE OF STRATEGIC TAXONOMIES

Typical for strategy–performance studies are (1) the advance identification of the strategies to be examined, and (2) the measurement of causal relationships between each single strategy and its performance.

Grant chooses four strategies to measure, most from Porter's (1980) generic strategy set: cost reduction through capital investment; product differentiation; up-market movement into higher-quality segments; and broadening the market scope through diversification. Why choose these four and not others? Perhaps other strategic taxonomies would apply better in this industry. And where are

Porter's strategies for declining markets – harvest and divest? These two latter strategies could also be a way to increase the profitability under the actual market conditions. Why, indeed, decide in advance the strategies to be measured and thereby make an *ex ante* construction of the reality to be studied? Why not instead begin the study with a reproduction of strategies currently in use in the pertinent industry and categorize them before attempting to measure the possible relationship of each to profitability? The motives encouraging this approach are especially strong in an industry dominated by small business firms. It is precarious to apply typical large-firm strategies to a sample of small firms, where formal strategic thinking is less developed. Changes in strategy are rare, especially in small owner-led firms (Melin, 1986).

On the whole, it is an action model for large firms which is used to formulate the hypothesis. The assumption is that an analytical valuation by the firm of its environment will give a basis for a decision consciously to change strategy. This model could be questioned regarding large firms (see below), but even more where small firms are concerned.

In fact, we often find firms that combine different (competitive) strategies in individual and varying ways. On the other hand, the researcher easily identifies separate and quite distinct strategies to measure. If a causal relationship between strategic change and later performance exists, it is surely the total strategy mix that determines the result.

The comments thus far are related to the concrete design of Grant's study, although the discussion is relevant for most strategy studies on content which have been put forth. In the next section I will be more general and will dip below the surface of traditional strategy–performance studies. These comments will be based on an alternative paradigm for research on strategy change.

SOME UNDERLYING ASSUMPTIONS

The theoretical framework supporting the mainstream of strategy–performance studies is (like Grant's) based on a number of underlying assumptions which certainly are worth a scholarly debate. Grant discusses some of these in a self-critical fashion, while other assumptions and their consequences are not directly apparent in the text.

The Objective Environment

It is assumed that the decision-makers objectively perceive an unambiguous and distinct environment. But is this a reasonable standpoint? Strategic decisions/actions are made by human beings, who tend to interpret their environment subjectively (Levin, 1951; Weick, 1979; and Smircich and Stubbart, 1985). As Mey (1972, p. 35) puts it, 'It is in the subjective environment that all real possibilities for action are to be found.' How, for example, do small business managers interpret their competitive environment when imported products from NICs turn up on the market? Do they really change their concept of their individual positions on the market according to a conscious analysis of the decreased competitive advantage for domestic producers arising from the low labour costs in South-east Asia?

Strategic Change as a Reaction to Environmental Change

Strategic change is regarded mainly as a deterministic adjustment to environmental change (objectively perceived). Environmental constraints consequently decide the possible strategic reaction. But if strategic change instead grows mainly from inside the organization (Greiner, 1983), as a result of the organization's history and mental frameworks, how much attention should be paid to the restricted model of strategy–environment fit?

This assumption is related to the black box syndrome in this type of strategy content research. Reality cannot be explained without some simplification. But here the whole organization, with its structure, culture and competences, is reduced to a black box. The following quotation from MacCrimmon (1985, p. 98) reflects one aspect of this mode of simplification: 'Although organizational decisions are usually the result of actions taken by many people, we can learn a great deal by thinking of the organization as a monolithic unit.'

A strategic change may have its roots in a turbulent and hostile environment; still, it cannot be assumed to be the result of deterministic forces in the environment (Bourgeois, 1984). It is always the internal understanding of the outside world which decides what is happening. This understanding is determined to a large degree by existing mental frameworks and ways of strategic thinking. Strategic actions are based on strategic thinking, composed of quite stable abstractions of reality (Nystrom and Starbuck, 1984). Strategic actions correspond to the values and preferences of management (Bourgeois, 1984). Furthermore, internal resources, especially human competences, will set the limits to which strategy will be developed and realized.

Grant takes a somewhat ambivalent attitude towards the role of the organization and its internal resources in strategy-making. In the beginning of his paper, he makes clear that comparative advantage is not determined exogenously: it is created by the firms themselves through strategic change. The capacity for strategic change depends, according to Grant, upon the resources of each firm. Yet, Grant disregards the role of internal organizational characteristics in the design of his study. In the only hypothesis concerning the relationship between strategy and the firm's resources, the latter are reduced to the size of the firm. But after comparing the results of the statistical test with the more qualitative observations, Grant admits that there is a close fit between specific skills and experiences of managers and the strategies pursued. So performance cannot, after all, be regarded as a deterministic outcome of a set of environment, strategy and resources variables.

Strategic Change as a Rational Problem-solving Process

Strategic change is regarded as the result of a rational problem-solving process containing three successive stages: (1) analysis, (2) strategy formulation, evaluation and decision, and (3) implementation. If strategic change is a much more incremental and, in part, unconscious process (Quinn, 1978; Mintzberg and Waters, 1985), with (from a rational perspective) the general weaknesses of decision processes (March and Olsen, 1976), then the results of traditional strategy–performance research become very difficult to interpret.

A World of Competitors

The competitors are regarded as the only actors of importance in the business environment. A strong belief in the market is related to this view, and the market war can be won only by superior competitive strategies. An alternative view is to see the market as much more organized and negotiated, especially concerning the interaction between suppliers and buyers in the vertical market system: i.e., the 'market-as-a-network' view (Johanson and Mattsson, 1984). With this view, co-operative strategies carried out in collaboration with suppliers and customers have as much influence on the strategic performance as pure competitive strategies. To understand the competitive advantage of a firm, we must understand the position of the firm in the integrated vertical market system of which it is a part, including the value of the mutual relationships the firm has with various customers and suppliers.

To illustrate the difference of these two images of the market structure, I present two quite extreme and absolute views on the British cutlery industry, the industry studied by Grant (see figures 4C.2 and 4C.3). Competitive advantage is of course not only a question of cost, price and quality. Grant gives examples from his qualitative data on customer-oriented, co-operative strategies, e.g., in his discussion of the difficulties of establishing a reputation and position as a new supplier of high-quality products as compared with already established supplier–buyer relationships. Dyads of firms are bound together in a quite stable pattern of ongoing interaction. This interaction is characterized by economic exchange (transactions), information exchange, and social exchange (commitments and trust) (Melin, 1987).

Grant's results show that firms holding a specific competitive position have an advantage over firms attempting to attain such a position. Further development of this conclusion spotlights the importance of having the competence both to maintain established customer relationships and to develop new ones in order to secure an improved position in the network of suppliers, competitors and customers. On the whole, the capability to deal with supplier and buyer relationships, as expressed through co-operative strategies, is a significant dimension of competitive advantage in a business environment.

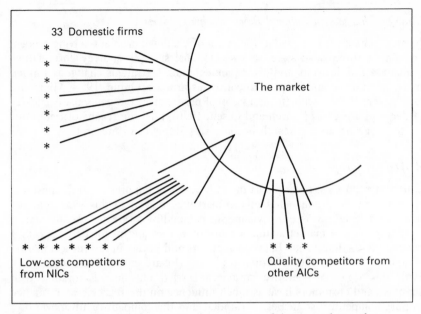

FIGURE 4C.2   View A: The world of competitors, fighting on the market

When trying to understand strategic change, we must consider a number of different forces, each having a different character. These range from strong external forces, which strike at nearly all firms acting in an industrial field, to invisible internal forces, such as the belief systems and other aspects of the organizational culture, which are specific to each firm. In between, we find each firm's strategic actions, which decide (1) the position of the individual firm in the field and (2) the structure of the entire field. This holistic view on forces explaining strategic change has been presented as the 'field-of-force' metaphor (Melin, 1985, 1987).

A POSITION DIAGRAM FOR STRATEGY RESEARCH

Building on some of the underlying assumptions just discussed and viewing them in combination with certain other aspects, I want to present a rough diagram through which different approaches in strategy research could be positioned. Figure 4C.4 consists of two dimensions. The first describes the direction of research – whether strategy research concentrates on *content* of strategy or on the strategic *process*. The content orientation refers both to descriptions of strategies in use (e.g. the taxonomy-oriented research of Miller

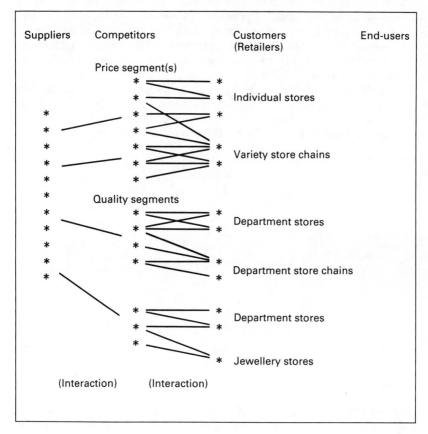

FIGURE 4C.3 View B: The structural vertical market system bound together by interaction; the market-as-a-network

and Friesen, 1984, and Galbraith and Schendel, 1983, but also Porter's, 1980, generic strategies) and to all studies on strategy–performance relationships. (See Fahey and Christensen, 1986, for a summary of this type of research.) The process orientation refers both to different studies of the strategic planning process (e.g. Lorange, 1982) and to studies of how new strategic actions take place (e.g. Mintzberg and Waters, 1985; Quinn, 1980).

The second dimension describes two completely different views on the way people behave in an organizational setting, especially regarding how they perceive information and make things happen (through decisions and actions). At one end of the axis I place research pursued on the assumption of a homogeneous organization making rational, strategic decisions at the top according to objective information; at the other end of the axis the research is based on an action frame of reference (Silverman, 1970), where instead strategic action is the result of intentional mental processes based on different actors' subjective interpretations and meanings. At this end the organization is also considered to be driven by political processes representing both internal and external interests.

It is a difficult and dubious undertaking to assign individual researchers specific positions in a rough diagram. Nevertheless, I shall give it a try. In figure 4C.5 individual researchers are not positioned in person; rather, a review of some main parts of their published works is attempted.

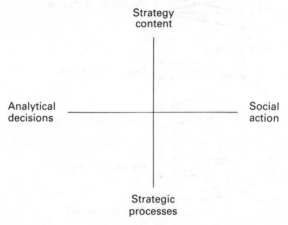

FIGURE 4C.4   A position diagram for strategy research

The purpose of all social science, including research in strategic management, must be to attain an increased insight in reality. The students of strategic management must be able to present an understanding of what really happens strategically in an organization. A theory of strategic management must in part be a theory of change, but at the same time it must consider the content of the change process. Furthermore, organizations are not monolithic, nor are decision-makers completely rational and analytical. From my point of view, scientific research in strategic management ought to avoid the extremes of the presented matrix and instead concentrate on the area around the intersection of the axes, and thus consider both the content and the process aspects of strategy with an eye specially on organizational actions that are not quite rational and analytical.

A CONCLUDING NOTE ON METHODOLOGY

Returning to Grant's study, it can only actually be viewed as two studies: as a formal test of the strategy–fit relationships, and as a more qualitatively-

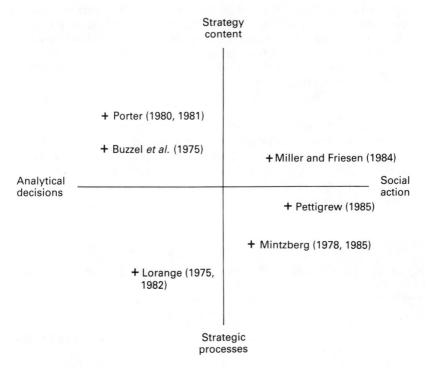

FIGURE 4C.5   The position of some directions in strategy research

oriented examination of the entire British cutlery industry. While the study is presented as a typical statistical measurement of strategy–performance relationships in a hostile environment, Grant seems to have a concurrent and broader interest. The study bears traits of a rather case-oriented analysis of the changes occurring in an entire industrial sector. This is interesting, because I believe that we can learn a great deal about strategic change through designing case studies of industrial sectors, e.g. of limited populations of business firms (Aldrich, 1986). But we must go further than Grant does if we are to reach the full potential of the case approach to the understanding of strategic change.

(a)   All external forces of importance must be identified in order to understand the degree of hostility and turbulence in the environment and the rules of the game for involved strategic actors in the industrial field.

(b)   The approach must be longitudinal, with the ambition to cover historical processes of change and important critical incidents.

(c)   To understand the relationship between performance and pursued strategies, we must understand the strategic action on the level of the firm, considering the specific organizational characteristics of each.

Using a process- and case-oriented approach has most often meant depending on pure qualitative analyses. But Miller and Friesen (1984) show promising research results after combining qualitative analyses of anecdotal data with quantitative analyses to find their taxonomies and configurations. Yet, they don't expect many followers: 'It is much easier to use common linear statistical analyses to establish samplewide multivariate relationships than it is to discover unanticipated regularities by groping in a complex data base' (Miller and Friesen, 1984, p. 268).

In conclusion, the reality of strategic management is complex and ambiguous with networks of mutual causation. Thus our approaches must try to capture and reproduce more of this complexity than is allowed by the dominating paradigm of strategy research. We must combine different, often divergent, methods if we want to build an advanced and more integrated theory of strategic management.

REFERENCES

Aldrich, H. (1986)   *Population Perspectives on Organizations*. Stockholm: Almqvist & Wiksell.

Bain, J. (1968)   *Industrial Organization*. New York: John Wiley.

Bourgeois, L. (1984)   Strategic management and determinism. *Academy of Management Review*, 9 (4), 586–96.

Buzzel, R., Gale, B. and Sultan, R. (1975)   Market share – a key to profitability. *Harvard Business Review*, 53, 97–106.

Chandler, A. (1962)   *Strategy and Structure*. Cambridge, Mass.: MIT Press.

Fahey, L. and Christensen, K. (1986)   Evaluating the research on strategy content. *Journal of Management*, 12, (2), 167–183.

Galbraith, C. S. and Schendel, D. (1983)   An empirical analysis of strategy types. *Strategic Management Journal*, 4, 153–73.

Greiner, L. (1983)   Senior executives as strategic actors. *New Management*, 1, (2), 13–14.

Johanson, J. and Mattsson, L G. (1984)   *Internationalization in Industrial Systems – A Network Approach*. Paper presented at the Prince Bertil Symposium, 'Strategies on Global Competition', Stockholm.

Levin, K. (1951)   *Field Theory in Social Science*. Cambridge, Mass.: MIT Press.

Lorange, P. (1982)   *Implementation of Strategic Planning*. Englewood Cliffs, NJ: Prentice-Hall.

—— and Vancil, R. (1976)   How to design a strategic planning system. *Harvard Business Review*, 54, September–October.

MacCrimmon, K. (1985)   Understanding strategic decisions: three systematic approaches. In J. Pennings, *Organizational Strategy and Change*. San Francisco: Jossey-Bass.

March, J. and Olsen, J. (1976)   *Ambiguity and Choice in Organizations*. Bergen: Universitetsforlaget.

Melin, L. (1985)   Strategies in managing turnaround: the Scandinavian TV industry. *Long Range Planning*, 18 (1), 80–6.

—— (1986) Entrepreneurship, Organizational Culture and Strategic Change. Paper presented at the Sixth Annual Strategic Management Society Conference, Singapore.

—— (1987) The Field-of-Force Metaphor: a study in industrial change. *International Studies of Management and Organization*, 17, (1), 24–33.

Mey, H. (1972) *Field-theory: A study of its application in the social science.* London: Routledge & Kegan Paul.

Miller, D. and Friesen, P. H. *(1984) Organizations: A Quantum View.* Englewood Cliffs, NJ: Prentice-Hall.

Mintzberg, H. (1978) Patterns in strategy formation. *Management Science*, 24, 934–48.

—— and Waters, J. (1985) Of strategies, deliberate and emergent. *Strategic Management Journal*, 6 (3), 257–72.

Nystrom, P. and Starbuck, W. (1984) To avoid organizational crises, unlearn. *Organizational Dynamics*, Spring, 53–65.

Pettigrew, A. M. (1985) *The Awakening Giant: Continuity and Change in ICI.* Oxford: Basil Blackwell.

Porter, M. (1980) *Competitive Strategy: Techniques for Analyzing Industries and Competitors.* New York: Free Press.

—— (1981) The contributions of industrial organization to strategic management. *Academy of Management Review* 6 (4), 609–20.

Quinn, J. B. (1978) Strategic change: logical incrementalism. *Sloan Management Review*, Fall, 7–21.

—— (1980) *Strategies for Change: Logical Incrementalism.* Homewood, Ill.: Richard D. Irwin.

Silverman, D. (1970) *The Theory of Organizations.* London: Heinemann.

Smircich, L. and Stubbart, C. (1985) Strategic management in an enacted world. *Academy of Management Review*, 10 (4), 724–36.

Weick, K. (1979) *The Social Psychology of Organizing.* Reading, Mass.: Addison-Wesley.

5 The Impact of Technological Change on Industry Structure and Corporate Strategy: The Case of the Reprographics Industry in the United Kingdom

Agha Ghazanfar, John McGee and Howard Thomas

INTRODUCTION

Over the last thirty years, a considerable body of research has focused on the process and incidence of the diffusion of technological innovations in firms, industries and society in general. Organizational conditions that favor or inhibit the innovative process have also been investigated and the problems and opportunities faced by the innovative firm discussed. Relatively little emphasis, however, has been placed on the process of substitution of one technology for another and on the behavior of firms and industries threatened by technological advances. Economic research following Schumpeter's theory of creative destruction has attempted primarily to determine the effect of market structure on technological innovation, although more recent studies (e.g. Scherer, 1980, p. 150, Phillips, 1971, pp. 7–12) focus upon technology as an endogenous variable and as a 'driver' of conduct in the context of market structures.

There have, for instance, been no case studies illustrating the process of creative destruction. It is hardly surprising, therefore, that the few strategic management analysts who have tried empirically to investigate the behavior of economic agents under the threat of what they perceive to be exogenous technological changes should conclude:

> The nature of substitution by one technology for another is not well known.
> (Cooper and Schendel, 1976, p. 62)

and:

> We know very little about technological change and its effect on competitive busines strategy except that it can have a profound impact. (Hofer and Schendel, 1978, p. 137)

and:

> Missing in both fields [the management of technology and industrial economics] is a comprehensive view of how technological change can affect the rules of competition and the ways in which technology can be the foundation of creating defensible strategies for firms. (Porter, 1983, pp. 2–3)

In a different vein, and a different tradition of investigation, insights into this process have come from historical accounts, notably those by Chandler in *Strategy and Structure* (1962) and *The Visible Hand* (1977), in which demand and technological changes are the progenitors of shifts in the business strategy and organizational structure of firms. The typical corporate response to technological change is one of diversification. Chandler's pioneering study (1962) and those that followed it (e.g. Rumelt, 1974) established the association between corporate diversification and organizational restructuring, but no attempt was made to focus on *corporate strategy* as the dependent variable, the emphasis having been on performance. Caves (1980, p. 74) points toward this vacuum:

> These studies [post-Chandler research] demonstrate the adaptation of business organization to strategy, but they do not explain the genesis of the whole process – the environmental forces that control the choice of corporate strategy.
> Chandler analyzed the association between large companies' organizational structure and the market structures of their basic business [1962, ch. 7] – a reduced-form relationship with the intermediate choice of corporate strategy solved out. (Caves, 1980, p. 74)

Studies by Cooper and Schendel (1976) and Abell (1980) use business policy and industrial organization concepts to analyze the strategic response of firms to technology changes. Abell studied nascent industries, while Cooper and Schendel analyzed declining businesses from the standpoint of the affected firms.

One of Cooper and Schendel's strong findings was that firms will continue with their traditional businesses in the face of sharp discontinuities associated with radical changes in product and process technologies. Abell viewed this failure to adjust as a problem in 'business definition.' Such firms defined their businesses narrowly and were unable to widen their concepts when technology imposed a widened definition on them and altered the boundaries of their industries.

A common feature of the aforementioned studies was that they confined their attention to the business unit. Corporate-level decisions and choices about rearranging the firm's portfolio of businesses were excluded from their analyses. Moreover, they did not examine most of the relevant features of the industries (in which the firms were operating) prevalent at the time the firms were confronted with strategic choices. Nor did they examine the nature of the technological threat – for instance, *how* it materialized, *why* it materialized and (most importantly) *when* it materialized – faced by each firm. Neither the antecedents nor the time element was taken into account.

In the present study of the impact of technological change on the strategic choices of firms in the reprographics industry (and their response thereto), the focus is not merely on the business unit. An attempt is made to analyze the strategic response of firms at each of the following three levels:

1   Product-level response – the positioning and repositioning of the product in the same market;
2   Business-unit-level response – the alteration of functional strategies within the product market;
3   Corporate-level response – diversification and redefinition of the firm's portfolio.

In so doing, the analysis underlines the process whereby firms lose their ability to differentiate their product and are obliged to reposition themselves *vis-à-vis* the old competitors as well as the new ones within the market-place. Changes in product–market boundaries are also analyzed, as are the strategic responses of firms to technological change. Particular attention is focused upon the nature of the technological threat and its likely impact on the competitive strategies of the range of firms in the industry.

Finally, the reprographics industry was chosen for this study because it is characterized by strong competition, technological change and UK-based firms with declining market shares. Consequently, it becomes possible to examine relationships between technological change and industry–market boundaries and between technological change and the strategic response of firms.

The chapter begins with a review of the findings concerning the longitudinal impacts of technology on products and market structures. Analyses of the effects of technology on market structures and strategies at both the business and the corporate level) are then made. Finally, its main conclusions and implications are discussed.

REVIEW OF THE EFFECTS OF TECHNOLOGY ON
MARKETS AND MARKET STRUCTURES IN THE
REPROGRAPHIC INDUSTRY (1880–1980)

The justification for using methodologies common to business and economic history to study the growth of firms and industries is provided by Hart and

Clarke (1980), Channon (1973), Pavitt (1980), Pope and Hoyle (1984), Schumpeter (1942, 1966) and Porter (1981b). Schumpeter (1966, pp. 83–4) notes that economists who look at existing market structures *ex visu* of a point of time miss the essential question which relates to the process of industrial change. Porter states the advantages of a multi-disciplinary, historical approach for understanding the complexity of strategic interactions and the industrial environment in the following terms:

> First, its emphasis is longitudinal, built around a careful re-creation of competitive moves and other events in the sequence in which they occurred. Second, it is broad and quite detailed in its coverage of firm behavior and industry events rather than focusing on one or a few elements of competitive behavior such as investment or pricing. Thirdly, it emphasizes the uncertainties present in predicting the future that bear on the decisions facing firms. (Porter, 1981b)

Therefore, it is appropriate at this point to summarize the changes that took place during the different phases of the evolution of the reprographics industry, focusing particularly on the actions of the 'players' (given larger supplier power), the sets of characteristics which identified the 'industry' at different points of time, and the rationales underlying the 'entry' and 'exit' decisions of firms.

1780–1880

The earliest of the technological innovations for office reprographics were James Watt's Copying Machine (1780), Brunel's Multiple Writing Pens (1799) and Wedgwood's Manifold Stylographic Writer (1806). All three innovations attempted to provide a means for retaining an extra copy of a handwritten document. However, owing to insufficient demand for written information, no *industry* as such came into being. These innovations attracted only a limited clientele, and they remained confined to the stationery–retail business. Their historical importance is that they foreshadowed later products for an office market. James Watt's Copying Machine was the precursor of the Victorian Copying Book a hundred years later, and it also bore a striking similarity to the offset-transfer principle of duplication. Wedgwood's Stylographic Writer was the precursor of carbon paper, which again came almost a hundred years later.

1880–1920

The first technology that permitted the making of a large number of duplicate copies for the office was Gestetner's stenciling process of the 1880s. Demand for duplication rose at the turn of the century because of the new management requirements of an expanding economy. By the 1920s an industry was established, and the market structure that emerged was distinguishable by the following characteristics:

1   the patents held by Gestetner;
2   the mass production (after 1920) of machinery;
3   a widespread distribution network;
4   the effective tying of the stencil duplicator with consumable supplies;
5   the high cost of direct-selling (further enhanced by the cost of training salesmen to sell the bundle of tied products);
6   the further differentiation of the product (brand name, free after-sales service)

These features reflected the strategic decisions of Gestetner, the pioneer and industry leader. They thwarted entry, and created an oligopoly of two firms, Gestetner and Roneo. (A. B. Dick, the only other firm to enter the business, remained confined to the US market.) Gestetner was thus to remain a profitable, specialized, single-technology firm for half a century (till the 1960s) serving a world market with a mass-produced, differentiated, tied bundle of products. Its 'product-market' strategy had created a market segment that was sharply defined, its attributes being high run-length, moderate quality, moderate volume duplication and low cost. In this segment the stenciling process, being the only method that could offer this bundle of attributes (or anything close to it), was thus immune from competition. Gestetner was to remain committed to the stenciling process, and the firm's 'product-development' strategy was limited to improvements in this technology alone.

1920–40

Hectographic or spirit duplication provided an answer to the lower-volume, shorter run-length needs of customers, and this filled a market segment in between carbon paper and the stencil duplicator. Hecto customers were those who would formerly have had to go in for the stenciling machine when their duplication needs exceeded the very low carbon-copy limits. Thus a new segment emerged. The incumbent firms, however, did not diversify into the new technology because they continued to define their business in terms of their original technology. They thus allowed the establishment of a separate oligopoly. This need not have been the structure of the market. Gestetner, for instance, could easily have acquired the hectographic technology, as, indeed, it could at any earlier stage have moved without much effort into the carbon paper and typewriter markets. As it was, the firms serving the new market segment remained small, and, because entry barriers were low, they were more vulnerable to external change.

1930–50

In a different market segment, a major technological advance was the diazo copying process, which superseded the blueprinting materials business. The diazo machine also provided customers with a superior alternative to the photostat (Projection Photographic Copying) machine, because it did not need a darkroom, use an expensive lens system or require silver halide. The diazo machine, however, had its limitations – for instance, the requirement of translucent originals – and its use was therefore restricted to engineering offices that needed large-size duplicates. For this narrow segment, the FESMM (Federation of Engineers' Sensitized Material Manufacturers) provided a highly differentiated bundle of products. Ozalid's strategy, based on proprietary knowledge (patents) and effective tying of consumables and machinery, was similar to Gestetner's.

It is noteworthy that the diazo and stencil industries remained independent of each other, despite the similarity in the manufacture of diazo and stencil papers on the one hand, and the marketing of all diazo and stencil products on the other. Here again, the strategic decisions of firms like Gestetner and Ozalid to stay with their particular technologies allowed the emergence in the 1930s of separate groups of suppliers serving the office reprographics market.

1950–60

The photochemical (including thermal) copying machine was the major technological breakthrough of the 1950s. It was developed by Agfa, Kodak and 3M, all of whom already had existing marketing networks for selling hardware and consumables. The entry barriers protecting firms like Gestetner and Ozalid did not, therefore, apply to these new suppliers. They not only created a new market segment, but also invaded and established themselves in some of the existing segments. For instance, Agfa-Gevaert's Diffusion Transfer machine ('Copyrapid') filled the latent demand for office copying and also penetrated the market for offset-lithographic duplication because the diffusion transfer process could be used for platemaking. The latent demand in offices was satisfied first in the USA and then worldwide through Agfa's international licensing policy. Kodak's 'Verifax' and 3M's thermographic copiers of the 1950s satisfied the same demand, primarily in the USA. The copying machines offered by these three firms penetrated and occupied the market segment delimited by the triple characteristics of low volume, short run-length and low quality reproduction. This was the segment previously occupied by spirit duplicators. The copying machines were not only a superior alternative to the spirit duplication process, but they were also compatible with it. Because of the same compatibility with other duplication processes (except stencil), they penetrated the diazo and offset-litho segments too.

The new market segment created by photochemical and thermographic copiers was that of customers requiring a limited number of copies of any document whatsoever, including incoming mail. Within this market segment, all of these machines had a number of drawbacks but also certain advantages, relative to one another. This allowed for fine product differentiation.

The possible ways in which these suppliers could differentiate their products were not limited to the factors of duplicating process, volume and run-length:

they were able to offer a greater number of combinations of product attributes, based on the following additional set of factors:

1   the kind of original required for reproduction;
2   inconvenience associated with handling skills and the chemicals required;
3   the intermediate stages necessary for reproducing a document;
4   the kind of special copying paper required;
5   the quality of reproduction obtainable;
6   the size of the machine.

Because sellers could segment the market in different ways according to the buyer's chosen bundle of preferences for machine attributes, with one drawback of a machine being traded off against another advantage, a highly differentiated oligopoly prevailed.

Kodak and 3M opted for a strategy based on vertical integration and aimed at monopolistic control. Agfa, on the other hand, made a creative departure from this norm: by licensing the applications of the new technology worldwide it opened up entry to a large number of licencees, manufacturers and sellers, making competition more international and intense. This diversity of entry strategies altered the entire market structure.

The new suppliers did not supplant Gestetner and Ozalid in the short period (1950s) of their emergence to the fore, because Gestetner's customers (long run-length duplication and Ozalid's customers (large-size drawings) had specialized needs that the photochemical copiers could not meet. In the long run, however, the research and development effort led by the new suppliers introduced a dynamism into the industry which posed a serious threat to the existing businesses. The possibility now existed of a product being developed which would be superior in all respects to the existing ones, invading all segments of the market and, by virtue of its overwhelming technological advantage, facilitating the establishment of a world monopoly.

1960–70

This new product was the Xerox–Rank Xerox plain-paper copier (PPC).

The detailed study and analysis of the Xerox phenomenon illustrates the manner in which the process of 'creative destruction' unfolds: how a new technology, allied to a particular entry strategy, re-segments and re-structures the market. Xerox, with its affiliate Rank Xerox, developed a wide range of copiers and positioned them in different markets comprising customers with different needs. This strategy weaned away customers from existing market segments and also created new customers. For instance, models such as the RX 914 and RX 813 created segments that not only overlapped with the electrofax users, but also included new buyers of reprographic equipment. With the second generation of PPC machines, the market expanded to encompass customers who had an even higher copying-volume requirement.

A series of sub-markets was captured sequentially as the Rank Xerox development program got underway: the diazo, hecto, stencil and offset duplicator markets were all invaded. Having attained monopoly power, Rank Xerox, with its superior technology, could also segment the market in an entirely new way. It segregated its customers into discrete blocks based upon the *intensity of their usage* of copiers, offering them machines specifically designed to meet their needs. It locked in its customers through a multiplicity of price schedules and discounts, discriminatory pricing (made possible by monopoly power) and higher switching costs.

The supply-side analysis showed the emergence in the 1960s of the Xerox Group as an international monopoly surrounded by a fringe of 'monopolistic competition' among electrofax suppliers, who were all licencees of Xerox. This structure was the direct outcome of Xerox's strategic decision to thwart entry into the most profitable segments, but not into the less profitable ones. Thus, while it licensed electrofax, it retained monopoly control over the PPC technology. It systematically erected a series of entry barriers, first through amassing patents, second by raising the capital cost of entry through the rental regime, and third by continually upgrading its machines and thus leaving potential competitors too far behind. Finally, it erected a substantial marketing and 'product differentiation' barrier by its investment in highly trained machine-specific salesmen and service and repair engineers.

During the 1960s, Rank Xerox was concerned less with the cost of production and more with 'differentiation' and product improvement, a policy which impelled it towards the manufacturing and renting of more and more expensive and higher-quality machines. This had two implications: first, it left room for entrants who could compete on the basis of a manufacturing cost advantage; second, it left the cheaper end of the market open for penetration.

1970–5

By this time, the PPC machine was the dominant product of the reprographics industry. This study showed that, in the PPC market, the height of entry barriers differed from segment to segment. The moderate- and high-volume segment differed from the low-volume, low-cost end in that the demand was more price-inelastic, the rental contract had a greater appeal, and the servicing requirement was greater and more expensive. Entry barriers were thus higher in this segment because of the high capital cost of the rental regime and of the sales-service–engineering network.

It was into this segment that the first four new entrants (IBM, Agfa, 3M and Gestetner) chose to make their entry. Their strategy was to compete not on the basis of price (customers being relatively price-insensitive) but on the basis of further 'differentiation' allied to established brand names transferred from other product markets. Entering this segment as self-manufacturers, they had the added disadvantage of an inadequate range of copying machines. They were, therefore, unable to shake Rank Xerox's predominance.

By contrast, the next eight entrants started from the low end, where entry barriers were lower. Customers were price-sensitive, there was less of a service requirement, and the rental regime held no great appeal. In this segment, therefore, outright sale and price competition were both possible. The Japanese entrants were able to choose these as the basis of competition because they possessed the enabling condition of a manufacturing cost advantage. They overcame the patent barrier by making substantial investments in new technologies. Entry was staged through a sharing of patents, a separation of production and marketing, and the provision of a wider line of products.

Following this round of entry, the low-volume segment expanded to form a larger part of an enlarged overall market. Photocopiers became more sophisticated and versatile and less expensive. This was the result of continual technological innovations, the main ones being:

1   the pioneering of better photo-conductive materials, which improved copy quality;
2   the development of liquid toners, which reduced the capital and running costs of machinery;
3   the application of microprocessors, which improved the reliability of machines and contributed to greater convenience and more efficient service;
4   the introduction of modular construction, which further reduced cost, and also allowed a multi-product, multi-segment entry through the addition of special features to a standardized design.

On the one hand, these innovations contributed to the relaxation of several constraints on entry (principally, cost and servicing constraints). On the other hand, they allowed the suppliers to segment the market in yet newer ways. Many new combinations of special features and product attributes could now be offered. For instance, it became possible to trade off;

1   reliability against serviceability;
2   copy quality against copy cost;
3   copying speed against the possibility and effect of breakdowns;
4   power and safety requirements against performance.

These segmentation variables were different from those along which the earlier suppliers had segmented the market in the 1950s and 1960s. The composition of the suppliers also changed. The new entrants had greater resources behind them and exploited brand names from a variety of markets. Very few of them were single-technology firms. The photocopying business was in most cases only a small portion of their overall portfolios. Their diversification was either technology-related or market-related (hardly any conglomerate or unrelated product diversification). Thus, the new industry now encompassed a variety of skills and backgrounds, and included in its fold firms whose functional (marketing, production, R&D) strategies were not uniform, leading to the emergence of several groups of suppliers. The Rank Xerox monopoly was replaced by highly competitive conditions.

1975–80

During the last five years of the 1970–80 decade, the advent of microelectronics provided yet another illustration of the same effect of technological change on product markets and market structure. It could be observed that by 1980 the new products based on electronic technologies had already displaced some of the electro-mechanical products of the reprographics industry.

The result of what is commonly described as 'the convergence of technologies' was that the distinctions between data processing, typewriting and composition, printing and reprographics were removed (since a single electronic product could now combine these previously discrete functions). This was so because the ability to input, store, process, reproduce, transmit and output information in digital or binary form conferred upon suppliers the possibility to serve multiple markets with the same building-blocks of a 'product'.

The cost differences between commercial printing and office reprographics also narrowed. As the market boundaries between printing, office reprographics and data processing became hazy, new ways of differentiation and segmentation came to the fore. One such new and significant variable was the quality and quantity of software provided. The market could be enlarged by the provision of additional software to enhance machine functions. An 'office systems' market emerged in which the suppliers sold a variety of complex, integrated, electronic systems. This 'office systems' market was distinguishable from the 'dedicated product' market by its higher selling costs and different marketing methods.

The market structure also reflected the changed cost conditions. The decline in the unit cost of semiconductor memory occasioned quicker entry from across several industrial boundaries, and greater competition across all markets, including those for small business machines, cash registers, electronic typewriters and word processors. The step-changes in microelectronics lowered the entry barriers associated with capital costs and service requirements: microelectronic-based products had fewer moving parts and therefore needed far less service and repair than electro-mechanical machines. With the resultant flood of entry, the reprographics industry now encompassed data processing firms, general office equipment suppliers, electrical firms and specialized high-technology firms. Thus, not only did several product markets coalesce, but there was also a convergence of the hitherto separate industries for office products, telecommunications and data processing. In the hundred years from 1880 to 1980, the stationery office supplies industry had evolved to become an integral part of a developing global electronic computing and communications industry.

Summary of Important Themes in the Evolution of the Reprographics Industry

This history of the office reprographics industry has highlighted certain recurring themes, which can now be summarized as follows.

1   Step-changes in technology – the changes in specifications or alteration of blueprints which result in new products – led to changes in market structure and competitive conditions, and to the formation of new sets of competitors. The height of entry barriers changed, cost conditions changed, and so did the extent and nature of product differentiation. These changes had serious implications for the survival of incumbent firms.
2   Technological change enabled firms from outside the industry to capture a series of sub-markets. Entry, however, was a gradual process.
3   The entry strategies and timing of entry of these firms were also important in determining the eventual competitive conditions that prevailed. Thus, the market structure observed at a given point of time was the result, to a great extent, not only of technological changes but also of the *strategic* decisions of firms.
4   With every step-change in technology, the market was enlarged. Product 'spaces' got filled up. Market boundaries were redefined. Segments got redrawn, and new ways of product differentiation and segmentation became available to suppliers. This created new dimensions of competition.

These recurring patterns constitute the Schumpeterian process of creative destruction. There are two steps to the argument here. The first, exemplified in figure 5.1, simply states that technology can change market structure. It can do so by changing the conditions on the demand side and/or by causing adjustments on the supply side. Thus, the nature of competition changes and the nature and level of entry barriers can alter, sometimes dramatically. The second step is more fundamental to an understanding of the process and concerns the role of the firm in the way in which it takes advantage of technological change. In figure 5.2 the centrepiece is the idea that technology changes the asset base of the firm. The key issue for the firm concerns its ability to invest in the creation of assets that are, relative to competitors, sufficiently distinct so that it can compete in the market in ways that cannot be imitated. The distinctiveness of the assets relates to the 'uncertain imitability' of those assets by competitors and thus constitutes the basis for economic rents. The ability of the firm to create distinctiveness for itself by investing in R&D is a prime source of competitive power and, taken far enough (as in the case of Xerox and plain paper copying), is sufficient to change market structure.

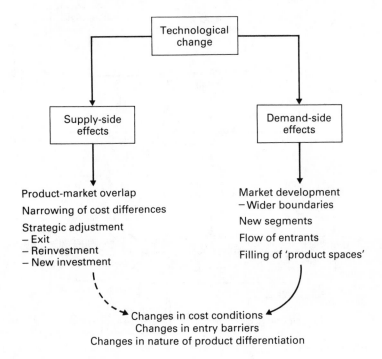

FIGURE 5.1 Technology and market structure linkages

This second point underlines the possibility for firms to act so as to make technological change endogenous to the system. It is evident from this that firms will be concerned to protect their distinctive assets (which *ex post* are sunk costs) with other kinds of differentiation strategy which could serve to lock in their customers in the face of similar or newer forms of competition. Not only is the asset base a potential entry barrier, therefore, but in the course of time it might also become a prison wall, inhibiting investment by the firm in new directions. In contrast, the successful firms are the ones (so our research suggests) that redefine their industry boundaries and engage in a continuous series of innovations.

TECHNOLOGY, MARKET STRUCTURE AND STRATEGIES

The historical survey of the reprographics industry has focused upon the relationship between technological change, firm strategy and market structure

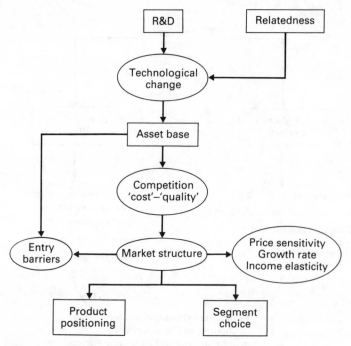

FIGURE 5.2   Model of change

over time. However, some of the relationships between these elements are well known. For instance, there is a vast body of literature on the effect of market structure on technological change. This tradition of industrial organization research derives from the Schumpeterian hypotheses (extended by Galbraith) that firm size or monopoly power or other structural features of the industry are the determinants of the rate of change in technology. Similarly, the effect of market structure on the behavior of firms ('conduct', in the industrial organization model) has been discussed extensively, (e.g. Phillips, 1971; Mansfield, 1968; Stoneman, 1983; Norris and Vaizey, 1973; and Freeman, 1982).

The reverse set of relationships, however, has not attracted as much research. There are fewer studies on the effect of:

1   technological change on market structure;
2   technological change on the strategies of firms;
3   strategic decisions of firms on market structure.

The focus in this chapter is on these three linkages, with particular concern for the role of the firm in sponsoring technological change and thereby changing market structures.

Technology–Market Structure

Technological change has been held to be the determining, rather than the dependent, variable by Phillips (1971), Samuelson (1976), Jewkes *et al.* (1958) and to some extent by Klein (1977). Historians (e.g. Chandler, 1962) have studied the long-term effects of technological advances. There have also been a number of doctoral dissertations on the effect of new products on the old: for instance, Knight (1963) on digital computers, Engler (1965) on typewriters, Yale (1965) on synthetic fibres, Gemery (1967) on the float-glass process, Golding (1971) on semiconductors, and Majumdar (1977) on calculators. Hill and Utterback (1979) provide a useful discussion on these studies. What is missing from all of them, however, is an examination, first, of the process whereby the structure of the old industry changes as a result of innovations, and, second, of the strategies of the firms involved. The present study paid attention to both sets of questions. How does the process of creative destruction unfold? What effect does the new technology have on segmentation in the market? How does the overlapping (of old and new products) occur? How do existing firms respond to change?

Technological change has been seen to be one of the important determinants of market structure. A new technology threatens existing businesses when, after a period of time, the markets for the two products (the old and the new) begin to overlap. Cost differences are abridged, and the new technology offers a superior alternative to existing and potential customers in one market segment after another, leaving the old technology firms with no unique differentiating factor or long-term competitive advantage. These firms are obliged either to exit from the business or to alter the concept of their business to accommodate the product-market change that has taken place.

On the demand side, it has been found that, with every step-change in technology, the market is enlarged. Product 'spaces' get filled up. Market boundaries are redefined. Segments get redrawn. Thus, new ways of segmentation become available to suppliers.

The overall effect of technological change on market structure noticed in this study can be summarized as follows. With every step-change in technology, the main elements of market structure change: cost conditions change, the height of entry barriers changes, and so do the extent and nature of product differentiation.

Technology–Strategy

The technology–strategy connection is another under-researched area. While it is obvious that a new technology will have some implications for the strategy of incumbent firms, the actual effect has not been examined empirically in any detail.

The findings of the present study indicate that not all the products of an industry are affected similarly or to the same extent by exogenous technological threats, and this provides firms with an opportunity to sub-optimize within the endgame. The threat emanating from the new technology is followed by an improvement of the traditional (threatened) product line, which reaches its most advanced stage after the threat materializes. The threatened firms' initial response is to increase, rather than decrease, their investment in the traditional business in the face of the technological threats. The history of the reprographics industry corroborates all these findings, but at the same time it suggests additional propositions: namely, that

1   sub-optimization within the endgame is a short-lived strategy, and
2   firms threatened by exogenous technological change are unable to build a position in the new technology which is the cause of the threat to them.

Unlike the earlier studies, this study analyzed the strategic options available to firms at different time periods. It also examined in detail the nature and timing of the technological threat to each business. The relevant features of the industry were taken into account and the strategic response was scrutinized at three levels: the repositioning of the product in the existing market, the change (if any) in business strategy, and the corporate-level change (if any). This detailed examination has led to the conclusion that, first, the strategic response of a firm is predicated upon the extent of its dependence on the threatened product line at the time that adversity sets in. Second, firms do have strategic choices: if they fail to exercise them, it is not because of cash constraints or lack of opportunity, but owing to some form of internal inertia. Finally, time is of the essence. The firm that inordinately delays its strategic reorientation is likely to find itself 'bound in shallows and in miseries'.

Strategy–Market Structure

Finally, this study has looked at the effect of strategic decisions on market structure. Econometric modeling has simply not been concerned with this relationship. In the industrial organization model, market structure is the determining, not the dependent, variable, although some economists have begun to raise the question of what makes market structure what it is. For instance, Scherer points out:

> A sophisticated explanation of how industry structures came to be what they are must blend the conventional, more or less static, determinants with the kinds of dynamic considerations introduced by stochastic growth process models. This is where future research on the determinants of market structure is most urgently needed. (Scherer, 1980, p. 150)

Abell (1980) and Porter (1981a) have argued that firms can, through their actions, fundamentally change the structure of their industries. However, they have provided little evidence in support of this proposition. The business policy literature has also shown little concern with this particular relationship, although it is these structural changes resulting from the strategic decisions of rivals that raise the most fundamental strategic problems for firms in competition (Porter, 1981a, p. 613).

In this study, the effect of long-term strategic decisions has been closely examined: for instance, the effect of Gestetner's strategic decisions of the 1920s on the market structure of the interwar years, the effect of the strategies of Kodak, 3M and Agfa-Gevaert on the structure of the industry in the 1950s and 1960s, the effect of Xerox's strategic decisions (during the 1950s) on the industrial structure during the 1960s and early 1970s, and the effect of the decisions of the Japanese manufacturers and the European and US marketing companies on the structure during the late 1970s. These effects suggest that the entry strategy and timing of entry chosen by firms is important in determining the eventual competitive conditions that will prevail. The existing market structure influences the 'conduct' of firms (as understood in the industrial organization literature), but this structure is itself, to a great extent, the outcome of the strategic decisions of firms. This is an extension of Abell's argument (1980, p. 191) that 'conduct determines structure' and that 'the way various competitors define their scope of activities, in particular, determines market boundaries.'

The ability of firms to affect the nature of competition and the underlying characteristics of market structure rests critically on the asset base of the industry. In particular, it hinges on the *ex ante* perception of firms of their ability to create distinctive assets (as 'first-movers') from which to gain rents, or (as later movers) to nullify or leapfrog the gains of earlier movers by investing in comparable or superior assets. Firms differ by virtue of the distinctiveness of their assets reinforced by the costs and uncertainties attached to replication by competitors.

Diversity of Strategies

The study identified differences in strategies between single-business and multi-business firms, which arose largely because of 'mobility barriers' (McGee and Thomas, 1986). In particular, the strategic behavior of the firms in the reprographics industry was found to depend upon, first, the time of entry; second, the life-cycle of the product (stage of industry evolution); and third, the nature of the firm (its scope of activities).

The evolution of single-product firms is first traced; this is followed by a discussion of the entry of 'dominant-product' firms, and finally of 'related-product' firms.

Evolution of Single-product firms

A single-product firm limits its growth to the prospects of its industry. In some cases this might be a deliberate and proper decision, but in others it

	Stage of growth of industry			1970–80 Stage of evolution of firm		
Technology firms to start with	Introduction	Growth	Maturity	Single-product	Dominant-product	Related-product
Gestetner	1880–1900	1920–1950	1950–1970 — — — — ➤ Dominant			
Ozalid	1928–1940	1940–1960	1960–1970 — — — — ➤ Dominant			
Rotaprint	1927–1950	1950–1960	1960–1970 ➤ Single			
Ricoh	1936–1960	1960–1975	— — — — — — — — — — — — — — — ➤ Related			
Xerox	1950–1960	1960–1975	— — — — — — — — — — — — — — — ➤ Related			

FIGURE 5.3   Evolution of single-product firms

may be a reflection of an inability to exploit opportunities outside the one industry. In either event, the firm can grow in size up to a point, as the examples of single-technology firms in this study (Rank Xerox, Gestetner, Ozalid, Rotaprint) demonstrate. However, in order to do so, a single-technology firm has to wean market share from its competitors, which may not be an easy task unless it starts with a de facto monopoly position, in which case it must retain its share. In order to retain its monopolistic control through the life-cycle of its product, the firm has to acquire a competitive advantage (e.g. cost leadership) stemming from factors other than the original ones (e.g. patents). Otherwise, its monopoly rents would be competed away. This necessitates a strategic reorientation of the firm some time after the initial product development. The perceived imperative of horizontal diversification thus stems from the difficulty of sustaining a permanent cost advantage within the original business.

Figure 5.3 depicts the movement of firms that started in the reprographics industry as their original business. The time of their start (the date being indicated in each case) was also the time of the start of their industry, because the firms were either themselves pioneers of a new technology or were set up specially to exploit a new technology.

The first of these was Gestetner, which pioneered the stenciling technology in the 1880s and founded a new industry. The 1920s and 1930s were a period of rapid expansion for the firm and the growth of the industry. Between 1950 and 1970 the stencil industry reached maturity, and it declined thereafter. Gestetner remained a 'single-technology' firm until well into the 1950s.

Thereafter, it began to diversify into the related business of offset lithographic duplication. In the 1970s, when its basic stenciling business was declining, Gestetner became a 'dominant-product' firm.

Ozalid's strategy followed the same course. It was founded in 1928 as a single-technology firm only to sell diazo products, the technology of which was pioneered by its parent (Kalle). The period between 1940 and 1960 was one of growth for the industry; during this time, Ozalid remained a single-technology firm. The 1960s witnessed the maturity of the industry. During this phase of maturity and subsequent decline, Ozalid diversified into very closely related product areas and became, like Gestetner, a 'dominant-product' firm.

Rotaprint, however, remained a single-technology firm during the mature phase of its industry. The historical record shows that Rotaprint did have the choice and the means to diversify out of its industry during the early 1970s but did not exercise that choice. Instead, it invested further within the industry. The difference between these three firms and Xerox and Ricoh, both of which also started as single-technology businesses, was that the latter two started diversifying out of their basic business while that business was still growing and had not yet reached maturity. Both Xerox and Ricoh were pioneering firms that became 'related-product diversifiers.'

Entry of Dominant-product Firms

These five firms were joined by four 'dominant-product' firms that entered parts of the reprographics market at different times but always when that part of the market was at a growth rather than a nascent stage. The most important of these was IBM, entering in the early 1970s when the plain-paper copying (PPC) business was growing very rapidly. IBM did not diversify further. However, the other three made various moves in different directions. Olivetti, basically a typewriter company, entered the field of telecommunications in addition to photocopying. A. B. Dick was the pioneer, in the USA, of stencil technology, but when it made a limited entry into the PPC business in the late 1970s it was a dominant-product company, although one undertaking an extensive diversification program (through in-house research and development) into areas unrelated to its basic business of stencil and offset duplication. Likewise, AM had started as a manufacturer of addressing machines, but in the 1950s it became a 'dominant-product' firm with its basic business being offset-litho duplicators but with a presence also in the electrofax copier business. It did not enter the growing PPC business, but attempted instead an ambitious program of acquisition of high-technology firms. Its subsequent diversification, like that of A. B. Dick, was unrelated to the basic business of office duplication, although both A. B. Dick and AM restricted their portfolios to the field of communications.

The significant feature of these 'dominant-product' entrants was the timing of their entry: it occured during the growth period of the market. This is shown in figure 5.4, which plots the corporate strategy posture (Wrigley-Rumelt classification) of the firm at the time of entry against the life-cycle of the industry entered.

Entry of Related-product Firms

A different set of firms that entered the industry were 'related-product diversifiers,' basing their strategy on their technical expertise and the exploitation of synergistic links between the manufacture of optical equipment (cameras), photographic film or paper and such supplies. Three of these firms were US-based multinational operations (Eastman Kodak, 3M and Nashua), one was European (Agfa-Gevaert) and three were Japanese (Canon, Minolta and Konishiroku). Of these firms, Kodak, 3M and Agfa-Gevaert entered twice, each time as related-product diversifiers.

These related-product firms appear to have had a settled or well defined corporate strategy. They selected their product markets on the basis of their relatedness to the firms' technologies or customer bases. Unlike the dominant-product firms A. B. Dick, AM and Olivetti, they did not grope in different directions in unrelated areas.

Agfa-Gevaert, 3M and Nashua were already in the reprographic supplies business; the PPC machine market was a complementary one. Canon, Minolta and Konishiroku could transfer their technical skills of camera manufacturing to the production of copying machines; they had a cost advantage here. Figure

	Scope of activity of firm (Corporate-level strategy)	
Stage of product life-cycle	Single-technology firm	Dominant-product firm
Early	Pioneers: Shown in figure 5.3	
Growth		IBM, Olivetti, A. B. Dick, AM
Advanced	Specialized firms: Copyer, Mita Kogyo	

FIGURE 5.4   Entry of dominant-product firms

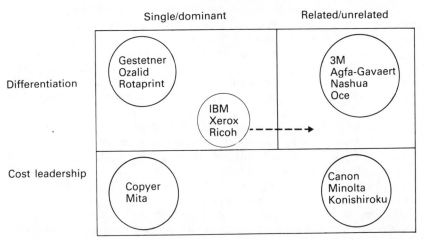

FIGURE 5.5   A broad classification of reprographics firms (1970s)
Note: Arrow shows direction of movement of firms. AM, A.B. Dick and Olivetti are hard to classify for the 1970s because their product portfolios were in a state of flux during this decade, and the firms were constantly undergoing reorganizations, venturing into new areas and then retracting.

5.5 maps the major reprographics firms of the 1970s according to the scope of their activities (horizontal axis) and business strategies (vertical axis).

Uni-dimensional and Multi-dimensional Businesses

The distinction in figure 5.5 is between single-technology and dominant-product firms on the one hand and related- and unrelated-product firms on the other. The rationale for this is that single-technology firms (specialization ratio between 0.95 and 1.0 – Rumelt, 1974) and dominant-product firms (specialization ratio between 0.70 and 0.95) are both dependent upon, and characterized by, their major product-market activity. They follow a strategy of growth that is constrained within defined industry boundaries. Their growth is, therefore, uni-dimensional. Single-technology businesses become dominant-product businesses by increasing some of their operations but not the *diversity* of these operations. Typically, the activities they add to their portfolio are extensions of the existing business. Examples of this are provided by Gestetner and A. B. Dick adding offset-litho duplicators to their existing range of stencil machines, Rotaprint selling duplicators in addition to printing presses, AM adding reprographic machines to addressing machines, and Ozalid adding spirit duplicators to its range of diazo machines.

On the other hand, both related- and unrelated-product firms have a multiplicity of product-market activities. They grow by an increase in the diversity of their operations, not merely in the size of those operations. For instance, camera companies entering the copying machine industry invest in new marketing methods (direct-selling and service networks that are not needed for selling cameras) or enter into partnerships with marketing companies that already have such networks. Firms marketing reprographic supplies undertake the manufacture of copying machines (Nashua, Agfa-Gevaert, 3M) which requires skills very different from those needed in producing sensitized and coated papers. The copying machine firm (Xerox) diversifies into computer equipment, telecommunications and publishing.

A firm comprising related-product businesses becomes an unrelated product diversifier by increasing the diversity in its product mix. The difference between the two is thus one of the degree only. Both are multi-business firms. Leontiades (1980, pp. 37–9) adds that, while single-business firms follow a functional organizational design (U-form), 'multi-business firms use a divisional strategy.' This is not only consistent with Chandler's thesis on strategy and organizational structure, but it also suggests that, while a single-business firm can achieve uni-dimensional growth by extending its current strategies, it cannot achieve multi-dimensional growth by replicating those strategies. If it 'jumps from a single-business to the multi-business classification, it has declared a dramatic change in its strategic posture' (Leontiades, 1980, p. 38).

The implication is that strategic planning for a single-business firm is fundamentally different from the strategic management of a multi-business firm. This distinction is already reflected in the strategy literature: in 'business strategy' the focus is on the functional strategies of single businesses, while the concern in 'corporate strategy' is with the multi-business strategies of the corporation as a whole. The first is concerned with uni-dimensional growth and 'static efficiencies' (Klein, 1977), while the second is concerned with the management of change or 'dynamic efficiency' (Klein, 1977). Klein explained the difference in terms of 'micro-stability.' The dichotomy between uni-dimensional and multi-dimensional growth also extends Penrose's (1959) argument about the limits to growth. Successful multi-business firms acquire, at some stage, the capability to seek and process new data and thus to remove the constraint on growth into diverse and previously unfamiliar areas (the 'Penrose effect'). Leontiades points towards exactly the same difference:

> Multi-business firms have at some point adopted an evolutionary management style. In order to progress from single business to related business, or from related business to unrelated business, implicitly requires evolutionary management. Indeed, it is impossible, conceptually, to move from one growth stage to another without an evolutionary-management orientation. By definition, steady-state management is concerned with ongoing operations while evolutionary management is continually evaluating the performance of its operating groups with an openness to change. (Leontiades, 1980, p. 59)

SUMMARY AND CONCLUSIONS

The present analysis of competition in the reprographics business from 1880 to 1980 has been a positivist study of the complexity of a dynamic industry. It has focused on the relationships between technological change, firm strategy and market structure. Its main conclusions and contribution to the existing literature will now be spelled out.

The field of strategic management has been the subject of scrutiny from a variety of approaches and paradigms, with each viewpoint providing a partial insight to a different slice of industrial and corporate behavior. Each discipline has made its own simplifying assumptions to keep the behavioral complexity tractable. Thus, the best-known corporate strategy model, the Wrigley–Rumelt model, ignores the conditions of the industry being diversified into or out of. It ignores the stage of industry evolution as a relevant factor in the firm's diversification decision. It also does not take into account the functional strategies of firms in particular product markets. The business policy models (e.g. PIMS, Porter, Abell) concern themselves with functional strategies but ignore the corporate-level strategies. In the present study, the analysis of competitive moves has been conducted at three levels:

1 the level at which the product is marketed;
2 the functional level at which the firm formulates its business strategies to gain advantages over its rivals in that product-market;
3 the level at which corporate strategy is formulated for the firm's entry into or exit from different product markets.

At the level of the firm, a close scrutiny is required of the differences between 'uni-dimensional' and 'multi-dimensional' firms. There are at least three important issues. First, it would be helpful to identify, from a different sample of firms, the systematic differences existing between these two kinds of firms in their resource allocation processes, incentives to encourage both the initiation and acceptance of change by top management and their organizational capacity to respond to exogenous threats.

Second, the process whereby single-product firms evolve into multi-business firms needs to be examined with a view to ascertaining whether this evolution is accompanied by a change in the functional strategies exercised in the chosen product markets. For example, do single-business firms become less concerned with the benefits of a vertical chain of value added as they become more diversified? Do they become more concerned with the management of diversity across product markets and with the synergistic links (or joint costs) between products? Are their strengths based on superior management of particular functions (e.g. R&D, production, marketing) for a variety of product markets, rather than on industry-specific barriers? If so, are there mobility barriers surrounding some functions or sectors of activity? Are transaction costs different for the two kinds of firms? These questions need empirically based answers.

The third issue is the costs of mobility. What are the costs and the constraints in moving from a single-business position to a multi-business one? Are these costs and constraints higher for a firm that was once the pioneer of a new technology (e.g. Gestetner, Ozalid)? The experience of the British reprographics firms suggests that what were once entry-deterring barriers (elaborate service and distribution network, high vertical integration, synonimity of firm with a particular technology) turned eventually into barriers to exit. When, how and why do these assets become liabilities?

These questions can be addressed by examining a wider sample of firms across industries or by an in-depth analysis of firms within the same industry. For example, 3M is an obvious candidate for researching issues related to the management of diversity across product markets. For management purposes, 3M classifies its products into ten groups, which in turn are organized into four major business sectors on the basis of technology: Electronic and Information Technologies, Life Sciences, Graphic Technologies, and Industrial and Consumer. It has 45 major product lines spanning several industries. These are sold through a variety of distribution channels to diverse customer groups. Each operating division has autonomy, including its own research and development, but there is also a central Technology Enterprises Division. What are the strategic differences between this diverse, yet 'related-product,' company (3M) and a comparable, or larger, single-technology or dominant-product firm (say, IBM)?

Oce van der Grinten provides a good example, in the reprographics industry, of the successful evolution of a single-product business. It started in 1955 as a small diazo firm, but by 1976 it had become (with the acquisition of Ozalid) the largest independent reprographics company in Europe. During the 1960s, it started marketing electrostatic, coated-paper copiers manufactured by Minolta. This range was later augmented with copying machines designed and manufactured in-house. During the 1970s, Oce followed a careful strategy of diversification into related areas, which included entry into the plain paper copying business. It first entered the PPC market with Japanese-built copying machines and then staged an entry into the higher-volume segments. This sequential entry was similar to that of Ricoh and Nashua.

The cost of mobility or of shifting the corporate orientation can be examined by an in-depth study of Olivetti, which provides yet another example of single-technology firm becoming a related-product company. One of the leaders in the typewriter industry, Olivetti changed its orientation, during the 1970s, from an electro-mechanical technology enterprise to an electronics firm. To the accompaniment of a series of organizational changes, it entered the reprographics market in addition to several related high-technology areas. It also veered towards a strategy of international co-operation (e.g., alliance with AT&T).

The study of the reprographic industry has also suggested that technological change creates a compulsion for firms to redefine their business. The quicker the pace of technological change, the more ready and better prepared the firms must be to acquire new technologies, enter new industries and adopt multi-market strategies. It was seen that the single-technology firms of half a century ago which failed to do this found themselves relegated to an insignificant position, while the successful firms were those that continually redefined the concept of their business across industry boundaries. Thus, Canon and Minolta enlarged their business definition and utilized the skills gained in the manufacture of precision optimal instruments to enter the copying industry; Nashua transformed itself quickly from a coating-technology business into an international copying machine business; Ricoh, from being principally a supplier of consumables to the Japanese market, made itself into a manufacturer of copying machines for the world market, as did Konishiroku, which was earlier a film and camera manufacturer. The example of Xerox is even more pertinent. Having built and sustained a remarkably profitable monopoly based on the exploitation of a single technology, it transformed itself between 1975 and 1980 into an information technology firm, consciously redefining its role to make a place for itself in the new electronic communications industry.

Redefinition of the business is an ongoing process, which continually calls for choices to be made in the face of technological uncertainty. The question of why some firms are able to change with the times while others are not has come to the fore in this study. Explanations of the phenomenon can probably be found by an examination of the following factors:

1 the effects of vertical integration;
2 the rigidity of managerial attitudes;
3 the behavioral consequences of organization structure.

As Phillips (1971) argued, vertically integrated firms often spend far too much time tying their products – jet engines to aircraft, spare parts to machinery, supplies to hardware. Rumelt (1974) also found the 'dominant-vertical' firms to be the worst performers. These observations seem to fit in with Klein's theory about the quest for micro-stability at the expense of dynamic efficiency. The case histories of Gestetner, Rotaprint and Ozalid support this view. It appears that vertical integration also reinforces the organizational factors constraining adaptation.

Rigidity of managerial attitudes is probably the prime cause of firms sticking to their narrow definition. Penrose (1959) argued that managers were conditioned by their past experiences and did not attempt to gain superiority under new conditions; rather, they attempted to set up protectionist barriers. This self-perpetuation and inability to exploit productive investment opportunity acted as a limitation on the growth of the firm.

Organizational inertia or managerial inability to cope with change do not, unfortunately, lend themselves to measurement or easy observation. There are serious difficulties here, not the least of which stem from the lack of workable concepts. Some of the existing behavioral frameworks, such as 'mechanistic' vs 'organic' structure (Burns and Stalker, 1961), could, however, be applied to track this important dimension. These organizational behavior concepts need to be integrated into the industrial organization and strategy models to form an eclectic paradigm of inquiry. Admittedly, this is an amorphous area for future research, but it also has the promise of leading to a strategic theory of the firm.

REFERENCES

Abell, D. F. (1980) *Defining the Business: The Starting Point of Strategic Planning.* Englewood Cliffs, NJ: Prentice-Hall.

Burns, T. and Stalker, G. M. (1961) *The Management of Innovation.* London: Tavistock Publications.

Caves, R. E. (1980) Industrial organization, corporate strategy, and structure (A survey). *Journal of Economic Literature,* 18 (1), 64–92.

Chandler, A. D. (1962) *Strategy and Structure: Chapters in the History of Industrial Enterprise,* Cambridge, Mass.: MIT Press.

—— (1977) *The Visible Hand: The Managerial Revolution in American Business.* Cambridge, Mass.: Harvard University Prses.

Channon, D. F. (1973) *The Strategy and Structure of British Industry.* Cambridge, Mass.: Harvard University Press.

Cooper, A. C. and Schendel, D. E. (1976) Strategic responses to technological threats. *Business Horizons,* February, 61–9.

Engler, G. N. (1965) *The typewriter industry: the impact of a significant technological innovation.* Unpublished doctoral dissertation, University of California.

Freeman, C. (1982) *The Economics of Industrial Innovation* (2nd edn). London: Frances Pinter.

Gemery, H. A. (1967) *Productivity growth, process change, and technical change in the United States glass industry, 1899–1935.* Unpublished doctoral dissertation, University of Pennsylvania.

Golding, A. M. (1971) *The semiconductor industry in Britain and the United States: a case study in innovation, growth and the diffusion of technology.* PhD dissertation, University of Sussex.

Hannah, L. (1976) *The Rise of the Corporate Economy.* London: Methuen.

Hart, P. E. and Clarke, R. (1980) *Concentration in British Industry 1935–1975.* Cambridge: University Press.

Hill, C. T. and Utterbank, J. M. (eds), (1979) *Technological Innovation for a Dynamic Economy.* Oxford: Pergamon Press.

Hofer, C. W. and Schendel, D. E. (1978) *Strategy Formulation: Analytical Concepts.* St Paul, Minn.: West Publishing.

Jewkes, J., Sawers, D. and Stillerman, R. (1958) *The Sources of Invention.* New York and London: Macmillan (2nd edn 1969).

Kamien, M. J. and Schwartz, N. L. (1982) *Market Structure and Innovation.* Cambridge: University Press.

Klein, B. H. (1977) *Dynamic Economics.* Cambridge, Mass.: Harvard University Press.

Knight, K. E. (1963) *A study of technological innovation: the evolution of digital computers.* Unpublished doctoral dissertation, Carnegie Institute of Technology, Pittsburgh.

Leontiades, M. E. (1980) *Strategies for Diversification*, Boston, Mass.: Little, Brown.

Majumdar, B. A. (1977) Innovations, product developments and technology transfers: an empirical study of dynamic competitive advantage: the case of electronic calculators. Unpublished doctoral dissertation, Case Western Reserve University.

Mansfield, E. (1968) *Industrial Research and Technological Innovation. New York: W. W. Norton.*

McGee, J. and Thomas, H. (1986) Strategic groups: theory research and taxonomy. *Strategic Management Journal*, 7, 141–60.

Norris, K. and Vaizey, J. (1973) *The Economics of Research and Technology.* London: Allen & Unwin.

Pope, R. and Hoyle, B. (1984) *British Economic Performance, 1880–1980.* Beckenham: Croom Helm.

Pavitt, K. (ed.) (1980) *Technological Innovation and British Economic Performance.* London: Macmillan.

Penrose, E. T. (1959) *The Theory of the Growth of the Firm.* Oxford: Basil Blackwell.

Phillips, A. (1971) *Technology and Market Structure.* Lexington, Mass.: D. C. Heath. (See particularly Chapter 1.)

Porter, M. E. (1981a) The contributions of industrial organization to strategic management. *Academy of Management Review*, 6 (4), 609–20.

—— (1981b) Strategic interaction: some lessons from industry histories for theory and anti-trust policy. In S. C. Salop (ed.), *Strategy, Predation and Economic Analysis*, pp. 449–506, Washington, DC.: Federal Trade Commission.

—— (1983) The technological dimension of competitive strategy. In R. Rosenbloom (ed.), *Research on Technological Innovation, Management and Policy*, Vol. 1. Greenwich, Conn.: JAI Press.

Rumelt, R. P. (1974) *Strategy, Structure and Economic Performance.* Cambridge, Mass.: Harvard University Press.

Samuelson, P. A. (1976) *Economics*, pp. 734–5. New York: McGraw-Hill.

Scherer, F. M. (1980) *Industrial Market Structure and Economic Performance.* Chicago: Rand McNally.

Schumpeter, J. A. (1942) *Capitalism, Socialism and Democracy.* New York: Harper & Row.

—— (1966) *The Theory of Economic Development.* Cambridge, Mass.: Harvard University Press.

Stoneman, P. (1983) *Economic Analysis of Technical Change.* Oxford: University Press.

Yale, J. P. (1965) *Innovation: the controlling factor in the life-cycle of the synthetic fiber industry.* Unpublished doctoral dissertation, New York University.

Commentary on Chapter 5

Paul Stoneman

Schumpeter defined technological advance as involving up to five possible types of change: new products, new processes, new management methods, new sources of raw materials, and new markets. Similarly, industrial structure is a multi–dimensional concept, encompassing the number and size distribution of producers, their degree of diversification, the extent of vertical integration and the degree of product differentiation within and across producers. That the two – technological change and market structure – should be closely interrelated should come as no surprise. Even within the now somewhat discredited structure–conduct–performance paradigm so favoured in the early industrial organization literature, this link was recognized, if not emphasized. That technological change might affect the degree of scale economies available to the firm, and thus the number of firms that might profitably co-exist in an industry, was a link in one direction; in the other direction, that firm size might affect the return to R&D goes back to Schumpeter.

This chapter by Ghazanfar, McGee and Thomas (G, M and T) attempts to move beyond this characterization of the link by emphasizing two particular themes.

1 Market structure should be treated as a dynamic rather than a static concept. The structure of an industry is in a continual process of change. This process is linked to changes in technology. Thus, as time passes and technology changes, markets and industries will, for example, experience changes in products and processes, the entry of new and exit of old firms, changes in relative sizes as some firms grow and others decline, and even changes in industry boundaries as product characteristics change. These latter changes may even lead to the integration of two previously separated industries, such as computers and telecommunications.

2 The mapping from technological change into changes in industry structure is neither unique nor automatic. Changes in technological opportunities will affect industry structure only as producers and potential producers exploit the opportunities. These exploitation decisions may be labelled strategic decisions. Thus, the link between changes in technology and changes in industry structure is corporate strategy.

G, M and T explore these themes within an analysis of the reprographics industry in the UK. The paper represents a useful and most interesting beginning to the analysis of this linkage between technology, corporate strategy and industry structure.

Within the paper I noticed on several occasions that observations were being made with regard to the reprographics industry that relate to findings in literatures with which I am more familiar. I pick out a couple of these:

1 G, M and T observe in the reprographics industry that new products often inspire updating or improvements of older products. I first came across this phenomenon in Harley (1973), where the change from wooden to iron ships was being discussed.

2 G, M and T lay emphasis at times on the patent system. The protection afforded by patents in this industry (especially to Rank-Xerox) may be atypical. Mansfield *et al.* (1981) suggest that, except in pharmaceuticals, patents offer very little protection.

The main point I wish to make, however, is that this paper is just a beginning. As an economist working on the economics of technological change in the industrial organization literature, I think that what I missed most in the paper was a degree of formalization with which I am familiar in my own subject area. It is no surprise that I should consider this as a possible way to proceed from this beginning. Hints of how one may do this might be discovered in three particular literatures.

1 There is now an extensive literature (see for example Williamson, 1975) on vertical integration that might usefully be explored to see how changes in technology may change the optimal degree of integration.

2 Recently, the work of Shaked and Sutton (1982), particularly on horizontal and vertical product differentiation, may provide some insight into how firms place themselves in product characteristics space and how changes in technology may affect this.

3 The growing and extensive literature on the diffusion of new technology (see for example Stoneman, 1983) may well provide some insight into the nature of substitution of one technology for another, which G, M and T consider is not well known.

These literatures may also give us an insight into why rather than what, and it is some understanding of why different firms select different strategies that I found to be a shortcoming of the paper. Similarly, I considered that the endogeneity of technological change did not receive sufficient attention. The determination of the direction of technical change is as much an instrument of corporate strategy as are reactions to exogenous technological advance. However, I do not wish to be particularly critical. I am in agreement with the general themes of the paper. The fact that I can see other lines of argument that might be pursued is completely consistent with the status of the paper. It is a beginning rather than an end.

REFERENCES

Harley, C. K. (1973) On the persistence of old techniques: the case of North American wooden shipbuilding. *Journal of Economic History*, 33, 372–98.
Mansfield, E. *et al.* (1981) Imitation costs and patents: an empirical study. *Economic Journal*, 91, 907–18.
Shaked, A. and Sutton, J. (1982) Relaxing price competition through product differentiation. *Review of Economic Studies*, 49, 3–13.
Stoneman, P. (1983) *The Economic Analysis of Technological Change*. Oxford: University Press.
Williamson, O. E. (1975) *Markets and Hierarchies*. London: Collier Macmillan.

6 Joint Ventures: A Mechanism for Creating Strategic Change

Kathryn Rudie Harrigan

Joint ventures are agreements among firms to work together to attain some strategic objective. They are a means for sponsoring firms to share their talents and resources in a manner that creates a superior competitive entity. The use of joint ventures (and other forms of co-operative strategy) has become particularly widespread since 1980 as successful competition within many types of industries has become more challenging (Berg *et al.*, 1982; Pate, 1969). Managers now recognize that they must learn to use joint ventures as a competitive weapon. Skills in using strategic alliances have become imperative because of the enormous potential that co-operative strategies possess as an instrument for creating strategic change.

Even if a firm itself does not enter joint ventures, its managers must understand the strategic impact of co-operative strategies, for they will undoubtedly face competitors that are jointly owned. Joint ventures can change an industry's profitability potential by allowing more firms to make the types of investments that were formerly reserved for leading players. They accelerate the pace of structural change. Strategic alliances permit firms to enter industries where they once lacked the wherewithal to do so alone, and they offer a frictionless means for hurdling the high exit barriers of industries where outright divestiture is infeasible. Finally, strategic co-operation accelerates the development of industry infrastructures and hastens technological obsolescence.

DEFINITIONS

Joint Ventures

'Joint ventures' are strategic alliances whereby two or more owners create a separate entity. They combine partners' resources and skills in the joint

Based on materials contained in K. R. Harrigan, *Strategies for Joint Ventures*, 1985, and K. R. Harrigan, *Managing for Joint Venture Success*, 1986, both published by Lexington Books, Lexington, Mass. Permission to use is gratefully acknowledged. Research support from the Strategy Research Center, Columbia University, and suggestions from its Chairman, William H. Newman, are also gratefully acknowledged.

venture's operations. Examples include Himont (Montedison and Hercules), General Numeric (Fujitsu and Siemens A.G.) and Rank-Xerox (the Rank Organization and Xerox). 'Minority investments' also involve shared equity, but they do not create a separate entity and are not the focus of this chapter.

Co-operative Agreements

For the purposes of this chapter, the term 'co-operative agreements' refers to all *non-equity* forms of co-operation. General Electric's arrangements with Northern Telecom, Hitachi, Volkswagen and Allegro Robots (which do not involve shared ownership) are co-operative agreements.

Profitability Potential

This study of joint ventures addresses changes in the profitability potential of industries, and changes in the sponsoring firms' relationships with the industries with which they co-operate, that result from their strategic alliances. The notion that an industry's structural traits determine its profitability potential draws on a body of research from industrial organization economics (which has been applied to the formulation of corporate strategy by Porter, 1980, and many others). Briefly, analysis of industry structure suggests whether firms can expect to enjoy the above-normal profits (that is, any profits above the 'normal' profits needed to pay capital costs, etc.) that would be needed to keep ongoing firms investing in an industry by competing in a particular industry.

Industry analysis is properly conducted in a 'dynamic' framework; that is, changes in the forces that affect an industry's profitability potential should be forecast, whether those changes are driven by (1) controllable (endogenous) forces, like an expansion of productive capacity, (2) uncontrollable (exogenous) forces, such as federal deregulation, or (3) something in between on the competitive continuum, like the ability of an individual firm to influence whether or not its competitors expand their productive capacity; and the changing profitability expected from these changes should guide firms' resource allocations to and competitive behaviors within that industry. The hypotheses of this study are concerned with how the use of joint ventures changes their respective competitive environments and how various industry forces affect each other. We would expect that changes in industry forces that determine an industry's profitability potential will affect whether sponsoring firms will use the *shared-equity* form of co-operative strategy (or a non-equity form) and whether they will grant substantial *operating autonomy* to their venture (regardless of their venture's ownership form). We would also expect that changes in certain structural traits move together with changes in other industry traits to create evolving industry environments. My investigation identifies this gestalt of change forces and examines their evolutionary effect on profitability potential in 23 US industries over the years 1924–85.

THE STRATEGIC IMPORTANCE OF CO-OPERATIVE STRATEGIES

The use of joint ventures is scarcely new; they are one of the oldest ways of transacting business in Europe, and were originally used as a commercial device by the merchants of ancient Egypt, Babylonia, Phoenicia and Syria to conduct overseas commercial transactions. The data base for this study is unusual, however, in the sense that it is concerned with 'domestic' ventures (those undertaken voluntarily in sponsoring firms' home markets) rather than those used as an instrument of a firm's international strategy and subject to host government coercion. The economy where these ventures were undertaken was mature, and its social services infrastructure – hydroelectricity, roads, hospitals and schools, for example – as well as its commercial infrastructure – such as sources of supply, distribution channels and the availability of skilled labor, – was well established (although the commercial infrastructure of a particular industry, such as genetic engineering, may as yet be undeveloped).

Motives for Co-operation

Previous studies of co-operation have suggested many motives for the forming of joint ventures. These include the creation of internal strengths, risk-sharing and uncertainty reduction (Harrigan, 1985, 1986; Pfeffer, 1972; Pfeffer and Nowak, 1976; Pfeffer and Salancik, 1978). Many firms have formed strategic alliances in the past because (1) the costs of investing in the skills and assets needed to keep pace with rivals has risen beyond their means of tolerance for risk (Orski, 1980; Williamson, 1975), and (2) co-operation was required as the ticket of admission into the overseas markets of industries like aerospace (Killing, 1983; Schwartz, 1975). Firms are now co-operating in environments where they never did in the past because competition within many industries has become more demanding. Adaptation to the skills of co-operation – rather than competition – has become particularly important as the success requirements within these industries have evolved to levels that many firms cannot satisfy alone.

Joint Ventures and Strategic Change

When firms form joint ventures, their co-operation functions as a structural change in the venture's industry because it has the potential to change (1) which firms can enter the venture's market-place (and how successful entry will be achieved), and (2) which firms are forced to abandon the venture's market-place (and how their exit will be effected), as well as (3) the optimum technological scale (and configuration of buyer–supplier relationships) for successful operations (Wilson, 1975). Co-operative strategies facilitate structural change because they enable firms to expand (or contract) productive capacities in a relatively frictionless manner that does not affect industry-wide price levels as adversely as large-scale capacity adjustments undertaken alone. Joint ventures may change the requirements for competitive success by (4) creating (or changing) component standards or product configurations, by (5) linking the value-creating activities of upstream and downstream firms to create more effective, vertically integrated entities, or by (6) changing firms' competitive behaviors. In such cases, co-operative ventures may be considered to be *strategic investments* in the parlance of Porter (1980, ch. 8).

Several assumptions (suggested by field interviews) underlie this investigation of how joint ventures act as a mechanism for strategic change. First, I assume that risk-averse, sponsoring firms prefer to maintain strategic flexibility as they venture; thus, I assumed that sponsoring firms prefer the form of co-operative strategy that seems to be less risky in the light of surrounding industry conditions. (For example, they will prefer highly flexible arrangements when they venture into highly volatile or uncertain situations.) Second, I assumed that sponsoring firms seek operating control over their sources of competitive advantage; thus, I assumed that their control preferences affect the range of operating autonomy granted to their ventures.

HYPOTHESIS DEVELOPMENT

Tests of joint ventures as a mechanism for strategic change involve an examination of the gestalt of dynamic forces which define an industry's competitive environment, as well as tests of the effects of co-operative strategies on competitive environments. Since these forces may interact with each other over time – each propelling subsequent changes in the other which, in turn, precipitates additional changes – a cascade of testable hypotheses was developed to capture these relationships. Categories of variables were used to isolate the dynamic relationships of joint ventures on competition and of competitive forces on the choice of co-operative strategy firms embraced. These variables are operationalized in table 6.1 and include: (1) venture form, (2) venture autonomy, (3) asymmetries in partners' relationships with their ventures, (4) partner-to-partner relationships, (5) asymmetries in partner's traits, (6) industry dynamics and (7) control variables (representing static industry traits). (Recent values of the industry dynamics variables were used as *dependent* variables in the tests that follow; earlier values of these variables were used as *independent* variables in tests of how changes in industry traits move together.)

Asymmetries in Partners' Relationshps with Their Ventures Variables

Asymmetries in horizontal linkages with ventures Informal (non-equity) forms of control over co-operative arrangements were expected to be sufficient when both parents were horizontally related to their venture. This relationship was expected because horizontal ties between owner and venture were expected to reduce the need for equity ownership and avoid destructive competition between parallel business units. Because the threat of jealousies (by sponsoring firms' wholly owned business units) regarding the venture's activities was expected to be greater between partners that were both horizontally related to their venture, non-equity forms of co-operation that do not create a separate entity were expected to be used more frequently where both partners were horizontally related to their venture. Thus, a negative relationship with both venture form and autonomy was expected. Co-operation to form ventures that were horizontally related to both parents was expected to encourage the venture's industry to develop a more formalized infrastructure, increase concentration, increase product viability (thereby encouraging demand growth) and accelerate the pace of technological obsolescence, because such forms of co-operation do not function like the entry of a new industry participant.

Asymmetries in vertical linkages with ventures Informal (non-equity) forms of control over co-operative arrangements were not expected to be sufficient when both parents were vertically related to their venture. Instead, buyer–seller (vertical) relationships between owner and venture were expected to *increase* the need for equity ownership. Because a formal buyer–supplier relationship between owners and their venture was more likely to exist where both partners were vertically related to their venture, a positive relationship with venture form was expected; but since the child of co-operation between vertically related parents was likely to represent the 'bottleneck' step in a vertical chain of processing, a negative relationship with venture autonomy was expected. Co-operation to form ventures that were vertically related to both parents was expected to encourage demand growth, increase concentration in the venture's industry and accelerate the pace of technological obsolescence, because such co-operation functioned like an infrastructure development investment.

Asymmetries in relatedness linkages with ventures Informal (non-equity) forms of control over co-operative arrangements were expected to be sufficient when the activities of both parents were closely related to those of their venture. Relatedness between owner and venture was expected to *reduce* the need for equity ownership. Because the venture was expected to be more likely to generate animosities (between partners' wholly owned business units) where the venture's facilities and activities duplicated those of its parents, non-equity forms of co-operation that did not create a new competitor were expected to be used more frequently where the ongoing activities of both partners were related to those of their venture. Thus, a negative relationship with venture form was expected. The greatest venture autonomy was expected where the venture's activities were *not* related to the ongoing activities of its parents. Co-operation to form ventures that were related to the ongoing activities of sponsoring firms was expected to accelerate the pace of industry infrastructure development, accelerate the pace of technological obsolescence in the venture's industry and lower industry exit barriers.

TABLE 6.1 Variable construction and hypotheses, as they relate to the co-operative strategy embraced

				Construction	Hypotheses
1 Horizontal linkages	0.4	0.5	−	Index: dummy variable indicating whether parent 1 is horizontally related to child times dummy variable indicating whether parent 2 is horizontally related to child	Informal (non-equity) forms of control over co-operative arrangements are sufficient when both parents are horizontally related to their venture. Horizontal ties between owner and venture reduce the need for equity ownership.
2 Vertical linkages	0.1	0.3	+	Index: dummy variable indicating whether parent 1 is vertically related to child times dummy variable indicating whether parent 2 is vertically related to child	Informal (non-equity) forms of control over co-operative arrangements are not sufficient when both parents are vertically related to their venture. Buyer–seller (vertical) relationships between owner and venture increase the need for equity ownership.
3 Relatedness linkages	0.6	0.5	−	Index: dummy variable indicating whether the activities of parent 1 are related to those of its child times dummy variable indicating whether the activities of parent 2 are related to those of its child	Informal (non-equity) forms of control over co-operative arrangements are sufficient when the activities of both parents are closely related to those of their venture. Relatedness between owner and venture reduces the need for equity ownership.
4 Horizontal partners	0.4	0.5	+	Dummy variable indicating whether partners are horizontally related	Horizontally related partners (which are more likely to be homogeneous in their outlooks) are more likely to use shared equity forms of co-operation.
5 Vertical partners	0.3	0.4	−	Dummy variable indicating whether partners are vertically related	Vertically related partners (which are more likely to have heterogeneous outlooks) are less likely to use shared equity forms of co-operation.
6 Firm nationalities	0.6	0.5	−	Index: dummy variable indicating whether parent 1 is a US firm times dummy variable indicating whether parent 2 is a US firm	Partners with common national origins tend to be more homogeneous and less likely to need shared ownership forms of co-operative arrangements.

7 Size asymmetry	20.7	15.8	−	Absolute value of difference between scaling (0–99) indicating the size of partner 1 and scaling (0–99) indicating size of partner 2	Partners of substantially different asset sizes are more heterogeneous and less likely to use shared equity forms of co-operation.
8 Experience asymmetry	4.0	4.5	−	Absolute value of difference between parent 1's no. of co-operative arrangements and parent 2's no. of co-operative arrangements	Partners of substantially different experience in the use of co-operative strategy are more heterogeneous and less likely to use shared equity forms of co-operation.
9 Changes in growth	2.4	8.8	−	Percentage change (pre-1971–8 and 1978–84) in sales growth rate	Substantial changes in demand increase competitive volatility and reduce the attractiveness of shared equity (and shared decision-making) arrangements.
10 Changes in infrastructure	9.8	8.3	−	Percentage change (pre-1971–8 and 1978–84) in the formality of industry structure (based on a scaling 0–99) indicating (a) extent of upstream and/or downstream vertical integration, (b) height of entry barriers, and (c) extent to which product standards are well established	Substantial changes in (a) vertical integration relationships, (b) product standards and (c) the height of entry barriers leading to a better established industry structure reduce the need for uncertainty-reducing arrangements, such as equity joint ventures.
11 Changes in concentration	−0.89	1.5	+	Percentage change (pre-1971–8 and 1978–84) in the market shares of the industry's four largest competitors	Substantial increases in competitors' market share concentration reduces the likelihood that competition will be volatile. Statesmanlike behavior increases the environment's relative attractiveness for using more enduring forms of strategic alliance, such shared equity ventures.
12 Changes in technology	1.3	2.6	−	Percentage change (pre-1971–8 and 1978–84) in the no. of years between obsolescing product and/or process innovations	Substantial changes in the rate of technological obsolescence reduce the attractiveness of equity joint ventures (and other less flexible forms of co-operation).

Cont'd.

TABLE 6.1 Cont'd.

Variable name	Mean	Std. Dev.	Expected Sign	Contruction	Hypothesis
13 Changes in height of exit barriers	0.14	0.3	+	Percentage change (pre-1971–8 and 1978–84) in an index: (a) the durability and specificity of physical assets, and (b) the significance of goodwill created by promotional and advertising investments	Substantial increases in exit barriers increases firms' propensities to use price-cutting forms of competition and reduces firms' strategic flexibility. Recognition of these risks decreases their willingness to use shared equity forms of strategic alliance.
14 Changes in the relative importance of personnel resources to value-creation	0.03	0.2	+	Percentage change (pre-1971–8 and 1978–84) in an index: (a) training and skill levels required personnel who deal with customers, (b) importance of product and/or process protection to competitive success, and (c) whether an individual's specific talents add significantly to a product's differentiation	Substantial increases in the importance of talented personnel to value-creation increases firms' needs for shared equity forms of strategic alliance, including joint ventures with firms' entrepreneurial employees

15 Demand uncertainty	53.7	27.7	+	Scaling (0–99) indicating perceived variability in growth of unit sales, pre-1971–84	High demand uncertainty increases firms' propensities to form equity joint ventures (and other stabilizing forms of co-operative arrangements).
16 Capital intensity	54.9	21.8	+	Scaling (0–99) indicating relative proportion of capital to labor in value-creating assets	Capital intensity (and inflexible assets) increases the attractiveness of forming equity joint ventures (and other less flexible forms of co-operative arrangements).
17 Products are services	29.6	40.1	+	Scaling (0–99) indicating proportion of product offering which is a service	The high co-ordination needs associated with delivering services of high quality increase the need to form equity joint ventures (and other less flexible forms of co-operation).
18 Customer sophistication	60.2	24.1	+	Scaling (0–99) indicating customers' abilities to discern meaningful differences among vendors' products	Highly sophisticated customers increase the need for the type of close co-ordination between parent and child associated with shared equity forms of co-operation.
19 Global markets	62.5	40.1	–	Scaling (0 to 99) indicating extent to which standardized products can be sold to customers in diverse geographic markets	The presence of diverse geographic markets that will accept standardized products reduces the attractiveness of shared equity (and shared decision-making) arrangements.

Partner-to-Partner Linkages Variables

Horizontal partners   Horizontally related partners – those firms that were engaged in making the same products, serving the same markets, using the same technologies and engaging in the same kinds of competitive activities – were expected to be *more* likely to use shared equity forms of co-operation. Since horizontally related firms were expected to be more likely to be similar in their outlooks and to value decisions more similarly than were partners that were not horizontally related, a positive relationship with venture form was expected. Moreover, co-operation among horizontally related ventures was expected to encourage demand growth (by creating viable products faster than if each partner entered alone), encourage industries' infrastructures to develop faster, increase concentration and accelerate the pace of technological obsolescence.

Vertical partners   Vertically related *partners* – those firms that have a buyer–seller relationship with each other – were expected to be *less* likely to use shared equity forms of co-operation. Since vertically related firms were expected to be more likely to have dissimilar outlooks and to value decisions differently (because of the constant tug-of-war between them to capture greater portions of profit margins available from their value-adding activity) than were firms that were not vertically related, a negative relationship with venture form was expected. Co-operation among vertically related partners was expected to encourage infrastructure development in their ventures' industries.

Asymmetries in Partners' Attributes Variables

Asymmetries in partners' nationalities   Partners with common national origins were expected to be more homogeneous and less likely to need shared ownership forms of co-operative arrangements in order for a venture to be formed. Because partners with common national backgrounds were expected to be more homogeneous in their outlooks and to value decisions more similarly, they were expected to need the formal shared equity forms of co-operation *less* frequently than partners from disparate national backgrounds, and a negative relationship with venture form was expected. Co-operation among partners of the same national origins was expected to increase demand growth, accelerate infrastructure development, increase concentration in the venture's industry, accelerate the pace of technological obsolescence and lower exit barriers in the venture's industry.

Sponsoring firms' size asymmetries   Because partners of substantially different asset sizes were expected to be more heterogeneous, they were expected to be less likely to use shared equity forms of co-operation. This relationship was expected because partners of substantially different asset sizes are less likely to be able to afford to fund and support their ventures in the same manner. For this reason, non-equity arrangements among them were expected to be used more frequently than formal, shared equity ventures; thus, a negative relationship with venture form was expected. Co-operation among partners of similar sizes was expected to increase concentration in their venture's industry, accelerate the pace of technological obsolescence and lower industry exit barriers.

Partners' venturing experience asymmetries Partners of substantially different experience levels in the use of co-operative strategy were expected to be more heterogeneous and less likely to use shared equity forms of co-operation. Because I expected an experience curve to be associated with the successful use of co-operative strategies (and because partners with substantial disparities in their experience base were expected to be less likely to have homogeneous outlooks regarding how their co-operative relationship should proceed), non-equity forms of co-operation were expected to be more likely to be used when such partners co-operate. Thus, a negative relationship with venture form was expected. However, co-operation among partners with similar experience levels in using co-operative strategies was expected to *increase* the venture's operating autonomy. Co-operation among partners with similar experience levels concerning the use of co-operative strategies was also expected to increase concentration within the venture's industry, accelerate the pace of technological obsolescence and reduce industry exit barriers.

Industry Dynamics Variables

Changes in demand growth Substantial changes in demand were· expected to increase competitive volatility and reduce the attractiveness of shared equity (and shared decision-making) arrangements. Positive changes in demand growth were expected to encourage the use of shared equity ventures, but large changes in demand were expected to reduce the venture's operating autonomy and the use of the joint venture form of co-operation because both decrease firms' strategic flexibility.

Changes in the formality of an industry's infrastructure Substantial structural changes (as an industry evolves from an embryonic one to an established one) in (1) the extent of upstream or downstream vertical integration relationships, (2) the extent to which product standards were well established, and (3) the height of entry barriers leading to a better established industry structure were expected to reduce the need for uncertainty-reducing arrangements, such as shared equity forms of co-operation. In defining the gestalt of industries' competitive environments, changes in the formality of an industry's infrastructure were expected to be found where technology changed rapidly, larger minimum efficient scale plants became required for competitive success and new firms entered the industry easily. Great shifts in the infrastructure were expected to be positively associated with the use of co-operative strategies, but venture autonomy was expected to be low where an industry evolved rapidly from an embryonic infrastructure to a better established infrastructure.

Changes in competitors' market share concentration Substantial increases in industry concentration were expected to reduce the likelihood that competition would be volatile. In defining the gestalt of industries' competitive environments, increasing concentration was expected to be positively associated with growing demand, more formalized industry infrastructures, rapid technological change and higher exit barriers. Increasing concentration was not expected to be positively associated with great infrastructural turmoil. Instead, the emergence of a few leading competitors was expected to reduce price competition and other volatile competitive behavior. Increasing concentration was expected to encourage the use of shared equity forms of co-operation and to increase venture autonomy.

Changes in the pace of technological obsolescence Substantial changes in the rate of technological obsolescence were expected to reduce the attractiveness of equity joint ventures (and other less flexible forms of co-operation). In defining the gestalt of industries' competitive environments, rapid changes in technological obsolescence were expected to be positively associated with growing demand, infrastructural turmoil (because product and/or process standards were expected to be constantly changing) and fragmented industry structures (Ewing, 1981; Gold, 1975). Rapid technological change was not expected to encourage the use of shared equity forms of co-operation, nor was it expected to encourage high venture autonomy (depending upon the nature of the parent–child relationship and on where the child obtained its technological resources).

Changes in the height of exit barriers Substantial increases in exit barriers – in (1) the durability and specificity of physical assets, and (2) the significance of goodwill created by promotional and advertising investments, for example (Caves and Porter, 1976) – were expected to increase firms' propensities to use price-cutting forms of competition and to reduce firms' strategic flexibility. Recognition of these risks was expected to decrease firm's willingness to use shared equity forms of strategic alliance and to decrease the venture's operating autonomy.

Changes in the relative importance of personnel resources to value added Substantial increases in the importance of talented personnel to value-creation – especially in (1) the training and skill levels required of personnel who deal with customers, (2) the importance of product and/or process protection to competitive success, and (3) whether an individual's specific talents added significantly to a product's differentiation – were expected to increase firms' needs for shared equity forms of strategic alliance, including joint ventures with firms' entrepreneurial employees. Such conditions were also expected to require the venture to enjoy greater operating autonomy.

Control Variables

The control variables include estimates of demand uncertainty, capital intensity, service content of products, customer sophistication and global markets. These are static measures (not dynamic ones) determined by industry conditions when the venture was formed.

Demand uncertainty High demand uncertainty is expected to increase firms' propensities to form equity joint ventures (and other stabilizing forms of co-operative arrangements). In defining the gestalt of industries' competitive environments, erratic patterns in shipment volumes and other sources of demand uncertainty is expected to be positively associated with very rapid increases or decreases in demand (as is found in the endgame as well as in the 'take-off' stages of new businesses). Demand uncertainty is also expected to be positively associated with the early years of industry evolution, with rapid technological obsolescence and with highly fragmented industry structures (Akerloff, 1970). Since joint ventures were expected to be undertaken in part to reduce demand uncertainties, a positive relationship with venture form was expected, along with a negative relationship with venture autonomy. (A venture's autonomy determined whether the venture (1) shared physical facilities, personnel, distribution channels and/or intelligence with one or more of its sponsoring firms, or was in some other way a captive of its parents, or (2) was free to use other market access, other marketing campaigns, outside suppliers (or distributors), outsiders' technical standards or technology, and/ or to hire personnel from the outside. The venture's sponsors were expected to co-ordinate its actions closely with their own when demand uncertainty was high.)

Capital intensity Capital intensity and inflexible assets increase the attractiveness of forming equity joint ventures (and other less flexible forms of co-operative arrangements). In defining the gestalt of industries' competitive environments, capital-intensive technologies were expected to be positively associated with environments of growing demand (which motivate firms to invest in new and often capital-intensive technologies with larger productive capacities). They were also expected to be positively associated with environments that were growing more formalized in their infrastructure relationships (especially those characterized by market share consolidation). Because managers may consider ventures based on the sharing of tangible, physical assets to be less risky than ventures based on the sharing of intangible and easily appropriated sources of competitive advantage, a positive relationship with venture form and venture autonomy was expected.

Service content of products   The high co-ordination needs associated with delivering services of high quality were expected to increase the need to form equity joint ventures (and other less flexible forms of co-operation). In defining the gestalt of industries' competitive environments, products with high proportions of services (rather than manufactured outputs) were expected to be positively associated with relatively young and growing industries. They were also expected to be positively associated with industries that were highly sensitive to the value-adding contributions of personnel resources, with fragmented industry structures and with a very rapid pace of technological change. Given their great dependence on flexible assets, products with high proportions of services were not expected to be positively associated with high exit barriers. Since the effective delivery of services requires careful co-ordination between owners and their ventures in all activities of a value-adding enterprise, a positive relationship with venture form was expected. But given the highly appropriable source of competitive advantage that lies in most service-intensive products, a positive relationship with venture autonomy was not expected.

Customer sophistication   Highly sophisticated customers were expected to increase the need for close co-ordination between parent and child often associated with shared equity forms of co-operation. In defining the gestalt of industries' competitive environments, highly sophisticated customers were expected to exhibit resistance to purchasing products at premium prices when they saw little justification to doing so and to resist standardized product solutions. Accordingly, the presence of sophisticated customers was expected to retard demand growth. Sophisticated customers were expected to be positively associated with fragmented and non-global industry structures, with rapid technological obsolescence and with high exit barriers. Sophisticated customers were not expected to be sensitive to the value-adding contributions of personnel resources. The strategic inflexibiity anticipated in the presence of strong customers was expected to be particularly intense where ventures and parents both served the same powerful customers. As with the example of effective service offerings, the presence of highly demanding customers was expected to require careful co-ordination between all parts of the value-adding activities of owners and ventures, and a positive relationship with venture form was expected. Venture autonomy was expected to be high in order for ventures to be flexible enough to satisfy highly demanding customers.

Global markets   The presence of diverse geographic markets that accept standardized products was expected to reduce the attractiveness of shared equity and shared decision-making arrangements. In defining the gestalt of industries' competitive environments, global markets were expected to be positively associated with growing demand, fragmented industry structures, an accelerating pace of technological obsolescence and a high sensitivity to the value-added contributions of personnel resources. Because the difficulties of co-ordinating actively involved partners' value-creating activities across several geographic boundaries (as would be necessary to pursue aspects of a global strategy) were expected to exacerbate partners' frustrations with each other, a negative relationship with venture form and autonomy was expected.

METHODOLOGY

Information concerning firms' co-operation strategies and the competitive environments where strategic alliances were formed was obtained in three stages: (1) construction of background papers on each industry using archival data; (2) validation, using field interviews and survey questionnaires (completed in advance of the delphi interviews), and (3), a three-round delphi-method questionnaire (see Harrigan, 1985).

Sample Design

The framework sketched above was tested by studying 895 strategic alliances competing in 23 industries during the years 1924–85. The industries were selected according to a taxonomy that was developed from observable traits, including the industries' (1) capital intensity, (2) service content as a proportion of total value added, (3) pace of technological obsolescence, (4) stage of infrastructure development, (5) product differentiability, (6) customer standardization from one geographic market to another and (7) growth in unit sales. This taxonomy was used to ensure that various features which make industries relatively attractive or unattractive environments for strategic alliances would be represented in my sample. Field studies were used to examine the following industries: automobiles (3.5 per cent of total sample), communications equipment (3.9 per cent), communications services (7.2 per cent), computers and peripherals (4.9 per cent), electronic components (12.1 per cent), engines (4.1 per cent), farm and industrial equipment (1 per cent), financial services (8 per cent), heavy machinery (3.3 per cent), light machinery (0.6 per cent), medical products (4.9 per cent), metals fabrication (0.8 per cent), metals processing (1.2 per cent), mining (2.9 per cent), office equipment (4.5 per cent), petrochemicals (14.2 per cent), pharmaceuticals (4.9 per cent), precision controls (3.3 per cent), programming – films (0.4 per cent), programming – packaging (4.9 per cent), software and data bases (2.9 per cent), steel (3.7 per cent), and videotape recorders and videodisc players (2.5 per cent).

Limitations

The many differences among industries in structural traits and competitive behaviors, the many differences in firms' co-operative strategies and the differences in their relationships with partners and with their ventures call for conservatism in the degree of confidence that can be placed in these data. Although great care was taken in conducting the study, delphi is an inherently subjective research methodology, and the findings should therefore be interpreted with great caution.

Replicating studies that did not question the same managers whom this study interviewed might obtain different estimates of these variables; however, similar values would be likely to result if the study were repeated with other subjects because managers were advised of their own previous estimates (as well as the range of estimates supplied by other respondents in their respective industries) as each round of the delphi inquiry progressed. If different industries were used, different estimates might result, but I would expect the relationships between industry forces and co-operative strategies to be similar.

Dependent Variable Construction

A description of measurements follows for the changes in the competitive environments where co-operative strategies were employed. (1) *Venture form* was estimated by a dummy variable indicating whether the strategic alliance involved shared equity (a joint venture) or not (other forms of co-operation) (2) *Venture autonomy* was estimated by a scaling (from 01 to 99) indicating whether the venture (a) shared physical facilities, personnel, distribution channels and/or intelligence with one or more of its sponsoring firms, or was in some other way a captive of its parents, or (b) was free to use other market access, other marketing campaigns, outside suppliers (or distributors), outsiders' technical standards or technology, and/or to hire personnel from the outside. (3) Changes in *demand growth* were estimated using the percentage change (from 1978 to 1984) in sales growth. (4) Changes in the formality of an industry's *infrastructure* (as it evolved from an embryonic condition to an established one) were estimated using the percentage change (from 1978 to 1984) in formality of industry structure (based on a scaling from 01 to 99) – indicating (a) the extent of upstream and/or downstream vertical integration, (b) the height of entry barriers, and (c) the extent to which product standards are well established. (5) Changes in *industry-wide concentration* were estimated from percentage changes (from 1978 to 1984) in market shares of the industry's four largest competitors. (6) Changes in the pace of technological *obsolescence* were estimated using percentage changes (from 1978 to 1984) in the number of years between obsolescing product and/or process innovations. (7) Changes in the height of *exit barriers* were estimated using the percentage change (from 1978 to 1984) in an index scaled from 01 to 99: (a) the durability and specificity of physical assets, and (b) the significance of goodwill created by promotional and advertising investment. (8) Changes in the relative importance of *personnel resources* to value added were estimated using the percentage change (from 1978 to 1984) in an index scaled from 01 to 99: (a) training and skill levels required personnel who deal with customers, (b) importance of product and/or process protection to competitive success, and

(c) whether an individual's specific talents add significantly to a product's differentiation. Change variables covering the earlier period, from pre-1971 to 1978, were used as independent variables to estimate more recent changes in the dependent variables described above.

Independent Variables: Measurement and Rationale

Independent variables were constructed as follows: (1) Asymmetries in partners' *horizontal linkages* with their venture were estimated using an index, a dummy variable indicating whether parent 1 is horizontally related to the venture multiplied by a dummy variable indicating whether parent 2 is horizontally related to the venture. (2) Asymmetries in partners' *vertical linkages* with their venture were estimated using an index, a dummy variable indicating whether parent 1 is vertically related to the venture multiplied by a dummy variable indicating whether parent 2 is vertically related to the venture. (3) Asymmetries in partners' *relatedness linkages* with their venture were estimated using an index, a dummy variable indicating whether the activities of parent 1 are related to those of its venture multiplied by a dummy variable indicating whether the activities of parent 2 are related to those of its venture. (4) *Horizontal partners* were estimated using a dummy variable indicating whether partners were horizontally related in a substantial portion of their products, markets, technologies and competitive activities. (5) *Vertical partners* were estimated using a dummy variable indicating whether partners are vertically related (that is, have a buyer–seller relationship with each other) in a substantial portion of their business activities. (6) Asymmetries in sponsoring firm *nationalities* were estimated using an index, a dummy variable indicating whether parent 1 is a US firm multiplied by a dummy variable indicating whether parent 2 is a US firm. (7) Partner *size* asymmetry was estimated using the absolute value of the difference between a scaling (from 0 to 99) indicating the asset size of partner 1 and a scaling (from 0 to 99) indicating the asset size of partner 2. (8) Partners' venturing *experience* asymmetry was estimated using the absolute value of the difference between parent 1's number of co-operative arrangements and parent 2's number of co-operative arrangements. (9) The independent industry dynamics variables were constructed in the same manner described above in the discussion of dependent variables, except that the independent change variables estimate the effects of forces that operated in the earlier period, prior to 1978. (The dependent variables measure changes that occurred in the ventures' industries in the period 1978–84.) (10) Demand *uncertainty* was estimated using a scaling (from 0 to 99) indicating perceived variability in the growth of unit sales. Demand uncertainty was considered to be high when there were large variations in yearly volumes shipped to the venture's market segments. (11) *Capital intensity* was estimated using a scaling (from 0 to 99) indicating the relative proportion of capital to labor in the value-creating assets used to serve the venture's customers. (12) The *service* content of a venture's products was estimated using a scaling (from 0 to 99) indicating the proportion of the product offering that was a service rather than a manufactured product. Since the effective delivery of services requires careful co-ordination between owners and ventures of all parts of a value-adding enterprise, the venture autonomy and service content variable were not used together as independent variables in model specifications. (13) *Customer sophistication* was estimated using a scaling (from 0 to 99) indicating customers' abilities to discern meaningful differences among vendors' products in the market segments served by a venture. (14) *Global markets* were estimated using a scaling (from 0 to 99) indicating the extent to which standardized products could be sold successfully to customers in diverse geographic markets.

Model Specification

An ordinary least-squares regression model was chosen to estimate the effects of industry dynamics on the gestalt of forces that make for a competitive environment and on venture form and operating autonomy because the individual contributions of each class of predictor variable (indicated by their standardized beta coefficients) were of interest. The model could be stated in the following form:

$$y_i = a_i + b_{ij} + e_i$$

where y_i equals the dependent variables – venture form, venture autonomy, changes in demand growth, changes in formality of industry infrastructure, changes in competitors' market share concentration, changes in the pace of technological obsolescence, changes in exit barrier heights and changes in the relative importance of personnel resources to value added, respectively. The independent variables, x_{ij}, correspond to a coding scheme where i (= 1, 2, –, 8) represents the structural equation's number, and where j (= 1, 2, –, 19) corresponds to the independent variables as numbered in table 6.1. Results are presented to illustrate how the competitive forces in ventures' industries has changed over time, and how the use of co-operative strategies changes in the presence of these competitive forces.

RESULTS

Results from the ordinary least squares models are presented and discussed in the following sections.

Venture Form

Asymmetries in partners' relationships with their ventures and with each other   The variable denoting asymmetries in partners' horizontal links with their ventures is negatively signed and statistically significant in the abbreviated results shown in table 6.2 suggesting that ventures that are horizontally related to both sponsoring firms tend *not* to be of the shared equity form. The variable denoting asymmetries in partners' vertical links to their ventures is positively signed and statistically significant, suggesting that ventures that are vertically related to both sponsoring firms *do* tend to be of the shared equity form. The partners' relatedness to their ventures' activities variable is negatively signed, but it is not statistically significant. The unrelated diversification relationship between parent and child variable is positively signed, but it is not statistically significant. The partners' horizontal relationships with each other variable is positively signed, but it is not statistically significant. The partners' vertical relationships with each other variable is negatively signed and is statistically significant.

Results suggest that horizontal ties between owner and venture led firms to avoid destructive competition between parallel business units by eschewing shared equity arrangements (but the relationship is not strong). Similarly, relatedness between the activities of parent firms and those of their venture were more likely to create jealousies (between partners' wholly owned business units and ventures). Buyer–seller (vertical) relationships between owner and venture *increase* the need for shared equity forms of co-operative strategy.

Asymmetries in partners' attributes The variable denoting ventures where partners are all US firms is positively signed, but it is not statistically significant. The variable denoting asymmetries in partners' asset sizes is negatively signed and statistically significant. The asymmetries in partners' co-operative strategies experiences variable is negatively signed.

Results suggest that significant differences in partners' asset sizes discourage the use of the shared equity form of co-operative strategy. Significant differences in partners' experience levels also *discourage* the use of the shared equity form of co-operation (but the relationship is not strong).

Industry dynamics variables The demand growth variables suggest that shared equity forms of co-operation are more likely to be used where demand is increasing. Results suggest that big increases in the rate of demand growth encourage the use of shorter-lived forms of co-operation – such as short-term sourcing arrangements, temporary cross-marketing arrangements and other highly flexible forms of co-operation – perhaps as stop-gap measures until demand stabilizes. The concentration variables are positively signed, but not statistically significant. Industry concentration does *not* appear to affect the form of co-operative strategy that firms embrace.

The industry infrastructure variables suggest that the shared equity form of strategic alliance is used more frequently where industry infrastructures are formally developed than in embryonic industries – where (1) upstream or downstream vertical integration relationships and (2) product standards, for example, are well established. The result reflects a pattern whereby 18.6 per cent of the financial services ventures were announced when the industry was

TABLE 6.2 Table of results – standardized betas

	Regression on:							
	Venture form (1)	Venture autonomy (2)	Changes in industry-wide demand growth (3)	Changes in formality of infrastructure (4)	Changes in industry concentration (5)	Rate of changes in technology (6)	Changes in height of exit barriers (7)	Changes in the importance of personal resources in value-creation (8)
Venture form	–	0.13***	-0.17***	-0.14***	0.06**	-0.09***	-0.11***	-0.07**
Horizontal linkages	-0.19***	-0.13***	0.01	–	0.17***	–	–	–
Vertical linkages	0.06*	-0.05***	0.07**	–	0.15***	–	–	–
Relatedness linkages	–	0.03	0.07*	-0.29***	0.02	0.06***	-0.20***	–
Unrelated diversification	–	0.06**	–	0.12***	–	–	–	–
Horizontal partners	0.03	0.05	–	0.13***	–	-0.01	–	–
Vertical partners	-0.08**	-0.03	–	–	–	-0.03	–	–
Firm nationalities	–	0.02	0.06**	–	-0.06*	-0.02	-0.04	–
Size asymmetry	-0.09**	0.03	0.00	–	-0.10***	0.05***	-0.04	–
Experience asymmetry	-0.03*	-0.12***	0.03	–	0.12***	-0.08***	0.04***	–
Earlier changes in growth	-0.15***	-0.13***	-0.14***	–	–	-0.19***	0.07**	–
Recent changes in growth	-0.12***	–	–	–	–	–	–	–
Earlier changes in infrastructure	0.02	-0.14***	-0.02	-0.39***	–	-0.01	-0.03	–
Recent changes in infrastructure	-0.15***	–	–	–	–	–	–	–
Earlier changes in concentration	0.03	0.14***	0.42***	-0.12***	-0.03	0.23***	-0.02	–
Recent changes in concentration	0.06	–	–	–	–	–	–	–

	(1)	(2)	(3)	(4)	(5)	(6)	(7)	(8)
Earlier changes in technology	0.07	0.67***	0.17***	−0.24***	—	0.81***	−0.10***	—
Recent changes in technology	−0.25***	—	—	—	—	—	—	—
Earlier changes in exit barriers	−0.09**	−0.23***	—	—	—	—	0.45***	—
Recent changes in exit barriers	−0.07*	—	—	—	—	—	—	—
Earlier changes in the importance of value-creating personnel resources	0.07**	−0.10***	—	—	—	—	—	0.48***
Recent changes in the importance of value-creating personnel resources	−0.03	—	—	—	—	—	—	—
Demand uncertainty	0.27***	−0.08***	0.18***	0.32***	−0.21***	0.10***	0.14***	0.16***
Capital intensity	—	0.12***	0.44***	−0.17***	0.15***	0.01	—	0.19***
Products are services	0.07*	−0.17***	0.17***	0.12*	−0.14***	0.11***	−0.13***	—
Customer sophistication	−0.02	0.20***	−0.07**	—	−0.05	−0.03	−0.08**	−0.11***
Global markets	−0.18***	−0.28***	0.14***	−0.02	−0.24***	0.04*	0.06*	0.07**
Intercept	0.00***	0.00***	0.00***	0.00***	0.00	0.00	0.00***	0.00***
Corrected R^2	0.3142	0.6024	0.3618	0.5660	0.2721	0.7901	0.4387	0.2755
F-statistic	18.25	62.98	31.11	104.70	25.33	206.56	49.13	56.28
(d.f.)	(872)	(873)	(878)	(883)	(881)	(875)	(880)	(885)
Significance	***	***	***	***	***	***	***	***
Mean	0.62	35.3	2.50	8.84	−0.89	0.71	0.14	0.03
(st. dev.)	(0.48)	(24.8)	(8.81)	(14.19)	(1.51)	(1.42)	(0.28)	(0.22)

*** $p = 0.01$ ** $p = 0.05$ * $p = 0.10$

very young. Similar patterns exist for medical products (22.9 per cent), pharmaceuticals (29 per cent), software (20 per cent), and videotape cassette recorders and videodisc players (28.6 per cent). Results suggest that environmental changes that increase infrastructure formality *reduce* the use of shared equity forms of co-operation, indicating that the co-operative arrangements that were once sufficient for industries' success requirements grow out-of-synch with those requirements over time as infrastructures evolve. The 'best' co-operative strategies for a particular competitive environment at a particular time cannot necessarily be used in the same way later as competitive conditions change.

The recent pace of technological change variable is negatively signed and statistically significant, but the earlier pace of technological change variable is not. Although the recent and earlier changes in the pace of technological obsolescence variables have conflicting signs, the pace of technological change variables suggest that rapid rates of technological change discourage firms from using highly inflexible forms of co-operation – such as shared equity ventures. The height of exit barriers variables suggest that recognizable increases in the height of exit barriers discourage the use of the shared equity form of co-operation. Instead, one infers that firms embrace more flexible forms of co-operation when exit barriers rise. The importance of personnal resources in value creation variables have conflicting signs. The earlier changes in the relative importance of personnel resources to the value-added variable is positively signed and statistically significant while the recent change variable is negatively signed and not statistically significant. Results suggest that, where the contributions of personnel resources to value added became more important during the period before 1978, they *encouraged* the use of the shared-equity form of co-operation (but the relationship is not strong).

Control variables The demand uncertainty variable is positively signed and statistically significant, suggesting that erratic patterns in shipment volumes are often one motivation for the use of shared equity forms of co-operative strategy. The services variable is positively signed and statistically significant, suggesting that the shared equity form of co-operation is used more frequently where services constitute a high proportion of product content, but the values of its standardized beta coefficients were not high. The customer sophistication variable is not statistically significant. The global markets variable is negatively signed and statistically significant, suggesting that non-equity forms of co-operation are used where industries are global to increase firms' strategic flexibility.

Summary The demand uncertainty, global markets, changes in demand growth, changes in the pace of technological obsolescence and size asymmetry variables offer the greatest explanatory power in estimating which form of co-operative strategy will be employed. The partner-to-partner linkages variables do not add much explanatory power to the models of venture form, but results concerning horizontal linkages between sponsors and ventures suggest that less formal forms of strategic alliance are preferred where the venture does not create a new industry entrant. These findings suggest that partners' traits are *less* important in determining which co-operative strategy to embrace than industry traits are.

Venture Autonomy

Venture form   The joint venture variable is positively signed and statistically significant, suggesting that shared equity ventures are associated with greater operating autonomy for ventures. In a pre-1978 sample, the standardized beta value indicated an even stronger explanatory power than for the later ventures, because more stand-alone ventures were formed during those earlier years than were formed after 1983.

Asymmetries in partners' relationships with their ventures and with each other   The variables denoting asymmetries in partners' horizontal and vertical links with their ventures are negatively signed and statistically significant, but the partners' relatedness to their ventures' activities variable is not statistically significant. The partners' unrelated diversification variable is positively signed and statistically significant. The partners' horizontal relationships with each other variable is positively signed, but it is not statistically significant. Nor is the partners' vertical relationships with each other variable. The variable denoting ventures where partners are all US firms is positively signed, but it is not statistically significant. Nor is the variable denoting asymmetries in partners' asset sizes. The asymmetries in partners' co-operative strategies experience variable is negatively signed and statistically significant. Results suggest that co-operation to form ventures that are (1) horizontally related or (2) vertically related to both parents *decreases* ventures' operating autonomy, but co-operation to form ventures that are unrelated to both parents *increases* venture autonomy. Market relationships among sponsoring firms do not have a strong effect on venture autonomy, but the relationship is not strong. Having parents that are not equally comfortable with the use of co-operative strategies reduces ventures' operating autonomy.

Industry dynamics variables   The earlier changes in demand growth variable is negatively signed and statistically significant. Results suggest that substantial increases in demand reduce the venture's operating autonomy – that is, whether the venture (1) shares physical facilities, personnel, distribution channels and/or intelligence with one or more of its sponsoring firms, or is in some other way a captive of its parents, or (2) is free to use other market access, other marketing campaigns, outside suppliers (or distributors), outsiders' technical standards or technology, and/or to hire personnel from the outside. The earlier changes in the formality of industry infrastructure variable is negatively signed and statistically significant. Results suggest that, as the venture's industry evolves from one with an embryonic infrastructure to a more established infrastructure, the venture loses its operating autonomy and is brought 'back into the fold' of its parents' operations.

The earlier changes in competitors' market share concentration variable is positively signed and statistically significant, indicating more operating autonomy. This result reflects the emergence of a few leading competitors, a change that reduces competitive volatility (by raising a pricing umbrella over the industry), thereby easing the venture's task of competing profitably with less assistance from its sponsoring firms. The variable's sign changes when the recent changes in concentration variable is tested. This result reflects the many new global competitors that have entered ventures' industries recently; concentration has decreased since 1978 in many ventures' industries. Results suggest that the recent influx of new rivals reduces venture autonomy; sponsoring firms wish to co-ordinate their defensive maneuvers closely with their child's activities when such changes occur.

The earlier changes in the pace of technological obsolescence variable is positively signed and statistically significant, reflecting the higher autonomy that should be enjoyed by ventures in fast-paced industries. The sign changes when the recent changes in the pace of technological obsolescence variable is used, reflecting the turmoil occuring in many ventures' industries. The earlier changes in the height of industry exit barriers variable is negatively signed and statistically significant, reflecting the lower operating autonomy that ventures enjoy in competitive settings where the risks of price-cutting are high.

The earlier changes in the relative importance of personnel resources to value-added variable is negatively signed and statistically significant. The sign changes when the recent changes in the relative importance of personnel resources to value-added variable is used, reflecting that many of the post-1983 ventures were announced in people-intensive industries where the skills and reputation of personnel resources played relatively greater roles in creating value within ventures. Results suggest that in such settings ventures enjoyed *greater* operating autonomy.

Control variables   The demand uncertainty variable is negatively signed and statistically significant in most specifications, suggesting that erratic patterns in shipment volumes are often associated with low venture autonomy. The capital intensity variable is positively signed and statistically significant, suggesting that venture autonomy is higher when technologies are capital-intensive. The services variable is negatively signed and statistically significant, reflecting that most of the service-intensive businesses in the sample do not enjoy much operating autonomy. The customer sophistication variable is positively signed and statistically significant, suggesting that ventures must have greater autonomy to satisfy highly demanding customers. The global markets variable is negatively signed and statistically significant. Results suggest that ventures do *not* enjoy operating autonomy when they are part of their sponsoring firms' systems for serving global markets.

Summary The strongest explanatory power describing venture autonomy is found in industry trait variables – in the pace of technological change, global markets, exit barrier height changes and customer sophistication variables. The venture form and horizontal linkages variables offer some explanatory power, but changes in industry traits influence venture autonomy more significantly.

Changes in Demand Growth

Venture form The joint venture variable is negatively signed and statistically significant, suggesting that shared equity ventures are associated with slow (or negative) growth in demand. Results confirm the use of joint ventures to consolidate excess capacity (thereby bolstering industry profitability) in very mature and declining industries, such as farm and industrial equipment (where all of the ventures formed occurred in the endgame), metal fabricating (50 per cent) and steel (66.7 per cent). Shared equity forms of co-operation were formed in 76.1 per cent of the industries where demand grew slowly (or declined). Most (31 per cent) of the non-equity ventures had been formed in environments, where demand had been growing rapidly; 49 per cent of all non-equity-ventures were operating in environments of rapidly growing demand in 1985.

Asymmetries in partners' relationships with their ventures and with each other The variable denoting asymmetries in partners' horizontal links with their ventures is positively signed. The variable denoting asymmetries in partners' vertical links to their ventures is positively signed and statistically significant, as is the partners' relatedness to their ventures' activities variable. The variable denoting ventures where partners are all US firms is positively signed, and statistically significant. The variable denoting asymmetries in partners' asset sizes is not statistically significant; nor are the asymmetries in partners' co-operative strategies experiences variable. Results suggest that co-operation to form ventures that are vertically related to both parents encourages demand growth, but the relationship is not a strong one. Similarities in partners' nationalities encourage demand growth, but the relationship is not strong.

Industry dynamics variables The earlier changes in demand growth variable are negatively signed and statistically significant although the variable's standardized beta coefficient does not indicate that it has as much explanatory power as the control variables. The earlier changes in the formality of industry infrastructure variable is negatively signed but not statistically significant. The earlier changes in competitors' market share concentration variable is positively signed and statistically significant, reflecting the early emergence of larger leading competitors, which encourages growth in demand because products offered by better established vendors are more credible to wary customers. The earlier changes in the pace of technological obsolescence variable is positively signed and statistically significant, reflecting that product and/or process improvements enable vendors to offer better products to their wary customers, which, in turn, encourages further demand growth.

Control variables   The demand uncertainty variable is positively signed and statistically significant, reflecting that erratic patterns in shipment volumes are often associated with extremes in demand growth – with very rapid increases or decreases in demand. The capital intensity variable is positively signed and statistically significant. Results suggest that capital-intensive technologies are associated with environments of growing demand, reflecting firms' investments in capacity expansions and new technologies while sales thrive. The services variable is positively signed and statistically significant, reflecting that most of the service-intensive businesses in the sample are experiencing increasing demand, especially in the portion of the sample where strategic alliances were announced after 1983. The customer sophistication variable is negatively signed and statistically significant, reflecting customers' resistance to purchasing products at premium prices when they see little justification in doing so. Results suggest that customers can be more demanding of their vendors when there is excess capacity in suppliers' industries. The global markets variable is positively signed and statistically significant. Results reflect that global industries enjoy the kind of growing demand that encourages firms to invest in global strategies, especially where strategic alliances were announced after 1983.

Summary   The changes in concentration and capital intensity variables exerted the strongest power over changes in demand growth. Although its explanatory power is less, the result concerning the venture form variable – which suggests that shared equity ventures squelch rapid dissemination of product information that might accelerate demand growth – is notable since it warns *against* excessively formal venturing arrangements when demand is growing rapidly.

Changes in Formality of Industry Infrastructure

Venture form   The joint venture variable is negatively signed and statistically significant, suggesting that shared equity ventures are not necessarily associated with developing greater formality in as yet poorly established or embryonic industry infrastructures. Results confirm the use of joint ventures within young industries such as medical products (37.1 per cent), which also ended while the industry was still young. (A similar pattern was found for the programming packaging (20.7 per cent) and petrochemical (22.8 per cent) industries; but using joint ventures seems to have *delayed* the consolidation of these industries, by allowing disparate approaches to serving market segments to survive longer, rather than accelerated them.) Thirty-six per cent of the shared equity ventures and 48 of the non-equity ventures were formed in industries where infrastructures had developed significantly greater formality; only 20 per cent of the shared equity ventures (and 38 per cent of the non-equity ventures) were formed in industries where infrastructures had changed little in their formality during an earlier time. One-third of the non-equity ventures (and 21 per cent of the shared-equity ventures) were in industries where infrastructures had increased substantially in formality in recent times.

Asymmetries in partners' relationships with their ventures and with each other The partners' relatedness to their ventures' activities variable is negatively signed and statistically significant. The partners' horizontal relationships with each other variable is positively signed and statistically significant, suggesting that, when horizontally related firms co-operate with each other, it encourages the industries in which they co-operate to evolve to more formalized infrastructures. The partners' vertical relationships with each other variable is positively signed and statistically significant, suggesting similar effects in the venture's industry when vertically related firms co-operate. Thus, although the standardized betas of the partner-to-partner linkages variables do not indicate the high explanatory power of the structural and technological change variables (reported below), their strong contributions indicate that, when horizontally related or vertically related partners co-operate, they help their ventures' industries to develop more formalized infrastructures. Results also suggest that co-operation to form ventures where both parents' activities are merely related to those of their ventures discourages their ventures' industry infrastructures from developing greater formality, perhaps by allowing disparate approaches to satisfying customer demand to coexist; but more study of this relationship is needed.

Industry dynamics variables The earlier changes in the formality of industry infrastructure variable is negatively signed and statistically significant, suggesting that the sample industries were subject to significant reversals in structural evolution trends. Structural turmoil in this sample was precipitated by (1) changes in industries' regulatory environments, (2) increasingly shorter product lives, (3) larger and riskier projects (hence higher capital requirements) needed to develop new processes and new product features, (4) entries by new competitors (that were supported by their respective federal governments), motivated by (5) industry maturation and/or stagnation in Japan and Europe, (6) improved communications and computational power and (7) the need for globalization in industries where competition was previously constrained to geographic boundaries. The earlier changes in competitors' market shares concentration variable is negatively signed and statistically significant, reflecting the structural turmoil suggested by the earlier structural variable. Finally, the earlier changes in the pace of technological obsolescence variable is also negatively signed and statistically significant, reflecting the riskiness of investments in product and/or process improvements that contribute to overall structural turmoil.

Control variables   The demand uncertainty variable is positively signed and statistically significant, reflecting that erratic patterns in shipment volumes are often associated with the process of industry evolution. The capital intensity variable is negatively signed and statistically significant, suggesting that the introduction of capital-intensive technologies is associated with environments that are consolidating. The services variable is positively signed and statistically significant, reflecting that most of the service-intensive businesses in the sample are relatively young and have been evolving better established infrastructures over the past decades. The global markets variable is negatively signed, but is not statistically significant, reflecting that savvy customers can prevent firms from offering them standardized product solutions. Knowledgeable customers may even keep the structures of industries fragmented and without well-accepted technological standards (although the evidence is weak in this specification).

Summary   The earlier changes in industry infrastructure, demand uncertainty and changes in the pace of technological change variables exerted the strongest power over subsequent changes in the formality of industry infrastructure. Although tests of the horizontal and vertical relatedness variables are not shown in table 6.2, other results suggest that joint ventures can delay the consolidation of some industries' infrastructures, rather than accelerate them. Horizontally or vertically related sponsors can encourage industry infrastructures to develop more rapidly, depending on how their venture is co-ordinated with their ongoing activities.

Changes in Competitors' Market Share Concentration

Venture form   The joint venture variable is positively signed and statistically significant, suggesting that shared equity joint ventures are associated with increases in competitors' market share concentration. Results confirm the use of joint ventures to consolidate excess capacity by creating longer surviving entities. Seventy-two per cent of the ventures in environments where concentration had increased substantially in earlier times were of the shared equity form, and 38 per cent of all shared equity ventures (and 25 per cent of all non-equity ventures) were in environments where concentration had increased substantially in earlier years; 20 per cent of all shared equity ventures were in industries where concentration had increased substantially in recent years.

Asymmetries in partners' relationships with their ventures and with each other The variable denoting asymmetries in partners' horizontal links with their ventures is positively signed, and statistically significant. The variable denoting asymmetries in partners' vertical links to their ventures is also positively signed and statistically significant, while the partners' relatedness to their ventures' activities variable is positively signed and statistically significant. The variable denoting ventures where partners are all US firms is negatively signed and statistically significant, as is the variable denoting asymmetries in partners' asset sizes. The variable denoting asymmetries in partners' co-operative strategy experiences is positively signed and statistically significant, suggesting that similarities in partners' experiences may also increase concentration in their ventures' industries. Results suggest that co-operation to form ventures that are vertically related to both parents increases concentration in the venture's industry, but the standardized beta coefficient's values suggest that the relationship is not as strong as those of the control variables. Similarities in partners' nationalities do not necessarily increase concentration, but similarities in their asset sizes may do so.

Industry dynamics and control variables None of the industry dynamics variables except the earlier changes in competitors' market share concentration variable has significant statistical power in predicting changes in concentration. The demand uncertainty variable is negatively signed and statistically significant, reflecting that erratic patterns in shipment volumes are often associated with fragmented industry structures. The capital intensity variable is positively signed and statistically significant. Results suggest that capital-intensive technologies are associated with environments of market share consolidation. The services variable is negatively signed and statistically significant, reflecting that most of the service-intensive businesses in the sample have not yet begun to consolidate. The customer sophistication variable is negatively signed but not statistically significant, suggesting that sophisticated customers may prevent the venture's industry from increasing in concentration. The global markets variable is negatively signed and statistically significant, and, like the demand uncertainty variable, its standardized beta coefficient is high. Results suggest that global industries discourage industry consolidation within a single national market.

Summary The demand uncertainty and global markets variables exert the greatest power over changes in industry concentration. Symmetry in sponsoring firms' relationships with their venture encourages concentration in the venture's industry, as do other similarities among sponsoring firms.

Changes in the Pace of Technological Obsolecence

Venture form The joint venture variable is negatively signed and statistically significant, suggesting that shared equity joint ventures are associated with slower paces of technological obsolescence. This result is scarcely surprising, because firms lose too much strategic flexibility by committing to shared equity arrangements in ventures with very short half-lives. Only 20 per cent of all shared equity ventures (and 37 per cent of all non-equity ventures) were formed in environments experiencing rapid rates of technological obsolescence in earlier years; 17 per cent of all shared equity ventures (and 38 per cent of all non-equity ventures) were formed in environments experiencing rapid rates of technological obsolecence in recent years.

Asymmetries in partners' relationships with their ventures and with each other The partners' relatedness to their ventures' activities variable is positively signed and statistically significant, suggesting that co-operation to form ventures that were related to the ongoing activities of both parents accelerated the pace of technological obsolescence in the venture's industry; but further study of this relationship is needed. The partners' horizontal relationships with each other variable is negatively signed, but not statistically significant. Nor is the partners' vertical relationships variable. The variable denoting ventures where partners are all US firms is negatively signed, but not statistically significant. The variable denoting asymmetries in partners' asset sizes is positively signed and statistically significant, suggesting that co-operation among partners of significantly dissimilar sizes *accelerates* the pace of technological obsolescence. The asymmetries in partners' co-operative strategies experiences variable is negatively signed and statistically significant, suggesting that significant differences in partners' venturing experience levels *reduces* the pace of technological obsolescence in the venture's industry, perhaps because their ventures cannot move as rapidly when parents are not equally comfortable with the use of co-operative strategies. Results suggest that the relationships between firms that co-operate to form ventures has little effect on the pace of technological obsolescence in the venture's industry. Similarities in partners' nationalities slow the pace of technological obsolescence, but the relationship is not strong.

Industry dynamics variables The earlier changes in demand growth variable is negatively signed and statistically significant. The earlier changes in the formality of industry infrastructure variable is negatively signed but not statistically significant. The earlier changes in competitors' market share concentration variable is positively signed and statistically significant, reflecting the power of leading competitors to encourage technological change. The earlier changes in the pace of technological obsolescence variable (which is positively signed, statistically significant, and has a very high standardized beta coefficient) suggests a *spiralling effect*, whereby the product and/or process improvements that made earlier technologies obsolete compound their effects by driving ventures' industries into further generations of technological obsolescence.

Control variables The demand uncertainty variable is positively signed and statistically significant, reflecting that erratic patterns in shipping volumes are often associated with rapid technological obsolescence. The capital intensity variable is positively signed but not statistically significant. The services variable is positively signed and statistically significant, reflecting that most of the service-intensive businesses in the sample are experiencing rapid technological change. The customer sophistication variable is negatively signed, but not statistically significant. Nor is the global markets variable. Results suggest that the recent globalization of several industries has contributed to the accelerating pace of technological obsolescence, but this relationship is weak since the variable's standardized beta coefficient value is not high.

Summary The changes in the pace of technological obsolescence variable exerts the strongest power over subsequent changes in the pace of technological obsolescence, reflecting the aforementioned spiralling effect in the pace of change seen in some ventures' industries. The changes in concentration and demand growth variables also exert greater influences over changes in the pace of technological obsolescence than do the partner-to-partner and sponsor-to-venture variables.

Changes in the Height of Exit Barriers

Venture form The joint venture variable is negatively signed and statistically significant, suggesting that shared equity-joint ventures are associated with lowered exit barriers. Joint ventures are being used as a form of 'fade-out divestiture' in industries such as steel, farm and industrial equipment, and perhaps even automobiles; hence these results should not be surprising. Thirty-seven per cent of all shared equity ventures were formed in industries with relatively low exit barriers in earlier years; 53 per cent of all shared equity ventures were formed in industries with relatively low exit barriers in recent years, suggesting that the exit barriers faced by some firms have *fallen* through the use of joint ventures.

Asymmetries in partners' relationships with their ventures The variable denoting asymmetries in partners' relatedness with their ventures' activities is positively signed, suggesting that co-operation to form ventures that are related to the ongoing activities of both parents lowers exit barriers (especially if parents pool their respective capabilities in their child). The variable denoting ventures where partners are all US firms is negatively signed, but not statistically significant; nor is the variable denoting asymmetries in partners' asset sizes. Results suggest that similarities in partners' nationalities *lower* exit barriers in ventures' industries, but the relationship is not strong. The asymmetries in partners' co-operative strategies experiences variable is positively signed and statistically significant, suggesting that significant asymmetries in experience levels *raises* partners' exit barriers in their ventures' industries.

Industry dynamics variables The earlier changes in demand growth variable is positively signed and statistically significant, confirming Harrigan's (1981) finding concerning the deterrent effects of expectations that an industry's environment will continue to be favorable. The earlier changes in the height of industry exit barriers variable is positively signed and statistically significant, as expected. The earlier changes in the formality of industry infrastructure variable is negatively signed but not statistically significant. Nor are the earlier changes in competitors' market share concentration variable. The earlier changes in the pace of technological obsolescence variable is negatively signed and statistically significant, suggesting that technological obsolescence overcomes the deterrent effects of other more favorable signals concerning the attractiveness of an industry's environment.

Control variables The demand uncertainty variable is positively signed and statistically significant, reflecting that erratic patterns in shipment volumes are often associated with high exit barriers because firms are less likely to exit from businesses where they harbor the belief that demand will strengthen (or resuscitate). The services variable is negatively signed and statistically significant, suggesting that most of the service-intensive businesses in the sample do not face high exit barriers in 1985. The customer sophistication variable is negatively signed and statistically significant, confirming Harrigan's (1981) earlier finding that unsophisticated customers' switching costs exert great negative effects on firms' abilities to exit. Reasoning from her findings, the deterrent effects of strong customer industries are expected to be especially strong where the venture's parents also serve these same customers and fear retaliation (against their wholly owned business units) by customers that they cut off from a source of supply. The global markets variable is positively signed and statistically significant. Results suggest that global industries require firms to pursue the kinds of strategies that increase their subsequent strategic inflexibility.

Summary No variable exerts as much power over changes in the height of exit barriers as the earlier changes in exit barriers height variable does. The venture relatedness variable suggests that joint ventures can reduce the exit barriers facing sponsoring firms by enabling them to divest incrementally.

Changes in the Relative Importance of Personnel Resources to Value Added

Venture form The joint venture variable is negatively signed and statistically significant, suggesting that shared equity joint ventures are not associated with activities where value creation is sensitive to the inputs of personnel resources.

The distribution of ventures by form was essentially identical regardless of the relative importance of personnel sources in earlier years, and this distribution changed little in recent years.

Industry dynamics and control variables The earlier changes in the relative importance of personnel resources to value added variable is positively signed, statistically significant and has the highest standardized beta coefficient values, as expected. Except for the changes in the pace of technological obsolescence variable (not shown), no other industry dynamics variable showed any explanatory power in this model. The demand uncertainty variable is positively signed and statistically significant, suggesting that erratic patterns in shipment volumes are associated with increases in the importance of personnel to adding value to the venture's products. The capital intensity variable is positively signed and statistically significant, suggesting that even capital-intensive technologies become more sensitive to the value-adding contributions of personnel resources as competition among firms progresses. The customer sophistication variable is negatively signed and statistically significant, suggesting that the contributions of personnel resources are less important when customers are sophisticated and choose to exert their bargaining power over vendors. The global markets variable is positively signed and statistically significant. Results reflect a commonplace confusion about the nature of global strategies: value that is added in marketing activites that are unique to each regional market *increase* the relative importance of personnel resources, while activities that can be standardized across the globe are less sensitive to the value-adding contributions of personnel resources.

Summary The industry dynamics variables do not exert much power over changes in the relative importance of personnel resources to value creation. Control variables and the earlier changes in the importance of personnel resources' contributions to value-added variables contribute the most explanatory power. Partners' attributes and sponsor–venture relationships had little effect on changing the importance of personnel resources' contributions to value added.

CONCLUSIONS

The longitudinal and cross-sectional tests presented herein have presented evidence concerning how the structural forces that determine an industry's profitability potential evolve over time, moving together (or in opposite directions) to change the competitive environments that firms face. From these results, we can predict which co-operative strategies are best suited to various competitive environments and what structural changes their use is likely to precipitate.

Conclusions Regarding the Impact of Structural Changes

Increasing industry concentration encourages demand growth and technological change. Rapid changes in technology encourage demand growth and create a spiralling effect whereby the effects of earlier product and/or process improvements are compounded in subsequent generations of innovation. Rapid changes in technology also overcome the exit barriers that expectations concerning demand growth may have created. Erratic swings in demand growth accompany changes in technology. Capital intensity is associated with industries that are developing greater infrastructure formality and increasing market share concentration, but the presence of sophisticated customers that exert their bargaining power over vendors can retard the pace of infrastructure development and slow the pace of market share concentration.

Results indicate that the contributions of personnel resources to value-added creation are less significant in the presence of sophisticated customers and global industries. The need for globalization also discourages industry consolidation within a single national market while it contributes to the accelerating pace of technological obsolescence in many industries. These results may be helpful for researchers seeking to represent industry forces in subsequent studies of competitive strategy. Knowledge of how industry forces move together is useful also to managers who use a dynamic analytical framework to forecast changes in the traits that will affect their venture's profitability potential.

Conclusions Regarding Form of Co-operative Strategy

Results from this study suggest that shared equity ventures are more likely to result where (1) sponsoring partners are both vertically related to the venture, (2) demand for the venture's product is increasing, (3) industry infrastructures are formally developed, (4) personnel contributions are very important to value creation, (5) growth in demand shifts erratically, and (6) services are an important part of the product offering. Non-equity forms of strategic alliance are more likely to result where (1) sponsoring partners are both horizontally related to the venture, (2) sponsoring firms are of very different asset sizes and venturing experience levels, (3) industry infrastructures are as yet undeveloped, (4) technologies change rapidly, (5) exit barriers are high, and (6) global strategies require sponsoring firms to maintain high strategic flexibility. Knowledge of the relationships between industry traits and venture form is useful to managers in predicting what types of jointly owned competitors they are most likely to face and how much operating autonomy from their sponsors these ventures will enjoy.

Conclusions Regarding Strategic Alliances as Change Agents

Results from this study have also established that joint ventures (and other forms of co-operation) have the potential to bring about structural changes in the forces which comprise an industry's competitive environment. Joint ventures consolidate excess capacity in slowly growing industries, while they may delay consolidation within embryonic industries. They are associated with increasing market share concentration, often brought about by consolidating the capacities of ongoing firms, and slower paces of technological obsolescence; also, they lower exit barriers' heights. Ventures among sponsoring firms that are horizontally related to their venture encourage infrastructure development and increasing market share concentration, while lowering exit barriers. Ventures among sponsoring firms that are merely related to their ventures' activities discourage the development of formal infrastructures (by allowing more disparate approaches to the satisfaction of customer demand to coexist longer) and accelerate the pace of technological obsolescence. Ventures among sponsoring firms that are vertically related to their ventures encourage demand growth and market share concentration, but slow the pace of technological obsolescence. Ventures between horizontally related partners encourage infrastructure development and market share concentration. Ventures between vertically related partners also encourage greater infrastructure formality. Similarities in sponsoring firms' nationalities encourage demand growth and slow the pace of technological obsolescence, while lowering exit barriers in the venture's industry. Similarities in sponsoring firms' asset sizes and venturing experience levels increase market share concentration and accelerate the pace of technological obsolescence, while possibly raising the heights of industry exit barriers. Knowledge of these change forces is useful to managers when selecting partners for their firms' respective venturing strategies.

The property of bringing about structural changes in an industry's competitive environment makes the decision to pursue co-operative alliances a strategic one that can have far-reaching structural implications for firms that do not use co-operative strategies to their best advantage. Results suggest that co-operative strategies can induce changes in firms' competitive environments by promulgating product standards, developing formal infrastructures in young industries and consolidating excess capacity in mature industries. The changes wrought by joint ventures, in turn, precipitate further changes in the profitability potential of firms' competitive environments. Thus, joint ventures must be added to the other competitive weapons in the strategist's arsenal, for they too have the potential to be a mechanism for promoting strategic change.

REFERENCES

Akerloff, G. A. (1970) The market for 'lemons': qualitative uncertainty and the market mechanism. *Quarterly Journal of Economics*, 84, 488–500.
Berg, S. V., Duncan, J. L., Jr. and Friedman, P. (1982) *Joint Venture Strategies and Corporate Innovation*. Cambridge, Mass.: Oelgeschlager, Gunn & Hain.

Caves, R. E. and Porter, M. E. (1976) Barriers to exit. In D. P. Qualls and R. T. Massson. *Essays in Industrial Organization in Honor of Joe S. Bain, chapter 3.* Cambridge, Mass.: Ballinger.

Ewing, K. P., Jr. (1981) Joint research, antitrust, and innovation. *Research Management,* 24 (2), 25–9.

Gold, B. (1975) Alternate strategies for advancing a company's technology. *Research Management,* 18, 24–9.

Harrigan, K. R. (1981) Deterrents to divestiture. *Academy of Management Journal,* 24 (2), 306–23.

—— (1985) *Strategies for Joint Ventures.* Lexington, Mass.: D. C. Heath, Lexington Book.

—— (1986) *Managing for Joint Venture Success.* Lexington, Mass.: D. C. Heath, Lexington Books.

Killing, J. P. (1983) *Strategies for Joint Venture Success.* New York: Praeger.

Orski, C. K. (1980) The world automotive industry at a crossroads: cooperative alliances. *Vital Speeches,* 47 (3), 89–93.

Pate, J. L. (1969) Joint venture activity, 1960–1968. *Economic Review* (Federal Reserve Bank of Cleveland), 16–23.

Pfeffer, J. (1972) Merger as a response to organizational interdependence. *Administrative Science Quarterly,* 17, 382–94.

—— and Nowak, P. (1976) Joint ventures and interorganizational interdependence. *Administrative Science Quarterly,* 21 (3), 315–39.

—— and Salancik, G. R. (1978) *External Control of Organizations: A Resource Dependence Perspective.* New York: Harper & Row.

Porter, M. E. (1980) *Competitive Strategy: Techniques for Analyzing Industries and Competitors.* New York: Free Press.

Schwartz, D. S. (1975) Comments on market-structure and interfirm integration. *Journal of Economic Issues,* 9 (2), 337–40.

Williamson, O. E. (1975) *Markets and Hierarchies: Analysis and Antitrust Implications.* New York: Free Press.

Wilson, J. W. (1975) Market structure and interfirm integration in the petroleum industry. *Journal of Economic Issues,* 9 (2), 319–36.

Commentary on Chapter 6

David Norburn

When I reviewed Kathy Harrigan's paper at the ESRC/Coopers & Lybrand Seminar at Warwick University, it exceeded 100 pages, each of which was concisely written. It is to her credit that, in the face of publication production constraints, this has been condensed to less than half of its previous length. However, just as wine increases its alcoholic potency when distilled, the strength of the paper is now analogous to cognac – wonderful in the after-taste, but difficult to take in large quantities. I view this paper as a refined and important contribution, unusual in its richness, but one which therefore demands distinct concentration.

My overall summary is that the chosen experiment has been carried out in a highly meticulous and scholastic manner, yet its clinical method of reporting unnecessarily bounds its impact. Of all academics active in joint venture research, Harrigan has made the largest contribution. Why, then, avoid interpreting these results from her perspective upon their implication for practitioners struggling to choose a weapon from their 'strategic arsenal'? To quote Larry Greiner, 'should any journal article be accepted without addressing the "practical implications" in more than two cursory paragraphs?' If the research had not been carried out as well as it has, this criticism would be entirely inappropriate. But the paper, being so important in its findings, has a responsibility to advance recommendations impinging upon the improvement of joint venture success in practice.

Right from the start, Harrigan emphasizes the importance of viewing joint ventures as a strategic choice, yielding potential competitive advantage. Methodically, she defines her terms of joint venture form, and its impact upon the profitability potential of industries, by underlining the 'dynamic' nature of the changing competitive position. She discusses the importance of co-operative strategies, grounding joint venture motives, and the logic of its intervention upon industry structures, from the literature. So far so good.

It is at this stage, however, that she makes a research choice which constrains the generalizability of her results. By restricting her source of data to US domestic joint venture activity, she deliberately chooses not to encompass joint ventures of a cross-national nature. While her research design undoubtedly strengthens the analysis within the geographic boundaries of the USA, I would much have preferred a wider geographic sample – for example, US joint ventures in the automobile industry within Pacific Rim and EEC countries. If joint ventures are to be regarded as strategic weapons impinging upon industry profit potential, it seems reasonable to study them within the context of global strategic choices. Despite this observation, however, I would be the first to acknowledge the research dilemma of intensive *v.* extensive choice.

The paper develops seven categories of variables from which to create hypotheses. This is carried out with great definitional precision, a characteristic of the author's style. In terms of the direction of expected relationships, I was pleased that she was prepared to advance her personal views based upon her own experience, rather than retreating into the current vogue of 'reference-dropping' so prevalent as a defensive habit in contemporary academic journals. (Galileo would find it tough to get past the review process of the twentieth century!) Her courage continues in the choice of delphi interviews in the collection of her data: far better to establish pieces of the strategic 'jigsaw' by subjective methodology than to abort the experiment on the altar of objective precision.

Given the welcomed element of personal subjectivity in hypotheses generation, and in the chosen research instrument, it is sad that, in contrast, the results are presented in such a dispassionate manner. Certainly they are extremely interesting; but, in terms of developing theory which is useful in practice, personal interpretation is both noticeably absent and badly needed. Even the final conclusion section merely summarizes the results already presented. If academic results are to be acted upon by the business world, it is the responsibility of scholars to provide direction.

I would therefore welcome certain additions, and certain modifications, to the paper. First, I would like to see a considerable increase in discussing the implications of these results from both an academic and practitioner perspective. The results need to be underpinned. Second, the longitudinal aspects of the data should be expanded. When should joint ventures be viewed as 'stepping-stones', and when as a vehicle leading to corporate metamorphosis? Third, given the availability of archival data, why not relate the form of co-operative strategy to measures of financial performance? Fourth, what hypotheses should now be advanced for further academic pursuit following these results? Fifth, what are the implications for government agencies in terms of anti-trust, and of interlocks? Despite these recommendations, I reiterate my judgement that the paper is a very important contribution to knowledge: perhaps, as with all good meals, one should leave the table feeling a little hungry.

So, what next for joint venture research? Three directions come to mind.

An obvious path would be to pursue this experiment on an international basis. I suspect that most joint venture activity will have a substantial element of global strategic implications – for example, the US automobile companies' involvement through equity stakes in Japanese, Korean and European corporations. Harrigan's methodology would be most useful here.

A second promising research avenue could be to develop the author's concept of the 'strategic arsenal'. Under what circumstances should joint venture be the chosen weapon, rather than outright acquisition? To what degree would companies be willing to trade corporate sovereignty and diminished control for financial benefit?

But it is a third avenue that I find the most appealing. Whereas the paper relates co-operative mechanisms to inanimate corporate or industry conditions, it is the process issues that are quite fascinating – the problems of integrating different managerial cultures and styles. Just as strategic management research has focused upon problems of implementation from its prior emphasis upon formulation, so too, I feel, will further research into the success or failures of joint ventures.

7 Management of Strategic Change in a 'Markets-as-Networks' Perspective

Lars-Gunnar Mattsson

INTRODUCTION

The theme of this book can be interpreted in different ways. My interpretation is as follows. If we agree that a firm's strategy describes major characteristics of its relations to the environment, then a strategic change implies major changes in these relations. However, strategic change can be caused both by the firm's strategy and by changes in the environment, e.g. by other firms' strategic activities. Thus the management of strategic change entails both the way in which management reacts to changes in the firm's relations to its environment and the management activities whose objectives are to cause strategic changes. A firm's strategy describes the principles by which the firm tries to realize strategic changes (or avoid unwanted such changes). Managing strategic changes involves managing activities that design, implement and control strategies.

Examples of strategic changes are a firm's entry to or exit from a market, change in the product/service assortment offered to customers, vertical integration or disintegration, growth or decline of a firm's sales volume in an absolute or a relative sense, or agreement on a co-operative venture with a competitor.

Strategic changes caused by others include those arising from a competitor's entry, an important supplier's exit, the acquisition of a distributor by a competing manufacturer, increased sales by the firm's customers to their own customers and co-operative ventures by the firms' competitors. Thus, individual firms' strategic changes are interdependent.

Strategic changes can be linked to a change in the firm's strategy or can be a part in a sequence of activities that implement a long-term strategy. For example, a change from indirect to direct distribution may be a strategy change, or part of a strategy to enter a market by indirect distribution and then sell directly to users as the firm's sales volume and market knowledge have increased.

It is obvious that this definition of strategic change, and the limited but nevertheless important link between the firm's own strategy and its strategic change, make it important how we describe the environment and the firm's relations to it. The aim of this chapter is to use a 'markets-as-networks' perspective on the environment and the firm's relations to it.

This implies some restrictions on what is included in the environment. I am concerned only with relations between firms in industrial systems, and not with the direct influence of the general social, economic and political environment.

This chapter was written as part of ongoing research efforts devoted to the development of the 'markets-as-networks' approach to which several Swedish researchers are contributing.[1] The application of these ideas to various functional fields such as marketing, purchasing and R&D, as well as to corporate and industrial policy issues, has resulted in some books and articles, but is still in a rather tentative stage.[2]

The chapter is organized as follows. First, a network approach is presented and some comparisons with other approaches to the study of industrial systems are made. Second, the general model for the analysis of management of strategic change, according to which my discussion is organized, is outlined. Third, network structure, the relationship between structure and strategy and the firm's strategic situation are treated as a preparation for the presentation, in the following section, of some generic firm strategies. After that I am ready to consider the management of strategic change. Finally, I arrive at some concluding remarks on research issues concerning strategic management which are raised by a network approach.

A NETWORK APPROACH[3]

Empirical studies of purchasing and marketing by firms on industrial markets have shown that firms devote considerable resources to interaction with other firms within rather long-term relationships, and that they are dependent on each other's resources in various ways (see e.g. Håkansson, 1982a). The relationships may reduce costs of exchange and production. They may also be helpful in a firm's knowledge development. Through relationships, the firm can acquire some control over its environment. It can also use a relationship as a bridge to a third party or to mobilize resources against other firms. Bonds of different kinds develop between firms, which means that there is a mutual adjustment between them. This has an influence on the exchange processes between firms, on the costs to switch to another seller or buyer and on the further adaptation processes. Industrial systems are composed of firms that are engaged in production, distribution and the use of goods and services. There is a division of work between the firms, but there are also changes in the activities of an innovative nature, the entry of new firms and the exit of old ones. We can regard the relations between the individual firm and its immediate, direct counterparts in the industrial system as individual relationships that are of some significance for both the firm and its counterparts. We can enlarge this notion of relationships to include all the other firms in the particular industrial system. Then the whole system can be regarded as a very complex network of relationships between firms. Each firm has direct or indirect relations to the other firms.

The activities in the network are complementary and/or competitive. It is easy to understand that a firm needs complementary activities performed by suppliers, distributors and users to make its own activities meaningful. It is also easy to see that other firms who sell substitutes carry out conflicting activities when they try to take over a customer's patronage. However, there are also important elements of conflict in the relations between complementary firms, which have to do with the characteristics of the exchange and adaptation processes. Between competitors there are also elements of complementarity between activities, not only when they co-operate to avoid competition or share common resources, but also, for example, when they are complementary suppliers to the same customer.

Co-ordination in the network takes place not through a central plan or organizational hierarchy, nor through the price mechanism of markets, but through interaction within the relationships.

Networks are stable in the sense that the dominant volume of products and services is transferred between firms whose relationships were established well before the individual transaction took place. However, the networks are also changing, in terms of the entry and exit of firms, the establishment of new relationships and in the disrupture of some of the old ones. A very important type of change is change within existing relationships and the indirect effects of such changes on other relationships. Changes within existing relationships are related to technical development, increases or decreases in volumes transferred, the adjustment of logistical systems and so on. Efforts are made by firms to maintain, develop and change such relationships. Bonds of various kinds that develop between firms include technical, planning, knowledge-based, social and legal bonds. These bonds can be exemplified by, respectively, product and process adjustments, logistical co-ordination, knowledge about the counterpart's strengths and weaknesses, personal confidence and liking, and long-term contracts.

Developments of relationships can be seen as investment processes, because the development takes time and resources, involves commitments for the future and creates assets that can be used by the firm in the future. The relationships give the individual firm access to external resources through exchange. Examples of such external resources are a supplier's capacity to manufacture products, a customer's financial capacity to pay, a distributor's sales organization, a customer's knowledge of the use situation and a customer's access to his own customers.

This model of the industrial system implies that the firm's activities are of a cumulative nature, i.e. that the activities in a specific time period and their effects are dependent on earlier activities and will have some influence on activities in the future.

The cumulative nature of the network activities makes the network 'positions' of the firm a seemingly useful concept (Mattsson, 1985). These positions characterize the roles that the firm has in the network. They can be defined according to:

1 the functions performed by the firm for other firms, e.g., a position as a full-function wholesaler of fine paper or as a manufacturer of stainless steel;
2 the relative importance of the firm in the network, e.g., its position as a dominant or a marginal firm;
3 the strength of the relationships with other firms, i.e., the strength of the bonds of different kinds that describe the relationships;
4 the identity of the firms with which the firm has direct relationships; e.g., firm A has a relationship with B and not with C.

We can define a firm A's position on a micro-level as a description of A's relationship to another individual firm, and on a macro-level as a description of A's relations to several firms in the network.

I define *strategic change* as a major change in the firm's network positions. The present network positions can be regarded as the firm's *strategic situation*. Present positions define restrictions and opportunities for the firm's future development.

To continue the discussion of the investment nature of activities in networks, let us make a distinction between the firm's internal assets, which it largely controls itself, and its market assets, which it only partially controls. The internal assets can be divided according to their functional use in, say, manufacturing assets and marketing assets. Examples of the former are factory buildings, machinery, manufacturing know-how and warehouse buildings, and of the latter, sales organization and market knowledge. The marketing assets give the firm access to some of the resources of other firms. A firm's position in relation to a distributor, for example, gives it some access to the distributor's facilities, know-how and customers. A firm's position in relation to a user gives it some access to the user's purchasing and problem-formulating capacities and to its own customers. It is obvious that there are interdependencies between investments in the different types of assets. There is a need to create some balance between these different assets. However, imbalances are also important, since they constitute driving forces for network development. The manufacturing assets might be too small for the marketing assets; for example, the position as dominant supplier cannot be upheld unless the firm increases its manufacturing capacity. The manufacturing assets might have changed qualitatively to create a mismatch with present marketing assets; for example, the positions to present suppliers may not generate certain input qualities. The marketing assets might be too small for the market assets; for example, the level of the salesforce's know-how may not match the increased need for technical assistance to the most important present customers.

The lack of balance between resources is an important driving force for investment processes to be initiated in different firms. There is never a perfect balance between the different assets. The network is too complicated for any firm, or group of firms, to be able to create a perfect 'balance'. Furthermore, investment activities in the network are not only of a complementary but also of a competitive nature. (See Johanson and Mattson, 1985, for a more detailed analysis of investments in networks.)

Comparison between a Network Approach and Some Other Bases for Analyses of the Management of Strategic Change

The network approach is here briefly discussed in relation to two research areas: research on marketing, and research on industrial organization.

Our 'network thinking' has been developed basically from studies of firms' behaviour in distribution systems and on industrial markets. It has been quite natural, then, to link our work both to industrial-organization-based studies of industrial systems and to frameworks developed by researchers on inter-organizational relations.[4] The links to literature on the individual firm's marketing and purchasing behaviour is evident in our publications. Comparisons are often made more or less explicitly with the typical 'marketing management' literature based on the 'marketing mix' concept (e.g. Kotler, 1984). The differences between the two approaches are emphasized (e.g. in Mattsson, 1985). Also, the industry-level studies often include a discussion about how the network approach differs from the traditional industrial organization studies and those analyses of competitiveness of firms and industries that are based on that microeconomic paradigm (Hägg and Johanson, 1982).

The marketing mix approach   The network approach stresses interaction over many time periods with individual counterparts, rather than one-period actions by sellers to stimulate reactions by aggregates of buyers. Marketing activities are of a more holistic nature, involving the whole company in the creation of exchange values. The development of resources is emphasized, rather than the optimal use of given resources. Our approach is less biased towards the output side of the firm. It specifically deals with the role of interaction between firms as a major determinant of the firm's innovative activity. Market information is to a large extent part of the commercial interaction, whereas the marketing mix approach stresses separate market research studies. Finally, the marketing mix approach puts rational planning by managers in selling companies into focus, while the network approach takes a less optimistic view on a firm's ability, in an analytical way, to 'plan' its future relations to the environment. As a marketing-oriented approach, the network model of the firm and the market seem to be closer to a corporate strategy orientation than the marketing management ideas, because of the holistic approach and the importance of long-term-oriented activities of an investment nature.[5]

Industrial organization studies In the traditional industrial organization literature, based on the structure–conduct–performance paradigm, the market is defined as comprising sellers of substitutes and buyers of substitutes. Thus, competitive behaviour between sellers is of major interest. Competition is lessened by co-operation between sellers. The structure of the market is defined by aggregated characteristics of the firms (concentration ratios, product heterogeneity, etc.). In the network approach, a 'market' is a system where both competitive and complementary activities are used as criteria for interdependency. The structure of the system is defined not by characteristics of the firms, but by characteristics of the relationships between firms. Activities that are instrumental in developing these relationships are 'equally important' as manufacturing activities themselves, whereas the latter are predominant in the economic analyses of an industrial organization nature.[6]

Corporate strategy writers, linked to the industrial organization perspective, tend to stress the competitive rather than the complementary nature of firms' activities (Porter, 1981). This is evident in Porter's basic model, where competitive pressures from firms presently among the sellers of substitutes, potential entrants, powerful buyers and powerful sellers are the basic driving forces. The subdivision of the competitive arenas into 'strategic groups' also emphasizes the structural characteristics of units rather than relationships. The idea that market share is an important measure and determinant of a firm's ability to compete successfully is a prevailing feature in many industrial-organization-based models of corporate strategy. In the network approach, both complementary and competitive interdependencies constitute criteria to be used to delineate the relevant networks.[7] The subdivision of these networks (comparable with the strategic groups) will contain not only 'sellers' but both sellers and buyers, possibly on more than two levels. The concept of 'market share' will be rather difficult to apply, since market share is an aggregated measure of certain aspects of the relationships, picked from a number of (possibly different) subsections of the network. This is not to say that the relative importance of the firm is irrelevant. Relative importance is part of the definition of network positions but, for example, the qualitative aspects of the relationships might be more crucial than the share of total sales of a specific type of product.

Traditional industrial organization analysis is a basis for many industrial policy programmes. Structural change initiatives are often based on scale economic notions. Production costs and investments or disinvestments in manufacturing resources are emphasized in the analyses. As to the relationships between firms, the need for mergers, for a rationalization of production through specialization and for co-operation between firms is a basis for programmes on the structural reorganization of industries (e.g. Shepherd *et al.*, 1983). On the demand side, usually more general environmental measures are taken, such as fostering or hindering international competition. Among the more specific demand-creating activities are government projects that require industrial activities among complementary firms. This is an example of industrial policies aiming at complementary activities, as is also government sponsorship of co-operation between firms for technology transfer projects. The latter types of industrial policies come closer to the network ideas.

A MODEL FOR THE ANALYSIS OF MANAGEMENT OF STRATEGIC CHANGE

Strategic change refers to a major (realized or anticipated) change in a firm's position in the network. By definition, strategic change for one firm implies strategic changes for other firms also. The firm's strategy is a major determinant of its strategic change. *Strategy* encompasses the principles governing the firm's conscious efforts to develop and direct its resources and its relationships to the environment. There are many ways in which such principles may be described. From an analytical point of view, strategies should be described in dimensions that are related to the theoretical framework used to analyse the firm's relations to its environment. *Strategic management* includes management activities to design, implement and control strategies, and may include direct conscious interaction with strategic management activities of other firms. Also, the direct relations between the firm's strategy and other firms' strategies are included in the conceptual scheme.

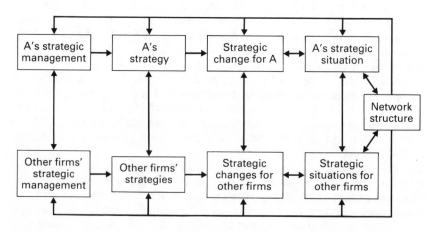

FIGURE 7.1   A model for the analysis of management of strategic change

Earlier, I stressed that the firm's present positions influence its development opportunities and restrictions. The present positions are part of the *network structure*, and the specific firm's present positions describe its *strategic situation*. The network structure and the strategic situation influence the design, implementation and control of the strategy.

There is also an influence in the other direction. Strategic changes for firms influence their strategic situations and thereby also, more or less, the network structure. Thus, the network structure influences the firm's strategies, but these strategies also influence the network structure (see figure 7.1).

CONCEPTUAL COMPONENTS IN THE MODEL

Network Structure

The following four dimensions are used to describe network structure: structuredness, homogeneity, hierarchy, and exclusiveness. They have been chosen because they describe aspects of the interrelatedness between positions in the network and the network's relations to other networks.

Structuredness refers to how interdependent the positions of different firms are. In tightly structured networks there is a clear division of work between firms, technologies are well defined, and the bonds between firms are strong. Entry and exit of firms are not very frequent. Loosely structured networks, on the other hand, feature a low interdependence between firms, unclear roles in terms of functions performed, weak bonds, and frequent entries and exits.

Homogeneity refers to how similar the positions are when relevant dimensions are compared. In a homogeneous network the bonds are of a similar nature in terms of types and strength; the relative importance of the few or many firms with a specific type of function is similar; and the functions performed by firms within the same type of function are similar (e.g. similar products and services, similar types of distribution channels). In a heterogeneous network, there is a wide dispersion between different positions as to strength of bonds, relative importance of firms and attributes of functions performed.

Hierarchy is a concept that is used to indicate the extent to which a few firms have a dominating influence over other firms. The network is more hierarchical, the more asymmetrical are the interdependence relations that describe the positions of a small number of firms with high relative importance. For example, if a few wholesalers have a dominating influence over both retailers and manufacturers, the network is highly hierarchical. The same is true if a few manufacturers dominate both suppliers and distributors.

Exclusiveness refers to the interdependence between positions in the network and positions in other networks. If the exclusiveness is high, the positions are not dependent on positions in other networks. This is the case if we define a nationally delimited network in which there are no internationally active firms. On the other hand, exclusiveness of this network is low if many international firms are sellers and/or buyers. The network boundaries can also be defined according to a specific technology used to carry out a generic function. If networks that carry out the same function using another technology exist, then exclusiveness is low. A network defined for transportation by rail has a low exclusiveness since the positions of those firms are interdependent with firms in road, sea and air transport.

Criteria according to which a network is defined and delimited can be of different nature and are, generally speaking, related to both complementary and competitive interdependencies. A very low exclusiveness indicates a need to redefine the network. Defining the network is in itself an important aspect of strategic management. There exists, naturally, many different network definitions and network interpretations for the same 'real' industrial system.

Various combinations of network structural dimensions are possible. We might describe one network as tightly structured, homogeneous, very hierarchical and highly exclusive, and another as loosely structured, hetero-geneous, not hierarchical and rather exclusive. Some combinations are probably less likely than others, such as the combination of loosely structured and hierarchical compared with tightly structured and hierarchical. Changes in the structural characteristics are probably not independent of each other. Major innovations in the early stages of diffusion tend, for example, to influence the network to become more loosely structured, more heterogeneous, less hierarchical and less exclusive. If the network is tightly structured, hierarchical, homogeneous and exclusive, innovating firms must be able to implement strategies with a high structure-changing effect. A discussion about the relations between strategy and network structure, and vice versa, will have to wait until we have treated the strategy concept.

STRATEGIES IN NETWORKS

The dimensions that are used to describe the strategies and their implemen-tation will be related to the basic attributes of the network approach, with its emphasis on disaggregated relationships, external resource dependencies and the importance of indirect relations. Three strategic dimensions will be discussed:

1   emphasis on efforts to adapt to the present network or emphasis on efforts to change the network;
2   emphasis on homogeneity in the relationships or emphasis on heterogeneity;
3   emphasis on internal resources or emphasis on external resources.

Network-integrative   or   network-changing   strategies   Integrative   strategies imply a close adaptation to the network. The firm does not intend to change the overall nature of the strategic situation of other firms (with the exception, perhaps, of some suppliers of substitutes) or the network structure. Rather, the attributes of network structure are strengthened by the strategy. An integrative strategy does not create major resource imbalances in the network, such as a surplus supply capacity of specific products. An integrative strategy by an entering firm is implemented by its acquisition of a firm that is already established in the network, instead of by investment in new capacity. If new capacity is added – say, by imports – the entrant grows slowly instead of trying quickly to make an impact so that present firms are not much affected. Another example of an integrative strategy is the use of existing distribution channels instead of developing alternative channels.

Network-changing strategies, on the other hand, imply structural changes in the network and have major influences on the strategic situation of other firms. Efforts to introduce a radically new production technology that changes the positions of firms (and leads to many new relationships) and the use of innovation in information technology to restructure distribution channels are two examples of network-changing strategies; major investments in new production capacity or major withdrawals of such capacities are further examples.

Homogeneous or heterogeneous strategies Homogeneous strategies imply that the firm has a standardized approach to its relationships in the network. There is little adaptation to individual counterparts. In heterogeneous strategies, on the other hand, the product and service offers are different depending on the specific relationship and its context. Selling standard products, at a price list common for all, using only one type of distribution channel would be an example of a homogeneous strategy. In heterogeneous strategies the firm sells both components and systems, sells both directly and through distributors, uses sub-suppliers or its own resources depending on the circumstances, adapts to individual customer needs and so on.

Strategies dominated by use of the firms' own resources or strategies dominated by the use of external resources The network approach generally defines firms as being dependent on external resources, but the strategies can be dominated more or less by internal or external resource use. A firm using mostly internal R&D activities for its product and process development, distributing directly rather than through distributors and taking 'make' rather than 'buy' decisions has a different strategy than a firm for which R&D co-operation with suppliers, buyers and competitors is important and which tries to externalize both manufacturing and distribution activities. It is important to note that a firm that has a more external resource-oriented strategy does not necessarily devote less internal resources in an absolute sense to a specific activity than a firm that has a more internally oriented strategy. A firm might actually have to increase its internal R&D activities in order to be able to co-operate successfully with other firms for product development.

The three strategy dimensions can be combined in different ways which may be more or less feasible in different situations. For example, it might not be feasible to implement a strategy that is both network-changing and internal-resource-oriented if the network is tightly structured. Table 7.1 shows the eight different combinations. The comments that follow are necessarily short, since the relations between strategy and network structure and between strategy and the firm's strategic situation have not yet been discussed (cf. figure 7.1).

TABLE 7.1   Combinations of strategy dimensions

	Internal resources		External resources	
	Homogeneous	*Heterogeneous*	*Homogeneous*	*Heterogeneous*
Network-integrative	1	2	3	4
Network-changing	5	6	7	8

Strategy 1   The firm's strategy is to give homogeneous offers to customers, and in its supplier relations not to demand specific adaptations of products or services. The relationships are adapted to the present position structure in the network. To implement this strategy successfully, the firm must be able to purchase, manufacture and distribute in a cost-efficient way and/or to have products that are generally superior to other sellers' offers.

Strategy 2   Here the firm adapts to the network through heterogeneous relationships. Offers are adapted to customers' specific need situations and the firm wants its suppliers to adapt to its own specific requirements, or else searches for suppliers whose offers fit these requirements. To be successful in this strategy, the firm needs to have purchasing, R&D, manufacturing and marketing organizations which can handle the heterogeneous relationships with only little dependence on external resources.

Strategy 3   Here, the dominant external resources are probably distributors that sell homogeneous products to many users, or a major customer to which the firm is a sub-supplier. Manufacturers of standard industrial supplies and small sub-suppliers to big customers are likely to have this kind of strategy.

Strategy 4   Firms that adapt to many different situations using (to a large extent) external resources are those that sell systems, or participate in building projects. If they follow a network-integrative strategy, the inter-organizational setup and the technology used are in accordance with accepted norms. If the strategy involves new technologies or new ways to organize the co-operation between the firms, the strategy is of type 8. To be successful in a type 4 strategy, the firm needs well developed positions to complementary suppliers, and an organization that can handle heterogeneous demand and supply situations in an effective way, for example through an experience-based repertoire of problem solutions.

Strategy 5   This strategy implies that a firm is able, rather singlehandedly, to change the network with a homogeneous strategy. This requires a high level of innovative ability ('a brilliant business idea'). The Swedish furniture retailer IKEA is an example of this type of firm, even though it could be argued that it has been so dependent on external subsuppliers that it is rather an example of strategy 7. Strategy 5 is not very likely to succeed in most cases. When it does succeed, it is regarded as a major successful innovation.

Strategy 6   This is not a very likely strategy because heterogeneous network-changing strategies probably require much help from external resources.

Strategy 7   See comments under strategy 5.

Strategy 8   This is a complicated strategy, since it involves co-ordination with other firms in order to change the network. It is likely that many of these relationships are new and that there are firms in the network that try to hinder the changes. See comments under strategy 4.

A firm might at the same time have more than one strategy. It might have a type 1 strategy for its standard, commodity-like assortment and a type 8 strategy for its advanced, innovative systems (in which the standard products may or may not be included as components). To handle multi-strategy situations, the firm has to develop separate organizational structures, and separate distribution channels. To the extent that the strategic change implies a change between two strategies that are 'far apart' in table 7.1, or the addition of a very different strategy, the firm will be faced with major strategic management problems, to be solved by reorganization and investments in internal assets and market assets.

The Strategy–Network Structure Relation

The structure of the network was discussed earlier in terms of structuredness, homogeneity, hierarchy and exclusiveness. The application of the different strategies will both be influenced by and will influence the network structure. The following offers some ideas about this interdependence.

How does network structure influence strategy? The more tightly structured the network is, the easier it will be to use integrative strategies. Strategies will mostly have to be external-resource-oriented since the bonds in the network are strong. It will therefore be easier for firms to implement this strategy through positions in the network that they have already established; otherwise, a firm will have to invest in building new strong bonds and will need to break or weaken some of the existing bonds between other firms. Using network-changing strategies in tightly structured networks will depend on a highly innovative and performance-increasing content of the firm's offer, especially if the firm is resorting mostly to internal resources and if the network is homogeneous; if the network is heterogeneous, a network-changing strategy can be directed to that part of the network where the conditions for its acceptance are best. Changes do not have to involve as many positions as when the network is homogeneous. If it is highly hierarchical, network-changing strategies that do not have the support from any or all of the most powerful firms will be very difficult to implement. On the other hand, if resources involving these powerful firms can be used in the implementation of the strategy, this will make such a strategy more feasible than if the network were non-hierarchical.

A homogeneous strategy will probably be easier to implement in a homogeneous, tightly structured and hierarchical network. There are, however, differences between a network-integrative and a network-changing strategy in these respects. If the exclusiveness is low – that is, if there are important interdependencies between positions in different networks – then a network-changing strategy is more feasible, because then resources from other networks can be used to effect the change. Typical examples are the influence on technical development or on distribution arrangements in a network by multinational firms and by firms from 'other industries' not considered to be members of the same network.

A low exclusiveness will also make it easier for firms with strategies requiring many resources to acquire such resources in other networks. The external resources (e.g. knowledge about the use of a new technology or the supply of components for such innovations) needed for a network-changing strategy may be acquired through a firm's positions in other networks.

How does strategy influence network structure? Network-integrative strategies tend to make the networks more tightly structured. Network-changing strategies tend to make networks more heterogeneous and less exclusive. Network-changing strategies might even cause people to redefine what they consider to be relevant network boundaries. Network-changing strategies might make the network either more or less hierarchical. Network-integrative strategies using external resources may increase the strength of the bonds and thereby also the structuredness of the network, while a network-changing strategy might make the network more loosely structured. The influence of an individual firm's strategy on the overall network structure may be very small. However, if there is a more general tendency among firms to use strategies of a specific nature, the influence will be important. We might then distinguish between two cases: one in which the present structure is reinforced and one in which there is a structural change.

If most firms pursue a network-integrative strategy in an already tightly structured network, this structure will be reinforced. If, on the other hand, many firms pursue a network-changing strategy in a tightly structured network, the structure will tend to become looser, at least initially.

Industry-wide and/or government/inter-government-directed industrial policies are important types of network-integrative or network-changing strategies that have as objectives the influencing of the network structure.

How does structural change influence strategy? Suppose instead we are interested in how structural change processes, rather than a specific structural situation, may influence the individual firm's strategy. If the network is changing towards a tighter or looser structure, if it gets more or less homogeneous, if the hierarchical structure is breaking down or getting stronger, if the network is getting more or less exclusive, such change processes will likely influence the individual firm's strategy. If the structuredness is getting looser, a firm might find that the receptiveness for a network-changing strategy is higher than if the development goes in the other direction. It is probably easier to find other firms that are interested in co-operating for network change. If the network is getting less exclusive, it will probably be easier for a firm with a heterogeneous strategy to use external resources, since 'outside' firms, such as suppliers in foreign countries, are more readily available. But it is also possible that decreasing exclusiveness is favourable for a homogeneous strategy, since customers that have similar needs and behaviour can be found also in other networks. International specialization among suppliers is an example of this.

The last example shows that it may often be difficult to link strategies logically or even empirically to structural change processes. The strategies and the structure are not that clearly defined, and the strategic situations of the firms vary. However, it seems that structural change processes are important to consider for the design, implementation and control of the specific strategies.

Influence of the Firm's Strategic Situation on its Strategy

It is a major idea in this paper that a firm's strategy is dependent on its strategic situation – that is, on the earlier development of the company that has led to its present positions. To demonstrate this idea, I will use three types of strategic situations as examples:

1   the firm is quite new in the network and has no positions in other networks;

2   the firm is established in other networks and is about to enter;
3   the firm is a well established and leading firm in the network.

Quite new firm   The quite new firm has to develop its relationships – in the extreme situation 'from scratch', in other situations from modest beginnings. It is usually quite small. Such a firm will find a network-integrative strategy easier to implement than a network-changing one. Suppose that the new firm is established on the basis of an invention. To transform this invention into an innovation that is diffused into the network, the firm must obtain access to external resources for distribution, manufacturing and use. If a network-integrative strategy is feasible (depending on the character of the innovation), this is probably easier to implement than a network-changing strategy, since the need to change existing relationships is of lower magnitude. If the innovation in itself implies changes in the network, the small new firm faces difficult resource acquisition problems. Both internal investments and investments in network positions are needed. Especially if the only feasible strategy is heterogeneous, the new firm will find the investment stakes so high that it will probably select a strategy with high dependence on external resources. In the extreme case, it will have to sell the invention as a licence to someone with established network positions. There are, of course, many examples of rapidly growing innovative firms , that have followed a network-changing strategy, (cf. Silicon Valley experience), but this has likely occurred in loosely structured networks with a great deal of external resources available.

Also, new firms who enter on other than an innovative basis will find it easier to implement a network-integrative strategy, especially if the network is tightly structured. Again, the reason is that it will be very resource-demanding to significantly change already established relationships. If the new firm is not innovation-based, there are also fewer incentives for other firms to contribute their resources to a network-changing strategy.

Established firm in another network   For firms that are already established in other networks, it is possible to use the positions that they have there for the entry. Especially if the network's exclusiveness is low, e.g. if the internationalization of the networks is high, the entry by firms that are themselves internationalized is facilitated. Not only do they have positions in other networks that generate income to finance the investments during entry, but also, some of the positions in relation to customers, distributors or suppliers in the other networks can be directly used, if these firms are also established in the network that is entered (Johanson and Mattsson, 1987b).

In the case of network-changing strategies, a firm established in another network might have developed an innovation there and be able to transfer it with the help of the experience thereby gained. If, however, the innovative firm is very dependent on external resources, a barrier to the successful entry might be the lack of such external resources in the network where the entry is to take place.

If the exclusiveness is high, involving various barriers for resource transfer between networks, entry of firms from other networks is more difficult. It might then be easier for them to enter with a network-integrative strategy, since this facilitates the establishment of relationships to other firms.

If the entering firm is strong enough singlehandedly to lower the exclusiveness, or if there is a general change towards less exclusiveness, the comments above need to be modified.

If the network is very hierarchical, entering firms will face either strong opposition to the entry or opportunities for help in implementing the strategy. If the network-integrative strategy involves the acquisition of powerful existing firms or some type of co-operative agreement, the outside firm might establish itself in its new network very quickly. Such a strategy (as followed, e.g., by the Swedish firm Electrolux) can also be part of a network-changing strategy, with the aim of reorganizing manufacturing activities among factories in different countries.

Leading firm   The firm that is one of the leading firms in the network has positions that imply that, regardless of its strategy, it has both internal resources and access to external resources, which gives it strategic opportunities, but also restrictions. A dominating firm adopting a network-changing strategy may or may not be helped by its present positions. Some of these positions, e.g. to suppliers or customers, might have to be abandoned or changed at high costs (cf. the notion of high resource commitments in strong bond relationships). The strategic opportunities given by the positions, however, are likely more important, especially if the firm has followed a heterogeneous strategy with a relatively high dependence on external resources. There are then many ways in which future developments can take place. If the structure is hierarchical and the network is tightly structured, the firm can use both integrative and change strategies, but integrative strategies are likely to be favoured because of the constellation of the firm's strategic situation and the structure of the network. The dominating firm is also resourceful enough to influence the exclusiveness of the network, for example to diversify into other technologies, enter other national markets or establish relationships to firms that are 'outsiders'. Furthermore, the firm can make entries from other networks more difficult, perhaps in co-operation with other dominating firms in the network, thus making the network more exclusive.

MANAGEMENT OF STRATEGIC CHANGE IN NETWORKS

In this section I will discuss what seem to be important management issues, given that markets are considered as networks of relationships between firms. By strategic change, I mean a major change in the firm's positions in the network. To what extent such changes can be 'managed', and be caused, by conscious strategies is of course a matter that has been discussed elsewhere.

What concerns us here is the contribution to strategic management that the network approach can offer. What types of questions are raised? What are the normative implications?

Management of strategic change has, as a base, the manager's perception and interpretation of the world, of structures and processes, of causes and effects. The network perspective offers a different 'view of the world' from, say, the microeconomic theory based 'industrial organization' or 'marketing mix' models, both on the general conceptual and methodological level and on the specific level concerning the individual firm and its environment. The interdependent nature of the positions, *a priori* unclear definition of the relevant networks and the obvious difficulties in operationalizing some of the major concepts leave much room for subjectivity. Individual managers perceive and interpret the network in different ways; they are influenced by their own, and other persons', experience, by the information through traditionally acknowledged business information systems (accounting information, market research) and through many other channels.

Perceptions and interpretations of the network are influenced by the interactions between firms within the relationships. Therefore, the firm's positions strongly influence the information on which strategic management is based. Since a firm consists of many individuals, and since interaction between firms usually involves several individuals in each firm, it follows that an important aspect of strategic management is the internal flows of information between individuals (and between organizational sub-units) within the firm. It also follows that the way in which the firm organizes for interaction with other firms and the quality and quantity of the resources it devotes to such activities influence the strategic management information.

Management of strategic change might be concerned with changes that have already occurred and which the firm wants to react to, changes that are expected to occur in the future which the firm wants to adapt to or influence, or future changes which the firm wants its own strategic activities to cause. From a network perspective, processes leading to strategic changes are not, in principle, reversible. To prevent a customer from developing strong bonds with a competitor is different from efforts to weaken already established bonds between the two. In the latter case, investments by the competitor and the customer have already been made which involve commitments for the future. Future strategic changes caused by the individual firm will in the network perspective also have to be concerned with the investment nature of strategic changes and the idea that investment processes in networks are interdependent. The network is changing during the time it takes to design and implement strategic activities, and the individual firm must react to those changes, but must also interact with other firms to influence them and perhaps co-ordinate various investment activities.

Thus, interdependencies between network positions make the 'time length' and 'timing' of strategic activities important and difficult issues to deal with. If production investments in a supplier firm are made 'too late' in relation to production investments in customer firms, the supplier firm's position might be difficult to defend since the customers must try to find additional supply capacity elsewhere. If a market investment takes a longer time than anticipated, production investments may be underutilized. The time length of a market investment process is influenced by the timing and other attributes of the marketing investments.

Individual position changes, such as developing a relationship to a new customer, achieving a well established macro-position in a new network and changing from a relationship involving simple products to one that includes more complicated products and services, often take a long time. Obviously, strategic management influences the timing and time length of investment processes. To be able to act at a specific time requires a preparedness to act. From a network perspective, preparedness is influenced by opportunities and restrictions implied by the firm's positions. Its positions in relation to complementary suppliers may make the firm better prepared to accept an invitation to bid on a big project than if no such positions exist. In general, the more the firm can use its present network positions to adapt to or create a strategic change, the easier the strategic management task will be. Market investments already made can be used, and complementary activities by counterparts may be expected. However, present network positions may not always be useful and may also hinder a strategic change. For example, the technical bonds to customers might be so strong that they act as deterrents to future changes of the firm's technology or to the development of new customer relations.

The network perspective offers a 'view of the world' that directs strategic management to focus on some major issues:

1 *The subjective and inter-subjective nature of descriptions and interpretations of the firm and its environment* Definitions and interpretations of the network are in themselves important and creative management tasks, which are influenced partly by information exchange within network relationships. The network can never be objectively and fully known!

2 *Positions in the network, which are interdependent and dependent on earlier investment processes* Thus, a firm's management of strategic change involves the management of investment processes that are interdependent with other firms' investment processes. This means that strategic change processes are irreversible. It also means that the time length and timing of the implementation of strategic activities in relation to other firms' complementary and competitive activities are given specific meaning. Furthermore, it follows from the notion of interdependent positions that the firm's preparedness and ability to undertake a strategic activity is dependent on its network positions.

Consider a multinational firm with geographically and technologically diversified positions which it can use to get early information about the networks, to adapt to or influence network changes, to quickly diffuse new products and to (partially) control and co-operate with competitors. The multinational firm can use its network positions, depending on their characteristics, for flexibility and for control.

What is said above influences the management of strategic change in all the three phases: design, implementation and control. To avoid repetition, I will just make a few comments on each phase.

Design   The description and analyses of the environment will emphasize the structure of the relationships between firms (i.e. the positions) and the changes in those relationships. A traditional market structure description will instead be in terms of organizational units. The emphasis on complementary activities and resources will widen the industrial environment to include parts of 'other industries', also. The subjective nature of the network descriptions makes it important to include decision-makers and not only 'analysts' in the analytical phase. The dependence on resources controlled by other firms makes it useful to include also their ideas about the network, and about their present and future positions. The network strategist will be much interested in intangible, internal investments and in investments in network positions (market investments).

The strategy formulation will naturally be in categories that are essential from a network perspective; i.e., intended attributes of the firm's relations to other firms define the strategies. This also has an effect on criteria for choice between different strategies. The network approach implies that the selection criteria are more in terms of how the strategies contribute to the firm's long-term survival and development than in terms of the highest economic return possible. The investment nature of the strategies does not imply that alternatives should be selected according to some 'net present value' criteria. However, it does mean that financial resources needed for the investments will play a major role in the design and selection of strategic activities. The market investments are especially important in this respect. A strategy that can use own and/or other firms' existing positions rather than requiring the development of new ones substantially lowers the financial burden on the firm.

Implementation of the strategy   This involves the development and deployment of resources and efforts to get resource commitments from other firms. Typical marketing and purchasing activities are at least as important implementation activities as investments in manufacturing resources. A reorganization of the firm's resources may be needed to reflect the strategy requirements. Radical strategy changes, such as changing from a network-integrative, homogeneous strategy based on internal resources to a network-changing, heterogeneous strategy with a high dependence on external resources, cannot be implemented without major changes in the organizational structure. A related aspect of implementation is to make the new strategy understandable and acceptable in the firm. This might amount to a need to change individuals' 'view of the world', and to change the 'corporate culture'.

Control of strategic activities Since the strategy is formulated in terms of relationships in the network, control information must also be possible to interpret in such categories. However, control information coming from the accounting systems, from investment/project control systems and from market research/market statistics is typically not relationship-oriented and does not acknowledge marketing investments and market investments. Resource development and resource deployment by other firms contributing to the strategic activities, are not shown. Thus, the 'network-oriented' manager will find it difficult and even misleading to use the control information that is available through traditional accounting and market information systems. If, as is often the case, entry on a new market takes a longer time and uses more resources than expected, because of the need to make market investments, a traditional control system might evaluate the entry as a failure and recommend exit as soon as possible. If, however, the control system had included information about attributes of the relationships, about effects of these relationships in other networks where the firm is established, about the negative long-term consequences of a withdrawal and so on, the evaluation and management reaction might be quite different. The network approach is commensurable with a long-term orientation and is, principally speaking, at odds with strategies that emphasize short-term economic performance to please financial markets.

The control phase naturally also involves efforts to get information about, and to influence, strategic activities in other firms, as well as adaptations and changes in the overall strategies, as experience accumulates or conditions change.

Some Research Issues

Finally, I will list some seemingly interesting issues for research on the management of strategic change that the network approach implies. I will be very brief as to the motivation for the research ideas, since the arguments should be rather evident from what has been said earlier.

1 To what extent do managers think and act according to ideas about networks? Can a 'theory-in use' approach (Zaltman *et al.*, 1982) be utilized to learn more about that question? One reason why analysts and planners often seem to have limited influence on the selection of strategies (Mintzberg, 1981) may be that managers have a different 'view of the world' from analysts/planners, being more 'network-oriented'. This idea is supported by the fact that our network approach is to a major extent built on interviews with managers in many different types of firms and markets, but has not yet been explicitly tested in any study.

2 How do managers in *different parts of the organization* perceive and interpret the networks and the changes in the networks? Are there any systematic differences between managers who are responsible for different functions in the firm, who are positioned on different hierarchical levels or

who are positioned in different national markets? For all the three phases of management of strategic change, it should be of interest to know more about the answers to such questions.

3   How do managers in *different interdependent firms* perceive and interpret the networks? Are there similar or dissimilar perceptions in firms that have important direct complementary relationships, such as a supplier and a buyer, a manufacturer and a distributor? Such comparisons between competitors would be of interest. Differences in perceptions can be, in terms of both structural and processual dimensions. Obviously, for strategies that involve a high dependence on external resources, such questions are important. If most managers perceive the network as tightly structured, homogeneous and highly exclusive, there is probably a greater similarity between them than if the network is characterized as loosely structured, homogeneous and not very exclusive.

4   The interdependencies between network positions suggest several questions about the management of strategic change (Mattsson, 1985). First, to what extent and how are changes in one position, or set of positions, dependent on other positions? How are changes in positions in one country dependent on positions in other countries? How are changes in positions in relation to users dependent on changes in positions in relation to suppliers? And so on. Second, there are many questions concerning the interdependencies between positions of firms that are not directly related. 'Parallel' investments in different sections of the network may in technological change processes be important for the implementation of a strategy (Håkansson, 1987).

5   Criteria of position interdependencies can be used to partition the networks into different network sections. This is similar to the idea of partitioning an industry into 'strategic groups'. Since the dimensions according to which strategic groups are defined are usually related to some measure of horizontal or vertical integration, this concept is rather close to network concepts. Also, the 'mobility barrier' concept, with its emphasis on the availability of resources and the ideas of entry as a first step in a long-term strategy, points to some potential linkages between research on networks and this well established conceptual scheme for research on strategy (McGee, 1985). The ideas about network positions as creating both opportunities and restrictions for change seem to be able to link to the concept of mobility barriers.

6   The time length and timing aspects of major changes in network positions suggest several research ideas of interest for strategic management, both for implementation and for control. Given that it will always be difficult to foresee the time length of a particular change that a firm wants to cause by its strategic activities, it is nevertheless useful to have some idea of the size order. Casual observations suggest that managers nearly always underestimate the time that establishment in a new network or in relation to a new customer takes. How does such an underestimation influence strategic change?

Finally, it is evident that research is needed to further develop and empirically use and evaluate the network strategy and structure concepts. In such efforts, as has been implied above, researchers could stress a subjective 'enacted' (or 'interacted') environment approach, where the focus is on processes, or a more objective idea about environmental descriptions, with an emphasis on network structures as determinants of strategic behaviour.

NOTES

1 The research on which this paper is based has been sponsored by the National Swedish Board for Technical Development (STU) and the Marketing Technology Center (MTC). I am indebted to Professors Jan Johanson and Håkan Håkansson, with whom for several years I have co-operated in research on 'markets-as-networks'.

2 Examples of such publications are Hägg and Johanson (1982), Hammarkvist *et al.* (1982), Håkansson (1982a), Mattsson (1985), Axelsson and Håkansson (1984), Johanson and Mattsson (1985, 1987a, 1987b), Håkansson (1987).

3 This section is mostly based on Johanson and Mattsson (1987a, 1987b).

4 Obvious links to the inter-organizational literature include Pfeffer and Salancik (1978) on resource-dependency, Weick (1979) on enacted environments, Aldrich (1979) on the discussion of rational *v.* natural selection and strategic choice, and Blau (1968) on social exchange.

5 The discussion about conceptual foundations for strategic marketing management that can be found in, e.g., Thomas and Gardner (1985) are related to some of the issues raised by the comparison above between the 'network' and 'marketing mix' frameworks.

6 Williamson's transaction cost approach (Williamson, 1975) is of course a development within the industrial organization field that specifically treats aspects of relationships between firms. There are basic differences between the transaction cost and network approaches, especially in terms of the nature and function of the relationships (Johanson and Mattsson, 1987a).

7 An example of a network analysis of a multi-industry character is Håkansson (1982b). In a study of technical development in the sawmill industry, Håkansson included firms in the steel industry and two mechanical engineering industries as well as the sawmill industry in the network. He also related his analysis to the electronics and forestry industries.

REFERENCES

Aldrich, H. E. (1979) *Organizations and Environments*. Englewood Cliffs, NJ: Prentice Hall.

Axelsson, B. and Håkansson, H. (1984) *Inköp för konkurrenskraft*. Stockholm: Liber Förlag.

Blau, P. (1968) The hierarchy of authority in organizations. *American Journal of Sociology*, 73, 453–67.

Dahmén, E. (1950) Svensk Industriell Företagarverksamhet – Kausalanalys av den industriella utvecklingen 1919–1939. Stockholm: Industriens Utredningsinstitut.

Håkansson, H. (ed.) (1987) Industrial Technological Development. A Network Approach. London: Croom Helm.

—— (ed.) (1982a) International Marketing and Purchasing of Industrial Goods – An Interaction Approach. Chichester: John Wiley.

—— (1982b) Teknisk utveckling och marknadsföring, MTC:s skriftserie 19. Stockholm: Liber.

Hägg, I. and Johanson, J. (eds) (1982) Företag i nätverk. Stockholm: SNS.

Hammarkvist, K-O., Håkansson, H. and Mattsson, L-G. (1982) Marknadsföring för konkurrenskraft. Malmö: Liber.

Johanson, J. and Mattsson, L-G. (1985) Marketing investments and market investments in industrial networks. International Journal of Research in Marketing, 2, 185–95.

—— (1987a) 'Interorganizational relations in industrial systems: a network approach compared with the transaction cost approach'. International Studies of Management and Organizations, XVII, (1), 37–48.

—— (1987b) Internationalization in industrial systems – a network approach. In N. Hood and J-E. Vahine (eds), Strategies in Global Competition. London: Croom Helm, forthcoming.

Kotler, P. (1984) Marketing Management: Analysis, Planning and Control. Englewood Cliffs, NJ: Prentice-Hall.

Mattsson, L-G. (1985) An application of a network approach to marketing: defending and changing market positions. In Changing the Course of Marketing: Alternative Paradigms for Widening Marketing Theory. Research in Marketing., Suppl. 2, pp. 263–88. Greenwich, Conn.: JAI Press.

McGee, J. (1985) Strategic groups: a bridge between industry structure and strategic management? In Thomas, E. and D. Gardner (eds), Strategic Marketing and Management, pp. 293–313. Chichester: John Wiley.

Mintzberg, H. (1981) What is planning anyway? Strategic Management Journal, 2 (3), 310–25.

Pfeffer, J. and Salancik, G. R. (1978) External Control of Organizations. New York: Harper & Row.

Porter, M. E. (1981) The contributions of industrial organization to strategic management. Academy of Management Review, 6 (4), 609–21.

Shepherd, G., Duchêne, F. and Saunders, C. (eds) (1983) Europe's Industries. Public and Private Strategies for Change. London: Frances Pinter.

Thomas, H. and Gardner, D. (eds) (1985) Strategic Marketing and Management. Chichester: John Wiley.

Weick, K. (1979) The Social Psychology of Organizing (2nd edn). Reading, Mass.: Addison Wesley.

Williamson, O. E. (1975) Markets and Hierarchies: Analysis and Antitrust Implications. New York: Free Press.

Zaltman, G., Le Masters, K. and Heffering, M. (1982) Theory Construction in Marketing. New York: John Wiley.

Commentary on Chapter 7

Roger Mansfield

Mattsson's chapter presents a very valuable contribution to the literature, and perhaps the most significant criticism one might make is that it does not go far enough. However, as it represents a report on an early stage in a large-scale research programme, that is merely a comment on the state of play rather than a criticism of the author's efforts. The approach suggested is clearly not new, but, despite that, it seems overdue for development. The 'markets-as-networks' perspective seems very appealing, particularly in relation to industries with few suppliers and customers, and where market conditions are clearly distant from the perfect competition model.

The position of a company in a network linking it with suppliers, customers and competitors is potentially a very valuable way of describing that company's strategic position. It clearly follows from this that one key element of strategy relates to the balancing of resource use and allocation, which, following the work of Howard Aldrich (1979), might be described as 'niche management'. However, the model suggested here, although potentially complicated, is far simpler than reality. The real networks in which organizations are involved do not relate just to the acquisition of equipment and raw materials and the sale of end-products or services, but also to relations with the labour market, the market for information and the market for finance. However, in the latter case the ownership question may complicate the relationships involved. Overall, in terms of flows, these networks may be seen as a system of interlocking cycles of production and consumption.

Viewing the networks in this way makes it clear that they comprise not just the immediate contacts of the focal company, although these may be important, but also the less direct relationships with all other parties to the cycles in question. This is a factor well understood in many industries, and perhaps shown most clearly when one examines the public relations and advertising activities of food manufacturing or food processing companies, much of which is aimed not at their immediate contacts (the large retail chains or wholesalers) but at the end consumer.

The reason that the network approach has probably not been more widely adopted relates to the general problem, whether faced by researchers or by managers, of having to deal with the amazing complexity of the environment in which real organizations operate. The great appeal of the market concept is that it provides a model for aggregation, although as economists have made the market model they use more realistic, the problems of aggregation have grown. None the less, the economic notion of markets still has great appeal in this direction. This is because senior managers must make decisions in terms of collections or aggregates of customers or suppliers where considering strategic issues to avoid getting bogged down in detail, leaving the process of dealing with particular individuals or organizations to functional specialists. What is needed is to replace the market concept with a model based on the idea of networks, which to some extent will allow for the aggregation problem to be solved.

It is possible that help can be gained by borrowing a model from another discipline, possibly from ecology: not, it is suggested, the population ecology model, which has been used to good effect in a somewhat different context by writers such as Campbell (1969) and Aldrich (1979), but the dynamic synecology model, which in conventional ecological research relates food chains to the actions of individual organisms. The utilization of this approach would allow the strategic position of the individual firm to be understood in the context of all the networks of which it is a part.

One must also consider the way in which networks are defined and whether the firm is really the appropriate unit of analysis. Viewed in terms of networks, it is not clear that one can draw a clear distinction between the firm and the environment in which it operates, although that may seem appealing to corporate lawyers, chief executives or uninformed shareholders. In reality, however, the relationships between the organization and its environment are in many ways similar to those between different parties within the organization. Cyert and March (1963) suggested that organizations were managed by a dominant coalition, and in reality coalitions can cross organizational boundaries. Williamson (1975) suggested that relationships within organizations are largely a question of hierarchical authority, while those between organizations or between organizations and individuals are governed largely by market forces. Reality, however, is more complex, and it is clear that virtually all relationships are a product partly of administrative hierarchies and partly of market forces. These relationships are further complicated and altered by factors stemming from the extent to which people have common values relevant to the situation and the transactions within it (Ouchi, 1980).

The dimensions of network structure suggested in Mattsson's paper seem somewhat limited and perhaps rather static. These four dimensions – structuredness, homogeneity, hierarchy and exclusiveness – provide a way of looking at networks, but in so doing dramatically oversimplify their properties. These problems are further confused if there are not clear-cut boundaries between organizations or a clear delimitation of particular networks.

In examining the range of possible strategies suggested by Mattsson, I would like to concentrate particularly on one that may at one extreme be regarded in the words of the paper as 'integrative', as contrasted with the other extreme of network-changing. However, I have some slight problem with the way the integrative strategy is conceptualized by Mattsson; it seems to me that no firm can enter a new market with an integrative strategy, because it must, by definition, change that market merely by the process of entry. What an integrative strategy would seem to be to me is one that changes a network in relatively *small* ways. In trying to analyse these two types of strategy, it may be worth considering what network changes are actually possible. There are four possibilities (Mansfield, 1986). The first of these might be regarded quite simply as substitution, where a company replaces wholely or partly the activities of another company in that particular network. In such a case the network itself is changed only to the extent that the identity of some of the actors has altered. Such processes or strategies depend on competitive advantage and the processes of market competition. The second and third ways in which the network may be changed are as a consequence of simplifying or elaborating strategies, and I will return to these in a moment. The fourth is where the network changes, but cannot be said as a consequence to be simpler or more elaborate, and this we may regard as a network metamorphosis.

Returning now to the question of simplifying and elaborating networks, it may be useful to illustrate this with a very simple example. If one considers two people on a desert island, they might each start by collecting enough food to eat every day. However, after a time one of them might consider that the whole process could be eased if tools were developed and manufactured. They might then go on to a system where one made the tools in half a day and the other used them for a whole day in order to collect enough food for both of them. To make this workable would involve creating a very simple network where the tools are exchanged for a proportion of the food. The advantage would be that both would eat as well as before and half a man-day would be freed by the system and could perhaps be used for other activities such as building shelters. This may be regarded as a way of elaborating the network and creating, in the process, the potential for development or economic growth. If, however, winter came, it might be that the individual involved in food collection could no longer collect enough for both of them to eat in a day, at which point it is likely that the network would be simplified by a negation of the earlier agreement, enabling both to return to food collection.

Translating this simple example into the modern industrial world, it could be argued that simplifying networks is typically done by companies when, and possibly only when, they are under enormous pressure owing to limitations on resources. This would be typical in a recession. On the other hand, elaborating the network will normally be easier in that it creates economic growth. However, this still is likely only where most or all of the parties gain in the process.

Clearly, these suggestions for elaborating the general idea of networks and the notion of network-changing strategies throw up the importance of power and resources in the system and relate to the question of investment in the network referred to by Mattsson. They also may provide a way of integrating the ideas of strategy relating to content and those relating to strategy formulation depending on process models. It is, however, worth noting that the pressure of time must be built into the approach adopted if a suitable explanatory and predictive model is to be developed. Clearly, the model must be made dynamic rather than static.

In concluding these rather limited comments, it may be useful to refer to Mattsson's first research issue relating to the extent to which 'managers think and act according to ideas about networks.' I would agree that many managers do, at least to some extent, think in network terms when considering strategic change. What is needed is the development of a more systematic approach to the analysis of such networks to assist them. It is in this context that Mattsson's paper should be judged, and within which one can say that he has made a useful and significant contribution.

REFERENCES

Aldrich, H. E. (1979)   *Organizations and Environments*. Englewood Cliffs, NJ: Prentice-Hall.

Campbell, D. (1969)   Variation and selective retention in socio-cultural evolution. *General Systems*, 16, 69–85.

Cyert, R. M. and March, J. G. (1963)   *A Behavioral Theory of the Firm*. Englewood Cliffs, NJ: Prentice-Hall.

Mansfield, R. (1986)   *Company Strategy and Organizational Design*. London: Croom Helm.

Ouchi, W. G. (1980)   Markets, bureaucracies and clans, *Administrative Science Quarterly*, 22, 129–41.

Williamson, O. E. (1975)   *Markets and Hierarchies*. New York: Free Press.

8 Strategic Challenges in the Financial Services Industry

Rajendra K. Srivastava and Allan D. Shocker

Those who would manage change must first understand its causes.

Anonymous

INTRODUCTION

This chapter provides a marketing perspective for the management of strategic change. In addressing these concerns, we recognize that a narrow perspective will be inadequate. Like others before us, we have found an integrative point of view to be necessary. In this paper we provide such a framework, one that attempts to juxtapose customer/demand perspectives (typically, the focus of marketing analyses) with firm/supply considerations, within an exogenous nd dynamic environment.

We discuss our conceptual framework in the context of the 'retail' (as opposed to institutional) market for financial/investment services in order to demonstrate how this framework can guide one in understanding and analyzing strategic change, and to suggest some particular methodologies for aiding this process. This market is undergoing major changes, at least in the USA, owing to deregulation, technological developments and the increasing encroachment by non-banking firms into traditional areas of concern (for example, by manufacturing firms in the credit arena and by stock brokerage firms in 'banking' products such as cash management/checking accounts. We hypothesize how demand is developed and how it shapes competition.) We also postulate how the firm develops its own initiatives and responses. The two perspectives are brought together in a discussion of the firm in relation to its customers in a competitive market-place affected by other environmental conditions. In doing so, we examine the twin concerns of feasibility and desirability which imply the need to understand better how both customers and firms assess market conditions. For products or services to be sold and purchased, the satisfaction of both concerns is necessary – customers decide what is more desirable from among alternatives that have been made feasible for them, and suppliers decide what is feasible to provide from among the possibilities they deem desirable.

The desirability and feasibility of options open to both customers and firms depend in part upon changes and trends in the environment. Fortunately, the essence of most change is that it is gradual. While there are occasions when change seems to occur in discrete jumps or otherwise appears very rapid, much of this is merely perceptual and a consequence of the fact that we do not monitor our environments on a continual basis. Consequently, many of the changes important to strategic thinking occur with ample warning if one is perceptive enough to see their signals. *Those who would manage change must first understand its causes.* The truth is that we live in a complex society and our ability to fathom its functioning is often quite limited. Thus, it is possible to miss and/or misinterpret such signals. But we must try, none the less. Since thinking and research are both costly activities, many firms do neither without considerable pain (Shugan, 1980). It helps to have a way of organizing and structuring one's ideas, and thus a framework such as is proposed here should provide exceedingly beneficial to the planning process.

THE FORMATION OF DEMAND AND COMPETITION

Overview

An overview of the integrative framework is provided by figure 8.1. We focus upon the market-place in a traditional way – as an intersection for forces of demand and supply. But we depart from tradition by viewing the organizing theme for a market not in terms of people or products *per se*, but in terms of usages or purposes. The idea is simply that customers have problems or purposes for which they desire solutions. Firms produce products and services as potential solutions. Sales are actualized by the judgements and behaviors of those for whom such purposes are relevant, which leads firms to research customer requirements. In this way, *a product market can be thought of as consisting of those people who have or are likely to have a coherent set of problems, and those products or services (and firms that provide them) that they would consider using to solve them.* An advantage to this view of a market is that the products in question need not be treated as all alike (i.e., as commodities); further, they do not even have to be products and services offered commercially by firms (so that a more accurate representation of competition can occur by including user-created solutions as well as commercial entries).

Starting with the perspective that customers purchase or create products to provide solutions to problems (upper left-hand corner of figure 8.1), we conceptualize a market as consisting of all products that meet benefit–cost criteria enabling them to satisfy user purpose. Those products (and the customers for whom the particular problem or purpose is relevant) comprise the potential product market. This market definition must be tempered by factors such as customer awareness of available product alternatives and

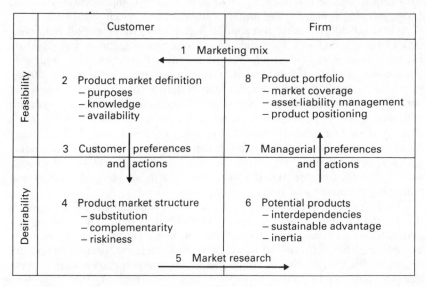

FIGURE 8.1　Overview of conceptual approach

knowledge regarding their ability to provide the benefits desired at an acceptable cost, as well as their availability in the customer's shopping area. Factors such as the features and benefits built into the product itself, its cost, customer awareness and distribution intensity are affected by the marketing efforts of firms. Through their pricing, product design, distribution and especially promotional efforts, firms also have some ability to affect the likelihood that customers will consider the product appropriate for a customer's intended purpose. Customers tend to be amenable to such suggestions, within limits. Thus, both customer and firm factors affect the set of products that will be considered feasible for a given purpose.

Which of the feasible alternatives will be selected and, indeed, how competitive the alternatives are can differ for different customers depending upon individual tastes and preferences, propensity for risk and economic circumstance, as well as shopping and other behaviors. Tastes and preferences, particularly, determine the desirability of the different feasible offerings. In the aggregate, the choices of the entire market determine product-market structure. This structure represents the degree of substitutability among the feasible alternatives. Recent studies (McAlister and Lattin, 1984) have argued that in some product categories variety-seeking takes place. The variety-seeking argument in turn implies that certain products that might otherwise be thought of as substitutes are in reality complements, in the sense that prior use of one increases the likelihood of use of another. Market structure can thus reflect the degree of both substitutability and complementarity (in the variety-seeking sense) among products feasible for a given purpose.

A firm conducts market research to better understand market behaviors. Analyses of market structure and the reasons that determine that structure help a firm in its own decisions regarding which markets to enter and with what kinds or types of products. The research is intended to reveal the set of products that is desirable for the firm in light of demand and competitive conditions. This analysis can be expected to reveal sustainable competitive advantages, interdependencies between potential new products and a firm's existing ones (e.g., cannibalization potential, synergies, etc.) and customer inertia or brand loyalty. All this information as well as the fit of the market with the scope of the firm's business or its traditions, cost considerations, manufacturing expertise and the like, affect the desirability of product and marketing actions by the firm.

The firm defines its business scope and, by so doing, the markets in which it has chosen to compete (Corey, 1975; Abell, 1980). The resources it assembles are necessary to serve these business objectives and, as such, become the raw material with which a firm seeks to develop its future opportunities. Conversely, the firm's traditions, reputation and resources serve also to constrain its ability to explore new opportunities. What the firm becomes and does with its resources, the extent to which it grows or languishes, is determined by management's tastes and preferences (within the framework of its objectives and existing resources). Foremost among the decisions that management is called upon to make are those concerning its product–service portfolio (Day, 1984). The product portfolio is important because products represent the bases of market exchanges with customers and their successful management affects the very existence of the firm (Day, 1977). Consideration of market opportunities affects the portfolio that is desirable to contemplate; the firm's inherent capabilities and resources affect what is feasible to implement. Factors such as a desire for market coverage, the ability to produce a credible positioning for any new products or repositionings of old, and the need (especially for financial services) to balance cash inflows and outflows (asset and liability management) are among those that affect the actions that management might take. The outcome of such managerial decision-making regarding feasibility is the implementation of a marketing mix (products, promotions, distribution and pricings) designed to achieve the ends it judges to be both desirable and feasible.

Both customers and firms formulate strategies, tactics and actions to achieve their objectives. Such objectives are necessarily interdependent. Certain of these interdependencies are identified in the product–market intersection of figure 8.2 and are described in the remainder of this paper. The dynamics of market behavior are captured by actions of firms and customers attempting to ensure that their decisions are both desirable and feasible with respect to each other. How they do that in the context of competition and other environmental circumstances is at the core of our approach to anticipating

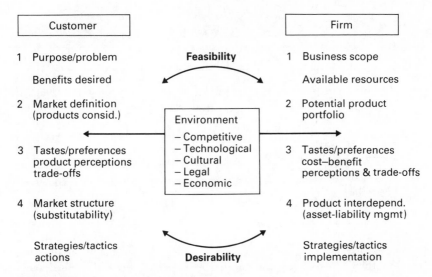

FIGURE 8.2 The conceptual framework

and understanding strategic change. What figure 8.2 affords, then, is a conceptual framework for looking at these issues. We illustrate this framework with reference to the market for financial services.

Customer Purposes and Business Scope

In the context of financial services, examples of *basic 'needs'* (generic problems or purposes for which solutions are desired) include the ability to borrow (for current consumption against future earnings), to save/invest (current earnings for future consumption), to safeguard (insure against uncertainties and/or potential catastrophes) and to transact (facilitate exchanges) with low cost (high return) and low risk. These needs provide one basis for understanding the more specific purposes which may guide market choices and are intended to be merely suggestive rather than deterministic of the needs that would guide a specific study. They appear fairly stable in that changes in the relative importance attached to them can be related to the evolution of customer value systems. For example, many individuals who were exposed to the vagaries of the great depression are enormously more concerned about the safety of their assets and are resistant to acquiring debt.

Derived needs emerge as a result of externalities such as regulation, technological changes and economic conditions. These may include objectives such as hedging against inflation and sheltering income from taxes. Their very nature suggests instability and susceptibility to environmental trends.

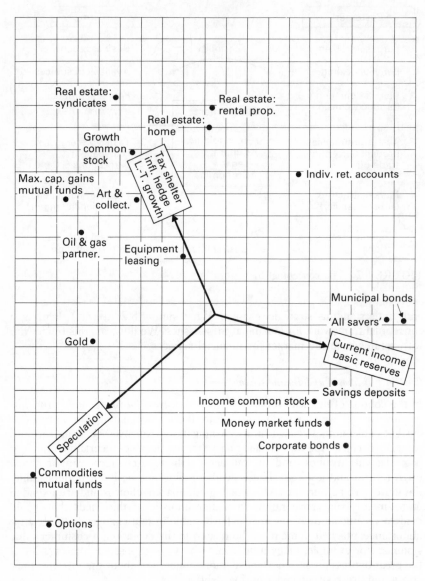

FIGURE 8.3 Joint space mapping of customer objectives and investment products

Figure 8.3 illustrates a joint space mapping of customer objectives and investment products arising from a specific study. It shows that money market funds and savings deposits are perceived as serving current income and basic reserves objectives, while real estate and other partnerships are seen as meeting objectives for growth, tax sheltering and providing a hedge against inflation. The relative desirability, and therefore the size of the market for these products, is influenced by both economic conditions and regulation. For example, the simultaneous reduction of inflation rates and maximum marginal tax rates have made partnerships less viable in the USA. They must now be justified more on their earning potential than on their tax benefits.

Customer purpose or problem, when determined, is presumed to dictate all that follows in the way of supplier selection and product-market construction. The strategic planning importance of this presumption is that such customer objectives normally will change only gradually, so that immediate or short-run market actions continue to be understandable in the light of such fundamentals.

Our description of the firm is laid out in a fashion analagous to that of demand. *Business scope* is meant to convey the firm's own concept of what it is about, what it can or should be. Such views of itself are tempered by realities imposed by the firm's several environments – particularly its customers, but also its competitive, cultural, regulatory, technological and economic environments. And they, in turn, are tempered by tradition (what it has been) and by inertia. One of the presumed advantages of any new firm is that it is usually not as constrained. Existing firms are strongly affected by their past actions and behaviors, which can lead to a heightened resistance to changing owing to the existence of a vested interest in the status quo. A bank, for example, may resist the legalization of interest-bearing checking accounts because it sees costs with certainty and benefits only potentially (i.e., with uncertainty). Thus, what is viewed as an opportunity by a small or new bank may be perceived as a threat by a larger, long-established institution.

As we shall discuss later, the benefits desired by customers (for example, higher interest rates on deposits) are often at odds with the profitability objectives of the firm (spreads on investments). Thus, the firm must decide how much it is necessary to give up in order to achieve satisfactory results. This depends, in part, on the nature of competitive action as well as on the firm's own resources and market position. For example, interest rate ceilings on depository accounts were phased out at the end of March 1986 in the USA. Therefore, a bank can acquire new customers/deposits by offering more attractive interest rates. But any advantage would be negated by competitors matching the strategy, and, if market growth were insufficient, all firms could have reduced earnings. Therefore, in oligopolistic geographical markets (banking operations in the USA are restricted to territories dictated by state and federal regulators), where market signals are likely to be heeded by competitors who also stand to lose revenues, it may be wise not to be first to offer higher rates. However, in fragmented markets, where smaller competitors may hope to offset reduced margins by increased deposits, a larger bank may want to offer higher rates as a pre-emptive strategy.

Since a product market is susceptible to environmental change, it is important that strategies be developed from an understanding of the causes of such change. *Contingency plans* should be developed for the less likely but salient events. But many managers merely observe historical trends and make straight-line projections for the future. Such practice can be dangerous. Rather, it is necessary for a firm to discover and challenge the assumptions behind any trends. For example, a growth in population and employment may lead to a boom in the real estate market with an attendant escalation of prices. But the very factors that have led to population and employment growth (such as a low cost of living, low congestion and high quality of life) deteriorate with such growth, thereby reducing the potential for future growth – and therefore will result in a slow-down of the real estate market. Hence there is a need for the monitoring of environmental forces and of customer decision-making. Financial institutions making blind projections for the increase in real estate prices are likely to consider loans to real estate developers as 'safe' and to emphasize such loans in the asset portfolios. This can, of course, have disastrous effects if the forecasts prove incorrect. Such scenarios are not restricted to the financial services industry; indeed, they provide one explanation for the boom-and-bust cycles observed in many arenas. They underscore the need for challenging the strategic assumptions upon which any continuation of trends is predicated.

For product markets based on basic needs (e.g. transaction and savings needs served by checking and saving accounts), the competitive ability of a financial institution is likely to be determined by efficiency-related factors, where costs can be expected to be related to market share/volume. But for product markets based on derived needs, served by product innovations that must be modified to suit environmental conditions, the competitive ability of firms must necessarily be a function of how effectively the firm can deal with threats and opportunities created by a changing environment. Effectiveness is enhanced by such objectives as the ability to adapt quickly to market conditions, the flexibility afforded by strategies chosen and the ability to anticipate and plan for additional change. These goals are aided by the analyses suggested by our framework because, as we have noted before, adaptation to change is assisted by the improved understanding of its causes.

Market Definition and Firm Constraints

As noted, customer objectives/purposes influence the set of benefits and costs that products and services targeted to those customers must provide in order to be considered for a market exchange. Products that meet such criteria constitute the relevant *potential* consideration set, or 'market definition.' That is, those products that serve the needs arising out of the same consumer problems, purposes or objectives can be considered in the same market because they are potentially interchangeable/substitutable. Since customers are likely to have multiple needs, firms could offer a portfolio of products to cover such multiplicity. But they may be constrained in doing so by the capital, skills, contacts, location and facilities and other resources available to them. Therefore firms may have to 'position' themselves in terms of the services they wish to provide, the customers they wish to serve and the manner in which such services are to be delivered. Moreover, there can be no guarantee that resources available will be sufficient to achieve and sustain a differential advantage.

Examination of figure 8.3 suggests that customers could simultaneously have tax shelter, long-term growth and speculation objectives. Further, products could serve two or more objectives. (For example, individual retirement accounts offer tax shelter benefits and provide a mechanism for both long-term capital accumulation and basic reserves.) This perspective allows one to move away from the restrictive logic that investors are always risk-averse. It also allows for the inclusion of seemingly different products within the same market (i.e., solving the same customer problems). For example, as is evident from the relative positions of real estate syndicates, growth common stock, mutual funds, oil and gas partnerships, equipment leasing programs and rental and personal property in the figure, these products meet the (correlated) purposes of long-term growth and protection from inflation and taxes.

Such a market definition is *potential* in the sense that it may be dependent upon factors such as availability and familiarity; i.e., are the services available to the customer via a convenient channel, and is the customer sufficiently knowledgeable regarding an alternative to recognize that it could satisfy his/her purposes? Customers vary considerably in their level of knowledge and their experience with complex financial products. Inadequate knowledge and/or experience lead either to higher perceived risks or and/or inaction *vis-à-vis* that alternative. Thus, the financial institution not only has to acquire the requisite skills in order to offer the product successfully, but, in order to convert potential clients into actual customers, it has to educate potential participants.

Unlike the case with many consumer goods, the provision of financial services requires an overlap in the production and consumption functions; i.e., customers must participate in the production process and therefore determine *how* the service is delivered (Parasuraman *et al.*, 1985). Thus, the firm must guide the 'producer's' interactions with customers in the delivery of services (lower panel of figure 8.4 (a)). By contrast, the role played by marketing in the context of most consumer goods is such that marketers often have little to do with the production processes, and even when they have influence, it is largely indirect (upper panel of figure 8.4 (a)). The role of marketing and production activities in determining profitability are further elaborated in figure 8.4 (b). Whereas marketing and production activities are

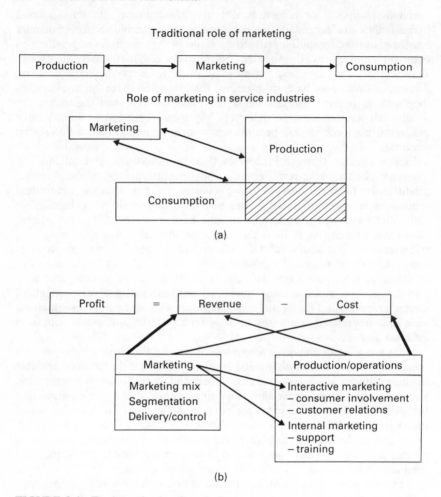

Traditional role of marketing

Role of marketing in service industries

(a)

(b)

FIGURE 8.4   Traditional role of marketing

traditionally more closely related to revenues and costs, respectively (dark lines), in the context of financial services the role played by marketers in managing the consumption–production interaction affects costs, and the manner in which services are produced and delivered affects demand or revenues (light lines). These suggest the need for the close co-ordination of production and marketing activities.

Environmental factors which determine the relevance of various customer objectives include the (1) stage in the family life-cycle and (2) life-styles. As posited by both economists and marketers (Tobin, 1967, and Katona, 1974, respectively), the need for credit decreases with age (which is positively correlated with both income and net worth). Individuals are likely initially to borrow against future earnings, then to save towards retirement and contingencies as earnings exceed cash needs, and finally to consume their savings during the years beyond retirement. Over the life-span, financial objectives can also be influenced by the presence of children: pre-school children represent a strain on household resources, and families save for their children's college education during the period when they are in school. Often, it is not till the children leave home that households have both the desire and the ability to invest substantial amounts of money. Of course, such objectives and abilities are also tempered by whether or not both spouses work. Figure 8.5 (a) provides an illustration of the distribution of income, debt and net worth by age of the head of the household. The fact that demographic changes are gradual and predictable enhances the ability of financial institutions to plan for them. Figure 8.5 (b) indicates that older household heads (age greater than 45 years) control the vast majority (about 75 per cent) of resources or assets available for investment and are therefore important to financial institutions.

Differences exist among customers in terms of the problems for which they seek solutions, or in their objectives. These in turn are associated with factors such as knowledge/experience or life-cycle, and lead to distinct preferences for specific benefits and costs. All of this suggests obvious criteria for market segmentation and product differentiation. For example, new payment technologies are generally more acceptable to younger population groups. Access to funds may be provided through paper (checks), card and electronic systems. But paper-based systems may be emphasized to the elderly, electronic access to the young and card technology to both. As others have argued, market segmentation and product differentiation are closely related. The purpose of market segmentation is to identify differences among buyers which may be important in developing distinct marketing strategies; product differentiation merely represents one of many such product portfolio strategies that may be targeted to the segments so identified.

A major part of the choice has been made when a customer decides upon a *consideration set* of alternatives. A firm is able to affect such choices primarily through its product design and distribution decisions, but also through its promotion and pricing. Product design seeks to build into the offering those features and characteristics which deliver the required benefits at acceptable costs. Distribution creates convenience and availability. Promotion seeks to make customers generally aware of the existence of the product and its features and where and how it might be obtained, but also to reinforce or create product–usage associations and to provide reminders to purchase. Prices are greatly affected by competitive factors but reflect the desirability of the features that have been built into the product and the costs of manufacture and distribution. A particularly inefficient producer would not survive long, so that products offering similar levels of benefits tend to be

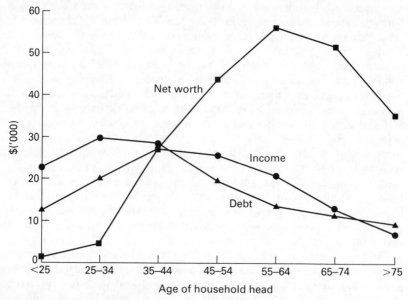

FIGURE 8.5(a)   Distribution of income, debts and assets

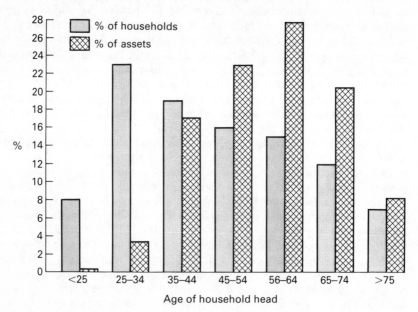

FIGURE 8.5(b)   Asset distribution by age group

comparably priced. It is worth noting, however, that product design and delivery are not cost-free to the firm. Hence, the firm has to consider important decisions such as

- *market coverage*: what markets (problems, purposes, objectives and geographical areas) it should serve, and
- *product variety*: how many products it should offer in each market.

If a firm through its product portfolio does not cover all purposes, not only may it be missing potential worthwhile opportunities, but it may also be less effective in marketing the products it does deliver because customers may prefer to maintain relations with vendors that provide a full line for convenience reasons. On the other hand, if its resources/skills are limited, broad market coverage may spread a firm too thin and inadequate performance on delivery/service in one market may negatively impact another. The decision to increase market coverage is not an easy one because managers must (often) make judgements with less than an adequate knowledge of both the clients they wish to serve and the products that will be used to serve them. In such circumstances, there is generally a bandwagon or herd effect and products are added to 'stay competitive' rather than having their *raison d'être* based on informed analysis. After all, a second entrant enters a market in which the first entrant already has a presence; a third entrant enters a market populated by the first and second; and so on. Thus, at a minimum, each faces a competitive and possibly also a demand environment different from that faced by earlier entrants so that simple imitation can increasingly make less and less sense.

For example, banks were limited in their ability to serve customer objectives related to long-term growth and tax shelters (see the top left hand quadrant in figure 8.3) and, at the same time, were faced with growing competition from brokerage houses in their traditional businesses through money market and cash management accounts. One response was to make inroads into the brokerage business via discount brokerage services. This objective was achieved by large institutions through acquisitions (e.g., of Charles Schwab by Bank of America). The success of these efforts led to efforts by others to jump on the bandwagon. Figure 8.6 (a) provides the growth patterns for the number of institutions offering discount brokerage services, the total revenues for that industry, and the revenues per institution. While it is obvious that the trend in revenue per institution (particularly late entrants) dropped dramatically in 1981–2, the number of providers increased steadily through 1984. Diffusion/growth models can be used to predict the growth in demand for services as a function of risk (Srivastava *et al.*, 1985). Figure 8.6 (b) illustrates how greater risk reduces the rate of diffusion and how higher initial investment requirements lower the potential market size for the product. A current interest in the US banking industry is in insurance products, where similar trends are being observed. In the provision of both discount brokerage and insurance services, banks (and savings and loan (S&L) houses) have, in the vast majority of cases,

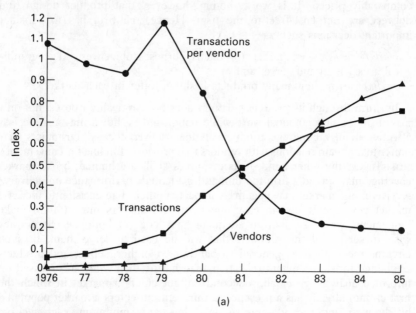

FIGURE 8.6(a) Discount brokerage industry

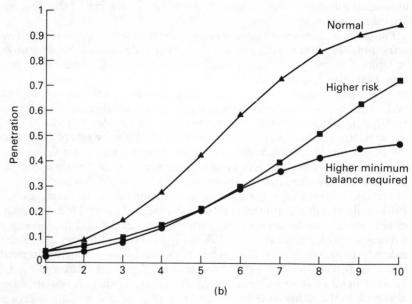

FIGURE 8.6(b) Diffusion patterns

been mere retailers for services actually provided by brokerage houses and insurance underwriters, respectively. Thus, unless they can market these products more *efficiently*, it is unlikely that such ventures will be profitable in the long run. But since efficiency is a function of accumulated experience in dealing with customer requests, complaints and the like, and because customers who have a need for these services are likely to have already established relationships, these ventures are, at best, likely to be only marginally profitable.

Thus, expansion into markets already adequately served may be dangerous unless the new entrant has a sustainable advantage in either the design, the pricing or the delivery of products. The financial services industry is unique in that its products are easily modified and duplicated, often by mere reprogramming of the computer. Thus, one way in which a firm tries to stay ahead of competition is through a constant effort to better serve customer needs, which requires investigations of the type implied by our framework.

Customer and Managerial Tastes and Preferences

The products in any individual customer's consideration set can usefully be thought of as bundles of features (e.g., interest rate paid, liquidity position, degree of safety of principal, likelihood of achieving financial targets, etc.) which represent *costs/benefits* to the customer. The specific features that are paid attention are again influenced, albeit in a different way, by customer purpose, but also by individual tastes and preferences with respect to the nature of existing products. Thus, for products designed to enable transactions (checking accounts, credit cards), convenience-related factors are relatively more important than for products designed for investment purposes, where interest rate, return and risk can play a more significant role. However, within a market, customers may exhibit differences in terms of trade-offs among features or other characteristics of the services under consideration. Of particular importance are the criteria (e.g., features) that are important determinants of choice. These can sometimes be influenced, but not dictated, by suppliers. (The existing set of product alternatives is one with which customers feel comfortable – their very existence having legitimized their necessity.) There may also be occasions when certain product characteristics define the category, and therefore promotion may be unable to change the importance of those characteristics for customer decision-making. For example, there has been consumer resistance to promotional efforts by banks in the introduction of debit cards (which eliminate the 'float' offered by credit cards) and truncated checking accounts (where checks are not returned).

Figure 8.7 presents checking accounts profiled in terms of minimum balances required to avoid service charges, the magnitude of service charge and the interest rate paid. These profiles were rated by two individuals. The preferences could be regressed against product features expressed as dummy variables to derive estimates of the utility of each feature to each customer or market segment. Analyses of these preferences reveal (see last two rows

Example: design of checking accounts

Product no.	Min. balance ($)	Service charge/ mo. ($)	Charge/ check ($)	Interest rate (%)	Preferences (10-pt scale) Subject A	Subject B
1	500	3	0	5	10	5
2	500	4	15	7	7	8
3	500	5	0	6	8	7
4	1000	3	15	6	6	5
5	1000	4	0	5	6	4
6	1000	5	0	7	5	9
7	1500	3	0	7	6	10
8	1500	4	0	6	4	6
9	1500	5	15	5	1	1

Subject A	−48	−27	−21	+4	
					Relative importance
Subject B	−10	−10	−25	+55	

FIGURE 8.7 Conjoint analysis; inferring actionable strategies via tradeoffs

of the table) that individual A dislikes higher minimum balance requirements, while B prefers higher interest rates. (The sum of the absolute weights across attributes = 100.) Analysis such as this can be used to aid *new product design*. Those options that are both desired by customers and viable (feasible and profitable) can be offered. Note that, with computerized bookkeeping services, a bank is not constrained to offering a single type of checking account. Thus, such analyses offer yet another basis for segmenting the market. In the previous section we discussed segmentation in terms of similar customer purposes, problems and objectives – i.e., in terms of the types or categories of service that they need. Here, segmentation is more refined and deals with the features deemed more desirable within a category of service.

Management's tastes and preferences affect how the resources of the firm are deployed (as well as the earlier question of what form those resources take). Managerial actions are determined only in part by perceptions of customer needs and how they may be profitably served by the firm. Much as was the case in our conceptualization of demand, such decision-making is strongly affected by the objectives of the firm and by the resources available to management. These affect the criteria management uses to evaluate its alternatives and, perhaps, the perceptions of the alternatives themselves (Choffray and Lilien, 1980). Beyond these factors are considerations of risk, both for the firm and for the manager's own career, and the manager's desire for flexibility to deal with contingencies.

Exchanges between firms and customers are generally easier to consummate when both parties objectively stand to benefit from the exchange. A problem prevalent in the financial services industry (but by no means confined to that industry) is that customer benefits often translate directly into firm costs and vice versa, so that the views of both parties must enter firm decision-making. For example, it is well known that higher interest rates on depository accounts are, *ceteris paribus*, more desirable to the customer. So also are greater liquidity, increased convenience of deposit and redemption, lower risk of loss, etc. However, these product features provide different levels of 'value' or satisfaction to different customers, and varying costs to the firm. If access to funds could be provided through cards, checks, tellers and automatic teller machines (ATMs) and other electronic systems, by using procedures similar to those that form the basis for figure 8.7, it should be possible to develop a measure of the utility or satisfaction associated with each delivery mechanism. Then, those providing the better value/cost ratios could be emphasized in marketing efforts.

As noted earlier, the criteria on which customers focus in determining their choice/actions can be influenced by the firm through its *communication* efforts. This is easier to accomplish if the customer has few well established preferences – possibly, for example, established at the time they first enter the product market (e.g., when they take their first job, or get married). Then the firm, through tactics based on educating the customer, may well be able to suggest criteria for selecting/using services. Even otherwise, incentives may be used to enhance customer trial, and (ultimately), through familiarity, preference for product features that are less costly to provide and may therefore lead to more desirable value/cost ratios. For example, banks could institute incentives for customers to use ATMs in the form of discounts or promotions. The use of human tellers (a more costly option) could be discouraged via fees. Thus, by influencing the trade-off among product features, the firm is able to influence the nature of demand and of product usage.

In evaluating trade-offs, managers often see costs with certainty and benefits only potentially. Even though market trends may warrant changes, there is a tendency for inertia to perpetuate past practices. For example, heavy regulation in the banking industry discouraged price-based competition. Therefore, firms competed in terms of the level/quality of services provided to clients. With deregulation, price competition has become more feasible. Yet, a large number of financial institutions have been afraid to cut back on services for fear of erosion in their customer base. In the process, they have become less profitable. The issues are complex, and it is often not easy to initiate actions unilaterally. But better understanding of price–quality trade-offs within the market, together with a knowledge of costs of providing service, should make for more objective, and hopefully more profitable, firm decisions.

Since it is not possible successfully to differentiate some services which by their very nature are 'commodity-like,' one is forced to compete on the basis of price. However, for services that can be differentiated, price competition is a less attractive option. It is important to draw the distinction between 'competing on price' and being 'price-competitive.' The former implies offering the lowest price, while the latter implies being in an acceptable price range. A financial institution in a competitive market can probably not afford to compete on the basis of price for each of the products it offers. It may compete on price for certain lead products ('loss leaders'), such as checking or money market accounts, in order to attract clientele and then cross-sell other products that are priced competitively so as to reduce incentives for existing customers to 'shop' around.

There are often substantial differences in the ways managers and customers perceive financial products/services. Managers tend to examine the services rather technically, owing to their greater level of involvement with and understanding of them. Customers, on the other hand, tend to rely on summary rules or heuristics to simplify their decision-making (Wright, 1975). After all, the services are not ends in and of themselves (as they may be to managers), but are instrumental in solving some larger customer problems. For example, in evaluating the risks associated with financial products, managers tend to examine the distribution of returns or outcomes and then tend to choose the one with the lowest variance ('risk'), given the same level of return. Risk, however, is seen somewhat differently by individuals who are less involved. For example, figures 8.8 (a) and (b) provide evidence of occasions where the 'riskier' alternative (as defined technically, based on variance) is often preferred by customers. In part (a), if the inflation rate were 15 per cent, alternative B (0.9 probability of a 10 per cent return) represents a definite loss while alternative B provides a 0.45 probability of beating inflation (often a target). In part (b) of the figure, alternative D provides a higher probability of loss and individuals often choose alternative C in order to minimize that probability. The second example may appear contrived, but it represents an 'exit' situation which occurs when an individual may have made an investment prior to a market downturn. This tendency to try to avoid losses is one explanation for why stock trading volume is almost always higher on market upswings than on downturns.

Other components of risk as perceived by customers are related to the high complexity and information cost and low confidence in one's judgement associated with some financial services. This implies that investors are likely

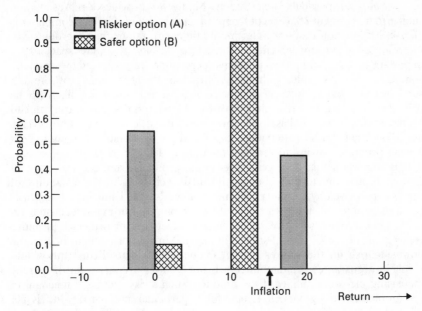

FIGURE 8.8(a) Choice among risky alternatives

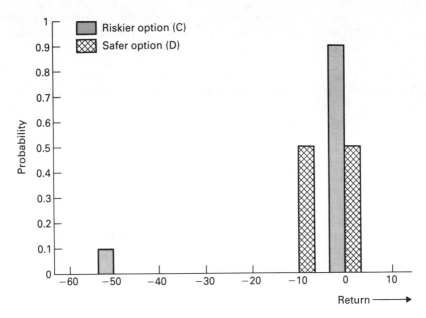

FIGURE 8.8(b) Choice among risky alternatives

to 'specialize' in particular investments. Figure 8.9 provides a representation similar to that of figure 8.3 except that product perceptions (various components of risk, information cost and selection confidence), rather than the objectives to which they are appropriate, are used to develop the joint space. It is important to note that product positions (perceptions) are affected by economic conditions. For example, with the recent dramatic gains made by the US stock market, products such as stocks and mutual funds are likely to be perceived as being less risky and providing better returns than those implied by figure 8.9 (which is based on data from an earlier period). The reverse would be true for real estate syndicates, oil and gas partnerships and equipment leasing programs, owing to reduced inflation and lower marginal tax rates.

It is important that management examine products from the viewpoint of customers in order to make better informed decisions. An understanding of the risks perceived by customers can aid product design. Table 8.1 summarizes some risk reduction strategies that could be employed. For example, customers could appear more sensitive to the likelihood of loss of principal (negative returns or downside risk), so that financial institutions could hedge the downside risk on the futures market on behalf of their clients (this would result in a guaranteed minimum return but a lower average return), thereby increasing the overall utility of the product. Such a risk reduction mechanism was implemented by Merrill Lynch for a particular municipal bond issue. That issue (over \$200 million) was targeted only to Merrill Lynch customers, and it sold out within one week.

Perceived risk can sometimes be reduced by simplifying products so that they are better understood by customers. Zero coupon bonds represent such an 'innovation' (actually, the concept is one that has been long used by US savings bonds). They are simple to understand – for a fixed investment, a fixed amount is promised at maturity. Risk can also be reduced by making the customer more familiar with products. This may be achieved via sponsorship of seminars or investment clubs and by enabling 'trial' by reducing the minimum amount that must be invested. Because of the risks inherent in financial products, and the reduction of risk via the provision of information and advice by financial institutions, customer loyalty is often much higher relative to that which exists in a consumer goods context. This enables a firm that already has an established relationship with a client to more easily cross-sell that client other services.

Changes in economic conditions influence the desirability of different types of investments. If customer motivations are not well understood, managerial responses to economic trends are likely to be inadequate. For example, recent gains in the stock market with the parallel reduction of interest rates have made certificates of deposits (CDs) less attractive relative to stocks, bonds and mutual funds. This has hurt the ability of banks and S&Ls to attract individual retirement accounts (IRAs), which have large account balances. IRA accounts at banks tend to be in CDs which are paying relatively low interest rates. Money from these accounts has thus been moving to IRA

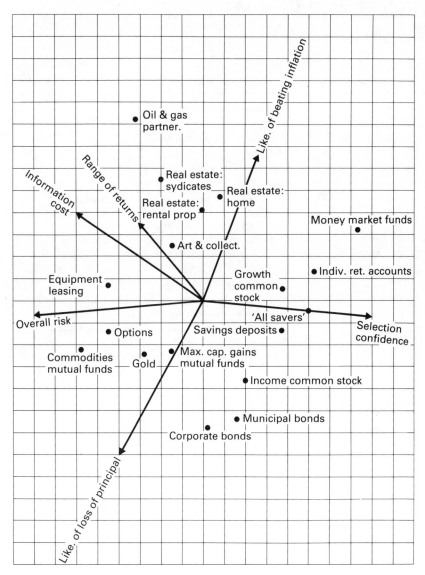

FIGURE 8.9 Product-attribute mapping

TABLE 8.1   Risk reduction strategies

Type of risk	Implication	Strategy/example
Complexity	Simplify products	Zero-coupon bonds
Communicability	Reduce information costs Reduce jargon Enhance selection confidence	Investment seminars Financial planning
Compatability	Market products that 'dove-tail' well with experience and assets held	Financial planning services
Observability	Illustrate with past performance	
Divisibility	Encourage sharing of investments Reduce minimum investment required	Investment clubs Money market
Relative advantage	Deliver products/services that offer distinct advantages relative to existing alternatives	Mutual funds Money market funds
Liquidity	Reduce/eliminate temporal restrictions	Hedged CDs
Downside risk	Hedge lower end of return distribution	Municipal bonds with 'puts'
Upside risk/aspiration levels	Cover aspiration levels and investment targets	Adjustable balance Deposits

accounts at brokerage firms, which allow a broader range of investments in stocks, bonds and mutual funds in addition to CDs – thereby providing the potential for higher returns through increased flexibility in moving funds among products as their relative desirability changes with economic conditions (which suggests that products which at first glance appear substitutable can also prove complementary).

If these inferences are correct, the response by many banks has been inadequate in that they continue to focus on magnitude of return issues, and not on customer flexibility concerns. Their response has been in the form of incentives, such as a higher (usually about 1 per cent) interest rate, *if* customers are willing to commit deposits for longer time periods. Such a commitment may be undesirable given current market conditions. Furthermore, how good is an interest rate of, say, 9 per cent (with penalties for early withdrawal) if higher rates are available in corporate bonds – which can offer an added bonus of capital appreciation when reductions in market interest rates can be anticipated. The important concern is not whether our particular analysis is correct, but whether it is grounded upon knowledge of which alternatives consumers see and how they see them and how they make decisions using that information. Needless to say, it is useful for management to monitor customer perceptions in order to develop appropriate responses. Management's own tastes and preferences are not adequate substitutes.

Owing to the dynamic nature of the environment for financial products, a desire for flexibility is high for both customers and firms. This leads to a situation where it is hard for either party to 'optimize.' Since uncertainties increase as we go further into the future, optimization is at best feasible only in the short run. But short-term optimization can result in long-run mistakes, particularly if the strategies followed involve high exit costs. Furthermore, there are many interdependencies among products that can make real optimization unfeasible and 'satisficing' a more reasonable goal. Certain of these interdependencies are examined in the next section.

Market Structures and Product Portfolios

It is the purchase decisions of many customers aggregated over time and space which define the extent of overall substitutability in a usage-defined product market. A *product-market structure* can be represented in terms of such substitutabilities. It should be pointed out, however, that this representation is not the same thing as an overall representation of substitutability between products, since a given product may have substantially different competitors in each of the different usage-defined sub-markets it competes in. For example, a personal check may be weakly substitutable for a credit card as a source of cash when out of town, but strongly substitutable for a credit card in one's home town. Overall substitutability of two services represents some aggregation of these usage-specific measures.

The mix of services, which collectively provides for multiple objectives or purposes, represents the customer's product portfolio. There are interdependencies among the products within this portfolio that are based on both synergy and substitutability. For example, checking or money market accounts may be used to facilitate the transfer of funds between different types of other investments and in that sense have a synergistic or complementary (not used in the strict economic sense) relation with other products such as stocks and bonds. At the same time, some individuals may use money market funds as investment vehicles, particularly when the desire for flexibility or liquidity may be high or when they are uncertain regarding their investment plans. Because perceptions and preferences are subject to change, it is important to monitor such changes in the market. In addition to mapping product perceptions (e.g., figure 8.9), it is also instructive to examine the flow of funds between products and co-ownership of products (a necessary condition for transfers to take place).

Focusing on IRA accounts, which serve the retirement savings and tax shelter objectives, table 8.2 provides information on the relationship between IRA accounts, checking accounts (CAs), money market accounts (MMAs), cash management asccounts (CMAs), tax shelters (TXSs), pension plans (PPs), life insurance (LIs) and certificates of deposit (CDs). Specifically, the table provides:

- percentage of owners of 'X' (PPs, CMAs, ...);
- percentage that owns IRAs and 'X';
- percentage of owners and non-owners of 'X' who own IRAs;
- the cross-selling efficiency of 'X'(difference between rows 3 and 4);
- the partial correlation between IRA and 'X' account balances if both are owned (while controlling for the overall size of the portfolio);
- the flow of funds to IRAs from 'X' over two consecutive quarters (in the form of indices).

These numbers are based on data collected and distributed by MRCA Information Services. For proprietary reasons the statistics are disguised, although the nature of the relationships has not been altered. The information reveals that IRA ownership is more likely if any of the 'X' products are owned, relative to what might prevail in the absence of such ownership (approximately 50 per cent), with the exception of CAs. The correlations among them suggest that IRAs are substitutable with PPs, TXSs and LIs and appear complementary

TABLE 8.2   Relationship between IRAs and Column Products (X)

Relationship	CA	MMA	CMA	TXS	PP	LI
Own X (%)	79	33	6	13	42	60
Own X & IRA (%)	42	25	5	11	26	34
ITA ownership by:						
Owners of X	48	69	78	75	56	50
Non-owners of X	47	35	45	43	40	42
Cross-selling efficiency of X	1	35	33	32	17	8
Partial correlations:	−0.02	−0.16	0.21	−0.36	−0.26	−0.21
X & IRA balances						
Sources of IRA funds:						
X to IRA index Q1	48	119	87	41	85	145
X to IRA index Q2	49	79	166	59	106	93

Key: CA = checking account
    MMA = money market account
    CMA = cash management account
    TXS = tax shelter
    PP = pension plan
    LI = life insurance
Source: MRCA Information Services; relationships are disguised for proprietary reasons.

with respect to CMAs. Finally, the flow of funds information suggests that LIs were the major sources of funds for IRAs in period 1 and that CMAs were important sources in period 2. Once the pattern of flows has been identified, one can try to discover reasons underlying those patterns. For example, stocks and mutual funds might be considered important sources for IRAs because individuals could shelter some of the gains in those products from taxes by investing in IRAs.

The analysis of the flow of funds between IRA accounts at different institutions reveals that brokerage houses gained at the expense of mutual fund institutions and banks, while mutual funds gained at the expense of banks. Brokerage houses were best able to retain deposits in IRA accounts. (See table 8.3, which indicates the flow of funds between institutions.) While we have focused on IRA accounts, however, similar analyses could be performed for other products. Such analyses as these provide for a richer understanding of the market and are therefore essential for informed managerial decision-making. Knowledge of how competitive one's own products are, whether or not there are gaps in one's product line, how much cannibalization exists between the firm's existing services, whether competitors have more complete or more general purpose products than does the firm, and so on are some of the questions that can be aided by such analyses.

Interdependencies among products based on customer usage provide important considerations for a number of decisions. Important among these

TABLE 8.3   Transfer of funds between IRA accounts (from row to column institution)

Source	S & L	Bank	Credit union	Broker	Mutual fund	Other	Total[b]
			Destination[a]				
S & L	36.32	1.62	2.27	21.92	2.96	34.91	7.90
Bank	16.60	16.48	7.13	6.55	42.24	10.99	13.27
Credit union	29.81	0.00	9.21	0.00	49.86	11.11	1.01
Broker	0.21	0.00	0.00	94.50	4.05	0.24	54.58
Mutual fund	0.00	0.00	0.00	40.26	24.24	35.50	16.04
Other	19.73	1.78	0.00	12.03	9.14	57.32	7.19
							100.00

[a]   Entries represent the percentage of IRA funds flowing from row institution to column institution (row entries sum up to 100 per cent).
[b]   The last column measures the flow from row institutions as a percentage of total flow (e.g., IRA funds from brokers accounted for 54.58 per cent of the total funds transferred; but brokers recaptured 94.50 per cent of these resources).

Source: MRCA Information Services. Data are disguised for proprietary reasons

are those having to do with the products and services of the firm. The portfolio of such products and services represents the reasons customers do business with the firm. They represent sources of funds and outlets for funds and so have implications for the present and future wellbeing of the firm. In making portfolio and other decisions, firm management faces a need to manage cash flows between already profitable products and newer ones whose potential has yet to be realized. This reveals one of the interdependencies that exist between products and suggests why a firm's product portfolio has become an important unit of analysis. Experience gained in the design, delivery and marketing of one product may generalize to others. Such experience may also permit the firm more quickly to modify its existing products to meet a competitive threat or adapt its offering to changing demand.

In the case of financial services, the joint management of assets and liabilities is critical. To have money to lend and provide loan services, an institution must also have ways of obtaining funds and hence be in the borrowing business as well. The items on the asset (loans made) and liability (deposits taken) sides of the balance sheet are interdependent in many other ways. The same customers may both borrow and deposit monies. Moreover, when credit is needed, deposits tend to be scarce. If the interrelationships are not adequately understood, major problems can arise. For example, during periods when banks are flush with deposits, they concentrate on marketing loan/credit products. To make it easier for the customers to borrow, they may offer credit lines. However, such lines may not be utilized extensively until adverse economic conditions are encountered (e.g., when unemployment is high) and deposits are harder to come by. Hence, when customers exercise their credit lines extensively, deposits often have become more expensive and lending is a less attractive option. Therefore, it is important for banks to understand the nature of demand for both their loan and their depository products. Ideally, one would want to forecast such demand based on not only economic conditions, which are largely uncontrollable, but also on actionable variables such as interest rates, maturities, incentives and disincentives that may be offered. Assets and liabilities have to be managed not only in terms of level, but also in terms of maturity. For example, Savings & Loan associations (S&Ls) experienced difficulty several years ago because they had in their loan portfolios many long-term, low interest mortgage loans and short-term deposits. As the cost of deposits increased, S&L profitability was adversely affected.

Other than asset–liability management, product interdependencies on both customer and firm sides suggest another reason to cross-sell financial services. Figure 8.10 provides information on groups of products used more frequently by the same segment of customers. The first group is a basic set, used by virtually all customers. The next includes these basic products as well as 'savings' products which have low risk associated with them. The third set consists of the basic group plus credit or loan products. Finally, the fourth group consists of the basic set, some of the 'savings' products, and 'investment'

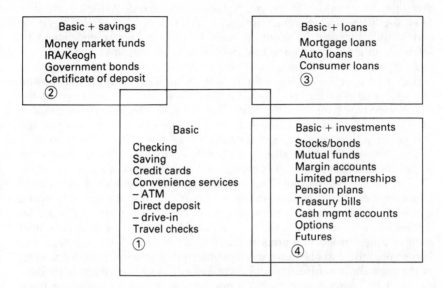

Basic + savings		Basic + loans
Money market funds IRA/Keogh Government bonds Certificate of deposit ②		Mortgage loans Auto loans Consumer loans ③

Basic	Basic + investments
Checking Saving Credit cards Convenience services – ATM Direct deposit – drive-in Travel checks ①	Stocks/bonds Mutual funds Margin accounts Limited partnerships Pension plans Treasury bills Cash mgmt accounts Options Futures ④

FIGURE 8.10   Grouping of products based on customer use

(somewhat riskier) products. Obviously, those who have money (the savers and the investors; generally older and richer) have less need for loans/credit. All individuals need the basic products to transact. These natural groupings suggest that *packages* of services might be developed to suit the needs of different market segments. For example, one package could consist of the basic products, another of basic plus credit products, etc. This would allow a firm to price the package rather than the individual services, thus preventing a direct price comparison of individual services. Additionally, the probability of holding on to a customer is greatly enhanced if the customer has multiple accounts owing to the greater efforts required on the part of the customer if he/she were to switch institutions.

IMPLICATIONS AND CHALLENGES

The demand/competitive side of the framework we have sketched out so briefly has been used by marketers to explore both tactical and strategic questions (Shocker and Srinivasan, 1979; Srivastava *et al.*, 1981). When linked to the firm's perspective, it provides a powerful diagnostic tool. Let us summarize some of the ways in which the framework could be utilized.

1   The framework offers a way of understanding demand and competition from a customer perspective. By accepting consumer sovereignty and competitive reality, a firm may be able to discover opportunities that are

desirable from a customer perspective and hence also desirable for the firm to pursue (if feasible). Several strategic options may be seen as both desirable and feasible because the profit consequences can be better understood by reference to analyses which led to creation of those options.

2   By organizing the analysis around customer problems and purposes, a logical basis is presented for defining both the products and the people who comprise a product market. Moreover, since these problems or purposes can be expected to remain relatively stable, changes in the structure or composition of the market-place can perhaps be better understood. For example, the success of a new product might signify its greater ability, versus existing products, to provide higher levels of already desired benefits or lower costs rather than indicating some basic change in the market's tastes and preferences.

3   Customer purpose implies benefit and cost constraints which help define a product market. Similarly, business scope dictates the resources and capabilities of the firm, which in turn serve to constrain new courses of action. Therefore, a logical basis is provided for deciding whether a strategic option such as a new product or product concept will be feasible for the firm, and how competitive it will be in any given product market. Improved understanding of the competitive set faced by the organization's existing products is similarly provided by knowledge of the purposes for which such products are used, the customers who have such needs, and the benefits necessary to compete in each product market or the costs that limit entry.

4   By viewing strategic options such as new products abstractly, in terms of benefit/cost bundles, it is possible to consider characteristics which, strictly speaking, are not part of the physical product or tangible service. By so doing, it is possible to examine the effects upon demand of benefits that may be creatable only through promotion, distribution, etc. (e.g., rapid delivery of the product, service with a smile, contact with an officer of the organization).

5   By developing a basis for modeling market choices as a function of perceived characteristics of the product–service offerings, some ability exists to predict how the market will behave under changed circumstances. Conceivably, so also might the model of firm decision-making predict how it might behave in the presence of changed market realities. The strategist is able to regard the framework as a kind of simulation of the market-place and to ask 'what if' kinds of questions. Answers to such questions are, of course, constrained by the assumptions upon which the framework is based, the continued validity of the data that are used to implement the framework, the inability to *know* what competitive reactions might be to any initiatives by the firm, and the firm's ability to implement its desired strategy, among others.

6   As one approach to developing an anticipation of possible competitive actions and reacitons, a firm can develop the simulation from the point of view of a competitor and use it to deal with its possible initiatives and reactions if faced with a specific competitive challenge from the firm (Hauser and Shugan, 1983).

7   By focusing upon a number of key aspects affecting demand and competition, this framework is also a framework for measurement. The entry

and exit of competitors from specific product markets, their specific positions in such markets, the existence and bases for decision-making by different customer segments, the goals and capabilities of major competitors, resources available for deployment, etc., all constitute constructs which can be measured and tracked. Therefore the framework becomes a basis for improving strategic and tactical planning for the future. Changes in model constructs can be related to changes in actions of the firm or its competitors or to changes in the environmental circumstances in which market activity takes place. Such systematic examination of relationships should lead to an improving ability to make forecasts of the likelihood and consequences of both the firm's actions and those of its competitors. And to the extent that the framework proves useful as a forecasting tool, it also becomes usable as a control device.

8   As we have several times emphasized, the framework offers the basis for assessing what is desirable as well as feasible (i.e., acceptable) from different customer and managerial perspectives. Desirability in this context is a normative question, providing guidance regarding how all market offerings, including those of any specific firm, might be improved. The framework can in certain instances deal with the question of what constitutes 'best' or 'better.' Issues, for example, of optimal product design or optimal positioning can be addressed within this framework (Sudharshan *et al.*, 1986; Gavish *et al*, 1983). Certain guidance to research and development can be provided by answers to questions such as, 'What share would be obtained by a product with such and so characteristics?' (Urban and Hauser, 1980), even if these characteristics are not feasible today. The framework can aid in deciding whether a specific strategic proposal (e.g., implying new terms for credit cards, improved access to funds, etc.) could be implemented and within what time span. Management may itself find that analyses of its own decision-making style are insightful. The representation of its goal structure, trade-offs desired and the like could provide analytic guidance leading to possible future change or improvement in organization capability.

9   Finally, we would note the potential of the framework as a communications device. Many of the components of the customer framework, i.e., the competitive array, product positions, segment desires and the like, can be represented in chart or diagram form (Green and Wind, 1975). Such a picture can be used to portray the current market situation and the intended configuration after the proposed strategy is implemented. By depicting the proposed strategy in the context of current market conditions, some of the rationale for the proposals may also be communicated. The effect of such a pictorial representation might also be to help those responsible for implementing the proposed strategy better understand its logic and objectives and, consequently, their own role.

Out of considerations such as the above come decisions about both the firm's strategies and tactics and the means for implementing them. The points made have several implications.

1   Except for the times when the firm is very new, it is both limited and aided by its history and tradition. What it has done legitimizes its future

endeavors and enables it to do more, but at the same time it may make certain new endeavors less feasible because they are less compatible with this past. This possibility once again stresses the importance of planning. The new firm has the potential to deploy its resources with fewest constraints, but may be less able to implement its plans because their very newness imposes larger risks on its environment. The older firm must bear both the advantages and limitations imposed by its history or 'track record'.

2   Similarly, a new product introduced to the market affords a firm the maximal capability in shaping the way the resulting product market will come to be perceived. The new product could, if properly planned, serve as a prototype or referent with which later entrants are compared. Where no standards currently exist, the new product may set them. On the other hand, a product new to the firm but not the market must conform to market norms and carry both the advantages and the liabilities associated with past and present products in the firm's portfolio. The firm's products and services are the most important elements in its strategic planning. As such, the longer-term effects of products must be planned with care since ill or incompletely conceived products may have longer-term effects which could go beyond sales of the specific item.

3   The scope of what it has accomplished serves sometimes to blind the firm to what could be. Measurement of success is more often than not made in relative terms, in comparison with the firm's competitors or its own past performance. When there are no absolute standards, a firm may be willing to accept less than it could have achieved with the same resources if only it was aware. This framework, by considering feasibiity and desirability from both firm and customer perspectives, may provide something approximating such standards and with them a foundation for examining more optimal use of the firm's resources.

4   Although according to some observers management should attempt only those objectives that best serve the interests of the firm's shareholders, this framework suggests that managers' own motives and ambitions play important roles in the decisions they make. These may not always be compatible.

5   Because of interdependencies that exist within a firm's set of products, the entire portfolio can become the appropriate unit of analysis for firm decision-making. New products and product additions and deletions need to be considered in terms of their effect upon this portfolio.

The firm and its customers are in a dynamic coexistence. Both sides have advantages to be gained from exchanges between them and thus are willing to spend time and other resources in searching each other out, understanding the nature of any offer, negotiating the transaction and dealing with any other details related to purchase. The marketing concept argues that firms should research the needs or desires of prospective customers and adapt their offerings to such objectives, thereby leading to enhanced customer satisfaction and greater firm profitability from such exchanges. Our framework also recognizes another approach to customer satisfaction and organizational profitability, namely, the ability of the firm to research different customer segments to discover which, if any, would be interested in what the firm, to satisfy its own internal goals, has chosen to provide. The original view of the marketing concept, which had the firm adapting to the needs of some pre-specified set of customers, ignores the fact that the firm has goals of its own which it will attempt to satisfy (although these do not arise in a vacuum). Moreover, its successful implementation is dependent upon the ability of the firm's research adequately to understand customer needs in relation to the offerings of competitors and to translate such needs into action while maintaining profitability objectives. However desirable in concept, this approach may not be feasible in implementation. The second approach of searching for customers for products the firm has chosen to provide has as its major limitation the possibility that insufficient numbers of such customers will be found, or that the costs of search and customer education will be too high.

None the less, these two approaches to customer satisfaction and firm profitability suggest the importance of the twin conditions of feasibility and desirability which much of our earlier discussion has emphasized. It is our conclusion that a more comprehensive framework, built around these powerful ideas, will aid the firm immeasurably in thinking through its important strategic as well as tactical concerns.

REFERENCES

Abell, Derek F. (1980) *Defining the Business: The Starting Point of Strategic Planning.* Englewood Cliffs, NJ: Prentice-Hall.

Choffray, Jean-Marie and Lilien, Gary L. (1980) *Market Planning for New Industrial Products.* New York: John Wiley.

Corey, E. Raymond (1975) Key options in market selection and product planning. *Harvard Business Review*, 53, 119–28.

Day, George S. (1977) Diagnosing the product portfolio. *Journal of Marketing*, 29–38.

—— (1984) *Strategic Market Planning: The Pursuit of Competitive Advantage.* St Paul, Minn.: West Publishing Co.

Gavish, Bezalel, Horsky, Dan and Srikanth, Kishanatham (1983) An approach to the optimal positioning of a new product. *Management Science*, 29, 1277–97.

Green, Paul E. and Wind, Yoram (1975) New way to measure consumers' judgments. *Harvard Business Review*, 53, 107–17.

Hauser, John R. and Shugan, Steven M. (1983) Defensive marketing strategies. *Marketing Science*, 2, 319–60.

Katona, George (1974) Psychology and consumer economics. *Journal of Consumer Research*, 1, 1–8.

McAlister, Leigh and Lattin, James M. (1984) Identifying substitute and complementary relationships revealed by consumer variety-seeking behavior. Working paper 1487–83, Sloan School of Management, Cambridge, Mass.

Parasuraman, A., Zeithaml, Valerie and Berry, Leonard (1985). A conceptual model of service quality and its implication for future research. *Journal of Marketing*, 41, 41–50.

Shocker, Allan D. and Srinivasan, V. (1979)   Multiattribute approaches to product concept evaluation and generation: a critical review. *Journal of Marketing Research*, 16, 159–80.

Shugan, Steven M. (1980)   The cost of thinking. *Journal of Consumer Research*, 7, 99–111.

Srivastava, Rajendra, Alpert, Mark I. and Shocker, Allan D. (1984)   A customer-oriented approach for determining market structures. *Journal of Marketing*, 48, 32–45.

Srivastava, Rajendra, Leone, Robert and Shocker, Allan D. (1981)   Market structure analysis: hierarchical clustering of products based on substitution in use. *Journal of Marketing*, 45, 38–48.

Srivastava, Rajendra K., Mahajan, Vijay, Ramaswami, Sridhar and Cherian, Joseph (1985)   A multi-attribute diffusion model for forecasting the adoption of investment alternatives for consumers. *Technological Forecasting and Social Change*, 28, 325–33.

Sudharshan, D., May, Jerrold H. and Shocker, Allan D. (1986)   A simulation comparison of methods for new product location. *Working Paper 82–126* (March), Owen Graduate School of Management, Vanderbilt University, Nashville, Tenn.

Tobin, J. (1967)   Lifecycle savings and balance growth. In B. Fellener (ed.), *Ten Economic Studies in the Tradition of Irving Fisher*. New York: John Wiley.

Urban, Glen L. and Hauser, John R. (1980)   *Design and Marketing of New Products*. Englewood Cliffs, NJ: Prentice-Hall.

Wright, Peter L. (1975)   Consumer choice strategies: simplifying vs. optimizing. *Journal of Marketing Research*, 12, 60–7.

Commentary on Chapter 8

Robin Wensley

This chapter raises a number of important issues at various levels in our discussion of strategic change within a market environment. Such issues are also at various levels, including technical, theoretical and philosophical. In this review I will start by considering some of the more technical issues in the detailed analysis and discussion presented, and then raise some broader considerations with respect to both our practical understanding and our researching of these and related phenomena.

TECHNICAL ISSUES

The technical issues principally concern the nature, validity and interpretation of the analysis and techniques actually used to interpret the nature of the market-place for customer financial services. These issues can be summarized under concerns with respect to predictive validity, customer characterization and the nature of competitive strategy.

Predictive Validity

In any marketing analysis, we should be concerned with predictive validity in a number of ways. We are first concerned with the relatively simple analysis of variance measure of validity in asking the question, 'How far does the relevant set of independent variables actually go to explain the variance in the dependent variable?' We are also concerned, however, with wider issues in terms of predictive validity, because we would wish to use the same framework to make estimates of likely behaviour in the future. This means that we have to be concerned not only with the likely stability in the attitude structures revealed, but also with the general relationship between attitudes and behaviour that we can expect. In other closely related work, Srivastava and Shocker (1984) have published detailed ANOVA tables for similar forms of analysis. These results suggest that any single-customer characterization scale (such as socio-demographic or usage situation) tends to explain only about 10–15 per cent of the variance in the dependent variable, which in this case is attitude perception of the appropriateness of a particular offering. Such explanatory power is of course very limited, although we should recognize that the oft-used relationship between return on investment and market share shows significantly lower explanatory power and yet has been widely and strongly influential in business and marketing strategy practice.[1]

Customer Characterization

The problems of the temporal stability of the attitude structures and the relationship between attitudes to actual purchase behaviour still need to be further researched. We do know, however, that in general it is quite possible that in both of these areas the linkages are relatively weak and therefore the explanatory power will be severely reduced. Srivastava and Shocker recognize the dynamic and evolving nature of the market-place, but a likely corollary of this is a dynamic and evolving structure of attitudes and perceptions among customers. The authors overcome this issue by postulating a set of customer purposes or problems which remain stable despite changing knowledge and the changing nature of specific offerings:

> Customer purpose or problem, when determined, is presumed to dictate all that follows in the way of supplier selection and product-market construction. The strategic planning importance of this presumption is that such customer objectives will normally change only gradually, so that immediate or short-run market actions continue to be understandable in the light of such fundamentals.

However, as they themselves recognize, this is indeed no more than a presumption and needs to be subjected to more extended empirical testing. Given what we know from other domains of marketing activity about the relatively 'subjective' characterization by individual customers of the options and their own purposes,[2] it is noticeable that in their chapter Shocker and Srivastava often have to characterize customer response as very much 'rational economic man' – this despite the fact that we are dealing with areas where such analytic frameworks are potentially most misleading, such as issues of savings and risk.

Competitive Strategy

For students of strategic management particularly, in a competitive market environment a further technical problem with the analysis is that the dependent variable is directly customer perceptions or indirectly customer behaviour, not either firm performance or competitive behaviour. This means that it is not always easy to see how the information about the evolving nature of customer perceptions can and should influence competitive strategy. At an epistemological level it is fair for Shocker and Srivastava to claim that, if competitive behaviour takes place against a backdrop of customer perceptions and behaviours, then we 'should understand more of the backcloth in interpreting the individual actions'. However, it is also probably true that it would help our interpretation if we could make more explicit links between particular characteristics of the backcloth and particular options in terms of competitive response. The paper mentions a number of these in a relatively *ad hoc* manner, but if we were to be more systematic we would need to consider both

1   the extent to which we might wish to modify our basically game-theoretical model of competitive behaviour to take into account competitors' differential positions from the point of view of their customers as well as from the point of view of their resources, and
2   the extent to which the competitive options are significantly different for different firms because of their current resource dispositions.

Such a refocusing of our interest in customer attitude structures might well indicate that we should be more selective, with a more cursory analysis of various aspects of the problem, compensated by a more detailed analysis of others.

THEORETICAL ISSUES

The theoretical issues raised by this paper can be considered in two main areas: first, how this method of understanding the process of strategy evolution compares and contrasts with other approaches; and second, the significance of some of the underlying assumptions in this approach.

Comparison with Other Methods

The most obvious alternative framework for understanding the process of firm behaviour in a competitive market-place is that developed under the general paradigm of structure–conduct–performance (SCP) and industrial organization economics. In such a wide field there is obviously a significant number of different approaches, but it is probably fair to regard Michael Porter as one of the key popularizers of the approach (see, e.g., Porter 1980, 1985). Porter, along with others, has extended the original SCP notion to take into account concepts such as strategic groups of similar firms, the impact of more complex industry infrastructure in terms of other independent channel members and the nature of the 'value chain'. Compared with the approach presented in the above paper, however, all these developments remain very strongly cost/resource-based. Indeed, it is arguable that Porter's notion of the 'value chain' should still be seen as a 'cost' rather than a 'value' chain, because there is only a limited attempt to map the structure on to a customer benefit or value perspective.

The approach presented by Shocker and Srivastava and my earlier critique of it also raises a number of analytically important questions with respect to approaches similar to Michael Porter's. In particular, it is clear that a resource cost perspective may not end up with a detailed industry structure that maps at all well onto a market structure as derived from customer perceptions and attitudes. Second, and equally important, the very fact that we can explain only a limited amount of individual behaviour from a customer-based analysis must also make us consider the extent to which we can expect to do no better from a similarly detailed analysis on the resource cost structure of the industry to explain individual firm behaviour and performance. Indeed, it is noticeable that very little of the Michael Porter-related work has been supported by systematic empirical analysis compared with the use of single or multiple selected anecdotes.[3] We can hardly expect to judge a customer-based perspective on one set of validity criteria and an industry-based perspective on another.

The Wider Significance of the Underlying Assumptions in the Model

The theories underlying the model presented in the paper are very consistent with an approach to competitive market evolution which considers the simultaneous interaction of both customer experience and competitor offerings.[4] In a technical sense, such an approach implies that we cannot 'solve' the equations for customer response unless we simultaneously solve those underlying the nature of the competitive offerings that they receive.

Equally importantly for understanding the nature of competitive strategy in such an environment, the paper implies focusing our attention on a market exchange definition of individual firm activity as 'the process of resource transformation to produce a product or service offering to a particular customer in a specific use situation.' This therefore suggests that we should consider three broad types of specialization or focus for individual firms in their competitive strategy alongside the obvious one of a pure volume and cost approach based on a standard product: product/resource specialization, context/use situation specialization, and customer/end-user specialization.

The paper emphasizes the extent to which we cannot effectively discuss the latter two forms of specialization without recognizing both customer organization and customer infrastructure, which are the analogies of industry organization and industry infrastructure, which we are more commonly used to looking at in terms of the resource cost perspective. This means that we have to consider much more carefully the assumptions often built into forms of market analysis which are popularized by strategic management and indeed many market management texts. In such texts the issues of use and then customer segmentation are still defined as within a notion of a clear product boundary. If we really start with our customers, we will tend to reconsider the nature of such boundaries and their interrelationships to recognize the fact that pure product boundaries can be relatively unimportant and insignificant. For instance, in the archetypal example of segmentation, we often describe the motor vehicle market as segmented into a number of categories including luxury vehicles, sports vehicles, family vehicles and economy vehicles. But if we look, for example, at the customers of economy vehicles, their portfolio choices may be better defined in terms of the options of public transportation *v.* the purchase of an economy vehicle rather than between the purchase of one type of vehicle and another. Similarly, if we look at multi-car household units, their choice of vehicle for a second car may depend on particular usage situations, and they may then compare this with other options such as hiring. We therefore recognize that the nature of the customers individually and the attendant customer clusters are such that we build up a different perspective on relative substitute offerings.

In terms of understanding the evolving nature of market-places, we clearly need to gather a significant volume of data about customer perceptions and behaviours in a systematic and comprehensive way so that we can develop a better understanding of the ways in which the market as a whole is organized to deliver and respond to individual customer demands. Such an understanding will almost inevitably throw new light on many issues which we currently may try and understand solely from a resource-based/industry infrastructure perspective. This should mean that we will begin to recognize the extent to which the whole market organization, including the actions of various intermediary agents, is to be seen as a dynamic and evolving response system to the nature of actual customer demand, rather than nearly a logistical distribution system for getting products from manufacturing entities to final end-users. As such, it is useful to remember Wroe Alderson's earlier notion that we should look at the stage activities of each intermediary in a distribution channel as one of actively 'matching and sorting' – in other words, matching their offerings to the specific demands they perceive from their customers while sorting through the offerings they receive from those further 'up' the channel to achieve such an appropriate match.

PHILOSOPHICAL/METHODOLOGICAL ISSUES

Finally, the Srivastava–Shocker paper raises a number of issues that are essentially of a philosophical or methodological nature. In particular, the very complexity of the analysis they represent raises the issue of how we can both know and understand about the phenomena we are attempting to explore. The very fact, as discussed above, that the available models, however well defined and well executed, cannot expect to explain anything near the majority of the variance in the system also suggests that we have to consider the relationship between our forms of analysis and the nature of the problem.

It is entirely possible that we need simultaneously to look for different forms of analysis and to consider the problem at a different level. The most powerful analogy to be applied to this issue currently would appear to be that of the domain of ecological research. This is not only because ecology has offered perhaps some of the most powerful current notions in competitive strategy, such as 'competitive survival' and 'niche', but also because it too faces the twin problems of classifying and understanding a process of interactive evolution between species and their habitat.

While it is instructive to consider directly some of the research informed by the ecological paradigm on issues of competitive strategy and survival,[5] it is also clear that, when we compare the understandings derived from such research with the approach represented in the paper, we see some additional problems and concerns.

In particular, the 'ecological approach' which has currently been applied has tended to be unidirectional in presuming that the 'habitat' is relatively univariate and passive. The Shocker–Srivastava paper emphasizes the extent to which the habitat, i.e. the customers, is, in fact far from either inactive or stable in its behaviour; indeed, it is interesting that a similar concern has been expressed by a number of leading thinkers in the study of evolutionary biology (see esp. Levins and Lewontin, 1985).

On the other hand, we must recognize that very great care has gone into trying to develop a systematic way of classifying species and phenomena which has yet to be replicated in the area of strategic management and marketing evolution. The seminal book by Bill McKelvey (1982) illustrates both the opportunities and the problems that await such an attempt. In particular, it is clear that those who, like the authors of this paper and indeed the author of this commentary, wish to encourage the adoption of a more marketing/customer perspective in our understanding of competitive evolution must respond to a severe 'unit of analysis' problem. To explain and understand what happens, we must not fall into the trap of arguing that more detail and more complexity is inevitably helpful. The search for greater detail may merely result in models that have less rather than more explanatory power. The above paper represents a stimulating and significant step in this direction but remains one of many that we will have to take if we are really to establish a way of incorporating a customer perspective in our understanding of strategic change.

NOTES

1 See the discussion, for instance, in Jacobson and Aaker (1985).
2 Many of these approaches are reviewed in Day *et al.* (1979).
3 A notable contrary example is Porter (1976), but this is not widely quoted because perhaps the results were not as consistent with the 'theory' of mobility and exit barriers as might have been hoped.
4 The background to the need for such an approach is argued in Day and Wensley (1983).
5 See, for instance, Chapter 2 ('Nature intervenes: organizations as organisms), in Morgan (1986).

REFERENCES

Day, George S., Shocker, A. D. and Srivastava, R. K. (1979) Customer-orientated approaches to identifying product markets. *Journal of Marketing*, Fall, 8–19.

Day, George S. and Wensley, R. (1983) Marketing theory with a strategic orientation. *Journal of Marketing*, Fall, 79–89.

Jacobson, R. and Aaker, D. A. (1985) Is market share all that it's cracked up to be? *Journal of Marketing*, Fall, 11–22.

Levins, R. and Lewontin, R. (1985) *The Dialectical Biologist*. Cambridge, Mass.: Harvard University Press.

McKelvey, B. (1982) *Organizational Systematics: Taxonomy, Evolution, Classification*. Berkeley: University of California Press.

Morgan, Gareth (1986) *Images of Organization*. Beverly Hills: Sage.

Porter, Michael E. (1976) Please note location of the nearest exit: exit barriers and planning. *California Management Review*, Winter, 21–33.

—— (1980) *Competitive Strategy: Techniques for Analyzing Industries and Competitors*. New York: Free Press.

—— (1985) *Competitive Advantage: Creating and Sustaining Superior Performance*. New York: Free Press.

Srivastava, R. K., Alpert, Mark I. and Shocker, Allan D. (1984) A customer-orientated approach for determining market structures. *Journal of Marketing*, Spring, 32–45.

9 The Influence of Product and Production Flexibility on Marketing Strategy

G. Easton and R. Rothschild

INTRODUCTION

The central concern of this chapter is the idea of 'organizational flexibility'. There are at least two ways in which this concept can be regarded as an element in the management of strategic change. The first can be expressed in terms of the tradeoff which organizations are typically required to make between the objectives of 'flexibility' and 'efficiency'. This tradeoff has been the subject of a substantial literature. For example, Ansoff's (1968) classic corporate strategy framework suggests the pursuit of the objectives of flexibility but warns of their possible conflict with those of financial efficiency. Burns and Stalker (1961) implicitly consider the problem in the course of relating organizational structure and its inherent flexibility to particular environments. Abernathy and Wayne (1974) examine the problems of maintaining manufacturing flexibility in the face of arguments for efficiency which derive from the idea of an 'experience curve'. Insofar as the present paper also analyses aspects of the tradeoff between flexibility and efficiency, it can be regarded as a contribution to this literature.

There is another sense in which flexibility becomes an element of strategic change. Strategic change must inevitably be, at least in part, a process of adaptation to a changing environment. In this paper we draw what we believe is an important distinction between adaptation and flexibility. The former may be regarded as a long term, discontinuous and resource-expensive change, while the latter is generally short term, continuous and resource-inexpensive. The capacity for adaptation within any given organization may or may not correlate with its ability to maintain flexibility, and indeed it is possible that in some cases flexibility may inhibit adaptation. However, an understanding of the nature of flexbility is crucial to an understanding of the process of adaptation. One of the concerns of this paper is an elaboration of the links between these two concepts.

Our focus in what follows has been deliberately restricted. The purpose in doing so is to generate specific and potentially testable insights. Two aspects of organizational flexibility will be examined: flexibility in the production processes which an organization may employ, and flexibility in the products which it produces. The implications of more or less flexibility in these two areas of activity are examined only insofar as they relate to marketing strategy. We concentrate on this relationship because it is of particular interest to economists and researchers in the field of marketing, and also because it lends itself to analysis within the framework of recent work being undertaken at the interface between marketing and production. Some of the themes addressed in this work are reviewed in the next section. There follows a general discussion of the nature of flexibility in organizations. This, in turn, leads on to a more specific consideration of the idea of flexibility in manufacturing processes. We next describe the impact of increased flexibility on marketing strategy. The concept of product flexibility is addresssed in similar fashion. Finally, we draw some tentative conclusions.

Manufacturing Strategy

Flexibility will be discussed here in the context of the relationship between two subsystems which exist within a firm: manufacturing and marketing. This relationship has attracted relatively little attention from scholars in the field of marketing. Shapiro (1977) has examined some of its organizational aspects, while Blois (1983) has charted the communication flows between marketing and manufacturing departments. Stobaugh and Telesio (1983) have looked at the manufacturing implications of various marketing strategies. These contributions notwithstanding, the most systematic attempt to examine manufacturing/marketing interactions has come from those researching in the area of production/operations management. In particular, the process-product life cycles matrix developed by Hayes and Wheelwright (1979) was an explicit attempt to examine the strategic interface between marketing and manufacturing.

The present paper is one of a number which attempt to identify the role of manufacturing in the strategic process. An early example of this approach is W. Skinner's 'Manufacturing – Missing Link in Corporate Strategy' (1969). The theme was taken up fifteen years later by Hayes and Wheelwright (1984) who wrote:

> The notion that manufacturing can be a competitive weapon, rather than just a collection of rather ponderous resources and constraints, is not new, although its practice is not very widespread. Even in many well-managed firms, manufacturing plays an essentially neutral role, reflecting the view that marketing, sales and R and D provide better bases for achieving a competitive advantge. (Hayes and Wheelwright, 1984)

Hill (1980), (1985) has made a similar point from a European perspective.

The arguments are broadly as follows. Manufacturing is essentially an engineering biased, day-to-day activity which is concerned with productivity and cost minimization. As such, it is subservient to the finance and marketing functions. Key capacity and technology decisions relate to capital, and as such are divorced from those of an operational nature. They are taken by senior management, who frequently lack manufacturing experience or knowledge and who use inappropriate financial evaluation techniques. This state of affairs may be attributed to history, operations management culture, promotion paths or lack of a suitable conceptual framework. The drive to establish manufacturing as a force in the strategic process has been fuelled by the debate on international competitiveness. A great deal of research has been carried out into the 'secret' of the success of Japanese industry, (for example, Hayes, 1981, Abernathy *et al.*, 1981, Wheelwright, 1981). Japan's lower costs, better delivery and superior quality are attributed, by those researching in the area of production, to the integration of manufacturing with other activities.

Manufacturing strategy, as a discipline, seeks to forge conceptual links with those of a cognate nature. It should not therefore be surprising that it affords a point of departure for much of what follows in this paper. A narrower focus is made possible by restricting the analysis to the flexibility of manufacturing processes and its impact on marketing strategy. Our argument is that it is at least as important to understand the essential elements of a single relationship as it is to understand a whole pattern of relationships.

FLEXIBILITY IN ORGANIZATIONS

Flexibility may be defined as the ability of a system to take on a variety of forms. A flexible organization may be capable of a diverse set of activities, be represented in a range of markets with a variety of products, use and incorporate different technologies and employ multi-talented, widely experienced people within a loose structure. Substantial cash resources facilitate the transition of such an organization from one state to another.

Another way of characterizing flexibility in organizations is in terms of 'cycles' of activities. The central feature of such a representation is that there are a variety of cycles which the organization, or parts of the organization, can perform, but in the course of doing so the system exhibits a tendency to return to its initial state. Figure 9.1 illustrates the phenomenon. Put another way, the organization may be seen as possessing the repertoire of behavioural responses which it can implement. Some of these may be undertaken simultaneously, as for example is the case when the firm operates in different markets. Here, the element of flexibility lies in the firm's capacity to switch resources among its various activities. Other behavioural responses may be implemented sequentially, as for example is the case when the firm undertakes different batch operations in production. Flexibility in this case is a function of the 'ease' with which the system can switch from one cycle to another.

FIGURE 9.1   The stability of the system

Such 'ease' can in turn be defined in terms of the time or resources required in order to make the switch. These quantities, which provide a measure of 'flexible efficiency', will be discussed in greater detail later. For the present they may be taken to provide a measure of the 'responsiveness' of the system.

It is useful at this point to distinguish between 'flexibility' and 'adaptability'. One extreme view is to regard the former as applying only to activity cycles which the system performs at any point in time, or which it has performed in the past. By way of contrast, if the organization carries out a new cycle then this may be regarded as adaptation. In practice, such a distinction is hard to make. No two activity cycles are exactly the same, and the question arises as to the nature and magnitude of the external change (e.g. machinery or new material) which must occur before the firm can be regarded as adapting in some way. A more interesting problem arises when changes take place in a given cycle as a consequence of organization learning, which can be regarded as incremental adaptation.

It may be more appropriate to regard the phenomenon identified here as being represented by a continuum, with 'flexibility' at one end and 'adaptability' at the other. In such a framework, flexibility relates to existing capacity and relatively small changes within it; adaptability relates to substantial changes in this capacity.

Flexibility entails a cost. The tradeoff is conventionally taken to be between flexibility and efficiency. A flexible organization sacrifices narrow functional specialization and the standardization of products and procedures which permit more efficient operation. As an example, a firm with a wide product range which sells into diverse markets will generally be able to shift resources between them in response to changing conditions. But the costs of production, distribution and marketing will usually be higher than is the case when the same sales volume is derived from fewer products and a smaller number of markets. In the sections which follow we shall consider such costs and benefits of flexibility, and give attention to the tradeoffs which it implies.

FLEXIBILITY IN MANUFACTURING PROCESSES

There is a great deal of scope for flexibility in a manufacturing organization other than at the level of the manufacturing process. At the highest level of aggregation, different manufacturing channels may be established both 'upstream' and 'downstream'. This makes it possible to exploit the options of 'make or buy', contracting and subcontracting. Alternatively, within the manufacturing plant itself, flexibility may be introduced by way, for example, of inventory systems and different methods of payment. Whilst there is much to be said about these possiblities, the demands of space and tractability make it necessary to focus attention on one type of flexibility in particular: that of flexibility in the manufacturing process itself.

The ways in which process flows are organized in a manufacturing plant may be categorised as project, jobbing, batch, assembly line and continuous flow (Hayes and Wheelwright, (1984)). In practice it is often difficult to distinguish these processes and many plants will exhibit characteristics of several of the categories. If flexibility is taken to relate to the system's capacity to manufacture new products or new product mixes, then in general the flexibility of the whole system decreases from the project level through to that of the continuous flow.

Project work stands out in this context. The project is almost invariably customized, targetted at a relatively small group of customers, produced over a long period of time employing non standard procedures and often involves a substantial degree of subcontracting. It is perhaps the ultimate flexible process. Organizations may be built to complete a single project and then disbanded. These characteristics suggest that project work should be treated separately from the other categories of process flow organization. This is not to say that some of the issues of flexibility that will be discussed later do not apply in this case; nor is it to argue that the marketing of projects has been adequately covered elsewhere, for it has not. The problem is simply postponed.

Since manufacturing has, until recently, been concerned in both theory and in practice with matters of efficiency, there is some evidence that the flexible end of the process flow organization spectrum has been regarded as primitive and deserving of improvement. Such a view is to be inferred from Abernathy and Townsend's (1975) description of the process life cycle:

> As a productive process develops over time it does so with a characteristic pattern: process flows become more rational, tasks more specific, process more capital intensive, product designs more standardized, etc.

Three definite stages may be identified – uncoordinated, segmental and systemic. In the early stages of the cycle, product and process changes are frequent, the process itself is unstandardized and often manual in nature, and the relationship among parts uncertain and unspecified. It is consequently inefficient in normal manufacturing terms. As the technology and market matures, specialization and standardization, where appropriate, become possible. However, this may occur at different rates for different parts of the process and so the process may be regarded as segmented. Finally the systemic process is highly specialized in procedures, standardized in products, but above all integrated. The equipment is expensive and redesign and reconfiguration slow and expensive.

If process evolution were to be regarded as inevitable then this would have significant implications for the links between manufacturing and marketing. However, this will not invariably be the case. Abernathy and Townsend argue that 'development requires consistent progress in four different factors: process continuity and predictability, product improvement and standardization, process scale and improved material inputs'. All must be present to a minimum level for development to continue. In addition, management may not be effective in promoting development. Finally, competition and particular patterns of market demands may stall the cycle. Thus, jobbing printers continue to exist at least partly because of the custom nature of their product and the fragmented nature of the demand for it. The cycle may in fact reverse as it is said to have done for the automobile industry in the US in the early 1920s. Perhaps the process life cycle should be regarded as a possible development path for certain products under certain technological and market conditions. It does not imply that flexibility will, in some deterministic sense, always be sacrificed for efficiency.

So far manufacturing processes, and their inherent flexibilities, have been discussed in an historical context but technological changes are occurring which look set to outdate traditional analysis. The key to these changes is information processing. Many of the problems of managing and controlling productive processes stemmed from an inability to acquire, store and process the information that they generated. With the advent of computers this constraint may be partially or wholly removed. One of the benefits which arises is that the nature of the flexibility/efficiency tradeoff is likely to alter.

However it is a mistake to believe that the process of automation is likely to be either a smooth one or that it is in anything but its infancy. Figure 9.2 provides a quasi-history of the development of information technology (IT)-based manufacturing. As in the case of the process life cycle it is unlikely that for all products the ultimate goal is production in an automatic factory. Some products may be suitable for computer aided design but not manufacture. Stand-alone robots may work more effectively in the manufacture of certain types of product. The links and integration required for the full flowering of IT-based production may be technologically feasible but not economically or strategically desirable. Thus, automation should be seen not as a unified concept with simple predictable qualities but as a heterogeneous group of technologies with the capacity but not necessarily the need for integration.

Such a view helps to put the following comment by Goldhar and Jelinek (1985) into context.

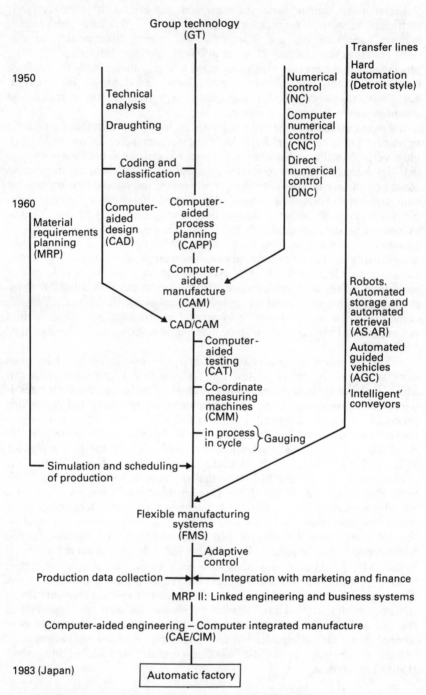

FIGURE 9.2 The development of flexible integrated manufacturing systems
Source: Macbeth (1985)

The computer allows us to integrate not only the factory itself, but also to integrate manufacturing with such functions as engineering and marketing at a level never before possible. In consequence, because process predictability improves as the level of integration rises, new demands for timely delivery, quality and low cost can be raised without the traditionally accepted trade-offs in variety and flexibility.

When the full fruits of IT-based manufacture are achieved, economies of scope replace economies of scale. The costs of producing a range of different products are no greater than those involved in producing larger quantities of the same product. The economic order quantity becomes one unit in the limit. Variety and flexibility are available without the penalty of inefficiency, and the philosophy of manufacturing is turned on its head.

Blois (1986) is one who remains unconvinced by this argument. Rather, he holds that current experience with flexible manufacturing systems suggests that flexibility is in practice much more limited than might be expected, at least partly due to the constraint of software limitation. Moreover, in his view, flexibility at anything less than the level of complete integration is likely to cause interface problems between processes, and with other functions. The counter-argument is that these are 'early days' and that IT-based manufacturing is simply experiencing the frustration of expectations that has characterized all major technological breakthroughs from computers to biotechnology. What seems undeniable is that flexibility, in whatever form it takes, will be more a feature of manufacturing in the future than it is at present and that this will create both significant opportunities and problems.

The Nature of Process Flexibility

Marketing strategy involves the matching of organizational competences to market needs. One such competence is the flexibility of the chosen production process. In this section we develop a framework for the characterization of process flexibility. We draw in particular upon the work of Slack (1983), and distinguish two related aspects of flexibility: 'dimensions' and 'efficiency'.

Flexibility must always occur within the context of a particular *dimension*. Slack suggests five such dimensions: product, product mix, quality level, output volume and delivery time. Gerwin (1982) suggests a similar set: mix, parts, routing, design change and volume. The measurement of flexibility does however present some quite considerable problems.

Flexibility, broadly defined, must be measured in part in terms of 'potential'. A plant will rarely realise more than a small subset of the tasks of which it is capable. It is sometimes difficult to establish the true potential of such plant, and its technical limits are often impossible to define precisely. There may be a tailing-off of performance with respect to a particular parameter and the question which then arises is who decides at what point the performance is sufficiently unacceptable to rule out the use of plant for that purpose. In these circumstances, not only are the measurements uncertain but the boundaries become blurred.

Flexibility is also multidimensional in nature. It is not sufficient for analysts to simply profile a system one dimension at a time. Some form of multidimensional flexibility 'mapping' is required. This will serve to identify the interactions and tradeoffs which must invariably occur where different dimensions are involved. For example, a printing shop may be able to print 6 colours on a foil/polyethylene laminate, overlacquer and slit to 6 cms but only print 4 colours with no overlacquer if the substrate is foil/polyester. At a higher level of aggregation one might expect to find interaction between, for example, product and delivery flexibility. Flexibility 'maps' would not necessarily be regular over their defined spaces: there would be irregularities, 'holes' and discontinuities. In fact, from the perspective of the firm, the latter might be seen as giving rise in competitors to the production-side equivalent of the discontinuities that strategists seek so eagerly in product markets, and so provide opportunities which could be exploited.

The measurement of flexibility has a great deal to do with the chosen level of aggregation. Slack and Gerwin discuss measures at a high level of aggregation, while Taylor (1983), in his treatment of the purchase of flexible manufacturing systems, refers to the parameters of a particular machine operation. At the lowest level it is relatively simple to define the 'range' of a given machine. The addition to the process of a second machine and a human operative with particular skills will make measurement more complicated. In practice there is a tradeoff between the level at which the measurement is undertaken and the degree of accuracy which can be achieved. The global measures required for strategic analysis (for example, product mix flexibility) are likely to be subject to substantial estimation errors.

A further difficulty which arises is one specific to the interface between production and marketing. This may be termed the 'translation problem'. Flexibility as defined by those involved in production refers, particularly at lower levels of aggregation, to process parameters. Marketing managers, on the other hand, are largely interested in determining the way in which these process parameters translate into product-related flexibility. The development of appropriate dimensions, measures, levels of aggregation and translation requires an iterative and interactive process. Of course, in many cases relatively few dimensions are relevant to strategic choices.

Flexible *efficiency* is defined as the ease with which a system can move amongst attainable states. It is the second key process flexibility variable in that, in a sense, it measures the 'cost' of flexibility. As such, it is essentially derivative or second order in nature. The rate of change may be measured in terms of any of the key objectives which an organisation recognises. Slack suggests as relevant criteria time (t) and money. The speed with which a system can modify a product, P, can be denoted by the derivative dP/dt. It is possible, in theory, to define a flexibility 'function' which would show how this rate changes over the product field in question. In practice, of course, this will be difficult to achieve with any accuracy. Nevertheless, broad estimates could in principle be made which would provide a basis for informing strategic decision making. The concept is also useful as a reminder of the phenomenon of inertia; that is to say, all changes are to a greater or lesser degree resisted by systems, and the recognition of this fact is crucially important when the flexibility of any such system is being assessed.

How, in general, does flexibility interact with and affect marketing strategy? The dimensions of flexibility provide an important link. The dialogue between the marketing and production functions in an organisation must, where flexibility is concerned, be conducted in a common language and with common definitions, i.e. those which generate the routes which are most likely to secure competitive advantage. The evaluation of strategies requires a knowledge of the efficiency of flexibility and the ease with which various configurations can be achieved. Problems of measurement themselves contribute to uncertainty in the minds of decision makers.

Process Flexibility and Marketing Strategy

The approach which we take in this section is to examine the costs and benefits involved in a small increase in process flexibility. The perspective is that of a firm which has the option of achieving this objective through the purchase of either additional conventional plant or plant which incorporates computer based flexibility. In order to narrow the focus and render the analysis tractable, a number of restrictive assumptions have been made. The discussion is largely concerned with the impact of process flexibility on product design and product mix, i.e. the variety of products of different specification which could be manufactured. In addition, the analysis is confined to the manufacture of industrial products. This enables us to eliminate the complications associated with the existence of distribution channels and mass marketing methods.

The most restrictive and formally analytical case is considered first; this relies on a form of economic analysis. In the remainder of the section we shall relax some of the assumptions in order to provide a broader and more qualitative evaluation of the consequences of a move towards greater process flexibility.

Marketing strategy may be said to involve a search for sustainable competitive advantage. In the first instance, therefore, the analysis will concentrate on the firm's existing competitors, i.e. those with limited process flexibility and a range of 'simple' products. We address in particular the question of how a switch to greater product flexibility might affect the competitive position.

Consider the following situation. The firm has open to it the possibility of using a process which is 'efficient' in the sense that it will produce a single variety of the product, embodying certain characteristics in fixed proportions; alternatively, it may employ a 'flexible' process which offers the potential for producing a number of varieties of the product. The analysis of this case employs a modified version of a model first used by Lancaster (1966). Figure 9.3 represents a Lancastrian 'characteristics space'. The space contains a fixed

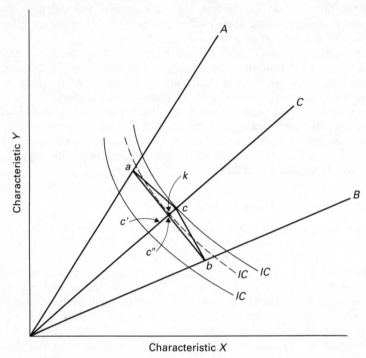

FIGURE 9.3   The process-characteristics space

number of 'processes', distinguished here by the letters A,B ... and each capable of producing varieties embodying in different proportions two essential characteristics (denoted X and Y) of the product class. The available quantities of these characteristics are represented on the axes. The points a,b ... show the quantities of the varieties which can be produced by these processes for given outlay. Thus, the further any such point from the origin, the lower is the unit price of the associated variety, while each point on the linear segments which link a,b ... is a combination of the outputs of the two processes which can be purchased for the given amount. We suppose that a representative buying organisation may either purchase one variety exclusively or combine varieties in any proportions represented on the linear segments.

The curves labelled IC show combinations among which the consumer is indifferent, while satisfaction is taken to increase with distance from the origin. The subjective rate at which one feature of the product (and, hence, of the process by which it is produced) is 'traded off' against the other is given by the slope of the *IC* curve between any two points.

Consider first the case where processes A,B and C give rise to varieties which sell at a common price. As constructed, the figure shows that the highest level of satisfaction for the representative consumer is attained through the consumption of the variety associated with C. If, however, the price of this variety were to rise (other prices remaining unchanged) so that the quantity available for the given outlay fell to c', then the consumer would obtain greater satisfaction from the combination of the outputs of processes A and B represented by the point of tangency k. Conversely, a fall in the price of the variety associated with C from the level corresponding to c'' would displace processes A and B from the market.

Suppose now that, in addition to a fixed number of efficient processes there is available one which is flexible. Figure 9.4 illustrates the case. Here, C is taken to be the flexible process, and the combinations of characteristics

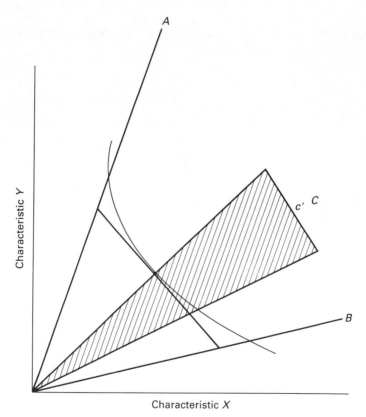

FIGURE 9.4 Flexibility *vs* efficiency in the process-characteristics space

which it offers can be represented by a cone rather than a single ray. The faces of the cone define the region of flexibility, so that the shaded area represents the attainable set of specification combinations offered by process C. The set of attainable combinations is taken to consist of only those varieties which are currently produced by efficient processes (i.e. A, B, and C). The mean output of the flexible processes which can be purchased for given outlay is given by the midpoint of the face of the cone. This quantity is represented here by the point c', but in general the relative mean price of the output of process C is a matter for conjecture. In any case, however, the extent to which C will displace other processes from the market will depend upon relative prices and upon the width of the cone (region of flexibility) relative to the competing efficient processes. Where the output of flexible processes can be sold at lower prices than those of efficient processes, the case is as represented in Figure 5.

In this example, in which it is assumed that varieties produced by A and B sell at a common price, the success of the strategy of replacing an efficient process by a flexible one, depends upon the width of the cone. If the faces of the cone are contained between the rays representing A and B, then the

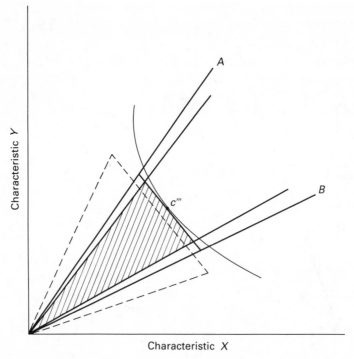

FIGURE 9.5   Flexible and efficient processes: pricing

flexible process does not displace its efficient neighbours from the market at a higher price than that which will allow the purchase of c'''. At any higher price, the flexible process will attract only the former buyers of the output of the efficient version of C, and the justification for the introduction of the flexible process can then be attributed only to lower production costs which permit higher profits at the higher price. If, on the other hand, the faces of the cone lie either on or 'outside' the rays A and B, then the mean output of the flexible process will have to be sold at a lower price than those produced by A and B, since if this were not so, the consumer could purchase a convex combination of these two processes and be better off.

Suppose now that the costs of output from process A exceed those from B. In this case, the reduction in the mean price of the output from process C from an arbitrary level will initially displace A from the market, while leaving B as the most preferred choice. With a further reduction in price, C will eliminate convex combinations of A and B as preferred choices, until ultimately process B is itself displaced. The rate at which these points will be attained clearly depends upon the relative prices of all three processes and upon the width of the cone.

The analysis contains a broad policy implication. As a general observation, it suggests that firms which contemplate the introduction of flexible processes should address market segments in which efficient processes are densely packed. Conversely, firms employing efficient processes should seek those segments which support only small numbers of clearly defined varieties. This prescription holds irrespective of the precise distribution of consumers' preferences over the product range, since the more concentrated are such preferences in any given segment, other things being equal, the greater are the potential gains from the employment of flexible processes, and conversely where preferences are less concentrated.

The foregoing discussion is based upon a set of simplifying assumptions which have been made in order to render the analysis tractable. A relaxation of some of these assumptions enables us to consider the more general costs and benefits of increased process flexibility.

What, in product/market terms, does process flexibility confer upon the firm which might lead to competitive advantage? The answer in broad terms is *width* and *depth* of market attack: width because products can now be made which allow entry into new and as yet unknown markets; depth in terms of the capacity to provide customers with products which more closely match their requirements.

In the section containing the formal economic analysis, we assumed that the flexibility 'cone' spanned only the existing range of simple products. In practice, there is no technical reason why this should be so, i.e. why process flexibility should be expected to map onto market structure in this way. The introduction of a flexible process is far more likely to lead to product, and therefore market, opportunities beyond those previously enjoyed. The benefits of this appear to be obvious – a reduction in risk, an increase in production volume, a gain in experience and the prospect of finding a market in which the firm's product has a substantial competitive advantage. The costs are rather less obvious. As an extreme example one might consider a jobbing engineering company which is able to enjoy a brief spell in a new market by virtue of its capacity to manufacture a wide range of components to an individual buyer's specifications. The problems which arise, from a marketing point of view, are threefold. First, when many markets and market segments are potentially accessible, which ones are to be chosen? As a general rule, market boundary definition and the analysis of market structure and competition require careful consideration. Because jobbing organisations face extremely fragmented markets, the resources required for studies of this kind are usually beyond those available to the firms concerned. Second, even if a set of potential markets can be identified, how are they to be managed? By what criteria are resources to be allocated? In practice, the control necessary to influence outcomes shifts from the marketing manager to the salesman, the production controller and the factory manager. Third, how can marketing synergies continue to be exploited? The set of products, and the markets which they serve, may not match the pattern which is necessary to use and reinforce the firm's marketing and other competences. In summary, incremental process flexibility cannot be allowed to drive marketing strategy; rather, there must be parity in influence between the two.

Flexibility in process which leads to variety in product promises the fulfilment of the marketing man's dream – that of being able to provide the customer with precisely what he wants. This notion corresponds to the idea of depth in market attack referred to earlier. Of special importance here are industrial markets where asymmetric customer size distributions are common. One aspect of this issue is the question of who specifies the product. As the variety of products increases a watershed in the marketing process is achieved. This occurs when the product changes from one which is producer-specified to one which is customer-specified. In practice this dimension is more likely to resemble a continuum than a dichotomy. At the boundary, products made to order from a series of producer-specified options (e.g. motor vehicles) come close to offering customer specification. Similarly, there occur situations where the production of 'specials' which are clustered, in product space, around a set of standard products provides localised customer specification. As the proportion of specials increases, so the firm moves towards the customer-specification end of the spectrum. In doing so, it opens up opportunities to tie in customers by establishing stable, long term relationships which create local barriers to entry (Håkansson, 1982). It achieves this at the cost of establishing a wholly different marketing system, and one in which the management of relationships rather than the manipulation of the product mix is the key skill. An improvement in the firm's ability to satisfy the customer changes the nature of the product positioning process. An acceptable marketing strategy requires the matching of the potential of the production process with customer requirements. This observation holds with equal force for both flexibility and the product dimension, but the argument here is concerned with distributions in product space rather than single points. Not all customers want different things from a product. The idea is illustrated in figure 9.6.

Clearly, in the case represented here, it would be unprofitable to provide much variety in the X dimension, whereas a concentration on Y might create a competitive advantage. In general however, this process cannot be implemented one dimension at a time. Customers will be prepared to make certain tradeoffs amongst specific features of a product, e.g. they may be willing to sacrifice colour shading in order to have high print definition in a printing process. Knowledge of these tradeoffs and the customers' willingness to make them is clearly valuable. On the other hand, there may be circumstances in which no tradeoffs are possible. This occurs, for example, when components are manufactured to fit into products under assembly. In any case, however, the opportunity for providing an exact match to customers' needs may well have to be evaluated in the light of the costs in time and effort of establishing what these needs are.

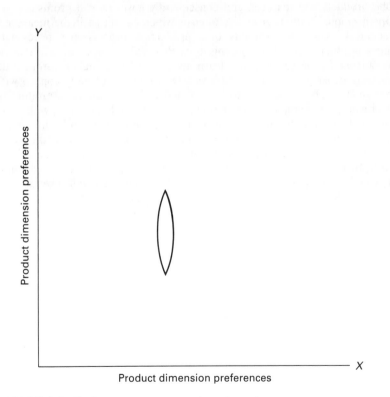

FIGURE 9.6   Preferences over two product dimensions

The formal economic analysis set out earlier was based on the assumption that flexibility can be achieved without cost or friction; that is to say, on the assumption that flexible efficiency is at a maximum. Clearly, however, this cannot be the case in practice. The larger the variety of products manufactured by a conventional plant, the smaller will be the proportion of effort devoted to production and the larger will be the proportion devoted to switching from one setup to another. Computer-based manufacture offers at least the potential for reducing changeover costs but not in the whole production process. Economies of scale may also be lost, and production costs will be higher in general, than they would be otherwise. The increased marketing benefits decribed earlier must result in larger sales if the firm is to offset the costs of greater flexibility. But not only will costs be higher; they will also be less easy to predict accurately. The costs of different system changes may vary a great deal. If, for example, the sequence of activities changes in some way, then so too will the overall costs. The process of allocating costs to products then becomes more difficult to implement, so that profit calculations are subject to the risk of greater error. The result may be the misallocation of resources among products and markets, and consequently lower overall profits.

Organizational friction gives rise to costs which cannot easily be measured. A technical change in flexibility in a production process may necessitate changes in other parts of the organisation. Production workers must become more adaptable; designers must learn to cope with a higher throughput; purchasing departments with a wider variety of inputs; inventory control with higher stock levels; accounting with more and varied transactions; production control with more complex programming problems, and marketing with more fragmented markets. In addition, all of these functions have to be integrated within the context of a continuously changing situation. If any of the parts, or combination of the parts, fails in some way, then friction may be said to inhibit process flexibility. This, in turn, increases the resources which must be devoted to change, and may even prevent it from occurring. Overall, one has to ask: 'What are the benefits in terms of competitive performance which flexibility will offer, and at what organisational cost?'

The *implementation* of marketing strategies within an overall increase in process flexibility creates additional costs. Computer aided manufacture works because it can manage and control the stream of information that the productive processes generate. It could be argued that in doing so it creates similar information processing problems for marketing. With fragmented markets and a variety of products the task of keeping track of events becomes a major preoccupation for a marketing executive. Forward planning is even more difficult. Moreover, the quality of information, from both internal and external sources, is likely to be poor, and product costing under these circumstances may become almost impossible. While in theory internal information flows can be processed electronically, much of what the marketing function deals with occurs outside the organisation and affords major data capture problems.

Communication in its turn may demand a more unconventional approach. Negotiation and involvement with individual customers is likely to become the norm and there may well be diseconomies of scale in advertising. Branding becomes less viable and image making may have to be concentrated somewhere between the 'brand' and 'corporate' level. Integration backwards by marketing into the organization will be required as negotiations may demand rapid changes in product design, costings and delivery schedules. The need to keep track of the product once it is ordered requires similarly powerful information systems. Finally, the selling of capabilities rather than products makes necessary a very different set of selling skills. All of these changes will have implications for resources.

An assumption which was made in the formal economic analysis is that only short run cost and demand considerations apply. In practice, of course, the concerns of marketing strategy relate to the need for sustainable (i.e. long term) competitive advantage. One aspect of long term flexibility relates to customer expectations. It may be tempting to believe that once a customer has attained a particular level of satisfaction he will not wish to undertake any action which might change it. Indeed, in an industrial context the expectation that requirements will remain unchanged in this sense may form the basis of a customer's own production process. In this case, the move towards flexibility may be uneven. A second long term consideration concerns the dimension of flexibility/adaptability. High short run flexibility will not necessarily lead to adequate adaptation in the long run. A highly flexible firm may be able to follow changing market developments without necessarily undergoing any fundamental transformation itself. The ability to do this may constitute an advantage in the short term, but at some point the market may move outside of the ambit of the flexibility 'envelope'. When this occurs, change must become discrete, and it is not obvious that a firm which can 'flex' in the short term has the ability to make the necessary long term adjustments. A similar argument has been put forward by Blois (1986) in relation to computer aided manufacture. The investment requirements of such systems are substantial, while the flexibility envelope, though wide, is relatively stable. If the market changes, or if it is incorrectly perceived by firms, then adjustments could be both difficult and costly.

The economic analysis offered earlier also omitted investment considerations. The long term returns to increased flexibility are, in theory at least, relatively easy to calculate with the aid of discounting techniques. In practice however, they could be extremely difficult to estimate, largely because investment gives rise to flexibility and it is precisely the longer term consequences of this phenomenon which it is so hard to anticipate.

At least one school of thought would suggest that flexibility arguments are largely inappropriate for a major section of the industrial market. Adherents of the Interaction Approach (Håkansson, 1982) argue that many industrial markets are characterised by highly stable, long term, relationships between customers and supplier companies which have made significant adaptations to accommodate one another. By definition, change in these relationships is likely to be infrequent. At first sight flexibility would not seem to be an important feature of such markets, but this may not be the case in practice. While any one relationship is stable, the variety of relationships and the products that characterise them may be highly variable. Campbell and Cunningham (1983) explicitly recognise this fact in their concept of the management of a 'portfolio' of customers. One of the problems is that of finding a common core of capabilities that match the diverse and inevitably changing customer distribution (Easton and Araujo, 1986). Increased process flexibility may be an answer.

To summarise, increased process flexibility allows access to new markets and, potentially, to better servicing of industrial customers. The price paid is in terms of increased costs, both visible and invisible, and greater uncertainty which in its own right makes the decision to go ahead a difficult one to take.

PRODUCT FLEXIBILITY

The same procedure will be used to analyse product flexibility as was applied in the case of process flexibility. Products, like processes, can take on a 'range' of states. However, the way in which they do so is somewhat more complex than it is for the process case. Two types of flexible product will be distinguished.

A *configured* product is one which initially has the potential for taking a variety of forms but is permanently fixed in character either at the last stage of the production process or by the consumer. Examples include some kinds of process controllers, shelving systems made from standard components and paint colouring systems. Since they are permanently configured they are in many respects equivalent to the range of products produced by a flexible process. The main difference lies in production. Such products may be manufactured largely by mass production methods with all the cost advantages that normally derive from doing so. This is possible when configuration can take place at low cost at the end of the production process or can be carried out by the customer. It may occur, for example, when final assembly is a relatively simple assortment process involving rather complex and expensive subassemblies or components, as in the production of some electronic products including various types of home computer. It may also occur when software is downloaded onto microprocessors, thereby customising the equipment for a particular application. Customers may buy a selection of components which are designed to fit together or interface in standard ways and then configure them permanently to fit their own individual requirements, e.g. industrialised building systems. Since the configured products case, at least in terms of the marketing dimensions, is similar to the process flexibility case, it will not be considered further.

Reconfigurable products are products which can take on a variety of states according to post-purchase customer requirements. Examples include computers, robots, food processors, music centres as well as any range of accessories which extend the functions of a product. In each case the producer is not to be seen as selling a single product even if it is packaged as such; rather, he sells a line of products which can carry out tasks which range from the limited to the almost infinite. It is not only possible to reconfigure the product as purchased, but by buying additional accessories or programmes the customer can achieve a higher level of configurability in discrete steps. The implications of reconfigurability for marketing strategy are substantial and will be discussed in the remainder of the section dealing with product flexibility.

The distinction between configured and reconfigurable products is not unambiguous. For example, products configured in software may be returned to the manufacturer for reconfiguring occasionally or customers might have the expertise to do it themselves. Exhibition stands may be permanent or temporary though made of the same components.

It is important to note that configurability is a relatively widespread phenomenon, and can be said to occur in both services and systems. We shall give these only brief consideration here. Services may be defined as people or systems which perform work for customers. It is a characteristic of services that production and consumption are one and the same: the process is the product. Since people may behave in a variety of ways, both as producers and consumers of services, it follows that there is at least the potential in service operations for a configurable outcome. Examples of customised, front room types of services – expensive restaurants and management consultancy – indicate how this might happen in practice.

Systems comprise a combination of products and services, which in theory might be sold separately, to provide 'a fulfilment of a more extended customer need than is the case in product selling' (Mattsson, 1973). Examples of systems include air traffic control systems, cooling systems, material handling systems and conference organization. The components – both products and services – are standardized so that the resulting economies can accrue.

> It is not a custom solution but a customised adaptation of the basic system to the customer's individual needs. This customised adaptation is called the configuration. (Page and Siemplenski, 1983).

A system has elements of both configured and reconfigurable products. While the hardware may be permanently configured, the software (or services) may respond, albeit in a programmed way, to the changing requirements of the system, e.g. installation, debugging, maintenance.

Characteristics of Product Flexibility

Where reconfiguration is concerned, it is possible to characterise product flexibility in the same way as is done for process flexibility. In this case the characteristics are not the characteristics of the organisation but of the product which it currently produces. Reconfigurable products clearly differ enormously in terms of the flexibility in use which they offer to the customer, but they are likely to be less flexible in general than the systems that produce them.

Flexibility dimensions may, at one end of the continuum, be fewer and better defined than they are for a system. In product terms flexibility dimensions describe what the product does, e.g. drilling or wordprocessing. In order to link them with marketing strategies it is necessary to define them in terms of customer functions (Abell, 1980) e.g. hole producing or writing letters. A drill can have attachments which will saw and turn wood but do no more. Their exact performance may be fairly accurately known. These are what can be termed producer defined dimensions. As the number of dimensions along which a product has flexibility grows there arises the possibility of consumer definition. Interaction among flexibility dimensions may create new areas of operation, e.g. adding communications capabilities to a microcomputer allows computer conferencing, electronic mail, networking, etc.

Measurement of flexibility remains a problem but for different reasons. A process, while it may be complex, is always under the scrutiny and control of the producer. However, the products may be used in ways which are unknown to those who produce them, and extensive research may be required to obtain the relevant information. This view is supported by the results of research into 'substitution-in-use' (Day, Shocker and Srivastava, 1979). It is clear that in many standard product fields the pattern of usage is a major determinant of the choice of suitable brand. If the 'brands' are in themselves capable of a range of functions this compounds the uncertainty in the measurement process, e.g. the use of a wordprocessing program for writing reports but not letters.

The characteristics of the efficiency of flexibility also differ between the product and process cases. At any particular configuration level the move from one mode to another is usually relatively easy in terms of time or money, e.g. the loading of a new program, the attaching of a different accessory to a robot or the switching from radio to tape on a music centre. However, the movement between configuration levels may be expensive and/or time-consuming. For example, a customer may have to buy a new accessory or write a new program.

Product Flexibility and Marketing Strategy

The analysis of product flexibility and its likely impact will take the same form as it did for process flexibility. We assume that a producer is considering the replacement of an existing product range by a single reconfigurable product, perhaps as a result of a technological development. If we further assume that the reconfigurable product can only be made at or above the cost of the products it is replacing then the producer would only do so in anticipation of increased volume. As in the case of process flexibility this might result from a combination of access to wider markets and increased ability to give customers what they demand.

A reconfigurable product will normally be capable of more than a simple combination of the products it replaces. In doing so it will, in theory, allow access to new markets. In particular it may attract customers for whom the particular flexibility envelope is precisely what is required. Such customers will at some time use all the functions provided, and for them the envelope of functions more of less exhausts the available set (e.g. woodworking). However, there will also be markets or segments with narrower sets of requirements. In this case, the reconfigurable product may be regarded as inferior to a dedicated product on a number of grounds. The first is that because of design compromises the product performs less well than might a dedicated product. This need not be the case in theory but it is often the case in practice. The second problem is that even if the reconfigurable product is better than a dedicated one it may not be perceived as such (i.e. the 'Jack of all trades, master of none' syndrome). A third difficulty is that a single function customer may resent paying (or apparently paying) for functions he does not require. The end result is that the marketing of a reconfigurable product represents a tradeoff between markets gained and markets lost.

The specificity with which a reconfigurable product can address sets of customer needs depends, as it did in the process case, on whether the configurations are largely producer or customer defined. Producer defined configurations are those where the variety of functions may be large but each is pre-specified and no interaction is possible, e.g. an electric drill with attachments. Customer defined configurations are those in which the modular nature of the product and the interaction of functions allow the customer to use the product in ways which the producer had not anticipated. At the producer specified end of the spectrum the producer's skill lies in providing a product envelope which covers a large number of markets and segments at low cost. This requires a detailed knowledge of the rather complex market maps that multifunctional products may generate. At the customer specified end of the spectrum the product is configured and reconfigured by the customer or the producer, to the customer's exact specifications. The assumption is that the product is flexible enough for this to be possible. Movement along the spectrum results in a product which is better able to satisfy the customer's multiple requirements, but this is almost certainly more costly to produce and the demand for it is likely to be much harder to predict.

Post purchase customer configuration opens up the possibility of the creative customer. In configuring the product the customer may be achieving performance the producer had not previously imagined. This is already the case in computing, where manufacturers are buying back software written by customers to license to other customers. This type of more equal producer–customer relationship is described by the Interaction Approach discussed earlier. It is possible that reconfigurable products might strengthen existing relationships and perhaps increase the number of relationships of an 'interactive' type. The balance of power may also shift to the customer.

Although reconfigurable products in use are clearly able to meet consumers' needs, in prospect they may appear less able to do so. Positioning in perceptual terms is often a major problem. In this case the marketing executive is selling a very versatile product and it is not always clear what is the best promotional strategy. On the one hand it is very difficult to sell versatility as such: there are problems of credibility, confusion and effective demonstration. On the other hand, a focus on specific functions invites the risk of 'selling the product short' or asking the customer to pay for functions he does not wish to use.

Dimensions of flexibility are, as noted earlier, best described in terms of Abell's functions. As in the case of processes, this provides a way of measuring the multidimensional distributions of consumer requirements in terms of these functions. However, the technology that provides the functions may not offer all possible combinations. There may in fact be technological discontinuities and 'holes' e.g. the wordprocessing program may link to the spreadsheet but not to the database. The process of researching the product is an attempt to discover the ways customers use the various functions open to them. Feedback from the market place is even more vital and more complex than is usually the case, since the producer may be said to be learning about the product from the consumer. A further element of uncertainty in modular or very powerfully configurable products, like computers, arises in the anticipation of the ways in which the modules can be made to interact. In theory a computer could be programmed to fulfil a very wide range of tasks. Consequently, with customer specified products it may only be by experience that a producer can begin to estimate the potential envelope of functions which the product is capable of performing. This clearly introduces a major additional source of uncertainty in the market assessment for new products.

The 'efficiency of flexibility' for products as compared with processes is a concept which relates to the ease with which a customer is able to reconfigure the product. As noted earlier, there are two elements to the process of reconfiguration. The first concerns the efficiency achieved in moving between functions at any level of configuration, e.g. the loading of a new program into a computer. What is of interest here are the perceptions of individuals concerning the efficiency of reconfiguration. Most people can manage to switch between manual and automatic modes on a machine tool. However, the loading of a new program may be difficult if a computer is networked, while many electronic PABX's are notoriously difficult to operate. The result has been that only a small subset of the possible functions are ever used. In post-purchase evaluation this must be regarded by customers as a major reason for buying something simpler at the next opportunity and for advising others to do the same.

The second type of reconfiguration involves the additional expense or effort in moving up a configuration level by buying an additional attachment or writing a new program. Such a step, depending on the resource required, will be something of a deterrent to customers and represents a major discontinuity in the flexibility envelope. The undertaking may be so large, for some systems software is more expensive than hardware, that the product effectively changes completely in character (e.g. the use of a payroll computer for process control). In terms of marketing strategy what is being offered here is a development path. As new needs emerge they can be met by adaptations of the base product. In addition the 'product' can develop in line with predictable consumer developments, e.g. increases in firm size, greater experience in the use of the technology, etc. The move is from short term flexibility to longer term adaptability. In the long term the flexibility/adaptability tradeoff would seem to be less important if the flexibility is built into the product. Providing that the process used to produce it remains standard then the switch to new products seems less likely to be as traumatic as the move from one type of flexible process to another.

The evaluation of the strategies which are suggested by the foregoing discussion involves the setting-off of demand factors against costs. Configurability can provide real competitive advantages but the question is: at what cost? In production terms a standard but configurable product need not cost any more than the range of products it replaces. The tradeoff may be more in terms of how close the substitution is on a function for function basis. The critical dimension must be the way that the product and its envelope of functions are matched, in the first instance, and then continue to adapt to markets, revealed and unrevealed. These processes of matching and adaptation involve a high degree of complexity and require more than usually good marketing decisions.

CONCLUSIONS

We argued in the introduction to this paper that organizational flexibility is a key decision variable for at least two reasons. First, as an intrinsic feature of any organisation it is the subject of strategic decision making and an element which must be explicitly traded off against 'efficiency'. Despite the relatively narrow focus of our analysis we have shown the complex nature of the decisions which bear on these issues. The natural question is how far the actors within organisations can be expected to deal with them adequately in practice. Flexibility, unlike most other organizational variables, is a second order dimension. It concerns changes in states rather than the states themselves. The measurement, even in gross terms and on a limited basis, of the current flexibility of an organization has been shown to be extremely difficult. Ideally, decisions about tradeoffs require knowledge of all relevant dimensions and of their potential for change. However, such is the counsel of perfection. On a practical level, it may be unreasonable to expect more than that the flexibility/efficiency tradeoff be explicitly recognized in major corporate decisions.

The second major issue, from a strategic point of view, which involves the idea of flexibility is its relationship to that of 'adaptation'. It is our view that organizational change should not be seen as a shift from one discrete state to another. Indeed, all organizations are more or less flexible, so that it may be impossible even to characterize a current 'state'. Nor are we considering here long-term underlying trends in organizational form and process. The notion of flexibility implies a range of modes of behaviour which are potentially open to an organization, and which can be attained quickly and at relatively low cost in terms of resources. The relationship between flexibility and adaptability is analogous to that between waves of short cycle and waves of long cycle, in which the latter are in some sense 'superimposed' upon the former.

Where processes are concerned, the distinction between the short and the long run often becomes blurred. It is tempting to view organizations as evolving in a coherent, incremental way in response to an orderly evolution of the environment itself. Of course, this may not be so. An organization may simply be following, in some sense, a line of least resistance which leads ultimately to disaster. A normative approach to the question suggests the need to think in broader terms and to stand ready to make the radical changes in direction which flexibility will allow. But in terms of the processes of adaptation and organizational learning, it may be the case that an organization's current flexibility, however appropriate to its short-term requirements, does not permit long-run adaptation. In this sense, insofar as such flexibility enables the organization to survive in a hostile environment beyond the point at which escape would be prudent, it can impose costs. The tradeoff then becomes one between flexibility and the capacity for survival.

A third issue of importance arises from considerations of product flexibility, particularly within the context of industrial markets. When products and services become flexible, the power which the supplier enjoys as a consequence of knowledge about the product may pass to the customer. The nature of the relationship between the supplier and the customer then changes. This phenomenon, where it occurs, provides further evidence to support the view that the traditional perception of the organization as the unit of analysis in industrial, and perhaps even consumer markets, is becoming outmoded. Alternative paradigms, such as the Interaction and Network Approaches, offer greater insight. It is easy to make the case that technological, economic and social factors are changing in a way that will ultimately render such conceptualizations more universally applicable than they are at present.

Flexibility, we have argued, is a key strategic variable. It has so far received scant attention and is both ill-understood and difficult to characterize. In this paper we have done little more than raise some issues. We would be defying academic convention if we did not argue that the subject deserves very much more attention than it currently enjoys.

REFERENCES

Abell, D. F. (1980) *Defining the Business: The Starting Point of Strategic Planning.* Englewood Cliffs, NJ: Prentice-Hall.

Abernathy, W. J., Clarke, Kim B. and Kantrow, Alan M. (1981) The new industrial competition. *Harvard Business Review*, September–October, 68–81.

Abernathy, W. J., and Townsend, P. L. (1975) Technology, productivity and process change. *Technical Forecasting and Social Change*, 7(4) 379–96.

Abernathy, W. J. and Wayne, K. (1974) Limits of the learning curve. *Harvard Business Review*, September–October, 109–119.

Ansoff, H. I. (1968) *Corporate Strategy*, Harmondsworth, Middx: Penguin Books.

Blois, K. J. (1983) The marketing concept and the manufacturing/marketing interface. In C. Voss (ed.), *Current Research in Production/Operations Management*. London: London Business School.

—— (forthcoming) *New Production Technologies and their Marketing Implications.*

Burns, T. and Stalker, G. M. (1961) *The Management of Innovation.* London: Tavistock.

Campbell, N. C. G. and Cunningham, M. T. (1983) Customer analysis for strategy development in industrial markets. *Strategic Management Journal*, 4, 369–80.

Day, G., Shocker, A. D. and Srivastava, R. K. (1979) Identifying competitive product markets: a review of customer-oriented approaches. *Journal of Marketing*, 43, 8–19.

Easton, G. and Araujo, L. (1987) Networks, bonding and relationships in industrial markets, *Industrial Marketing and Purchasing.*

Gerwin, D. (1982). Do's and don'ts of computerised manufacture. *Harvard Business Review*, March–April, 107–116.

Goldhar, J. D. and Jelinek, M. (1985) Computer-integrated flexible manufacturing: organisational, economic and strategic implications. *Interfaces*, 15 (3), 94–105.

Håkansson, H. (1982) *International Marketing and Purchasing of Industrial Goods: An Interaction Approach.* Chichester: John Wiley.

Hayes, R. H. (1981) Why Japanese factories work. *Harvard Business Review*, July–August, 56–66.

—— and Wheelwright, S. C. (1979) Link manufacturing process and product life-cycles. *Harvard Business Review*, January–February, 127–36.

—— (1984) *Restoring our Competitive Edge.* New York: John Wiley.

Hill, T. J. (1980) Manufacturing implications of determining corporate policy, *International Journal of Product Management*, 1 (1), 3–11.

—— (1983) Manufacturing strategy – building the concepts. Prod/OM Workshop, London Business School, 5–6 January 1983.

Jelinek, M. and Goldhar, J. D. (1983) The interface between strategy and manufacturing technology. Columbia Journal of World Business, 18:1, 26–36.

Lancaster, K. (1966) A new approach to consumer theory. *Journal of Political Economy*, 74, 132–57.

Macbeth, D. K. (1985) The flexible manufacturing mission – some implications for management. *International Journal of Operations and Production Management*, 5 (1), 26–31.

Mattsson, L-G, (1973) Systems selling as a strategy on industrial markets. *Industrial Marketing Management*, 3, 107–20.

Page, A. L. ad Siemplenski, M. (1983) Product systems marketing. *Industrial Marketing Management*, 12, 89–99.

Shapiro, B. P. (1977) Can marketing and manufacturing coexist? *Harvard Business Review*, September–October, 104–13.

Shocker, A., Zahovik, A. J. and Stewart, D. W. (1984) Competitive market structure analysis: a comment on problems. *Journal of Consumer Research*, 11, 836–41.

Skinner, Wickham (1969) Manufacturing – missing link in corporate strategy. *Harvard Business Review*, May–June, 136–45.

—— (1974) The focused factory. *Harvard Business Review*, May–June, 113–21.

Slack, N. (1983) Flexibility as a manufacturing objective. In C. Voss (ed.), *Current Research in Production/Operations Management*. London: London Business School.

Stobaugh, R. and Telesio, P. (1983) Match manufacturing policies and product strategy. *Harvard Business Review*, March–April, 113–20.

Taylor, I. (1983) How to realize the benefits of FMS. *The Production Engineer*, 62, 44–8.

Utterback, J. and Abernathy, W. J. (1975) A dynamic model of process and product innovation. *Omega*, 3 (6), 639–56.

Wheelwright, S. C. (1978) Reflecting corporate strategy in manufacturing decisions. *Business Horizons*, February, 21, 1, 57–66.

—— (1981) Japan – where operations really are strategic. *Harvard Business Review*, July–August, 67–74.

Commentary on Chapter 9

Malcolm T. Cunningham

A refreshing feature of the paper by Easton and Rothschild is its genuine interdisciplinary nature. The authors use economic analysis to evaluate and compare the concepts of 'efficiency' and 'flexibility' as strategic options for business. The paper draws together ideas concerning both manufacturing and marketing strategy by means of the dominant theme of the benefits of flexibility and the management decisions to achieve this, primarily in the areas of manufacturing processes and in the product range. While the perspective adopted is primarily strategic, with its focus upon the firm as the unit of analysis, the analysis and discussion delve into operational issues which have equal appeal to both the manufacturing and the marketing academic researcher. Finally, the topicality of the paper is assured in its concern for addressing the problem of gaining and maintaining competitive advantage in the marketplace. Competitiveness through flexibility is the central message. The management of change in market positions, products and manufacturing systems are the means proposed for reaching this goal.

Essentially this is a conceptual paper, with no pretence at offering substantial empirical evidence or consistently selected contemporary illustrations to support the propositions. The very general nature of the paper, with its lack of specificity, may give it an aura of practical usefulness which may not be fully justified. The theme of flexibility is presumed to be appropriate for all sizes of firms in different markets and technologies. In some respects the authors assume that the firm is not concerned with the financial paybacks from past investment in existing processes and products. Investments to achieve flexibility through the choice of an optimum product mix and the appropriate flexible manufacturing processes are not discussed as constraints on strategic decisions. This may seem to fly in the face of realism, but it is characteristic of many studies in strategy.

The management of change, whether it be of a radical or an incremental nature in existing market positions, products and manufacturing systems, in order to achieve flexible positions is a major issue which is developed at a later stage in the paper.

The authors view flexibility as an attractive goal for a business, and one that manifests itself in such characteristics as flexibility of product mix, quality levels, output volume and delivery times. They recognize that such basic performance characteristics of a firm are at the heart of the competitive advantage which UK firms need to achieve both in domestic and international markets. Other research shows how vital these are and how they are often found lacking in many industrial markets in the face of Japanese and German competitors. At first glance, flexibility is not the dominant feature associated with suppliers from these countries. It is, however, the authors' proposition that flexibility is 'a capability to exhibit a variety of forms in a comparatively short space of time'. This is a useful and attractive definition which implies neither unplanned adaptability nor the accession to every whim of the market, but instead a strategic capability by which manufacturing processes can respond in a systematic manner to market demand.

The paper argues for a distinction between adaptability and flexibility and this receives thorough discussion, particularly in the conclusions.

The pleas and exhortations by advocates of manufacturing for a greater say in strategic decision-making are unconvincing and unsupported by evidence. Such pleas come from other functions, such as purchasing, personnel, etc. The authors' treatment of various organizational forms of process flows in manufacturing places emphasis on the 'project' form, but no evidence is offered to support its inherent superiority over jobbing, batch or assembly line flow systems. Flexibility cannot be said to be the sole objective of various organizational forms, however attractive this would be.

In discussing the impact of information technology (IT) on a business, the authors realistically but unconventionally advocate that automation should not be the ultimate goal for IT-based manufacturing systems. Instead, it should facilitate the better integration of manufacturing, marketing and design functions and in this way be a significant contributor towards flexibility. The lack of availability of suitable proven software is noted as a current constraint.

With flexibility (as compared with efficiency) being the preferred aim, the authors address the difficulties of measuring flexibility because of its multi-dimensional nature. However, as one might expect, the deeper analysis still leaves many unanswered questions.

The economic analysis of the efficiency and flexibility options for a business uses both costs and demand criteria. However, the notion of 'a representative consumer' adopted by the authors seems an illusion, and certainly is an alien one to a marketer or strategist in industrial markets in which there is often considerable heterogeneity of customers. I must confess to a lack of understanding and conviction about this part of the paper. As with most economic analysis, the constraints and assumptions are hardly compatible with the earlier qualitative discussion of the dichotomy between efficiency and flexibility. Apparently 'all's well that ends well', because the paper goes on to conclude, in a pragmatic manner, 'that firms which contemplate the introduction of flexible processes should address market segments in which efficient processes are densely packed'. This is an interesting conclusion, and it is hoped that it can be tested by applying it to some companies. There is ample scope here for research into this aspect of managing strategic change.

The section of the paper dealing with marketing flexibility and the problems of matching resources to a changing portfolio of market and customer needs is thoughtful as is the comparison between flexibility issues in consumer and industrial goods markets. These ideas are worthy of further development and empirical investigation.

The paper addresses a host of issues in its later stages, but perhaps raises them in a way that does not always illuminate the central argument. One of the more interesting of the latter sections is that on 'competitive advantage of flexibility'. The benefits of process flexibility are claimed to be 'width' and 'depth' of market attack: width enabling products to enter new markets, and depth allowing products to be more closely matched with customers' requirements. The authors should explain their views on how a product–market matrix can be developed to guide the strategy or how incremental moves into contiguous markets can be undertaken from the existing product line. This is only tenuously linked with the concept of flexibility.

The authors raise some provocative issues in their discussion on the organizational costs of flexibility:

1 organizational *friction* arises in changes in product design, working practices, output levels and inventory costs;
2 organizational *mechanisms* have to be developed to achieve better integration between the functions in a firm;
3 new management *information systems* and data bases have to be created;
4 historical patterns of *adaptability* to satisfy powerful customers need to be appraised because short-term adaptability can impede longer-term strategic flexibility.

These costs of flexibility are important areas of research investigation, and as such are worth measuring in juxtaposition with the benefits of flexibility.

The paper has genuinely attempted to integrate the areas of marketing and manufacturing. Therefore it is worth postulating how some reconciliation might be effected between the investment and performance criteria in the marketing and manufacturing domains of a business. In practice, this is not readily attained. Marketing investments may have to be made in market positions, product brand reputation and customer relationships. Manufacturing investments are often found in processes, equipment and labour skills. There is also a conflict to be found in evaluating the performance of a marketing activity as compared with that of manufacturing. Although the common corporate goals of flexibility, organizational responsiveness and competitive advantage prevail, sub-optimum goals for marketing may be imposed by management in terms of order intake, profit margins, new customers gained and market share performance. Simultaneously and in an equally sub-optimum manner, the performance of manufacturing may be judged according to output levels, machine utilization, control of cost variances and the like.

10 Review Essay: Four Requirements for Processual Analysis

Andrew H. Van de Ven

Although there is great diversity in subject matter covered in the previous chapters, a common objective is to understand processes of strategic change, or the ways in which organizational strategies emerge, grow and decline. Four requirements are necessary to undertake research on the process of change in general, and strategic management in particular:

1 a clear set of concepts about the object being studied;
2 systematic methods for observing change in the object over time;
3 methods for representing raw data to identify processual patterns;
4 a motor or theory to make sense of the process pattern.

While simple to set forth, these requirements are challenging to achieve. As Pettigrew (1985), Mohr (1982) and Nisbet (1970) indicate, they represent basic methodological steps in processual analysis and for building 'process theories' as distinct from 'variance theories.' While the previous chapters make significant contributions in suggesting ways to accomplish the first three requirements, the fourth received relatively little attention and represents a significant challenge for further work. Since methods for processual analysis have received far less attention and codification than methods for variance analysis (Mohr, 1982), this chapter will consider how these four requirements might be met in order to study processes of strategic organizational change over time.

I gratefully acknowledge stimulating comments and ideas developed in this chapter from Raghu Garud, Douglas Polley, M. Scott Poole and S. Venkataraman, as well as other colleagues involved in the Minnesota Innovation Research Program. Support for this research program has been provided in part by a grant to the Strategic Management Research Center at the University of Minnesota from the Program on Organization Effectiveness, Office of Naval Research (code 4420E), under contract no. N00014–84–K–0016, as well as other sources.

The four requirements derive from definitions of change and processes of change. By definition, *change is an empirical observation of differences in time on one or more dimensions of an entity*. All four elements in this definition are necessary. As Nisbet (1969) describes, a mere array of differences is not change, only differences. Time is also a critical element, for any differences necessarily involve earlier and later points of reference. Mobility, motion or activity in themselves do not constitute change, although each is in some degree involved in change. Certain dimensions or categories of an entity are the objects being transformed. Change without reference to an object is meaningless.

The process of change adds an additional and more abstract element to the above definition of change. Whereas change is an empirical or manifest observation, *the process of change is an inference of a latent pattern of differences noted in time*. Thus, change processes are not directly observed: instead, they are conceptual inferences about the temporal ordering of relationships among observed changes.

With these definitions, the relationships among the four requirements for processual analysis become apparent. While the first requirement specifies the objects being investigated, the second deals with empirical observations of changes in these objects. The third requirement addresses methods for inferring processes of change, and the fourth is concerned with theories or conceptual motors that can explain these processes of change. The remainder of this commentary elaborates on these four requirements.

A CLEAR SET OF CONCEPTS ABOUT THE OBJECT BEING STUDIED

Implicitly or explicitly, observation of any strategic organizational issue entails examination of a set of categories or variables. As should be expected, different categories will produce very different substantive inquiries. For example, witness the wide array of concepts examined in preceding chapters under the umbrella of 'strategic management of change':

- Whipp/Rosenfeld/Pettigrew: Automobile and banking changes
-    Content, process, context (inner and outer)
- Tushman/Anderson: Minicomputers, cement, airlines
-    Core values, strategy, structure, power, controls and executive succession
- Doz Prahalad: Cases of strategic change
-    Variety generation, power shift, refocusing
- Grant: 33 firms in cutlery industry
-    Firm and profit, competitive advantage, resource-sharing
- Ghazanfar/McGee/Thomas: Reprographics industry
-    Technology, industry, strategy levels
- Harrigan: Joint venture in 23 US industries

- Supply side, demand side, profit potential
- Mattsson: No specific empirical references
- Network structuredness, homogeneity, hierarchy, exclusiveness

Whatever the concepts and organizational settings examined in a study, research on strategic change processes requires a clear understanding of how change can be observed. Measurement of change necessarily implies not only a longitudinal study, but also rigorous methods for observing differences over time in the conceptual categories of the organizational unit being investigated.

SYSTEMATIC METHODS FOR OBSERVING CHANGE OVER TIME

Most studies of innovation or change to date have been retrospective case histories conducted after the outcomes were known (Van de Ven and associates, 1987). However, it is widely recognized that prior knowledge of the success or failure of an innovation invariably biases a study's findings. While historical analysis is necessary for examining many questions and concerted efforts can be undertaken to minimize bias, it is generally better, if possible, to initiate historical study before the outcomes of a strategic change process become known.

Moreover, time itself sets a frame of reference which directly affects our perceptions of change. As Pettigrew (1985) notes, the more we look at present-day events, the easier it is to identify change; the longer we stay with an emergent process and the further back we go to disentangle its origins, the more likely we are to identify continuities. Appreciating this dilemma requires that investigators carefully design their studies in order to observe changes that are relevant to the purposes and users of their research.

For example, if the purpose of a study is to understand how to manage the formulation or implementation of an organizational strategy, it will be necessary for researchers to place themselves in the manager's temporal and contextual frames of reference. Presumably, this would initially involve conducting a retrospective case history to understand the context and events leading up to the present strategy being investigated. However, the major focus of the study would entail conducting real-time observations of the strategy development effort as it unfolds over time, without knowing *a priori* the outcomes of the actions taken.

Regularly scheduled and intermittent field observations are necessary for a processual analysis of how changes occur over time. Repetitive surveys and interviews provide comparative-static observations of the organizational concepts or dimensions being tracked over time. As defined above, difference scores between time periods on these dimensions would determine what changes occurred in the organizational unit or program. But to understand how these changes came about, there is a need to supplement regularly scheduled data collection with intermittent real-time data. This would involve, for example, observing key committee meetings, decision or crisis events, and conducting informal discussions with key organizational participants. Both regularly scheduled and periodic observations are necessary in a processual analysis because, while difference scores between regularly scheduled observations will identify *what* changes occurred, real-time observations at key intermittent periods are needed to understand *how* these changes occurred.

As Argyris (1968; 1985) has forcefully argued over the years, significant new methods and skills of action science are called for to conduct this kind of longitudinal real-time research. In addition, it implies significant researcher commitment and organizational access, which few researchers have achieved to date. And as a consequence, very few processual studies of strategic change processes have been conducted. Our processual research experience (Van de Ven and associates, 1987) suggests that one reason why gaining organizational access has been problematic is because researchers seldom place themselves in the manager's frame of reference to conduct their studies. Without observing a change process from a manager's perspective, it becomes difficult (if not impossible) for an investigator to understand the dynamics confronting managers who are involved in a strategic change effort, and thereby to generate findings that are relevant to the theory and practice of strategic management. If organizational participants perceive little potential use of a study's findings, there is little to motivate their providing access and information to an investigator.

METHODS FOR TABULATING RAW DATA TO IDENTIFY PROCESSUAL PATTERNS

Obtaining systematic observations of a strategic change process over time using multiple methods quickly produces an overwhelming amount of rich raw data about an organizational development effort. Drawing inferential links between these data and theory requires methods for organizing and evaluating the raw data in a manner that facilitates identifying processual patterns.

While the task may seem formidable on quantitative data, an extensive methodology has developed over the years to codify procedures for handling longitudinal panels of such data, including procedures for constructing computer data files and analyzing longitudinal data (Tuma and Hannan, 1984). Far less has been written about methods for analyzing longitudinal qualitative data. Here, I will briefly outline four basic steps that I have found useful for tabulating qualitative data in a manner that helps to identify processual change patterns.

Chronological Listing of Qualitative Events

The first step in tabulating qualitative data is to develop a chronological listing of events that occur in the development of the organizational unit or program being investigated: i.e.,

Month/year	Event	Data source
:	:	:

Events require careful definition, and vary with the concepts being investigated. For example, Whipp, Rosenfeld and Pettigrew (chapter 1 above) would probably define an 'event' as a point in time when a change occurs in either the content, process or inner/outer contexts of strategic management of the automobile and banking firms they examine. The chronological listing of events would be obtained by combining data collected through multiple methods and sources over time, including surveys, interviews, participant observations, archival sources and published information.

Coding Chronological Events into Conceptual Tracks

The next step in organizing the longitudinal data into a format that facilitates identifying change processes is to code the chronological listing of events into multiple tracks which correspond to the conceptual research categories. Poole's (1983) Multiple Sequence Model provides a useful descriptive system which specifies tracks used for recording process activities. Poole's method avoids the problem of preordaining the existence of stages or phases to the process, yet provides a way of identifying cycles or transitions among activity tracks, and in this way facilitates the development and testing of models or theories about innovation and change processes. Instead of picturing the strategic change process as a unitary sequence of phases or stages, Poole suggests portraying events as a set of parallel strands or tracks of activities.

In the illustration below, each track represents a different concept or category in a research framework. For example, a tracking of the core concepts in the Whipp/Rosenfeld/Pettigrew research program would require at least four tracks. As Poole (1983) indicates, a coding scheme is also necessary to enumerate the kinds of activities or issues occurring at each point in time in the tracks:

Content topics   _____

Press issues   _____

Inner context   _____

Outer context   _____

|—|—|—|—|—|—|—|—|—|—|—

Time →

Analyzing Process Patterns or Cycles in Activity Tracks

After the chronological data are coded in these conceptual tracks, a search begins to identify processual patterns that may be reflected in the activity tracks. Cycles and breakpoints are useful for identifying processual patterns. A recurrent pattern of behavior is called a *cycle*. Cycles are identified when repetitions occur within tracks over time. *Breakpoints* are of key importance to understanding change processes because they represent transitions between cycles of activities; they indicate the pacing of activities within tracks and possible linkages between tracks of activities. Poole (1983) and Mintzberg *et al.* (1976) describe four types of breakpoints: normal breakpoints or topical shifts, delays, internal disruptions, and external interrupts.

Poole (1983) points out that, when breakpoints interrupt cycles within a track, this suggests that the track is loosely coupled or operating somewhat independently of the other tracks. On the other hand, when breakpoints occur in many tracks, those tracks are likely to be highly interdependent, and the rupture may presage major events or shifts in developmental activity. Thus, when cyclical breaks in multiple tracks occur in some coherent fashion, phases or stages similar to those in classical models may be found. However, at other points there may be no relationship in the cyclical breaks between tracks, and therefore no recognizable phases. In this case, each track is analyzed in its own right, but the entire ensemble of tracks does not yield a coherent analysis.

Vocabulary for Describing Processual Progressions

New concepts about developmental processes are often needed to describe and analyze longitudinal processual patterns in the above activity tracks. Based on mathematical set theory, van den Daele (1969; 1974) proposes a rich vocabulary of operational concepts for describing and analyzing change processes. Space limitations permit these concepts only to be outlined here.

1   Simple, unitary progression; U, V, W.
2   Simple, multiple progression: U, V, W may contain subsets; in set theory $[Ui] \rightarrow [Vi] \rightarrow [Wi]$.
Multiple progressions can be of three forms:

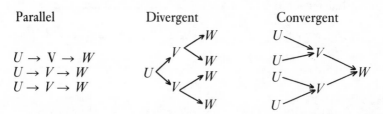

| Parallel | Divergent | Convergent |

$U \rightarrow V \rightarrow W$
$U \rightarrow V \rightarrow W$
$U \rightarrow V \rightarrow W$

3   Cumulative progression (unitary or multiple): more than one stage may belong to a unit at a time; in set theory: $U \supset a$, $V \supset ab$, $W \supset bc$ (unitary model). For example, a multiple parallel partially cumulative model would look like this:

$U \supset a \rightarrow V \supset a \, b \rightarrow W \supset a \, b \, c$
$U \supset a \rightarrow V \supset b \quad \rightarrow W \supset b \, c$
$U \supset a \rightarrow V \supset a \, b \rightarrow W \supset c$

4   Conjunctive progression (unitary, multiple or cumulative): the elements of subsets may be related, such that aRb, or $AR'b$.

Van den Daele (1969) points out that these forms of progression do not occur independently. Every developmental model makes a commitment (implicitly or explicitly) to some form of invariant sequential order, between-unit variation (unitary or multiple sequence), within-unit variance (simple or cumulative structure), and in the relationship of developmental elements (conjunctive or disjunctive). Given model relations among these dimensions, van den Daele develops four typical patterns of change processes:

1   simple, unitary progression (which includes most of the stage models of strategic management change in the literature);
2   simple, multiple progression patterns, which provide alternative developmental sequences for different units, but with only one stage belonging to a unit at a time. Binary fission is a good example;
3   cumulative, unitary progression patterns, which assume the maintenance of some earlier and later stages of a single sequence. The model implies one 'proper' path. Progressive ossification of cartilage is a good example;
4   cumulative, multiple progression patterns, which imply the coexistence of earlier and later stages along with the option of developmentally alternative characteristics, accommodating to between-unit as well as within-unit differences. This cumulative pattern of multiple progression is captured

in Alexander Gray's adage, 'No point of view, once expressed, ever seems wholly to die. Our ears are filled with the whisperings of dead men.'

Obviously, this processual analysis of longitudinal tracks cannot go far unless it is driven by an explicit motor or theory of change processes.

MOTORS OR THEORIES OF CHANGE PROCESSES

Theories of choice and decision-making processes have perhaps received the greatest attention to date by strategic management scholars. Indeed, Schroeder et al. (1986) reviews the literature, showing that most models of individual, group and organizational change or innovation appear to rely uncritically upon choice process models. If knowledge of strategic decision processes is to advance in the future, study of alternative choice processes should be emphasized. Special emphasis should be given to evaluations of the conceptual motors. They are:

- rational: logical necessity motor;
- contingency: situational congruency motor;
- incremental: political–negotiative motor;
- random: systemic–probabilistic regularity motor;
- structuration: socially constructed sense-making motor.

Although very little is known about the conditions for which these different theories of choice processes apply, they are in all likelihood descendants from a few basic theories of change in historical social theory.

As discussed in Van de Ven and Poole (1987), social theorists have historically relied upon one of three basic theories to explain change: evolution (or developmentalism), accumulation (or epigenesis), and punctuated equilibrium theories. While evolution and accumulation theories of change have deep historically opposing roots, their differences can be reconciled with a punctuated equilibrium model of change processes.

Evolutionary/Developmental Models

Evolution is a continuous and gradual change which proceeds endogenously, that is, directly from within the unit that is undergoing change. In an evolutionary/developmental model, the forces for change lie within the system. While external events can and do affect development through deceleration, acceleration, distortion or even obliteration, the seed or genetic structure for change is contained within the social system. An evolutionary theory of change underlies processes of differentiation in structural–functional social theories, the sequential stages of variation, selection and retention in social Darwinism and of thesis, antithesis and synthesis in dialectical theories.

Accumulation of Epigenesis Models

There are many social units the emergence of which cannot be adequately explained by evolution. Instead, 'adult' units often seem to emerge through a process in which parts that carry out new functions are added to (or subtracted from) existing ones, until the entire unit is assembled. Earlier parts do not include the 'representation' of later ones. Accumulation theories explain change as externally (exogenously) and discontinuously produced by the addition of totally or radically new components or deletions of other components of a social system.

Etzioni (1963) suggests that periods of initiation, startup and takeoff are useful for examining accumulation processes. *Initiation* is the time when people decide to form a new unit (if successfully launched, it will become the unit's birthday), and *takeoff* is the time when the unit can do without the support of its initiators and continue growing 'on its own.' The period between initiation and takeoff could be called *startup*, where the new unit must draw its funds, staff and power from the founding leaders and groups in order to accumulate followers and contributors directly committed to developing and sustaining the new unit.

The image here is like an airplane that first starts its engines and begins rolling, still supported by the runway, until it accumulates enough momentum to 'take off,' and continue in motion 'on its own' energy to carry it to higher altitudes and speeds. Thus, while relying initially on external support, the necessary condition for autonomous action is produced through a process of accumulation.

Punctuated Equilibrium Model of Change

A punctuated equilibrium model (as described in Tushman and Anderson's chapter) uses time as one avenue to reconcile and incorporate both evolution and accumulation theories of change. In a punctuated equilibrium model, accumulation best describes the process of occasional discontinuous reorientations in part or all of a social system, while evolution characterizes the periods of continuous convergence and morphogenesis. Accumulation appears to be the basic process underlying discontinuous punctuations because the resulting transformation represents a metamorphic or radical change which no longer includes representations of the earlier organization. Evolution describes morphogenic change, i.e., where an organization converges over time toward increasing order, complexity, unity or operational effectiveness. Thus, change in a given organization may be empirically observed either to result from evolutionary embodiments of old functions, or to consist of punctuated accumulations of totally new functions.

Accumulation and evolutionary change processes may be observed to occur at different times in the same organization. As Tushman and Romanelli (1985) indicate, most of the time an incremental, continuous and imminent process of evolution may occur, punctuated by occasional discontinuous periods of externally stimulated epigenesis. Thus, as we argue elsewhere (Van de Ven and Poole, 1987), time provides the vehicle for incorporating contradictory change processess in a punctuated equilibrium model to explain both internal and external sources of organizational change.

TOWARD A THEORY OF STRATEGIC MANAGEMENT OF CHANGE

In conclusion, I must touch upon a few basic normative questions. Where do we go with this processual analysis and search for process models? Where do we want to end up? While each reader is likely to have different answers to these questions, it seems to me that we want not only to describe observed changes in strategic management, but also to explain how and why they occur. Scientifically valid explanation not only requires systematic procedures for observing and tabulating longitudinal data (as proposed with the first three requirements for processual analysis); it also requires the development and evaluation of theories or motors of the change process itself. It is hoped that the destination of this journey will yield some practically useful and theoretically robust theories for the management of strategic change.

We must therefore ask, What are the requirements for a good theory of change? Hernes (1976) and Dahrendorf (1959) have proposed standards for a theory of change which are useful in answering this question. Adapting their criteria to strategic management suggests that our theory should attain the following four requirements for a good theory of strategic change.

1   It should explain how structure and individual purposive action are linked at micro and macro-levels of analysis. The dominant paradigm of social science rests on the firm belief that any macro-theory of organizational or industrial change must be grounded in the purposive actions and ambitions of individuals (Coleman, 1986).

2   It should explain how change is produced both by the internal functioning of the structure and by the external purposive actions of individuals. If one concludes that innovation is totally controlled by natural or structural forces imminent to the social system, no room is left for individual purpose, and no theory of action can result. And vice versa: if one concludes that organizational change is totally controlled by purposive individual action unconstrained by natural or structural forces, only a teleological or utopian theory can result.

3   The theory should explain both stability and instability. In its fundamental structure a theory of organizational innovation or change should not be remarkably different from a theory of ordinary action (March, 1981, p. 564). Without this requirement, any theory of innovation would explode and be

unable to explain the amazing persistence and fixity observed in common organizational life.

4 It should include time as the key historical metric. By definition, change is a difference that can only be noted over time in an entity. *Chronos* (or calendar time) tends to predominate in studies of structural change, while *kiros* (periods of peak experience – as in the planting and harvesting periods of a growing season) appears to be the most common metric of time in studies of individual creativity and purposive action. A theory of innovation and change that links structure and action must therefore link *chronos* and *kiros* time metrics (Van de Ven and Poole, 1987).

REFERENCES

Argyris, C. (1968)   Some unintended consequences of rigorous research. *Psychological Bulletin*, 70 (3), 185–97.
—— (1985)   *Strategy, Change, and Defensive Routines*. Marshfield, Mass.: Pitman.
Coleman, J. S. (1986)   Social theory, social research, and a theory of action. *American Journal of Sociology*, 16, 1309–35.
Dahrendorf, R. (1959)   *Class and Class Conflict in Industrial Society*. Stanford: University Press.
Etzioni, A. (1963)   The Epigenesis of Political Unification. In A. Etzioni (ed), *Social Change: Sources, Patterns and Consequences*. Chapter 55. New York: Basic Books.
Hernes, G. (1976)   Structural change in social processes. *American Journal of Sociology*, 82 (3), 513–45.
March, J. G. (1981)   Footnotes to organizational change. *Administrative Science Quarterly*, 26, 563–77.
McKinney J. and Tiryakin, E. *Theoretical Sociology*. N. York: Meredith.
Mintzberg, H., Raisinghani, D. and Theoret, A. (1976)   The structure of 'unstructured' decision processes. *Administrative Science Quarterly*, 21 (2), 246–75.
Mohr, L. B. (1982)   *Explaining Organizational Behavior: The Limits and Possibilities of Theory and Research*. San Francisco: Jossey-Bass.
Nisbet, R. A. (1970)   Developmentalism: a critical analysis. In J. McKinney and E. Tiryakin (eds), *Theoretical Sociology*, Chapter 7. New York: Meredith.
Pettigrew, A., (1985) *The Awakening Giant: Continuity and Change in ICI*. Oxford: Basil Blackwell.
Poole, M. S. (1983)   Decision development in small groups. III: A multiple sequence model of group decision development. *Communication Monographs*, vol. 50.
Schroeder, R., Van de Ven, A., Scudder, G. and Polley, D. (1986)   Managing innovation and change processes: findings from the Minnesota Innovation Research Program. *Agribusiness*, 2 (4), 501–23.
Tuma, N. B. and Hannan, M. T. (1984)   *Social Dynamics*. Orlando, Fla.: Academic press.
Tushman, M. L. and Romanelli, E. (1985)   Organizational evolution: a metamorphosis model of convergence and reorientation. In B. Staw and L. Cummings (eds), *Research in Organizational Behavior*, vol. 7, 171–222. Greenwich, Conn.: Jai Press.
Van de Ven, A. H., and Associates (1987)   The Minnesota innovation research

program. *Final Report to the Office of Naval Research Program on Organizational Effectiveness.*

Van de Ven, A. H. and Poole, M. S. (1987) Paradoxical requirements for a theory of organizational change. In R. Quinn and K. Cameron (eds), *Paradox and Transformation: Toward a Theory of Change in Organization and Management.* Cambridge, Mass.: Ballinger.

Van den Daele, L. D. (1969) Qualitative models in developmental analysis. *Developmental Psychology.* 1 (4), 303–10.

—— (1974) Infrastructure and transition in developmental analysis. *Human Development,* 17, 1–23.

11 Review Essay: First- and Second-Order Errors in Managing Strategic Change: The Role of Organizational Defensive Routines

Chris Argyris

All but two of the papers presented above described important errors made by the participants in the cases while they were managing strategic change. The question with which I began my inquiry was, Why did the executives make these kinds of non-trivial errors in the first place?

The inquiry led to the hypothesis that a second set of errors probably existed. This second set, which I will call 'second-order errors,' deserves study for two reasons. First, second-order errors may cause the executives to repeat similar errors in the future. Second, if scholars do not include them in their descriptions, they may unrealizingly be acting with the same unawareness that the practitioners showed. Research reports that contain the same omissions may help to maintain the conditions that reinforce both sets of errors.

EXAMPLES OF FIRST-ORDER ERRORS IDENTIFIED

Here are five examples of non-trivial first-order errors cited in the papers presented above. In the left-hand column, I cite the researchers' description; in the right-hand column, I infer the nature of the error that was made.

Errors Identified by the Researchers	*The Nature of the Error*
1 The assertion by the players that there was a compatibility between	1 Major incompatibilities in market structure, dominant

Chrysler and Rootes that would be a source of strength was not the case (Whipp *et al.*, p. 26 above).

design and product cycle were overlooked by the players.

2 Heavy investment in plant and equipment was not, as thought by many executives, synonymous with cost reduction (Grant, p. 145 above).

2 Executives invested in plant and equipment to reduce costs under assumptions that the intended consequences would not occur.

3 The original understanding was not sufficient to trigger collaboration and integration in the absence of change that affected the power of management (Doz and Prahalad, p. 80 above).

3 Requiring new collaboration and integration without changing the old structures and managerial patterns will not work.

4 Most managers do not monitor environment complexity, and hence they experience gradual change as rapid (Srivastava and Shocker, p. 290 above).

4 This results from a lack of monitoring of the economic environment.

5 Rigidity of managerial attitudes is probably the prime cause of firms sticking to their previously held positions (Ghazanfar, McGee and Thomas, p. 189 above) ...

5 ... producing rigid managerial attitudes.

There are, I suggest, two different types of recommendation embedded in the analysis above. The first is what the executives should know; the second is how they should act.

Know
1 The Chrysler–Rootes executives should know the incompatibility between their market structure, dominant design and product life.

Act
1 The Chrysler–Rootes executives should make the incompatibilities and their consequences on the merger explicit.

2 Executives should know the economic conditions under which investment in plant and equipment does not lead to cost reduction.

2 Executives should invest in plant and equipment only when costs can be reduced.

3 Executives should know that when the new way of managing contradicts the old way, then the

3 Get rid of the old structure of managing if the new one is to work.

old has to be changed if the new is
to be implemented effectively.

4 Executives should know the rate of change in the environment.	4 Executives should monitor changes more adequately.
5 Executives should know that rigid managerial attitudes and policies inhibit formulating and implementing strategic change.	5 Executives should reduce rigid managerial attitudes and policies.

Examining the nature of the errors in thought and action, one might ask, Why didn't the executives know the information described in the left-hand column, or why did they not act appropriately? Neither the knowledge nor the action required seems particularly difficult or subtle.

Focusing on why the executives thought and acted as they did in these cases may, I suggest, be a worthwhile exercise. For example, if the Chrysler–Rootes executives were unaware of the differences, then that says something about their competence. The same is true for those executives who invest heavily in plant and equipment in order to reduce costs when such reductions will not follow. Or, what executives do not know that if they impose a new management structure on top of the old one, the latter may inhibit the effective implementation of the former?

Another possibility is that the executives knew the information and knew what action would follow: if so, then why didn't they use the information and act appropriately? One hypothesis is that there were factors in their world that they could not ignore, and that made it necessary for them to think and act as they did.

In presenting as complete and valid an account of what happened, these conjectures should be addressed, because recent research suggests that organizations can have defensive routines that produce these kinds of errors, especially as related to strategy change. (Ansoff, 1984; Argyris, 1985; Hall, 1984).

For example, executives have been observed knowingly to produce errors such as those described above in order to protect themselves, others and the organization. The Chrysler–Rootes statement could have been used to cover up some other issues. The apparent inability to change the rigidity of managerial attitudes may stem from the fear that the known cures could make the illness worse. The ineffective monitoring of the economic environment may be caused by a line senior executive who believes that such activity would add costly and unnecessary bureaucracy. It would have been helpful if researchers had collected data to at least rule out these additional explanations.

THE RELEVANCE OF SECOND-ORDER ERRORS

We now open up the possibility that more profound errors may have occurred and gone undocumented. Ignorance is one thing, but not acting when one is informed is another. Not acting responsibly violates managerial stewardship, but covering this up compounds the error. Covering it up is detrimental, but covering up the cover-up can prevent organizational learning.

The reason that these second-order errors are more profound is that they have the quality of being self-reinforcing. It is not easy to detect and correct errors that are covered up when the cover-up is also covered up. Such errors are undiscussable. Their undiscussability makes them self-sealing and unmanageable. Finally, if they cannot be managed, then they can become self-proliferating.

Error-producing activities that are self-reinforcing, difficult to manage, self-sealing and self-proliferating could easily spread and influence other strategic decisions and changes. Once this happens, the management of strategic change can be inhibited by organizational defensive routines that make it difficult for executives to act on what they know or to know what they do not know in order to act to acquire the knowledge they lack.

Unless researchers expand their inquiry to include organizational defensive routines, they run the risk of unrealizingly colluding in the most basic function of defensive routines: namely, to bypass that which is embarrassing, bewildering or threatening, and to bypass the bypass.

HOW ORGANIZATIONAL DEFENSIVE ROUTINES CREATE ERRORS AND INHIBIT DETECTING AND CORRECTING THEM

Organizational defensive routines are any routinized policies or actions that are intended to prevent the experience of embarrassment or threat and simultaneously make it unlikely that they can help to reduce the factors that caused the embarrassment or threat in the first place. Organizational defensive routines are anti-learning and over-protective.

Organizational defensive routines differ from individual defensive routines in that they exist even though (1) individuals move in and out of the organization, (2) psychologically different individuals use them in the same ways, (3) the source of learning them is socialization, and (4) the trigger to use them is concern and being realistic rather than a personal anxiety (Argyris, 1985).

Let us explore an example of a prominent organizational defensive routine that is often found in decentralized organizations, but is certainly not limited to such organizations.

MIXED MESSAGES AND DECENTRALIZATION

Built into genuine decentralization is the age-old dilemma of autonomy versus control. Subordinates wish to be left alone but held accountable. Superiors agree but do not want surprises. The subordinates push for autonomy, asserting that letting them alone is the best sign that they are trusted by the top. They push for a solution that combines trust with distancing. The superiors, on the other hand, push for no surprises by using information systems as controls. The subordinates see the control feature as confirming mistrust.

The point is not how to get rid of the dilemma; that will never occur, for it is built into the concept of decentralization. The point is how to deal with it in a way that we can make decentralization work.

The more frequently used strategy that I observed executives using to deal with this dilemma is mixed messages. The top keeps communicating, 'We mean it – you are running your show.' The divisional heads concur that the message is credible except when the division or corporate gets into trouble or when a very important issue is at stake. In the eyes of the divisional heads, corporate begins to interfere precisely when they want to prove their own mettle. In the eyes of corporate, they intervene precisely when they can be of most help, that is, when the issue 'requires a corporate perspective.' Divisional heads described the mixed messages they received as:

'You are running the show; however, ...'
'You make the decisions, but clear with ...'
'That's an interesting idea, but be careful ...'

THE LOGIC EMBEDDED IN THE MIXED MESSAGES

Mixed messages contain meanings that are simultaneously ambiguous and clear, imprecise and precise.

Anyone who deals with mixed messages experiences the dilemmas that are embedded in them. The designers know that designing a message to be clearly ambiguous requires skill and knowledge about the receiver. They know that to be both vague and clear is inconsistent. Furthermore, to be clearly vague is not only inconsistent, but is designed inconsistency. Because of the construction, the designer is vulnerable – unless, of course, the receiver does not question the inconsistency.

There are therefore four rules about designing and implementing mixed messages. They are:

1 Design a message that is inconsistent.
2 Act as if the message is not inconsistent.
3 Make the inconsistency in the message· and the act that there is no inconsistency undiscussable.
4 Make the undiscussability of the undiscussable also undiscussable.

Thus, the strategies embedded in this logic are: when dealing with organizational defensive routines, be inconsistent, yet act as if you were not being inconsistent. Make the issues undiscussable and uninfluenceable, and act as if this were not the case. Thus the undiscussability and uninfluenceability become undiscussable.

Organizational defensive routines can lead people to feel helpless and cynical about changing them. This leads people to distance themselves from trying to engage the defensive routines in order to reduce them. As a result, organizational defensive routines not only become unmanageable (it is difficult to manage what is undiscussable), but they become the source of much distorted information. The distortion of the information is taken for granted because it is seen as necessary for the survival of the players as well as for the organization.

In some recent studies of strategic change, the following examples were reported (Argyris, 1985).

- The top ten directors of a large organization were unaware of two fundamental inconsistencies in certain financial policies. Once they became aware of their error, they were helped to see that they had had had all the information required to be aware of the inconsistency, but the group defensive routines had prevented the information from being surfaced.
- Strategy professionals (both internal and external) knowingly suppressed their views about how top management's behavior caused them to become anxious. They adapted by producing more complete analyses, hoping to satisfy their superiors. The top, in turn, saw the more complete studies as excess paper. They did not confront the issue directly. Instead, they diplomatically distanced themselves from the planners. The planners sensed the distancing on the part of the top, which upset them very much. However, they too acted diplomatically and covered up their feelings.
- The same financial information is interpreted in several different ways in order for planners to cover themselves and their divisional superiors from the corporate CEO and his top group. The planners, of course, cover up the cover-up. After years of skilful translation of the data, the players no longer see it as an aberrant activity, but as one that makes it possible for no one to get hurt.

IMPLICATIONS

One implication for research and practice is that scholars and practitioners would find it useful to focus on second-order errors that result from organizational defensive routines. Scholars as well as practitioners naturally focus on first-order errors. The former do so because they are alerted by their respective academic discipline; the latter do so because that is what getting the job done means to them.

It is the second-order errors that make the first-order errors more likely to occur, and, once they do, to reinforce them and to make all these consequences undiscussable and hence difficult to manage effectively. It is the second-order errors combined with the organizational defensive routines that make it more difficult for management to manage strategic change effectively.

PROPOSITIONS PRODUCED BY SCHOLARS TO GENERALIZE THEIR FINDINGS COULD LEAD TO THE REINFORCEMENT OF ORGANIZATIONAL DEFENSIVE ROUTINES

Often scholars produced generalizations in the form of propositions which, if used by practitioners to design and implement their actions, could get them into trouble. One reason is that the propositions do not identify the organizational defensive routines as part of the conditions under which they are valid. If practitioners choose to use the propositions, they may unrealizingly reinforce the defensive routines. For example, Tushman and Anderson (p. 115 above) report the proposition that the frame-breaking changes are most frequently initiated during financial crises. But one important reason that this proposition may be correct is that frame-breaking requires the existence of financial crises in order for the actors to feel free to violate the undiscussability and cover up features of existing organizational defensive routines that protect the existing frames.

Some executives may take propositions such as the one above as a guidepost for producing change. They may actually wait until a financial crisis cannot be denied. Indeed, they may even feed the crisis in order to speed it up. Once the crisis is so big that it is undeniable, then the executives take action even if it violates the overprotective feature of the organizational defensive routines.

Doz and Prahalad describe a success in organizational change instituted by a senior executive. Briefly, the strategy the senior executive used was (1) to leave the formal structure alone, (2) to take small incremental steps designed not to create trauma, and (3) to do so in ways that would make it hard for the subordinates to disagree or resist.

There was, I suggest, a fourth component in the executive's strategy. The executive took the actions described above and covered up the reasoning that underlay them. I make this inference because it would be difficult for the strategy to work if, for example, the executive stated openly to the subordinates that his actions were designed to reduce their resistance and power. Moreover, it may be that the subordinates sensed the reasons behind the strategy used by their superior. They may have also sensed that their superior was covering up, and they too covered up what they sensed. All these actions are illustrations of organizational defensive routines.

There is one other interesting example of how researchers may unrealizingly reinforce defensive routines in this case. Doz and Prahalad (pp. 73–4) conclude that 'By the time [the managers] realized that power was taken away from them, the logic for global integration was prevalent .... It thus became very difficult to disagree with and local managers no longer had the power to oppose it.'

If I interpret the authors correctly, they recommend to other practitioners the easing-in process used by this senior executive. If so, then maybe the strategy worked because it was consistent with existing organizational defensive routines as how to deal with potentially threatening information to subordinates. If this is true, then the strategy strengthened the organizational defensive routines.

MANAGING STRATEGIC CHANGE REQUIRES THEORIES OF CONTROL

Managing strategic change – or any activity, for that matter – means designing intentions and implementing them. Managing entails producing intended consequences. Theories of managing must deal with the question of how well the intended consequences were implemented. This is a question of effectiveness.

Theories of effectiveness are part of the more general category of theories of control. Theories of control deal with how to design and govern behavior in such a way that intended consequences come about (Ashby, 1966; Bateson, 1971; Weiner, 1965). One reason why the focus on defensive routines is important is that the routines create conditions where it is difficult for management to be in control. (Ironically, this is a condition created by management in their attempt to be in control.)

Theories of control must meet the same requirements of scientific theories regarding their testability and comprehensibility. The theories must be disconfirmable. Also, the number of concepts used should be as low as possible, yet the comprehensiveness of their explanatory power should be as strong as possible.

One important feature of theories of control is that their propositions should be producible by practitioners, and the action to produce them should also be an act to test their validity. In order for propositions to be producible by human beings under everyday conditions, they must take into account the way the human mind works when being used to take action. For example, Miller (1956) and Simon (1969) have shown that the human mind is a finite information processor. It cannot deal with the normal complexity of the environment all at once. In order to act, therefore, human beings are likely to simplify reality to the point where it is manageable. They may use heuristics in order to act rather than rigorous propositions that specify the relationships among all the relevant variables.

Scholars, however, may focus on describing reality as completely and rigorously as possible. Chapter 1 by Whipp, Rosenfeld and Pettigrew, for example, illustrates that managing strategic change is very complex and requires studying many factors that are related to content, context (inner and outer) and process. In a recent book, Pettigrew (1985) has shown that fulfilling these requirements means identifying, understanding and interrelating factors from many different disciplines. Moreover, some of the factors and their impact may not be known ahead of time. *Ad hoc* observations and explanations are necessary to provide a complete description. Although it is possible to use these comprehensive studies to alert practitioners to important factors to which they must attend, more work is required by scholars to show us how their propositions about understanding can be translated into propositions about taking action.

Some social scientists might suggest that propositions about control can be produced after knowledge becomes more additive. Unfortunately, social science knowledge does not have a good track record when it comes to being additive (Argyris, 1980). More importantly, however, propositions about understanding reality and propositions about designing and implementing actions may have different characteristics. It is one thing to produce propositions that describe the universe; it may be quite another to produce propositions about how to create the universe (Argyris and Schön, 1974, 1978; Argyris, 1980).

Some insight into the differences beween theories of understanding and theories of control could be obtained if scholars reflect on how they go about conducting their research and producing their publications. For example, scholars rarely publish their ideas in the sequence that they came to mind; they rarely publish the errors and misunderstandings that they made while analyzing and writing their material; they rarely make explicit the rules that they use to say 'that's enough information.' Yet knowing this kind of information would help to make explicit the theory of control used by scholars to produce theories of understanding. Moreover, practitioners are in situations where the sequence of their actions cannot be ignored, where their errors cannot be wiped clean, and where they must make decisions about what is enough information that satisfies many participants in the organization.

The second feature of theories of control is that the validity of the propositions is established by showing that the consequences predicted do actually occur. The criteria for effectiveness to be used to test the validity of the proposition cannot be stated objectively to hold for all people and all organizations. The criteria are a matter of personal choice, and personal choice, in turn, is related to governing values of the actors or of the organizations. Theories of control must therefore make explicit the governing values which the actions are intended to satisfy.

For example, Doz and Prahalad do attempt to state propositions about how executives behaved as well as suggestions on how they might behave in the future. They organized the executives' actions in a sequence of phases or steps. They showed how the sequence seemed to lead to the superiors' intended consequences being achieved. Hence, they suggested that other executives, when faced with similar problems, might use the actions their executive used.

The executive did achieve his objectives. However, as suggested above, he may also have reinforced important existing organizational defensive routines. What if 'effectiveness' meant not only achieving intended consequences, but doing so in such a way as to reduce, or at least not strengthen, the organizational defensive routines? Then the results are not as effective as the authors suggest.

But why do the authors have to include such governing rules (reducing or minimizing defensive routines)? The answer is that they do not have to in order to meet the requirements of normal science. The requirement they must meet is to make explicit the conditions under which their propositions would lead to the strengthening of defensive routines. The choice of whether this is effective or not is related to the governing values. Theories of control are therefore also normative theories. They not only take a position on what is effective or ineffective action, but they also take a position on what governing values should be used to make the judgement if the actions were effective.

REFERENCES

Ansoff, I. H. (1984) *Implanting Strategic Management*. Englewood Cliffs, NJ: Prentice-Hall International.

Argyris, C. (1980) *Inner Contradictions of Rigorous Research*. New York: Academic Research.

—— (1985) *Strategy, Change, and Defensive Routines*. Cambridge, Mass.: Ballinger.

—— and Schön, D. (1974) *Theory in Practice*. San Francisco: Jossey-Bass.

—— (1978) *Organizational Learning*. Reading, Mass.: Addison-Wesley.

Ashby, R. (1966) *Design for a Brain*. London: Chapman & Hall.

Bateson, G. (1971) *Steps to an Ecology of the Mind*. New York: Ballantine Books.

Hall, Roger, J. (1984) The natural logic of management policy making: its implications for the survival of an organization. *Management Science*, 30 (8), 905–27.

Miller, G. A. (1956) The magical number seven, plus or minus two: some limits on our capacity for processing information. *Psychological Review*, 63, 81–96.

Pettigrew, A. (1985) *The Awakening Giant*. Oxford: Basil Blackwell.

Simon, H. (1969) *The Science of the Artificial*. Cambridge, Mass.: MIT Press.

Weiner, N. (1965) *Cybernetics*. Cambridge, Mass.: MIT Press.

Author Index

354   *Author Index*

Subject Index

Most references are to Britain unless otherwise indicated

Indices compiled by
Ann Hall